Land Use Issues
of the
1980s

Land Use Issues
of the
1980s

Edited by
James H. Carr
and
Edward E. Duensing

CENTER
FOR URBAN
POLICY   RESEARCH

© Copyright 1983. Rutgers—The State University of New Jersey
All rights reserved.
Published in the United States by the Center for Urban Policy Research
Rutgers University, New Brunswick, New Jersey 08903
Manufactured in the United States of America

Library of Congress Cataloging in Publication Data
Main entry under title:

Land use issues of the 1980s.

    Bibliography: p. 304
    Includes index.
    1. Land use—Government policy—United States.
2. Land use—United States—Planning. I. Carr, James H.
II. Duensing, Edward. III. Rutgers University. Center
for Urban Policy Research.
HD205.L36 1983   333.73′17′0973   83–1888
ISBN 0–88285–085–7

Contents

III—Modifying Land Use Regulation

IV—Future Land Use Considerations

Acknowledgments

We express our sincere appreciation to each of the contributors whose articles appear in this volume and to the publishing companies, journals, and professional associations that have been most gracious in granting permission for publication.

We extend our gratitude to Dr. Robert W. Burchell for his assistance in the preparation of the format of this text and to Mary Picarella and Barry Jones for their invaluable administrative and editorial assistance. A special note of thanks is also due to Joan Frantz and Lydia Lombardi for their typing of various segments of the manuscript, to Arlene Pashman for her assistance in proofreading the final text, and to Judy Lyon Davis for preparing the index.

Introduction

L AND USE and development patterns are the result of a complex interaction of demographic trends, economic circumstances and social
attitudes. Technological advancements in areas such as transportation
and construction, and the availability and cost of key natural resources, including land, fresh water and energy, also have a profound impact on urban
spatial patterns.

The forces that influence land development decisions are constantly
evolving. Consequently, the determinants of urban spatial form are
dramatically different today from the forces which acted to shape American
cities at the turn of the century. Life-style preferences, size and configuration of households, levels of personal income, available transportation
modes and the composition of our industrial complex are a few of the
variables responsible for the current geographic distribution of urban activities, all of which have experienced significant shifts since the early 1900s.

In order for land use controls to be effective in achieving efficient
development patterns, regulations on the use of land must keep abreast of
changes in the complexity of factors affecting the demand for land. Regret-
tably, most of our existing system of land use controls is based on planning
principles developed almost a half-century ago. Zoning ordinances, subdivision regulations and building codes, initially designed to regulate development of densely populated, built-up urban complexes of the early twentieth
century, have drawn increasing criticism in recent years from land use planners, developers, environmentalists and others involved in or concerned
with the land use planning process. The myriad problems associated with
the rapid growth and expansion of suburbia and, more recently, of exurbia,
have been answered with traditional land regulatory mechanisms which
have had only mixed success. In fact, many land use controls have actually
exacerbated problems of suburban sprawl by strictly prohibiting less costly,
more efficient development configurations.

How have controls been adapted to meet the demands of increasingly
complex development patterns? How successful have these modifications

ix

been in achieving more efficient spatial configurations and less costly building practices? What factors will have the greatest impact on development choices throughout the 1980s?

These issues are the subject of the readings which have been assembled in the following pages. Beginning with factors affecting land use demand in the 1980s, this volume presents an analysis of current state-of-the-art land use controls, reviews the shortcomings of the current land regulatory system and suggests certain modifications to improve urban spatial development patterns. The concluding chapters discuss emerging land use issues for future consideration.

Land Use Controls: The Last Decade

By the early 1970s, the sweep of post-World War II development had changed the face of the nation. Perhaps as a reflection of more somber appraisals of the future—or simply a pause for consideration—alternative tools and approaches in land planning were called for. Rising dissatisfaction with standard zoning laws produced numerous new concepts and techniques for more efficient management of future land development. Techniques such as transfer of development rights and impact and performance zoning were introduced to add flexibility to the planning process. Concern for rapidly dwindling agricultural and forestry lands and for construction in flood plains, wetlands and mineral resource areas encouraged the use of tax differentials for active farm lands and the introduction of a broad array of sensitive-lands legislation.

Changing attitudes toward unbridled growth combined with rising fiscal pressures and a desire by communities to exert more influence over new construction also prompted changes in the ways in which communities regulated new development. Some municipalities totally prohibited uses considered to be undesirable, others placed a moratorium on new construction, and still others invested in sophisticated growth management programs. Comprehensive planning also gained widespread attention during the last ten years, and regional planning agencies and metropolitan governments were formed to address land use-related problems which did not respect jurisdictional boundaries.

The federal role in land use control has grown considerably during the last decade. Federal legislation has been enacted to influence, directly and indirectly, land use and development patterns to achieve articulated national objectives. Although the principal focus of direct federal involvement has centered on environmental issues of greatest concern to suburban and nonmetropolitan jurisdictions, national programs have also played an important role in encouraging redevelopment activities in the nation's central cities.

Finally, the courts, in recent years, have been instrumental in modifying land use control. They have both expanded and narrowed local government's land use regulatory powers. On the one hand, municipal power to control land use and development has been expanded through a series of judicial determinations, primarily at the state court level. Zoning, traditionally employed as a means to promote the health, safety and welfare of residents of a community and to protect property values, has been upheld as a means of protecting the environment and character of a community, to control the pace and timing of development, to protect historic landmarks and, to a limited extent, to regulate aesthetic aspects of new construction. At the same time, both federal and state courts have diminished much of the automony local planning bodies historically enjoyed by greatly expanding the rights of individuals to challenge municipal land use ordinances. Legal challenges of exclusionary zoning have been the most visible example of this development.

Land Use Controls: The Next Decade

Although significant strides were made during the last ten years to improve land use planning and control in this country, substantial work is still needed. Many of the land use control reforms of the last decade have proven to be more injurious than the problems they were devised to remedy. Some critics see them as unnecessarily complex, confusing, overlapping and in many instances contradictory; they have stifled new development and have encouraged continued costly and inefficient sprawl-type development.

Compounding the inefficiency of current land use regulations are the trends which are developing with regard to America's demographic profile. The far-reaching consequences of a rapidly changing population–age structure, declining household size, fewer children and an increasing divorce rate will have profound impacts on the organization and location of future urban activity. These trends, when combined with concerns for the availability and cost of energy and a stagnating economy, will make projecting future development parameters difficult. The readings which follow examine those trends which are likely to be the most influential in the coming years.

Organization of Readings

The readings that follow are arranged under four principal headings: (*1*) Factors Affecting Land Use Demand; (*2*) Institutional Controls on the Supply of Land; (*3*) Modifying Land Use Regulation; and (*4*) Future Land Use Considerations. The first two sections establish the basic supply and demand parameters for future land development patterns. The last two sets of readings offer suggestions to improve the efficiency of current land use management practices and offer insight into emerging trends and opportunities in land use planning and control.

Factors Affecting Land Use Demand

What factors will have the most profound impact on land use and development patterns in the coming years? In the lead article of this section, the Council on Development Choices for the 1980s discusses evolving and emerging demographic and economic trends which are likely to exert the greatest influence on the demand for land throughout the 1980s. The Council also reviews significant social changes which have occurred during the past two decades and speculates on the ways in which life style preferences in the 1980s are likely to be reflected in the geographic distribution of urban activities.

Richard H. Jackson explains how the demand for land over the last two decades has altered the distribution of America's land resources among major use categories. Citing various reasons for shifts in land use which have occurred over that 20-year period, Jackson concludes that past trends may not be indicative of future actions, since demand factors such as housing preferences, shopping patterns and other aspects of community life are likely to be different in the years to come.

Housing choices for the 1980s is the subject of Lawrence O. Houstoun's article. Detailing major demographic and economic trends and the resulting demands in household size, configuration and cost, Houstoun offers insight into the housing market of the 1980s and discusses the impact this demand will have on residential land consumption.

The effect of the interstate highway system on America's urban pattern is, by now, well known. Rapidly improving transportation technology of the late 1960s, combined with spiraling energy costs of the 1970s, led many urbanologists to believe that rail transit would, in the near future, play a prominent role in the demand for urban land. In his article, Robert L. Knight casts doubts on the future of rail transit. He maintains that, based on available data, rail transit has not encouraged urban spatial development patterns, as earlier expected. Knight cautions that his findings do not support the argument that rail transit has no role in the future city. On the contrary, he suggests that the potential role of rail transit in an overall strategy for reaching larger urban goals deserves further attention.

In only a decade's time, uncertainties in the availability and cost of energy have become prominent issues with respect to future land development patterns. George Sternlieb and James W. Hughes view future development trends with particular attention to the impact of new energy constraints. Despite increasing energy concerns, Sternlieb and Hughes do not envision dramatic shifts in land use and development configurations within the next ten years. Rather they look forward to a modest but significant alteration of basic developmental trends which are currently in existence. They conclude that, with appropriate government action, energy realities present substantial opportunities for important land use readjustment.

In the concluding article of this section, Forrest M. Cason probes the relationship between urban fiscal stress and future land use patterns. From a case study of the Denver metropolitan area, Cason argues that fiscal pressures on local governments are changing the patterns of land use in metropolitan areas from the specialization of land use and economic function by jurisdiction that currently characterizes metropolitan areas to metropolitan complexes composed of communities indistinct in terms of their land use.

Institutional Controls on the Supply of Land

The first three chapters of this section review government intervention in the land development process at the local, state and federal levels. In the lead article, Victor Moore discusses the development of legislation for the public control of land use in the United States and compares the American experience with that of Great Britain. Although concentrating primarily on local controls, Moore discusses the need for greater regional, state and federal involvement in the regulation of land use and development.

David E. Hess reviews judicial reaction to state land use laws. Hess concludes that the courts have overwhelmingly affirmed the legitimacy of statewide, shoreland and regional land use programs aimed at controlling environmental and growth-related problems.

Richard H. Jackson concludes the general overview of the current status of land use controls by examining federal policies affecting land use and development decisions. In addition to discussing direct regulation and public ownership, Jackson reviews the ways in which federal spending affects land use patterns and how the federal government indirectly controls land use through programs which encourage or require land use planning for receipt of federal funds.

The final two articles of this section are concerned solely with environmental land use controls. Jon A. Kusler begins his review of sensitive lands legislation with a general overview of regulatory approaches and then examines regulations affecting each major category of sensitive land—flood plains, coastal zones, wetlands, etc. Kusler's overview of sensitive lands legislation encompasses local, state and federal laws.

John J. Rhodes concludes this section in an article pointing to the need for development of a national water policy. Rhodes advises that failure to implement a broad-scale water strategy, taking into account federal, state and local governments, may be disastrous with respect to the nation's water supplies. Inasmuch as water-rights issues involve a multiplicity of competing interests, Rhodes outlines several of these conflicting interests which must be overcome in order to develop a meaningful water policy.

Modifying Land Use Regulation

Each of the articles in this section highlights specific deficiencies in existing land use regulatory mechanisms and either proposes specific curative actions or argues for dramatically altered control devices.

David E. Dowall begins this section by discussing the inflationary effects of local land use controls and proposing a monitoring system to measure the supply of and demand for residential land. Dowall argues that planners, by monitoring the performance of land and housing markets, can gauge the performance of land use and regulatory systems and adjust them to avoid unnecessary price inflation. He outlines the process of creating a local monitoring system and presents a hypothetical case demonstrating his ideas.

Charles Thurow and John Vranicar address the procedural aspects of local land use regulation. Pointing to the current system of control as one that is punctuated by overlapping and often conflicting regulatory procedures which straddle local, regional, state and federal jurisdictions, Thurow and Vranicar summarize some central issues and review what they consider to be the most promising techniques available to improve local regulatory administration. They also suggest a few ways in which states can assist in improving local land use control and intergovernmental cooperation.

Cheryl Farr directs her attention specifically to ways in which current land use regulatory practices stifle economic development ventures. Farr examines where and how regulations can be both inflationary and time-consuming and offers some suggestions on streamlining controls to encourage local economic growth.

Douglas W. Kmiec argues that streamlining existing controls addresses merely cosmetic and not the substantive difficulties with our current land use regulatory system. In his article, Kmiec suggests the implementation of an alternative system of control wherein private decisions would determine the use, location and design of land development. Public intervention would be required only in instances where private decisions do not reach an optimal result when measured by an articulated community policy and the maximization of economic resources.

George Lefcoe also considers the case for dominance of the marketplace in land use policy. Lefcoe cautions against a false juxtaposition of planning and the marketplace and states that each has a role to play in the land development process; the pricing system is effective in determining consumer demand and encouraging productivity, whereas public controls are better suited for determining the distribution of externalities of development.

Curtis J. Berger investigates a final, modified method of land use regulation. Citing the use of tax policy as a method of encouraging favored activities such as low-income housing, historic preservation or preservation of farmland, Berger asserts that, inasmuch as this is a relatively recent practice, careful evaluation of this approach is advised to ensure that stated policy objectives are being achieved.

Future Land Use Considerations

Two articles comprise this concluding section. In the first, Michael Halpin explores new land use economics and opportunities for the 1980s. Halpin suggests that new growth will occur in divergent directions. On the one hand, selected central city sites will attract significant new investment. At the same time, major new development will occur in nonmetropolitan areas. Pointing to difficulties in identifying specific growth areas, Halpin concludes that public policy should avoid attempting to manipulate the market; rather, policy should be formulated to adjust to free market trends and demands.

Where new growth will occur over the next ten years will depend on a broad spectrum of variables. Not the least of these influencing factors is the increasing sophistication of communications technology. In the closing article of this reader, Ithiel de Sola Pool traces the impact of communications technology on the shape of urban America today and suggests future development trends which are likely to be encouraged by future advancements in telecommunications.

James H. Carr
Edward E. Duensing

I

Factors Affecting
Land Use Demand

1

Factors Shaping Development
in the '80s

Council on Development Choices
for the '80s

THE COMMUNITIES in which we live and work must adapt to emerging trends and forces in this nation's economy and society. People's choices about where they want to live, the kind of home they prefer, their shopping patterns, their demands for public services, and many other aspects of community life in the '80s will be different from their preferences in the '60s or '70s because the conditions in which these choices are made will be different.

What are the trends and forces most likely to affect the choices people make? The Council determined that the following conditions, policies, and demands will be important shapers of American communities over the next 10 years, and possibly beyond.

Growth and Diversity of
Households

Approximately 17 million new households are projected for the '80s, the actual number depending on economic circumstances, housing supply, and social trends such as divorce rates, marriage ages, and housing choices of the elderly. Although the rate of household formation will be only slightly higher than in the '70s (1.68 million per year), the age, composition, and size of new households will differ significantly from last decade's new households. The increasing number of households will put pressure on the supply of housing units. Changes in household characteristics and cir-

Reprinted with permission from *Urban Land*, December 1981, published by the Urban Land Institute, 1090 Vermont Avenue, N.W., Washington, D.C. 20005.

cumstances will change consumer perceptions and preferences on housing types, sizes, and locations.

The postwar "baby boom" is maturing. In the '80s, the age group 25–44 will increase by 33 percent. Of the 17 million new households formed, almost one-third will be in the 25–34 age group and another two-fifths will be in the 35–44 group. On the other end of the spectrum, the elderly population will grow rapidly. The number of persons aged 65 or over will increase by more than 19 percent. Almost one-quarter of the new households formed in the '80s will be elderly households.

The changing age structure of population, housing supply and affordability, increasing divorce rates, and decreasing fertility rates are among the factors that will affect the size and composition of households in the '80s. Household sizes have been shrinking since 1950, and this trend is expected to continue.

For several decades, approximately seven out of 10 households have been composed of married couples, with or without children. The buyers of new housing have typically been households comprised of a husband, wife, and two or three children. Increasingly, however, the types of households seeking to buy housing are diversifying. By 1990, only six out of 10 households will be married couples, with or without children. The types of households that are growing in proportion to this decline are one-parent households, single households, and households composed of unrelated individuals. Of the 17 million new households formed in the '80s, it is anticipated that 51 percent will be composed of single persons (many of them elderly) and unrelated individuals, that 22 percent will be single-parent families, and that only 27 percent will contain married couples.

Where new households choose to settle and where existing households choose to relocate is a matter of a great number of variables. Some current growth trends are expected to continue through the '80s, such as the turnaround in rural areas from population decline to population growth that began to become evident in the early '70s and the back-to-the-city movement in selected near-downtown neighborhoods in many cities. In the '80s, the suburbs will be key growth areas, with population increasing from about 63 million in 1975 to 86 million in 1990. This increase represents a relative gain from 30 percent to 35 percent in the suburban share of total population, a gain that will be offset by decreases in the population shares of central cities, small urban areas, and rural areas.

The many shifts in population characteristics that are occurring entail changes in perceptions of community and housing, which will translate into changed demands for land and housing. Old ways of building communities will not fit the demography of the '80s. Communities that attempt to persist in outmoded ways are likely to face stagnation or to become the focus of homeseeker politics. The baby boom generation represents a voting bloc of substantial size, capable of exerting political pressures at all levels of government to make its need heard, not the least of which will be affordable housing.

Energy—Rising Costs and
Supply Problems

For many decades before the recent rounds of interrupted energy supply and increasing prices, the way in which U.S. cities, towns, and suburbs were growing was expressive of the fact and the perception that energy was and would continue to be cheap and plentiful. How little or how much energy was consumed by buildings was of little concern to most project developers, building owners, homebuyers, architects, engineers, and public officials. Energy's share of total operating costs tended to be relatively small, so that trying to cut building energy consumption by some percent through the use of better construction techniques, better siting, or more efficient systems was not an important decision-making criterion. Cheap energy, a rapid rise in the rate of car ownership, and the building of an impressive roadway network enabled homeseekers to discount the distance between their employment and their home in choosing a location.

Energy, however, is no longer cheap. As the nation searches for alternatives to dwindling and uncertain supplies of petroleum-based energy, the ways in which it is used are being reconsidered. It is clear that patterns and characteristics of physical development are significant influences on energy consumption.

Development patterns affect the use of energy for transportation. More than one-quarter of the energy used in this nation is for transportation, and the energy used for transportation is almost all petroleum based. Americans use cars for 90 percent of all personal travel. Moreover, people are traveling much more than they used to. The number of passenger-miles each person traveled nearly doubled from 1950 to the early '70s, reaching 9,285 annual miles. This high degree of personal mobility—almost all by auto and by autos more often than not carrying one or two rather than three or four passengers—has made automobiles a major consumer of energy. Half of the transport sector's energy consumption is ascribable to cars, which account for 85 percent of the energy consumed for personal travel.

The fuel efficiency of cars is rising. Whether this factor will compensate for rising gasoline prices through the '80s is a matter of debate, however. Whatever the case, cars will continue to use a substantial proportion of the nation's petroleum budget. How much they use will depend on how peoples' driving habits are affected by fuel prices, by the availability of alternative modes of transportation, and by land development patterns that influence the distances traveled by automobile, the speed and efficiency of automobile travel, and the frequency of automobile trips. Petroleum consumption affects household, business, and government budgets. Given the country's dependence on imported oil and the role of petroleum in the economy, it is an issue of national security and economic well-being.

In recent years, Americans have begun to think about alternatives to the automobile for certain situations. At the least, they are considering using automobiles less to save money. The problem is that not many alternatives are currently available. Public transportation service is often inadequate, inconvenient, and uncomfortable. Many people live in communities that are built at unsuitably low densities for cost-effective public transit.

Public transit ridership has increased for the past six years, but even so it accounts for a smaller share of total passenger-miles than it did in the '60s. The challenge of maintaining or improving present levels of mobility while conserving transportation energy will have to be met by renewed attention to public transportation systems, to highway systems, and to patterns of urban growth.

Similar concerns can be raised about the energy consumed in homes and businesses. Between 35 and 40 percent of the national energy budget goes to operate equipment in buildings for space heating and cooling, water heating, and appliances. The nation's most popular kind of residence, the single-family detached house, has proven to be an energy glutton. Even with good insulation and storm windows, this type of structure consumes much more energy for heating and cooling than other housing types. A single-family townhouse with the same amount of space as a detached house, for example, uses 25 percent less fuel. Detached houses, in addition, are more difficult to serve with innovative energy-saving systems, such as district heating.

Regional and super regional shopping centers also consume tremendous amounts of energy with large covered spaces to heat and cool often remote locations, escalators to connect several levels, and vast parking lots that entirely eliminate walk-in trade. Most office buildings in this country consume much more energy per square foot than necessary had they been designed with energy conservation in mind and were their heating, cooling, and lighting systems operated more efficiently.

Clearly, opportunities exist for energy conservation in land development—in where we build, how we build, and what we build. In the '80s, energy costs and supply constraints will demand that community building respond to the opportunities for conservation.

Increasing Costs of Housing

Nationwide, the average price of a new single-family home in 1980 was $76,300. In many markets, average prices are much higher. Homeseekers are being priced out of the market in larger and larger numbers. While in 1970 almost half of all American families could afford the median priced, single-family new home, today less than one-quarter can. Renters have been faced with equally difficult problems of affordability and with a growing scarcity of rental units.

Housing to fit the needs and the pocketbooks of today's (and tomorrow's) households is, to put it simply, not being built. A recent survey showed that over half of the nation's homebuilders are building houses that cannot be considered affordable to median-income families. First-time homebuyers, without equity in a previous house, are most severely affected by rising prices. Surveys show that the lack of a downpayment is now the principal obstacle to purchasing a house by prospective, first-time buyers, followed closely by inability to meet monthly payments.

The high cost of housing exacts more than a personal economic toll. There are signs that housing costs are hampering peoples' mobility—the employee trying to relocate to a better job in an area where housing prices are beyond reach; the elderly couple trapped in their old neighborhood in a house bigger than they can afford to maintain but unable to find affordable housing elsewhere; even the middle-income family that would have to swap an eight percent mortgage for a 12 percent one in order to move. By hampering mobility, housing costs are becoming a negative factor in the nation's economic growth. Communities with little but high-priced housing are facing the prospect of economic and fiscal decline because young, first-time homeseekers—often the children of current residents—who would add social and economic vitality to the community are forced to seek affordable housing elsewhere. Many older suburbs are facing the prospect of becoming communities of fixed-income older households, because younger households cannot afford housing in them.

Many factors are at work. Some of the most important are skyrocketing interest rates, inflation of land costs that has outstripped the inflation in other components of housing cost, inflation in the cost of many building materials, increasingly strict standards imposed by local regulation on such components of housing development as streets, sewers, and lot sizes, and longer regulatory delays that add to developers' carrying costs. In many local housing markets, growth controls have kept the levels of housing production far below potential demand, thereby artificially inflating local housing prices.

Frustrations over housing costs are becoming a force in public policy. Unfortunately, they may lead consumers to seek regulatory answers. The conflicts over rent control and condominium conversion erupting throughout the nation, for example, discourage production of affordable housing. Local elected officials are forced into making their housing policies explicit as increasing numbers of moderate-income renters and homeseekers vie for relatively decreasing supplies of moderately priced housing. At the same time, current owners may be attempting to protect the value of their housing investment by keeping moderately priced housing off the market and out of their neighborhoods and communities.

In the past 20 to 30 years, Americans have become accustomed to increasingly high standards of housing. In the '50s, the average house had 1,100 square feet and one bathroom. By contrast, in 1979 more than half the houses built were 1,600 square feet or larger and more than three-quarters had two or more bathrooms. While houses have been getting bigger, households have been getting smaller. The proportion of households living in "crowded" conditions has dropped by two-thirds for owners and three-fifths for renters. Home ownership is up to 65 percent from 55 percent in 1950. In 1950, very few houses had air conditioning. Today over half do. In the coming decade, however, large houses and detached houses are likely to become less important to many homebuyers who choose to emphasize other housing amenities, such as location, design, and recreational features. While the single-family detached house is still the overwhelming preference of homeseekers, smaller houses and attached housing are gaining in market share. Homebuyers are adjusting their preferences to fit the realities of their budgets, their needs, and their personal spending priorities. While owning a house will remain an important goal for the majority of households, alternative forms of tenure combining rental and equity features may become popular, especially as a means of achieving eventual ownership.

Declining Urban Economies

Many communities throughout the nation have experienced outflows of employment which leave behind empty factories, warehouses, rail centers, and office buildings, and unemployed or underemployed residents. Manufacturing employment is declining in most parts of the country, in large cities and small ones, in core areas and older suburbs.

The most substantial declines, however, have been recorded in older, large central cities and industrial suburbs, especially in the northeastern and midwestern regions of the nation. Once the home of much of the industrial might of this nation, these cities have steadily lost ground, first to suburban areas and newer cities, and more recently to rural areas as well. In 1958, central cities' share of metropolitan manufacturing employment stood at 76 percent. Fifteen years later, only half of metropolitan area manufacturing jobs were located in central cities. Not only has cities' relative share of manufacturing employment declined, but also they have experienced absolute decreases in the number of blue collar manufacturing jobs. The older suburbs of many cities have suffered a similar fate. This decentralization of manufacturing employment has been matched and even exceeded by outward movement in other major employment sectors, namely retail trade, wholesale trade, and selected services.

Fundamental regional as well as sectoral shifts in economic activity have been responsible for much of the problem. In the first half of the '70s, the northeast region experienced a net loss of 36,000 jobs, while employment in the south grew by over 3.3 million and in the west by almost 1.8 million. More striking, perhaps, is the loss by the northeast region of 781,000 manufacturing jobs. Accompanying the shift in industries has been a massive migration of people to the west and south.

Unfortunately, the cities affected and people left behind by this movement of jobs have found it hard to adapt to changed circumstances. Three-quarters of the 147 largest cities in the United States experienced over a 50 percent increase in unemployment rates from 1970 to 1975. Incomes were also affected. In almost three-quarters of the largest cities, per capita increases in incomes were below the national average.

One consequence of urban economic decline is a growing number of cities in fiscal distress. Cities with economic problems tend to spend more than economically healthy cities. In a sample of 28 cities representative of the nation's large cities in 1973, per capita expenditures for declining cities were 70 percent higher than for growing cities. To some degree, higher expenditures may reflect higher quality services, but is is also true that expenditures for in-place services do not correspondingly shrink to match declining population and employment.

What is the prognosis for places caught in economic decline? Some experts see little hope for reviving employment in distressed larger cities where rates of economic growth are lower and rates of job losses are higher than in more prosperous cities. Other experts see some signs of recovery in some older cities, especially in service employment generated by construction of new offices in downtowns. The nation's transition to a service economy may favor economic recovery of central cities. Recent statistics suggest that the economic decline of distressed cities may be slowing. Once prosperous manufacturing cities that are now distressed cities may have started to adapt to changed circumstances.

Inflation and Growing Competition
for Development Financing

Financial support for real estate development in the '80s will come under increasing pressure as other sectors of the economy demand growing shares of capital. Competition for capital may restrain production in the development industry and will almost surely cause interest rates for development financing to remain high throughout the decade.

The development industry has always attracted a substantial share of the nation's capital investment. Residential mortgage credit has accounted for an annual average of 26 percent of all funds raised in the economy over the last 30 years; in the last five years (1976–1980), it has ranged from 22.3 to 26.7 percent of total funds raised. Nonresidential construction financing accounts for another 4.6 percent of current capital expenditures. The development industry is in fact an important participant in the nation's capital markets.

In the '80s, however, capital for development will be exposed to increasing competition from other sectors of the economy. The amount of capital required for energy exploration and development of alternative energy sources, for replacement of aging plants and equipment, and for updating equipment made obsolete by high energy costs is huge. Furthermore, borrowing from the federal treasury is taking an expanding share of available capital.

Inflation has a powerful impact on development finance. Traditional long-term, fixed-rate loans are unpopular with investors during periods of inflation and upwardly volatile interest rates. Throughout the '80s, housing mortgage credit shortfalls in terms of demand could become very significant, unless the way mortgage debt is financed is adjusted substantially.

Inflation affects the size and time frame of project commitments. Real estate investors try to limit their exposure by investing smaller amounts of capital over shorter periods of time; expected inflation curtails investment in large-scale and innovative projects. Public officials, likewise caught in an inflationary bind, attempt to minimize public investment and avoid long-term commitments. For the development product—the houses, stores, offices, factories, and public buildings and facilities that will be in demand in the '80s—financing uncertainties will prove troublesome.

Mobility and "buying up" are also threatened by inflation. Greater numbers of households may choose to remain in their current residences rather than sacrifice their low-interest housing loans. Reduced mobility could lessen the demand for newly constructed housing but it would also diminish the supply of less expensive resale houses available to first-time buyers. Reduced mobility could also adversely affect the economy during a period of structural economic shifts that compel jobholders and jobseekers to move.

Risk and Uncertainty in the Development Industry

Almost all building in this country is undertaken by private developers and builders, who must make profits if they are to continue in business. National economic cycles and changing factor costs are everyday business risks that developers and builders face. But in the past decade or two, the business of development has been complicated and constrained by an enormous expansion in public regulation of development. Continued increasing regulatory activity in the '80s will dampen the productivity of the development industry and hamper its ability to respond to changing market demands.

Regulation of development has reached extreme heights of complexity in the past few years. Many cities, counties, and towns have taken steps to more closely control the type, location, and rate of development. Localities have expanded requirements for site and building design beyond necessary tests of health, safety, and prudent fiscal management.

State and federal governments have enacted development restrictions and required new development procedures to preserve environmental resources, reduce flood damage, improve water quality, preserve historic sites and buildings, and achieve many other goals. Requirements and procedures affecting new development, many of them overlapping and some working at cross purposes, have been piling up. Moreover, the layers of agencies at all levels of government that review and process applications for construction are sometimes competitive rather than cooperative, often understaffed, and usually slow to act.

Most but not all regulations are intended to meet a legitimate public purpose. Taken together, however, they can add up to a costly and time-consuming process that ultimately penalizes the consumer. The developer or builder making his way through the maze of development regulation may find his path blocked or plans altered at any stage. A subdivision plat that once required only a preliminary drawing, a set of plans, and two meetings of the local planning commission may now require a number of special studies, several additional detailed plans, and three or four stages of hearings and reviews. A development plan once needing clearance from a single agency now is likely to need approvals from four or five agencies. More detailed review takes time, which is money. One study concluded that 15 to 21 percent of the purchase price of a typical house may be attributable to government regulatory excesses. The process of gathering all the necessary public approvals for a project of a certain size often takes two to three years, a fourfold to sixfold increase in time over a decade ago.

The effects of overregulation go beyond the direct costs of the developer's or builder's time and effort. As with any other business, risks are covered by raising prices, and uncertainties are avoided whenever possible by "playing it safe" in the marketplace. Excellence and innovation become too risky. It is the consumer who suffers most, who pays the price, and who finds his choices in the marketplace limited.

Economic and Social Mobility

Millions of people remain outside the mainstream of the American economy, unable to find jobs or decent housing. The number of people living in poverty decreased by eight percent from 1969 to 1976, but that decrease still leaves almost 25 million people living on poverty level incomes. In the central cities of this nation, moreover, the number of poor people has been increasing, representing 17 percent of all central city residents in 1976. In contrast, the number of poor residents in areas outside of large central cities has declined. Poverty in the suburbs, for example, dropped by 15 percent in the period 1969–1976.

Washington, D.C. is typical of many cities of America: it is developing into an area, whose central city is occupied by the very rich and the very poor. The area's major challenge will be to provide for the poor people at the edges of the city. They need jobs, adequate housing, and costly public services. Whether they are ignored or treated fairly, their problems will touch city and suburb alike.

The link between poverty and lack of employment opportunities is inescapable. Cities with shrinking employment bases, particularly in manufacturing, have experienced high growth in the rate of poverty. Unskilled, low-income people left behind in cities are increasingly separated from job opportunities. The challenge is two-pronged: to get job opportunities to where needy people live, and/or to get needy people to where the jobs are. Job opportunities, more often than not, are in areas where low-income housing is not available. The dilemma of this imbalance in jobs and housing for the disadvantaged is very obvious, and it will continue to demand attention through the '80s.

Choices in Shelter and Location

A major obstacle to more widespread acceptance of the need to modernize development policies is the popular assumption that Americans have a single preference for lifestyle and shelter. This myth has never been less true. Varying economic circumstances and increasingly diverse household types are accompanied by new patterns of preferences and consumption.

While the detached single-story ranch-style structure is the overall favorite, first-time buyers prefer two-story houses and are more inclined than the general homebuying public to buy attached housing. Small units in convenient locations are increasingly viewed as more suitable to the needs of older households as well as younger singles and couples. Neighborhoods designed for raising children make up a reduced share of the new market, because the proportion of households with children has dropped so dramatically.

Prospective homebuyers in general increasingly favor locations closer to work. An increase in the number of families with two wage earners has probably contributed to the desire to reduce driving time to work and stores. Increasing congestion on our aging highway network is another factor. In Santa Clara County, California, the average morning trip in 1975 took 23 minutes at an average speed of 26 mph. By the end of this decade, the average trip time is expected to increase by 50 percent to 36 minutes at an average speed of only 19 mph. Similar congestion problems will be experienced on many other highways systems.

One consistent market force has been the desire of many people to live in a house of their own in a community of compatible neighbors and pleasant appearance. Peoples' attraction to small towns and identifiable city neighborhoods in part reflects this search for community. Families are also concerned with privacy and safety, protection for their property, and a secure economic future for their housing investment. In recent years, home ownership has been considered an investment to hedge against inflation.

New market preferences combined with the age-old desire for community and security place new challenges before the development industry and require regulatory reform and updating on the part of local governments before they can be put into practice.

Resistance to Change

Citizen groups resist many of the changes that would benefit consumers and communities for various reasons. In mature communities, neighborhood resistance to change may take the form of political opposition to new rental housing, mixed-use development, use of manufactured homes or other cost-cutting construction techniques, infill on previously vacant land, increased densities, or other changes. Such alterations to the status quo may be feared for different reasons—the introduction of new types of residents, changes in aesthetic values, or possible adverse effects on property values. As a result, much of the affordable housing that has been built in recent years has been located in fairly remote places where resistance is less likely to occur or where regulatory procedures are less likely to be applied to delay and thwart changes.

Use of zoning, subdivision regulations, and environmental reviews for the purpose of maintaining the status quo has become common practice.

They give leverage to small groups of citizens, not only to bar opportunities to those housing consumers who may not yet be residents of the community, but also to block new revenues desired by the community at large or housing opportunities for the parents or children of established residents.

Desire for Amenities and
High-Quality Public Services

Homeseekers are increasingly interested in the quality of amenities and public services in their communities. As household ages and compositions change, so will the types of facilities and services demanded. Schools and playgrounds will be less important and adult recreation facilities—tennis courts and swimming pools, for instance—more popular. Demand for new basic public services such as water supply, sewage treatment, road maintenance, and police and fire protection will keep pace with the formation of households.

In developing areas, public facilities must be provided through the expansion of existing systems or new construction. In the past, public entities have taken responsibility for providing most of these facilities. But fiscally pressed localities have been pressuring developers to provide public facilities directly, through the payment of fees, or by the formation of associations to own and operate community facilities.

In already developed areas, increased intensity of development may require some revamping of existing facilities. Changes in household composition will also require adaptation of facilities for new uses, such as conversion of school buildings to facilities for the elderly. Whether in developing or developed areas, the provision of public facilities must keep pace with development needs if the quality of development is to be maintained.

Households of the '80s will be putting a premium on design features, special recreation facilities, and other amenities in both residential and commercial development. Yet they will continue to be cost-conscious. In these circumstances, developers and builders will have to be highly sensitive to the cost tradeoffs between the "basic" product and optional amenities. House and lot sizes can be pared in the interest of affordability, for instance, if extra attention is paid to site design, common outdoor space, and interior design arrangements.

Efficiency of Public Services

It is one thing to want more and better public services and quite another to obtain them at a reasonable cost. Many of today's communities, particularly suburban communities, came to full bloom in a period of rapid growth, unlimited resources, and high optimism. There seemed to be no limit to the new roads, sewers, community centers, schools, parks, and other public accouterments of development. Voters regularly approved bonds for new facilities. Schools, roads, and other infrastructure were planned to be oversized, something to grow into.

Many such communities have learned two expensive lessons: growth is not inevitable and capital construction and operating bills come due. Today, many communities are closing schools that they are still paying for. Other communities face years of operating deficits for overextended facilities that population growth has not caught up to. Meanwhile, many other communities are just beginning to grow and are finding that public revenues do not seem to stretch very far when it comes to providing the essential facilities for urban development, especially for low density, dispersed development. When they go to the bond market to secure financing, they are experiencing the same rise in interest costs as the private sector.

Facilities in some older cities need major repair and reconstruction. Other cities with good systems find that the facilities are used less and less as residents move away. Costs are going up, revenues are going down, and taxpayers are resisting new taxes to fill the gap. These factors, combined with high inflation, are requiring most cities—and suburbs—to do more with less.

Urban governments—and not just those with severe unemployment—are finding it more and more difficult to deliver expected standards of services with their present revenues. Many cities and towns have been forced to curtail services and to postpone needed maintenance, repairs, and new facilities. The property tax base of many older cities and suburbs has failed to keep pace with public expenditures, in part due to losses in employment and population, but also because assessments have not kept up with inflationary changes in property values. In contrast, expenditures of local governments have risen relentlessly. From 1960 to 1975, while the gross national product rose by only 200 percent, municipal expenditures rose almost 350 percent and municipal debt tripled.

It is not surprising that many cities and towns are thinking twice about building new facilities. Taxpayers are reluctant to authorize new bond issues, especially for facilities that will accommodate growth. If possible, they are shifting much of these costs to project developers, who pass them along to customers in the form of higher prices.

Passing the costs of new facilities to the consumer may produce knotty problems in the '80s. Facilities provided by developers may be owned and managed by special districts or community associations, having responsibilities separate from the general purpose governmental jurisdiction in which they are located. Aside from the interjurisdictional squabbles that this arrangement can easily foster, most communities have not yet addressed other issues such as long-term capabilities for maintenance and replacement of facilities.

Increasing Competition for Land

More people and an expanding economy will require land for development. Renovation, redevelopment, and infill can make more space available in already developed areas. Most of the expected growth of households and associated development, however, must be accommodated on land not now developed. The density of future land development is obviously a key determinant of future rates of land consumption.

There are many signs that competition for land will be increasing in the decade ahead. Land under cultivation is expanding to meet growing export demands for food and fiber. Large land areas are being set aside in open space and natural environments as interest grows in the conservation of natural resources. More land is being used for mining, production of gasohol, and other energy needs. Concerns are increasing for protecting farmland from conversion to nonagricultural uses. Whether the nation's land resources can satisfy all of these pressures for their use is under debate. Experts do not agree on measurements of land supply for various uses and projections of land needs. It can be expected, however, that concerns over this issue will continue to feed public debate in the decade ahead.

Protecting the Natural Environment

Concern for the environment was a major factor affecting development in the '60s and '70s. In some communities, development was virtually halted to preserve environmental qualities; in other communities, the character and amount of development was drastically altered.

Public demands to protect the environment will continue to affect development in the '80s, but other concerns will have a balancing effect on environmental policies. The public is becoming increasingly aware that the costs of some environmental protection actions may exceed perceived benefits. For example, citizens are becoming more concerned that maintaining or expanding a community's job base may be precluded by strict adherence to existing environmental standards. Citizens are also concerned that development policies designed to achieve environmental objectives can result in sharply increased housing costs. Environmental protection permitting processes are frequently the most time consuming of all permitting steps, adding a great deal of uncertainty to the development process. Delays and uncertainty translate into added development costs that are passed on to homebuyers.

Environmental protection policies can also add to housing costs by forcing low density development. The most frequent change required of developers as a result of environmental impact reviews is to reduce residential densities. The rationale for this requirement is that lower densities mean less development and therefore fewer adverse environmental impacts. While this result may hold true for a short time for the particular site in question, the larger urban area may actually suffer adverse environmental impacts. Housing costs are increased because more land is required for each housing unit.

Costs of public facilities may also increase substantially. Adverse environmental impacts can occur because the development that was not allowed on the site may simply occur on other, perhaps less appropriate and less regulated sites in the same market area. The likely effect of spreading out development is more auto travel, which in turn increases pollutants in other areas. Moreover, depending on travel patterns, the site with the reduced density may end up no better off than it would have been with a higher density.

As public awareness of these problems continues to increase, it can be expected that there will be a search for new solutions for meeting environmental needs. The challenge of the '80s will be to accommodate environmental preferences while allowing the private sector to deliver development products at a cost the public can afford.

Institutional Limitations

Many development problems and solutions do not respect jurisdictional boundaries. This phenomenon is especially true in metropolitan areas, many of which are divided by state as well as county, municipal, and special district lines. Different building codes and differing interpretations of identical codes, for example, add to housing construction costs. No-growth rules in one community drive development into other, frequently more remote, ones. Most of the nation's 26,000 municipalities, 3,000 counties, and 50 states need substantial changes in their general plans, regulatory apparatus, and tax policies to meet changing conditions. The most pervasive institutional problem associated with the need to modernize public development policies is the lack of awareness on the part of voters and many lay board members. Other institutional problems include a lack of technical capacity in some towns and counties, absence of appropriate public/private development mechanisms in cities, and inexperience with mixed-use development by developers, localities, and lending institutions.

These problems have increasingly constrained the development process in many communities and will continue to add costs and block needed innovations to development through the present decade.

2

Land Use in America

The Dilemma of Changing Values

Richard H. Jackson

THE UNITED STATES OF AMERICA is one of the world's largest countries. With 3.68 million square miles, the United States ranks fourth after the Soviet Union (8.6 million square miles), Canada (3.85 million square miles), and the People's Republic of China (3.7 million square miles). The vastness of the United States led to the idea that because there was such a surplus of land there was no need to control any but the most extreme forms of land use. In 1800, there were only approximately 5 million inhabitants of the U.S. territory, and concern for preserving the land was low. By 1900, the population had surged to 76 million due to massive migration coupled with a high birth rate, but there were still nearly 30 acres of land for every man, woman, and child in the country. The population growth of the 20th century has now cut this figure to only about 10 acres per person in the U.S. This figure is still high when compared to China (about 2 acres per person) or India (less than one acre per person), but the quality as well as quantity of the land resource base must be considered. If the land resource were divided evenly, a typical American would have 2 acres of cropland, 2½ acres of grass pasture and rangeland, 3⅓ acres of forest land, and 1⅓ acres of wasteland, ½ acre of land used for recreation and wildlife, and ¼ acre of roads, airports, and other urban components.

The relative abundance of the American land resource when compared to other areas of the world should not obscure the fact that it is still finite. There are very real limits to the productive capacity of our land resource. Changes in technology may increase the productivity of cropland and forest, but expanding population and urban sprawl can offset this. The adequacy of our land resource to meet future demands of the citizenry of the United States will largely center on how well we use it today. Actions which positively or negatively affect the land resource need to be analyzed in terms of both short- and long-term impact. Such analysis is made difficult (if not impossible) by existing land use controls which are diffused among private individuals, business, and local, state, and federal governments. The powers and actions of each are multi-faceted and often overlap.

The federal government, for example, directly manages large land areas (particularly in the West), but also affects land use decisions through government spending and taxation. The effect of federal action on land use may be as local as the construction of a post office in a suburb, or as broad as the multi-state impact of a large water development project. Likewise, states have broad powers which affect land use, including, in some states, specific legislation to regulate land use for selected regions or the entire state. Local government can also undertake an array of actions affecting land use, including land use planning, zoning, capital expenditures, and taxation.

It would appear that American land use is already overcontrolled, and yet in the last decade there has been an upsurge in interest in land use controls. States have passed new legislation, several bills have been proposed for national legislation of land use, and the question of control of land use has become important to all Americans. The basic reason for the increased interest in land use controls is the rapidly growing population that is demanding products and services of the land which are different from those required in the past. If America is to resolve the dilemma of use of its land, it will be necessary to develop workable and acceptable laws and programs to guide decisions which are made concerning the land resource.

America's Land Resource

The total gross area of the United States (including Alaska and Hawaii) is 2,314 million acres (Table 1). It should be noted that about 2% of the total gross area of the country consists of inland water bodies such as the Great Salt Lake. Inland waters are included in Table 1 only if they are ponds or lakes 40 acres or more in area; streams, rivers, or canals 1/8 of a mile wide or wider; or deeply indented embayments or other coastal waters behind or sheltered by headlands or islands separated by less than 1 nautical mile of water. (The Great Lakes, Long Island Sound, and Puget Sound are not included as part of the inland waters.)

Approximately one-third of this land is controlled by agencies of the federal government (762 million acres). The Bureau of Land Management controls 60% of the land administered by the federal government, and the

TABLE 1. *The Land of the United States, 1970*

State	Land		Inland water		Total	
	Square Miles	*Acres*	*Square Miles*	*Acres*	*Square Miles*	*Acres*
Alabama	50,708	32,453,120	901	576,640	51,609	33,029,760
Alaska	566,432	362,516,480	19,980	12,787,200	586,412	375,303,680
Arizona	113,417	72,586,880	492	314,880	113,909	72,901,760
Arkansas	51,945	33,244,800	1,159	741,760	53,104	33,986,560
California	156,361	100,071,040	2,332	1,492,480	158,693	101,563,520
Colorado	103,766	66,410,240	481	307,840	104,247	66,718,080
Connecticut	4,862	3,111,680	147	94,080	5,009	3,205,760
Delaware	1,982	1,268,480	75	48,000	2,057	1,316,480
District of Columbia	61	39,040	6	2,840	67	42,880
Florida	54,090	34,617,600	4,470	2,860,800	58,560	37,478,400
Georgia	58,073	37,166,720	803	513,920	58,876	37,680,640
Hawaii	6,425	4,112,000	25	16,000	6,450	4,128,000
Idaho	82,677	52,913,280	880	563,200	83,557	53,476,480
Illinois	55,748	35,678,720	652	417,280	56,400	36,096,000
Indiana	36,097	23,102,080	194	124,160	36,291	23,226,240
Iowa	55,941	35,802,240	349	223,360	56,290	36,025,600
Kansas	81,787	52,343,680	477	305,280	82,264	52,648,960
Kentucky	39,650	25,376,000	745	476,800	40,395	25,825,800
Louisiana	44,930	28,755,200	3,593	2,299,520	48,523	31,054,720
Maine	30,920	19,788,800	2,295	1,468,800	33,215	21,257,600
Maryland	9,891	6,330,240	686	439,040	10,577	6,769,280
Massachusetts	7,826	5,008,640	431	275,840	8,257	5,284,480
Michigan	56,817	36,362,880	1,399	895,360	58,216	37,258,240
Minnesota	79,289	50,744,960	4,779	3,058,560	84,068	53,803,520

Mississippi	47,296	30,269,440	420	268,800	47,716	30,538,240
Missouri	68,995	44,156,800	691	442,240	69,686	44,599,040
Montana	145,587	93,175,680	1,551	992,640	147,138	94,186,320
Nebraska	76,483	48,949,120	744	476,160	77,227	49,425,280
Nevada	109,889	70,328,960	651	416,640	110,540	70,745,600
New Hampshire	9,027	5,777,280	277	177,280	9,304	5,954,560
New Jersey	7,521	4,813,440	315	201,600	7,836	5,015,040
New Mexico	121,412	77,703,680	254	162,560	121,666	77,866,240
New York	47,831	30,611,840	1,745	1,116,800	49,576	31,728,640
North Carolina	48,798	31,230,720	3,788	2,424,320	52,586	33,655,040
North Dakota	69,273	44,334,720	1,398	890,880	70,665	45,225,600
Ohio	40,975	26,224,000	247	158,080	41,222	26,382,080
Oklahoma	68,782	44,020,480	1,137	727,680	69,911	44,748,160
Oregon	96,148	61,557,760	797	510,080	95,981	62,067,840
Pennsylvania	44,966	28,778,240	367	234,880	45,333	29,013,120
Rhode Island	1,049	671,360	165	105,600	1,214	776,960
South Carolina	30,225	19,344,000	830	531,200	31,055	19,875,200
South Dakota	75,955	48,611,200	1,092	698,880	77,047	49,310,080
Tennessee	41,328	26,449,920	916	586,240	42,244	27,036,160
Texas	262,143	176,765,760	5,204	3,330,560	267,338	171,096,320
Utah	82,096	52,541,440	2,820	1,804,800	84,916	54,346,240
Vermont	9,267	5,930,880	342	218,880	9,609	6,149,760
Virginia	39,780	25,459,200	1,037	663,680	40,817	26,122,880
Washington	66,570	42,604,800	1,622	1,038,080	68,192	43,642,880
West Virginia	42,070	15,404,800	111	71,040	24,181	15,475,480
Wisconsin	54,464	34,856,960	1,690	1,081,600	56,154	35,938,560
Wyoming	97,203	62,209,920	711	455,040	97,914	62,664,960
Total	3,536,855	2,263,587,200	78,267	50,090,880	3,615,122	2,313,678,080

SOURCE: U.S. Department of the Interior, *Public Land Statistics, 1976*, p. 3 (Washington: GPO, 1976).

Forest Service controls an additional 24%. Other federal agencies administering public lands include the National Park Service, the Fish and Wildlife Service, and the Bureau of Reclamation. In addition, the federal government holds 50 million acres of land in trust for Indian tribes and individuals.[1]

The remaining two-thirds of the United States land resource consists of approximately 1.1 billion acres and is controlled by private individuals and corporations or state and local governments. State, county, and municipal governments received title to 328 million acres of land for support of schools, roads, and other economic development, but only 134 million acres remain in their ownership today.[2] Noteworthy among corporations controlling land are railroad companies. Between 1850 and 1976, slightly more than 94 million acres of public land were granted to railroads as an incentive to expand the rail links of the nation. Although much of this has since been sold by the railroads, they are still major landholders. The balance of the nation's land is controlled by other corporations or individuals.[3]

Land Use in the United States

The land of America is used for a multitude of activities. Land use includes everything the land is used for by residents of the country, from farms to golf courses, houses to fast food establishments, hospitals to graveyards; and all uses are interconnected. The Illinois corn farmer's use of artificial fertilizer affects fishermen on Lake Erie, and the erection of a factory in rural Nebraska precipitates loss of prime corn land to the ubiquitous subdivision. Although land use types are almost limitless, America's land use can be broadly categorized into intensive and extensive types. Extensive land use includes the bulk of the land in the categories of cropland, grazing land, forest land, wasteland, and recreation and wildlife areas. Intensive land uses include urban uses and land for transportation purposes (Table 2).[4]

The cropland resource of the United States is estimated to be at 472 million acres, or 21% of the land area, representing neither the acreage actually harvested each year nor that which could conceivably be used, but land that is now involved in cropland rotation.[5] In any given year, the cropland resource consists of land actually in crops, land used for pasture, and fallow land. The amount of land classified as cropland has not changed significantly in the past few decades, but there have been important changes in individual use components. The record high for land actually used for crops occurred in 1949 when 387 million acres of cropland were planted. Since that time, there has been a general downward trend to 333 million acres in 1969. Land planted remained at this low figure until 1973 when it increased sharply to 354 million acres.[6] The decline in cropland planted was a result of increased productivity in the 1949–1969 era in which productivity

TABLE 2.—*Major Land Use in the United States, 1969*

Major land uses	Acreage[a] (million acres)	Percent of total
Agricultural:		
Total cropland	384	17.0
Grassland pasture and range	692	30.6
Forest land grazed	198	8.7
Farmsteads, farm roads	9	.4
Total agricultural land	1,283	56.7
Nonagricultural:		
Forest land not grazed	525	23.2
Special uses	169	7.5
Urban areas, roads, and other built-up areas	(61)	(2.7)
Recreation parks and wildlife	(81)	(3.6)
Public installations and facilities	(27)	(1.2)
Miscellaneous land	28	12.6
Total nonagricultural land	981	43.3
Total land area	2,264	100.0

[a]It is almost impossible to provide adequate statistics on land use in the United States because of differing definitions of what constitutes forest, or grazing land, or even cropland. Publications of the U.S. Department of Agriculture give differing figures depending on the purpose of the publication. Consequently all figures used here will refer to those developed from the (1969) census of agriculture unless otherwise indicated. Although they have changed in the ensuing decade, they show relative magnitude of uses.

SOURCE: U.S. Department of Agriculture, *Our Land and Water Resources* (Washington: Economic Research Service, 1974), Misc. Pub. 1290, 1974, p. 3.

per acre increased over one-half. As a consequence, marginal lands were abandoned and other land was diverted into fallow under government programs. Cropland in soil improvement and other government programs ranged from 37 to 65 million acres between 1950 and 1972.[7] After 1973, cropland planted increased dramatically as a result of world demand for foods and associated price increases which cut diverted land to only 8 million acres. By 1974, only 2 million acres of cropland remained in the government-sponsored diversion programs.[8]

Another trend affecting the nation's cropland has been associated with expansion of cropland through reclamation projects. New cropland has appeared in a number of well-defined areas, particularly along the Mississippi River as a result of drainage, in the western states as a result of expanded irrigation, in Florida associated with both drainage and irrigation, and in northern Montana as a result of improved dryland farming techniques. There has also been expansion of cropland throughout the corn belt associated with contouring, drainage, leveling, and other management techniques.

Cropland has also been changed to non-cropland use in the United States.[9] With the exception of the Mississippi Delta states and Florida, the entire south is a region of such cropland "abandonment." Lands "abandoned" were infertile, unsuited for mechanization, or both. The northeastern states have also been the scene of land abandonment as marginal land was allowed to revert to brush, or transferred to other types of uses. Between 1952 and 1972, the nation lost 6% of its taxable farm acreage. In the same period, New England lost half of all its farm acreage, and New Jersey lost 45% (Fig. 1).[10]

Pasture and Range

Livestock graze on 890 million acres, or 39% of the land area of the United States. The land used for grazing includes not only grassland, but cropland and forest land which is grazed. The total amount of land used for pasture and range has declined since 1950, but cropland pastured has increased 31 million acres. The 88 million acres of cropland used for pasture contributes half of total pasture land needs.[11] Approximately two-thirds of land used for pasture or range is on private farms. This includes the 88 million acres of cropland pastured, 452 million acres of permanent pasture and range, and 62 million acres of woodland used for grazing. The 288 million acres of non-farmland used for grazing consist of 72 million acres of private or state-owned woodland, 72 million acres of federal woodland, and 144 million acres of federally administered grazing lands, primarily in the more arid western states.[12]

Forest Land

About one-third of the United States (754 million acres) is categorized as forest land by the Census Bureau. The quality of the forest land varies, with one-sixth in Alaska where little timber is harvested for commercial use. There are 633 million acres of forest land in the 48 conterminous states, and an estimated 80% (493 million acres) of this is commercially useful. During the decades of the '50s and '60s, the area of commercially productive forest declined 8.4 million acres (2%).[13] This decline is largely concentrated in the south, especially in the Mississippi Delta region where bottomlands are being drained and forest land transformed into cropland. The most productive forest land is found in the Pacific Northwest and the southern states.

Special Land Uses

Twenty percent (456 million acres) of the land in the United States is classified as land other than cropland, pasture-grazing land, or forest land. Areas unsuited for use in deserts, swamps, tundra, and bare rock comprise 287 million acres, and an additional 169 million acres (8% of the total land

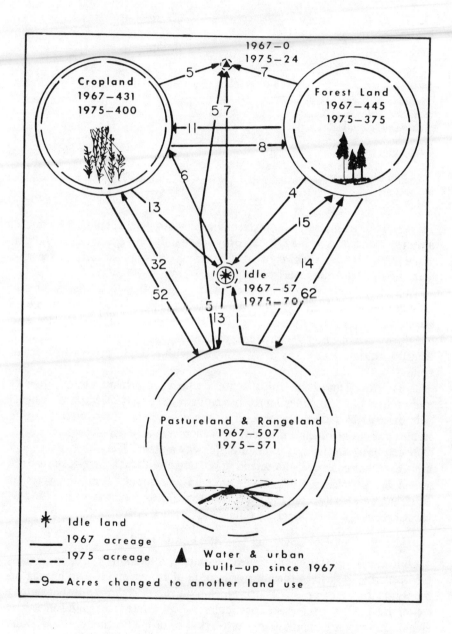

FIGURE 1.—*Changes in land use: 1967-1975.*

TABLE 3.—*Special Land Uses, 1959, 1969*

Special uses	1959	Million acres 1969	Change
Urban areas	27.2	34.6	7.3
Transportation areas	24.7	26.0	1.3
Recreation and wildlife areas	61.5	81.4	19.9
Public installations and facilities	27.5	27.4	-.1
Farmsteads and farm roads	10.1	8.4	-1.7
Total	151.0	177.8	26.8

SOURCE: U.S. Department of Agriculture, *Our Land and Water Resources* (Washington: Economic Research Service, 1974), Misc. Pub. 1290, 1974, p. 10.

resource) are in the special-purpose land use category (Table 3).[14] Land in swamps, tundra, and bare rock is low-use land. The special-use lands include intensive uses such as urban and transport uses, as well as extensive uses such as recreation and wildlife.

There are some 35 million acres of land classified in urban or urban-related uses. This includes land in all urban places, plus all land in incorporated and unincorporated places of 1,000 or more population. The land use in the urban category includes residential, commercial, industrial, and transportation uses as well as vacant land within the boundaries of urban areas.[15]

The road system of the United States exclusive of urban areas occupies 21 million acres and includes lands in roadbeds and right-of-ways of systems administered by federal, state, and local governments. This system is quite stable in amount of land utilized, with increases associated primarily with completion of the federal interstate highway system. The interstate system utilized 1 million acres in 1969, and approximately 100,000 acres per year are added to it.[16] "Rural" airports include an additional 1.8 million acres of land, including airports serving large urban areas which are classified as rural because of their location outside of the urbanized area.

The Changing Use of Land in the U.S.

Land use is not static, but rather a dynamic, interacting system. Changes are occurring in each of the categories of land use which have an impact on the residents of the nation. Those which have received the greatest attention center around the special uses, particularly those related to urban functions. Urban sprawl with its attendant destruction of prime farmland, the second-home phenomenon which destroys the tranquility of highly prized natural environments, and the seeming spread of tract housing over hill and dale have received attention in popular and scholarly works. Examination of the trends in land use in the United States seems to indicate that these problems are less severe than popularly supposed. If so, it is because the statistics are macro in scale. At the micro scale, serious problems of land use are being created by these trends.

The general trend in land use for the past 20 years has involved two facets. The first of these has shifted land from agricultural, forest, or other extensive uses into such intensive uses as roads, airports, and other urban-related activities. At the same time, a change has occurred affecting land shifts within the extensive uses, as land is shifted from cropland or forest land to recreation or wildlife activity. During the 1959–1969 decade, an average of 1.2 million acres of rural land per year was shifted to intensive urban related uses. One million acres per year were shifted to extensive uses (Fig. 1).[17]

The trend in land use associated with the 1960s continued in the '70s. Recent estimates indicate that on non-federal lands, 79.2 million acres were removed from cropland use between 1967 and 1975. In the same period, only 48.7 million acres were converted to cropland use, resulting in a net loss of 30.5 million acres of cropland.[18] Pasture land and rangeland increased by 64 million acres as cropland or forest land was converted to pasture use. Forest land declined by about 70 million acres during the 8-year span, and acreage in miscellaneous other uses increased by 13 million acres.[19] An estimated 17 million acres of land were shifted to urban-related activities during the same time, and an additional 7 million acres were flooded by reservoirs or used for flood control.[20] In general, it can be said that the land use trends of the 1960s intensified in the '70s, with increasing amounts of land being transformed into urban-related uses each year.

The importance of the trends in American land use centers around their impact on the ability of the nation to maintain sufficient land to provide for future food, fiber, and forest products required by the population. When viewed at the micro scale, the amount of land being lost to intensive uses is a small percentage. Only an estimated 600,000 acres of land transformed to urban uses each year comes directly from land used for crops. Although the rate of conversion of land to urban and built-up areas is increasing, the majority of the land affected is not prime agricultural land. Such a micro analysis of land use trends masks important regional differences, however.

The mountain states, the Pacific states, and the northeastern states are regions in which the availability of prime land is limited, and yet these regions are seeing rapid conversion of land to urban uses. The semi-arid mountain states are faced with restrictions of topography which result in serious competition for the use of the more level land, with resultant loss of cropland as their population rapidly increases (Table 4). The Pacific states have been growing rapidly for the past several decades, with a California

TABLE 4.—*Estimated Population Growth in the United States, 1970-1980*

Region	1970 population (millions)	1980 population (millions)	Growth (%)
Northeast	49.157	50.3	2.3
North central	56.673	59.0	4.1
South	63.032	72.7	15.3
West	34.947	40.5	15.9
United States	203.810	222.5	9

SOURCE: U.S. Census Bureau, "Population Estimates to 1980" (Washington: Commerce Department, 1978), n.p.

study indicating 134,000 acres per year converted from agriculture, a rate of change which, if continued, would consume three-fourths of the state's agricultural land by the year 2000.[21]

In addition to loss of land to urban uses, important land use shifts occur as the demand for recreation increases. From 1965 to 1972, participation more than doubled in such activities as camping, picnicking, fishing, swimming, and canoeing. By 1976, the Bureau of Outdoor Recreation estimated a total of 6.8 billion visitor hours on federally administered lands alone.[22] Over 1 million acres are converted annually to recreation-related activities. Increased leisure time, more disposable income, increased concern for the environment, and greater mobility indicate that there will be even greater demands for recreation land in the future. Changes in land use in America and the pressures affecting their use pose important questions concerning how our land resource is controlled, managed, and used. . . .

NOTES

[1]*Our Land and Water Resources* (Washington, D.C.: U.S. Department of Agriculture, Economic Research Service, Misc. Pub. 1290, 1974), p. 21.

[2]*Public Land Statistics, 1976*, U.S. Department of the Interior (Washington, D.C.: Government Printing Office, 1976).

[3]Ibid.

[4]*Our Land and Water Resources*, op. cit., p. 1.

[5]Ibid., p. 2.

[6]Ibid., pp. 2-3.

[7]Orville Krause and Dwight Han, *Perspective on Prime Lands*, U.S. Department of Agriculture (Washington, D.C.: Government Printing Office, 1975), p. 13.

[8]Ibid., p. 3.

[9]This trend is usually erroneously referred to as "land abandonment." The land is not abandoned, it is converted to woodland, pasture or second home development. Only the cropping is abandoned.

[10]*Conservation News* (National Wildlife Federation, Washington, D.C.), Vol. 43 (1978), No. 1, p. 3.

[11] *Our Land and Water Resources*, op. cit., pp. 7–9.

[12] Ibid.

[13] Krause and Han, op. cit., p. 17.

[14] *Our Land and Water Resources*, op. cit., p. 10.

[15] *Major Uses of Land in the United States* (Washington, D.C.: U.S. Department of Agriculture, Economic Research Service, Agricultural Economic Report No. 247), pp. 16–17.

[16] *Our Land and Water Resources*, op. cit., p. 11.

[17] Ibid., pp. 10–11.

[18] Raymond I. Diderikson, Allen R. Hildebaugh, and Keith O. Sihmude, *Potential Cropland Study*, Soil Conservation Service, Statistical Bulletin No. 578, 1977, p. 1.

[19] Ibid., pp. 10–11.

[20] Ibid.

[21] *State Open Space and Resource Conservation Programs for California*, California Legislature, Joint Committee on Open Space Lands, April 1972.

[22] *Environmental Quality, 1977. Eighth Annual Report of the Council on Environmental Quality* (Washington, D.C.: Government Printing Office, Dec. 1977), p. 80.

3

Market Trends Reveal
Housing Choices for the 1980s

Lawrence O. Houstoun, Jr.

THE UNITED STATES is very different than it was in the 1950s, 1960s, and 1970s when current development rules and practices became widespread. Today, local governments increasingly apply strict tests of fiscal survival to development proposals; state governments are saddled with gargantuan highway maintenance bills while gas revenues are declining; federal subsidies for development in growing and declining areas are dropping in real dollars. The per capita use of land for urban purposes doubled from 0.2 acres to 0.4 acres between 1950 and 1970. Metropolitan densities have dropped like a rock since 1950, and the current build-up in population across the vast stretches of non-metropolitan America is expected to continue in the 1980s, adding the cost of dispersion to the mounting bill for public services and facilities.

The American people are different, too. Changes in household composition are having as profound an impact on the size and form of new and remodeled housing as are economic changes. The popular vision of the typical household—father, mother, and two or three children—is fast assuming the proportions of folklore.

One of many remarkable phenomena is the explosion in the number of households. Even central cities that lost population steadily for the past decade or two have gained households. At the same time, the composition of households is remarkably different from that which was typical in the 1950s and 1960s when so many residential areas were planned, zoned, and built. While the number of households has grown by approximately 45 per-

Reprinted from Lawrence Houstoun, Jr. "Market Trends Reveal Housing Choices for the 1980s." *Journal of Housing* (February 1981), 73–79. Copyright © 1981, National Association of Housing and Redevelopment Officials. Reprinted by permission.

cent since 1950, the number of single-person households has increased more than 70 percent, the number of multi-person households without children has grown by about 55 percent, and the proportion over 65 years of age has increased almost 60 percent. Divorce will affect 40 percent of all marriages in the 1980s, inducing a chain reaction of moves among housing units and changes in the number, ages, and marital status of those within units.

The seven-room home that sheltered two adults and three children from 1950 to 1970 is likely to find only one adult in residence in 1985; often, she will be hard pressed to meet the combined burdens of taxes, maintenance, and energy costs in a home that provides an abundance of no longer desired land, but that lacks adequate amounts of insulation.

Today, 61 percent of households include two adult incomes. Two incomes have helped many families overcome the economic pressures of a decade in which disposable family incomes declined in real terms despite the surge of wives in the work force. Households now spend a larger share of incomes on transportation and housing, leaving less for savings and purchase of durable goods. Dual wage earning households have less time for yard and home care, and, with fewer children, are less inclined to spend heavily for the private outdoor space considered a must 10 years ago.

Changing tastes and beliefs also affect housing and community choices. A University of Michigan research study found that American women want their 18-year-old children to have an average of 2.5 children; in 1962, they hoped for four children for themselves, and indeed that's what the study group averaged in practice. More Americans are reported satisfied with manufactured or "mobile" homes, while an entirely different group is delighted to restore and enjoy Victorian housing styles rejected by their parents.

Northeastern planners worry because older suburbs lack the vitality sought by young adults; they forsee a decline in revenues and services as the tax base increasingly becomes dependent on retirement incomes. A decade ago, everyone "knew" that American families would never purchase new row houses. Today, attached dwellings are the hottest sales item among builders in many major markets. Five years ago, America remained mesmerized by the inexorable growth of automobile travel. Today, builders report that half of all potential purchasers want their new homes closer to work. Time, perhaps more than money, impels this shift. *Texas Monthly* magazine reported, for example, that a driver in rush hour could go almost 20 miles in 30 minutes on Houston's Katy Freeway in 1969; today, he or she would be lucky to progress 10 miles in the same time. . . .

Since 1950, the number of persons per square mile residing in central cities has dropped 46 percent from approximately 7,500 to 4,000, that is, from 11 to six persons per acre. The thinning trend in older central cities and suburbs is the result of shrinking household size, abandonment, and demolition of residential and nonresidential structures and clearance for highways and other activities. Reduced demand for central locations by manufacturing, warehousing and railroads offers significant opportunities for conversion of this land to new uses. Many parcels of land in suburbs and cities have been kept from the market as the result of public regulations that set excessive standards for minimum size or that needlessly limit the uses to which they can be put. Low property taxes on unimproved or underutilized land encourage withholding land from the market, awaiting the possibility of higher sales prices.

In a recent study of 86 cities, approximately 25 percent of the land was determined to be vacant; perhaps half of this may be available for development. Opportunities for redevelopment are also substantial. Revitalization is occurring in many cities, but it must be expanded to other cities, older suburbs, and declining nonmetropolitan towns.

In the last three decades, the number of persons per square mile in metropolitan areas has dropped 47 percent (from 450 to 305) and, in suburbs, 11 percent (from 200 to 180). Much of this decline is the result of the expansion of metropolitan areas where new growth typically has been noncontiguous and marked by larger lot sizes.

Newer residential projects tend to be denser by the acre, but are widely dispersed with respect to other residential and nonresidential uses. The latter trend helps contain land costs for residents, but increases household transportation costs and the costs of government services and facilities. . . .

For the past 50 years, and particularly since 1950, communities have increasingly segregated the activities of daily life—homes, work sites, recreation, shopping. Originally, these rules were adopted to mitigate the adverse effects of manufacturing and transportation activities. More recently, they also have been applied to separate unattractive commercial development from residences, particularly in areas zoned for single-family detached homes.

With declining densities, public transportation has become less available to more people. Local plans and regulations increasingly require that movement among activities be accomplished through the use of private motor vehicles. However, an increasing number of Americans cannot use private cars. Also, the growing percentage of dual wage earning households requires more cars per household, increasing both personal and public costs. The number of cars per household continued to rise between 1973 and 1980, even though the number of persons per household dropped dramatically. . . .

Although 65 percent of American commuters drove to work alone in 1975, recently more Americans appear to be ride-sharing and using transit. The number of cars per capita in 1975 was .45, amounting to approximately

95 million cars. Barring critical price or supply changes or altered development patterns, the Department of Transportation projects per capita car
ownership rates ranging from .50 to .57, thus adding 40 to 55 million cars to
the total stock in 20 years.

In spite of the higher total trip rate reported by households where transit
is available, DOT notes that these households had a monthly gasoline expense of under $45, while those with no transit spent $61. DOT officials say
that persons choosing to reside in the types of areas served by transit can
fulfill their travel needs with significantly less use of gasoline (and money).
Changes in the rules that govern development—such as allowing more compact, mixed use development, and allowing more persons to use their homes
as business sites—will enable more Americans to reduce overall transportation costs and/or travel time by using transit or by living closer to more of
the activities associated with daily life. . . .

The changing income structure of home owners, rising real costs of purchase, operations and maintenance, demographic changes, and shifting
preferences have recently stimulated significant changes in housing form.
New construction increasingly features attached housing; manufactured
units and components are being widely utilized; zero lot line construction
offers many of the external benefits of detached homes without the added
costs and maintenance responsibilities; one in five new homes is owned as
part of a condominium.

A few older communities are modifying their codes to permit large
homes, no longer attractive to the market or unavailable for resale, to be
used by more than one household. In many older suburbs, however, a new
underground housing market has arisen through which persons needing
very inexpensive shelter rent one or more rooms in spite of local codes that
prohibit this practice. Modernization, rehabilitation, adaptive reuse, and
expansion of existing homes are occurring at record rates, creating higher
quality and larger units on present lots, and providing profitable new
markets for the housing construction industry. These economically and
socially beneficial market trends should be encouraged rather than thwarted
by regulations that impose unwanted sizes and types of structures and unnecessary costs of construction and rehabilitation. . . .

The "urban village" concept is an organizing principle that offers attractive, efficient, and marketable development forms that incorporate all of
the council's development objectives—compact new growth, infill, and
redevelopment; mixed uses; transportation alternatives; and diversity and
affordability of housing. . . . Planned transportation systems offering alternatives to driving alone make compact growth workable without congestion
and environmental degradation. Compact, mixed use centers lessen the
need for car use and provide destinations of sufficient scale to assure suc-

cessful transit. Diversity of housing supply, both through new construction and conservation, is best achieved through built environments that are themselves diverse and that offer sufficient scale to assure profitability to the investors and social compatibility to the community. All of these features are embraced in the urban village concept.

Phoenix, Arizona, a rapidly growing, low density city, has adopted a concept plan that encourages, through selective code modification, the formation of nine urban villages, including an enhanced central business district with new residential opportunities. The city anticipates that this approach to development and redevelopment will support the population's need for an effective bus system to link the new centers, will provide a greater sense of identity and attractiveness to the sub-city centers, and will substantially reduce the future rate of land consumption and government facility and service costs.

Other low density, growing city, and suburban areas in the South, the West, and elsewhere can apply this concept by encouraging planned employment, shopping, and higher density residential facilities in compact, well-integrated settings. Different opportunities for creating urban villages exist in the rapidly growing Western mountain states where energy development is occurring. There, the need for moderate-priced housing, nearby shopping, and bus transportation to work has been identified as essential to the stability of the work force, a major cost reduction requirement associated with power plant construction and mining.

Perhaps most important, however, are the opportunities in older cities to expand uses in existing neighborhoods or to form complete new urban villages in central locations on land no longer used for railroads, warehousing, or manufacturing. Major infill projects of this sort are often needed to facilitate the changing economic base of cities and to reflect their renewed use as residential sites for all income groups. . . .

The quality and size of single-family residences improved dramatically over the past 30 years. The proportion of households in "crowded" conditions has dropped by two-thirds for owners and three-fifths for renters. Moreover, the proportion of households that own their homes has risen to 65 percent.

On the other hand, in the past five years, other changes have occurred that threaten to limit opportunities for home ownership and improved housing quality. Increased financing costs, rising land prices, and the impact of public regulation have contributed to a housing supply crisis concentrated among those now just entering the housing market (a group that is at record numbers), those over 65, and the poor. Various responses are occurring. Home ownership is being postponed by young families without property to sell. Older home owners, legally or otherwise, are renting portions of large homes to offset the rising costs of maintenance, energy, and taxes. Conflicts over rent control and condominium conversions are erupting throughout the nation. In the course of the rent control struggle there, the mayor of Santa Monica, California, said that if the country doesn't attend to the housing affordability problem, we'll have a revolution on our hands. The proportion of total personal consumption allocated for housing is rising significantly, lessening choices for other goods and services. Lower-income families are increasingly concentrated in central cities where great numbers remain unable to pay sufficient rent to afford standard housing.

In addition, the United States lost more than three million housing units, or one in every 20 of the total stock, between 1973 and 1977. One in 16 rental units extant in 1973 had been removed by 1977. The loss of rental units occupied by blacks amounts to 2.5 percent per year. Much of the low- and moderate-income housing crisis is heightened by the removal of the units they can afford. Minority households also are disproportionately affected by failure of maintenance procedures; black-occupied units typically have two to three times as many maintenance defects as their white counterparts. . . .

Conclusion

Of the more than 80,000 governmental entities in the United States, 26,000 are general purpose counties and municipalities. All, however, affect development to a greater or lesser degree. Many civic, environmental, consumer, and other interests that play important roles in the development process have yet to appreciate the significance of recent shifts in market trends. State level organizations representing development interests have limited experience working with organizations representing counties and municipalities on common legislative agendas. There is even less experience with an equally necessary process: bringing development and environmental interests together to sort out mutually acceptable ways to reduce housing costs, conserve land, and improve community building. Clearly, substantial public education is necessary in order to make such widespread cooperation possible. National organizations representing both development and governmental interests will need to help convey the message through their policy and educational processes.

Seemingly diverse interests can reach accord on troublesome land and housing issues. To achieve implementation by state and local governments, however, will require public and private leaders respected in each state and sub-state region to consider comparable issues in the light of their own political traditions, growth trends, and preferences; each area must frame its own agenda for implementing regulatory and tax reform and adopting new planning and development tools. Failure to do so would add additional cost burdens to consumers and taxpayers that the nation can ill afford, and would deny improved community and housing opportunities to a growing segment of the population.

4

The Impact of Rail Transit
on Land Use

Evidence and a Change of Perspective

Robert L. Knight

IN THE CONTINUING battle among the larger U.S. cities to lay claim to some of the limited Federal funds available for new urban rail transit systems and extensions, great efforts are expended in trying to prove that the transit investment will lead to large and desirable changes in the pattern of urban development. It is typically claimed that such changes will occur through some combination of improvements in accessibility, the generation of new points of major activity (transit stations) and hence development market potential, and joint development of sites around the transit stations along with the transit system itself. These changes in land use, it is argued, will create higher urban densities and thereby expand the transit system's ridership base as well as help in reducing the region's private vehicular travel needs, fuel consumption, air pollution, noise, and generally enhance the quality of life.

All of this is intuitively appealing, and is also in reasonable accord with the limited theoretical foundations we have for understanding the determinants of land value and use. However, in view of the very high cost of such transit systems, the relatively limited capital generally available for in-

ACKNOWLEDGEMENT. The author gratefully acknowledges the support of the Office of the Secreatry, U.S. Department of Transportation, in the research and evaluation efforts which led to the conclusions in this article. However, views expressed here are represented as the author's alone and do not necessarily reflect the official position of the Department or opinions of individual staff members.

Reprinted from Robert L. Knight. "The Impact of Rail Transit on Land Use: Evidence and a Change in Perspective." *Transportation* 9 (1980): 3–16. Copyright © 1980, Elsevier Scientific Publishing Company. Reprinted by permission.

vestment in urban systems, and the need to assure the effective use of such capital as is available, more definitive proof is continually sought.

Against this background, a major purpose of this paper is to review the experience of the post-World War II period in rapid investment and its apparent effects on urban development. The intent of this review is to draw inferences concerning the potential strength of that relationship and to indicate why success in achieving such effects on land use seems to have varied so much between places such as Toronto and San Francisco.

It should be reported at the outset that the results to follow are not very satisfying. Available evidence does not show that recent American and Canadian rail rapid transit investments have had major effects on urban structure, as determined by activity locations, resulting patterns of travel, and related secondary effects. Within our ability to identify such effects, they simply do not seem to have occurred within the ten- to twenty-year period we have had to observe modern transit systems such as San Francisco's BART, the Toronto subway, Montreal's Metro and the major new extensions of older systems elsewhere. This seems to be the case even under the best of circumstances, such as in Toronto, in which the transit investment is fortuitously coordinated with other forces such as an expanding local economy, land available and attractive for development around the transit stations, other nearby public investments, zoning incentives, and a supportive community.

Predictably under such circumstances, rail transit has many detractors. In addition to its apparent lack of provable effectiveness, it costs huge sums, which are increasingly hard to obtain either locally or from central sources. And yet even most of the detractors would like to be proven wrong, for they, just as those who support rail transit, seek solutions to the pressing urban problems which rapid transit is intended to address. They merely wish for clearer evidence that the massive public investments required by transit are indeed justified by the likelihood of the desired effects on urban development.

Unfortunately, such wishes for clear empirical proof of rapid transit's effects on urban development cannot be met. We simply do not have the experience needed to yield the necessary information. Rail rapid transit may well have the effects sought, but apparently not within the first ten to twenty years after construction. In addition, older transit systems—which do appear to have had such effects—were built under very different circumstances which may have permitted much greater impact.

The evidence and reasoning to support these pessimistic conclusions is summarized later in this article. However, the pressing needs for solutions to our very real problems of energy use, traffic congestion, environmental degradation, land overconsumption and sprawl, all provide incentives to attempt to go beyond the all-too-easy conclusion that rail rapid transit is not an effective tool. Consequently the paper continues in order to serve a second purpose: that of indicating structural deficiencies in the way the issue is being formulated and suggesting an approach which results in very different policy implications. In brief, that approach shifts the focus of debate from proof of transit's direct land-use effects to the justification of risks.

This writer conducted a nationwide study for the U.S. Department of Transportation in 1977 to assess the effects of rapid transit on land use (Knight and Trigg, 1977). Developments since that time have not materially affected the validity of that study's findings. Those findings and related policy implications are worth repeating here in some detail, together with some observations on events since that study's completion. This updated review constitutes the basis for this paper's further conclusions.

This review begins with comments on this century's early rapid transit systems and their effects, followed by a brief analysis of the effects of modern American and Canadian urban rapid transit investments. Further comments are provided on the recent U.S. experience with related fixed transit modes such as light rail, commuter rail and busways. Brief mention is also made of the European experience. A series of conclusions and policy implications follows these synopses of study findings.

Pre-World War II Experience

Urban transportation in the past century has been characterized by a series of technological innovations ranging from horsecars through modern subways and beyond to the private automobile operating on high-speed roadways. Each succeeding wave of innovation has permitted an almost explosive expansion of the city. Behind this, throughout the latter half of the 19th century and into the 20th when most of these improvements were made, the country's urban population was growing rapidly through immigration as well as rural-urban migration. All of this was fueled by a rapidly expanding and industrializing economy built on natural resource exploitation.

The consequence of these urban growth pressures, together with the subsequent transit innovations, and the lack of competition from more effective methods of travel such as the later auto, was a shaping of urban growth along transit lines. In older cities many of these patterns persist today, even as more effective methods of movement have replaced their slower predecessors in the same corridors. However, forces other than transit were also important. In addition to those already noted, the geographical restraints and inducements of ethnic groupings, natural topography, prior development and its value, and early land use controls and taxation policies also had significant effect.

This situation was different from the current one in at least one very important way. Today's transit improvements do not provide the kind of drastic improvement in overall accessibility which was typically associated with earlier transit improvements. The auto provides a superior competitive alternative for many travelers. Consequently in today's world the lesson of the past seems to be that future transit-induced land use impacts can approach pre-war proportions, if at all, only in two ways: first, through now-unforeseen innovations which create major improvements in accessibility, and second, through greatly increased coordination of transit with other complementary forces.

Modern Rapid Rail Improvements

Recent improvements in conventional rail rapid transit in the U.S. and Canada vary widely in their potential as well as actual land use impact. In general, experiences of the past 25 years in cities such as Toronto, Montreal, San Francisco, Boston, and Philadelphia demonstrate that some impacts on land use have occurred. Typically where such impacts have occurred, they involve increases in intensity of use of land near transit stations. These land use effects have ranged in size from nil to quite large, at least with respect to the small size of these transit station areas (typically only a few blocks in each direction). A careful study of experience in each city indicates that successful cases have been those in which transit and a variety of other complementary factors were present together. These factors included land availability, its ease of assembly, the social and physical characteristics of the area, general economic conditions, community support, and public land use policies. Conversely, when these forces were absent or weak, few land use impacts were found.

Land use impacts of new full-scale systems in Toronto, Montreal and San Francisco have tended to be substantial in facilitating downtown high-rise office development. Evidence accumulating since the USDOT study's completion suggests that similar effects may be occurring in central Atlanta and Washington, D.C., where new rail systems are now only partially open for service. Except in Toronto, impacts elsewhere along these new transit lines have generally been small. In Toronto, intensive high-rise apartment and mixed-use development has occurred at many (but not all) outlying stations. These differences in impact appear to stem from the strong support given transit's impact potential by other forces in Toronto, notably zoning incentives plus historical, economic and social forces. In contrast, negative forces such as community composition and opposition, physical constraints, and lack of regional demand for new development appear to have overshadowed the positive potential of the San Francisco (BART) and Montreal (Metro) systems in suburban areas.

Impacts of smaller systems, new lines and extensions built since World War II have also been mixed. Substantial transit-related intensification of development has been experienced, notably at some stations along Philadelphia's Lindenwold Line and Boston's Red Line extension to Quincy. A particularly interesting example of coordinated development is found in New York's Roosevelt Island and the Crosstown Subway, now under construction. Conversely, virtually no effects are apparent for the Cleveland system and its airport extension as well as for the line extensions of Chicago's rapid transit system. Here again the difference is found in other factors, especially the attractiveness of the station site, zoning encouragements or hindrances, and overall demand for new intensive development.

An important perspective on these results is provided by a finding not cited in the 1977 study: the amount of development induced to concentrate around rapid transit stations has been only a very small fraction of all new regional development occurring in the decade or two following construction of modern rail transit systems, and an even smaller fraction of any region's total building stock. This is true even for Toronto, where high-rise buildings around some stations have been widely cited as evidence of transit's potential for shaping urban development.

Other Transit Modes

Commuter rail system improvements in coverage as well as quality of service were reviewed in all cities in which such improvements were substantial. One all-new system, Toronto's "GO," was also studied. It was found that such improvements varied greatly both in their own magnitude and their land use effects. Such effects were generally weaker than those observed with conventional rail transit, and depended heavily on the same factors.

Particularly at downtown terminals, evidence indicates substantial impact potential in cases of downtown expansion. Notably in Chicago, the service improvements and the resulting consistently high patronage on the rail lines using the Union and Northwestern stations were apparent encouragements to the high-rise development of nearby areas outside the Loop. Likewise, in Philadelphia the prospect of the yet-unfinished Center City Commuter Connection has been a factor—though by no means the only one—in redevelopment now taking place in the Market Street East area.

The recent light rail improvements available for study in the U.S. and Canada are inadequate to provide a proper indication of this mode's potential. Major improvements now in progress in Edmonton, Calgary, San Diego, San Francisco, Pittsburgh and elsewhere are not yet or only recently in operation, and evidence of early impact is inconclusive. Other improvements involve only restoration or minimal upgrading of old systems, as in Chicago (Skokie Swift) and Boston (Green Line). Consequently no evidence of impacts was found. Given the current interest in light rail, this should be a focus of further evaluation of land use impact.

Busway improvements have had no discernible impacts on land use to date. Here again, however, the cases studied were characterized by an absence of consideration of land use impact potential in their original planning, and were implemented in situations in which few if any complementary factors existed to enhance the potential for such impacts. Consequently, as with light rail improvements, the American experience to date is not sufficient to allow firm conclusions on land use impact potential.

The European Experience

The planning of transit improvements and urban land development is much more coordinated in most European countries than in the U.S. However, it is not often controlled so absolutely as commonly believed in this country. Most often the guiding force is suburban land development with active participation by the metropolitan government. Transit access to the city is often a complementary feature, amounting to a classic joint development process. Examples of such efforts can be found in most European countries.

The government often has more influence on such a development than is usually the case in the United States. However, the usual approach is interagency and public-private coordination of land development, which could be applied more in the U.S. as well. The key difference between the American and European approaches resides not simply in irreconcilable philosophical differences regarding the role of government; more basic is the European's higher level of expectations and stronger preferences for public transportation services. These attitudinal differences may be based on differences in the degree of experience with effective modern rapid transit between the typical American and European, and suggest that American attitudes may change as experience with high-quality transit increases.

Conclusions and Policy Implications

Recent major rapid transit improvements have been important inducements to intensified development near stations both in CBD's and in outlying areas, although only when supported by other favorable forces. In downtown areas, transit projects in cities such as Toronto, Montreal and San Francisco have enhanced accessibility by providing additional commuter capacity in some major congested radial travel corridors. However, the primary factor behind the intensification of land use in such areas has been the existence of a strong and effective demand for new office, retail, and apartment development.

Other key factors, as shown in Figure 1, have included local land use policies and other government policies, other nearby land investment, the availability of developable land at reasonable risk and cost, and the attractiveness of the site for development. Each of these factors is in turn influenced by several other determinants, as the figure indicates. Federal policy must acknowledge these many forces and the need for their coordination in general urban development as well as transit planning. Impact-potential assessments for proposed transit improvements should include site-specific evaluations of the effects of these factors, and such evaluations should include knowledgeable real estate development perspectives.

Although it does appear that rapid transit can help to induce intensification of urban development, that effect is most likely to be very small in rela-

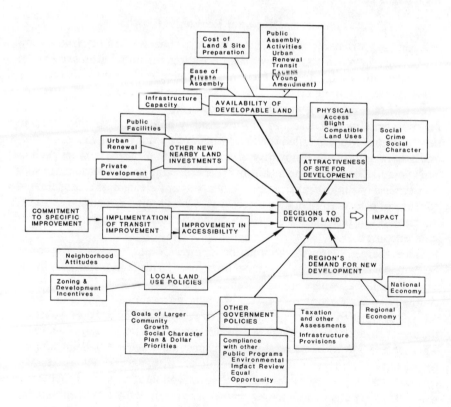

FIGURE 1.—*Factors influencing land use impacts (Knight and Trigg, 1977).*

tion to the overall size or development activity of a given metropolitan area. A study undertaken by this author as part of the BART Impact Program indicated that even if clustered high-rise development similar to that seen in Toronto were to occur around every BART station, the locations of no more than ten percent of the Bay Area's projected growth through the year 2000 would be affected. Consequently, the effects of such development impacts on travel patterns, overall residential densities, and related fuel consumption are likely to be only marginal.

This suggests, for example, that energy policy should not rely on rapid transit's development-focusing power as a key element, although it may be a useful contributor. Some further research—which could be done quite quickly—is needed to test this preliminary judgment and estimate the likely "energy payoff" of further rapid transit investments in terms of fuel savings versus cost.

Impact on Regional Economic Growth

Recent experience provides no evidence that any rapid transit improvements have led to net new urban economic or population growth. In particular, the BART Impact Program's detailed evaluation failed to find any such net economic effects. This suggests that land use impacts are shifts from one part of the city to another. However, evidence of the lack of net regional benefits is sparse and not necessarily binding on future efforts in this direction. More detailed research is needed on this important issue, particularly in light of the innovative attempts now in progress in cities such as Buffalo and Detroit. In the meantime, Federal policy might reasonably support the use of major transit improvements as one element of a coordinated package of efforts to revitalize a declining urban economy and social order, but should not rely upon transit investment as the sole or primary tool for such purposes.

Since the 1977 study's completion claims of new regional economic benefits of new transit systems have intensified. This is most notable in the case of Atlanta, where a net "impact" of some $500 million so far is claimed in private economic growth brought in from outside the state due to the yet-unfinished Metro system. Apart from the difficulty of substantiating such a claim, this raises a major issue for the Congress—namely whether it ought to be Federal policy to provide massive financial support for such public works in already economically strong areas such as Atlanta, if that investment encourages the further attraction of capital to such areas from other regions of the country which are presumably less economically healthy environments. Such Federal investment is perhaps reasonable in economically depressed cities such as a Detroit or Buffalo, but hardly so—if the claims of net economic gain are true—in the growing urban areas of the South and West.

Significance of Local Land Use Policy

Local land use policy changes have often been instrumental in facilitating transit's land use impacts. Land use policy was found to be one of the most important factors in the generation or prevention of impact. Zoning near stations, in particular, must usually allow intensification of use if any significant impact is to occur. Other local policies concerning factors such as provision of needed infrastructure to sites have also been important. When these policies work at cross purposes, a crucial source of impact encouragement is lost. Federal policy should urge the rationalization of land use controls and other local policies with transit-related land use impact objectives.

The transit improvement itself has often led to changes in land use policies. Experience indicates that major transit improvements often act as catalysts in the process of land use change, coalescing support for previously contentious policy changes. This appears to have been based largely on a widely shared belief in the likelihood of impact which the transit investment instills in decision-makers and the general public. This indirect influence may in fact be one of rapid transit's most powerful means of generating land use impacts. It is not always positive; fear is often the motivation and downzoning the outcome when transit stations are placed within established residential neighborhoods. In view of the size of transit investments, this is a substantial threat to the achievement of a justifiable level of societal benefit. Federal policy should not depend solely on the appearance of favorable local land use policy after the transit investment is made, but should stress the need for its advance demonstration as well as assurance of stability over time, where possible.

Changing the Perspective

Certainly the evidence provides little encouragement to the use of rail transit investment for reshaping our cities. But the urban problems remain. There seems to be substantial consensus that we need to reduce transportation energy use, through shifts of both travel mode and activity locations; improve residential environments through traffic reduction; save personal travel time; conserve our existing urban investment, notably in the central areas; save valuable urban-fringe land; improve individual access to open space; and improve the quality of life of disadvantaged persons. There is probably also reasonable agreement that no single action or program can fully solve any one of these problems. Finally, it is likely that rail transit does contribute at least marginally to the achievement of not just one or two but most or all of these goals whether or not definitive proof is possible.

Notice, too, that all the results presented earlier in this paper do not disprove the power of rapid transit investment to contribute meaningfully to major urban reshaping, but only fail to substantiate that such power exists. The potential may in fact be there, yet beyond the possibility of empirical proof. However, as long as the burden of proof is on the advocates of rapid transit and factual, quantitative evidence is required to establish that proof, it is unlikely that major new transit investment will win the broad support required for its implementation.

This may be an unduly limited view. There is the possibility that in focusing only on the effects we are able to measure, we could be ignoring or discounting other effects which are less tractable but far more important in the long run. We cannot hope to find clear evidence from the recent past which confidently predicts the future, for at least two reasons as noted earlier in this article. First, our recent experiences are too limited and brief. Second, the evidence indicates transit does not seem to have distinctly separable effects on urban form and activity, but rather acts as an element—and also perhaps a precondition, to some degree—of a mix of forces which produce such effects only when in concert. Consequently its "unique" effects on urban land use cannot be found in recent experience, for they probably do not exist in isolation.

The present rationale and formal process of qualifying for Federal aid in the construction of rapid transit systems requires an exhaustive effort to justify costs through definite benefits. Because of the high costs, such benefits must include significant effects on land use. Even so, such aid is less and less likely at present, since available Federal funds are not expanding significantly and the demands for prior proof of benefits are stiffening. Thus the present impasse: benefits, particularly those related to effects on land use and urban development, must be proven; yet no matter how plausible, such benefits are, by their nature, unprovable. One result has been that in attempting to provide such proof, some applicant cities have been forced to rely on weak data and arguments, thereby undermining their own credibility. But perhaps the wrong game is being played. Given the great importance of solving the many problems which are related to urban structure, our present logic may be too conservative. Maybe the mandatory search for *a priori* assurance of desirable land use impacts should even be abolished, since it appears to be both fruitless and possibly even countereffective.

This intemperate statement requires some explanation. Such suggestions are dangerously subject to misunderstanding and misuse by uncritical advocates of high-cost rapid transit construction, who have sometimes argued in favor of such heavy investment on the grounds that massive urban restructuring and revitalization *will* occur—citing European and turn-of-the-century American experience—despite our inability to demonstrate it from our own recent experience. But this article does not suggest a turn to reliance on blind faith in rapid transit's salutary effects on urban structure; quite the argument over the size of rapid transit's impacts on land use, we need to be shifted to a higher level. Instead of the present tedious, unresolvable arguement over the size of rapid transit's impacts on land use, we need to be considering what kind of cities we want, how much we want them, and how to maximize our chances of achieving those wants.

Investment in rail transit must be only one part of a strategy for achieving a particular future; but we are not even sure of what future we want—let alone in possession of a real strategy for reaching it. That the current argument is only over rail transit's specific land use effects is testimony to our lack of common vision and purpose, at the local level as well as nationally. Certainly the simplest remedy for this situation is an explicit national urban policy backed by national and local goals including physical form and function. In the extreme, if the goals were agreed to be important enough, virtually any action with any chance of contributing to their achievement could be included almost irrespective of cost. A broad range of actions, from rapid transit investment to focused development tax credits, could then be pursued jointly to reach those goals. However, hardly anything could be less likely. The U.S. society is one built on diversity, and its decision-making processes emphasize negotiation and compromise among diverse interests. The kind of consensus required in the simplistic scenario just described virtually never occurs, and especially not in topics involving as many competing interests as urban development and the allocation of very large sums of public funds.

In this society, public actions are taken incrementally, with both the results and actions—and even the goals themselves—continually being re-evaluated and revised. Given this reality, how might we improve our perspective on the issue of rail transit investment? An important first step is to openly acknowledge the limitations of what we can predict; as shown by the research results presented earlier in this article, there is much that we do not understand. Decision-makers must not be misled to believe otherwise.

Let us summarize that limited knowledge once more. At best, it appears that major direct effects of transit investment on urban form, activity patterns, and related effects such as fuel savings and environmental enhancement will emerge only over several decades and only with close coordination with other factors. That coordination is extremely difficult to achieve. Even then, major effects cannot be guaranteed. There is also some evidence of a less direct but potentially more significant role for transit in the urban development process. The firm assurance or actual presence of a new rapid transit system may provide an important impetus to other complementary changes in local public policy, which in turn help to focus and intensify urban development around the framework provided by the transit system. For example, land use controls and incentives may have much more power than rail transit to help generate desired development patterns, but the required changes in such land use policies may become politically possible only with the impetus provided by a rapid transit investment.

This suggests that such major transit investments may be crucial catalysts in the process of generating long-term changes in urban structure. This cannot be proven. However, such catalysts, or "levers," are particularly important in our incremental style of societal guidance. In the case of urban development, at the moment there seem to be almost no other promising candidates for this role. For example, the many local and Federal incentives to central-city revitalization of the last three decades have generally failed to promote local land use policy changes and other innovations which seem necessary to foster the large-scale land-use effects which are needed. Thus despite its high costs and uncertainty of success, rapid transit investment may literally be the "only game in town" if major and desired urban-structure changes are to be generated within the foreseeable future.

Such a possibility cannot even be considered within the current approach to transit investment decision-making. Instead, skeptics as well as advocates of new rapid transit systems tend to argue in terms of the "definite" land use impacts of such investments. Skeptics want proof; many advocates insist (without such proof) that the hoped-for effects on urban development are virtually certain. Risk and uncertainty are essentially ignored. But our actual experience, as reviewed in this paper, shows that uncertainty is the central feature of the entire process. Thus, we need a means of dealing with that uncertainty in making rapid transit investment decisions.

From this discussion four key factors emerge. Two have to do with urban objectives; they are the *desired urban development effects* of some program of actions and the *degree of importance* attached to those effects by the public and their decision-making authorities. The other two factors are related characteristics of alternative programs of actions (one or more of which includes rapid transit). These are their *costs* and the *uncertainty* of their achieving the desired urban-development effects. Together these factors provide the framework for an improved approach to rapid transit investment decision-making.

Essentially this proposed approach bases the transit investment decision on an explicit recognition and trade-off of these factors. In effect, the importance of achieving the desired urban-development results is weighed against the cost *and uncertainty* of the transit investment (along with the complementary forces as outlined earlier) as a means of achieving those results. The conventional multi-modal transportation alternatives analysis procedure concentrates on costs and benefits without due and explicit regard for either the uncertainty of success or the importance of the objectives. But in fact, if an objective is important enough even a very high risk may be justified. For example, if nothing short of a major renewal and restructuring of the CBD will stop a particular city's rapid slide into virtual economic collapse, and a major rapid transit investment is widely believed to be the only chance to effectively encourage that scale of renewal, then the stakes are so high that a rapid transit investment may be reasonably justified even at very high cost and under the greatest uncertainty regarding its eventual success. In less extreme cases, the principle still holds; rapid transit costs and uncertainties, and those of alternative actions (or inaction), should be weighed not just against the desired achievement of urban development objectives but also the importance of achieving those objectives.

All very well. But how to assess that importance, and that uncertainty? How to compare the two and reach the necessary degree of consensus on what costs and risks are justified? This article cannot encompass the details of procedural options. However, there are several models and methods for reducing the procedural problem to manageable pieces. Uncertainty can, for example, be assessed in relative terms by the presence or absence of factors which are known to complement transit investment in guiding land use change. Importance can be assessed, in part, through studies of the societal consequences of *not* achieving crucial national objectives such as reduction of energy use in urban transportation without serious mobility problems. Ultimately the two must be weighed along with cost in the political process to determine whether the investment and risk are justified. At the local level this may occur at the polls in the form of a tax referendum; for the government's funding decision it is likely to continue to be an administrative judgment, perhaps based on risk-acceptance criteria established by some future legislation in place of some aspects of the present alternatives-analysis procedure. Under such legislation it might be possible to vary the level of Federal support depending on the consonance of a project's objectives with national needs and the degree of uncertainty involved.

This method is particularly appropriate for situations in which one or more urban development objectives of overriding importance are generally agreed upon. In such situations the inherent uncertainty of transit's effectiveness is most likely to be balanced by the importance of the objectives and the apparent lack of alternatives. That is, risk is most likely to be justifiable in such cases. The emerging urgency of the need for transportation energy conservation may create just this sort of situation, in which a consensus gradually develops in support of the need for massive restructuring of cities to reduce vehicular travel.

The approach to decision-making suggested here is intended to help correct the imbalance now evident in the Federally mandated process of providing technical justification for locally proposed rail transit investments. Very large amounts of technical evaluation could and should be eliminated by relaxing the emphasis on objective evidence of direct land use effects. Instead, as argued above, much more attention should be given to demonstrating the linkages between specific social and environmental goals—such as energy independence or accessibility—and alternative patterns of evolution in city form and function over the next thirty to fifty years. Similar attention should be given to assessing the consequences of not achieving those ends, so as to judge the acceptability of taking risks in funding efforts—such as a rail transit system—intended to catalyze and move the process of change in the desired direction.

Naturally, more research is needed. We should not stop trying to understand specific cause-and-effect relationships in the urban development process. But more importantly, we need to do much more in identifying the effects of the divergent evolutionary paths that cities might be induced to take, not only in currently pressing aspects such as energy use but also with respect to broader social needs. We must learn how our cities need to evolve to serve us best—or at least to avoid the worst.

In short, we need to change our perspective. We seem to be asking and working hard to answer the wrong questions. Rapid transit may or may not be a good investment, but we can judge effectively only if we view the need and justification for it in terms of our larger urban objectives. Above all, we must learn to go beyond a deterministic style of transit investment evaluation to one more suited to decision-making needs in an uncertain world. We must deal with needs and risks, not guarantees, if we are to make intelligent decisions about rail transit investment in the future.

REFERENCE

Knight, R. L., and Trigg, L. L. (1977). "Land Use Impacts of Rapid Transit: Implications of Recent Experience." DOT-TPI-10-77-29 (Final Report) and DOT-TPI-10-77-31 (Executive Summary). Office of the Secretary, U.S. Department of Transportation, August.

5

Energy Constraints and Development Patterns in the 1980s

George Sternlieb and James W. Hughes

D O THE NEW energy constraints—destined to exert their full force
in the decade of the 1980s—involve a wholesale revision of the
spatial patterns of land use that have dominated the post-World
War II era? Have history and market experience lost their value as guide-
posts for future development, i.e., have the geographic and economic parameters of the recent past been rendered obsolete? With building cycles now
typically taking upwards of four years from initial land purchase to finished
product, and with the results fixed in place and exerting their influence for
many decades, these questions are not philosophical abstractions but rather
the essence of required present day decisionmaking.

In broad terms, land use in the United States has moved in a single
mature lifetime through three stages. The first period was one in which
there was a concatenation in space of industry, commerce, recreation and
residence. Its historic manifestation was the central city. The second stage
of the life cycle was an initial spatial fragmentation of these functions, with
inexpensive transportation providing the linkage. The development of
classic suburban bedroom communities was the most visible symbol of this
evolution, but the central city still preserved the major role of sheltering
most nonresidential urban activities. The third stage of the life cycle, which
is presently with us, is founded on the development of a critical mass of
population and buying power in selected suburban ring areas, such as to
either replicate or provide appropriate surrogates for activities which at one
time were dominated by the core. The latter area, in turn, in all too many
cases, has found it very difficult to maintain its "pulling power" against the

Reprinted from *Energy and Land Use*, edited by Robert W. Burchell and David Listokin.
Copyright © 1982, by the Center for Urban Policy Research, Rutgers University.

frictions that have arisen in it—not least of them racial—and in the face of competing alternatives.

It is striking to note in this context that nonmetropolitan territories of America have recently shown the greatest level of activity. The nation's population—and by definition, housing—has moved from city to suburb and increasingly, out of both into a whole new dimension of dispersal. Much of this redistribution is the consequence of shifting employment concentrations to outer suburban locations, particularly along metropolitan circumferential freeways. Land which had once been remote from the central city—both inside and outside the formally designated metropolitan boundaries—gained increased residential attractiveness as the 1970s employment dispersal gained momentum.

What can we anticipate from the fourth stage of development? In our estimation there is an enormous inertia of events, of historic capital investment patterns, of job and population shifts, which once set in motion as powerfully as has been the case in the United States require not a decade, but literally a generation, to be shifted in a meaningful fashion.

Changes of a much more radical and rapid nature could very easily bring into question the entire political foundation of our government and its institutions. The United States has invested the bulk of its capital development since World War II in an increasingly centrifugal fashion. We cannot declare this obsolete without bankrupting the country. Within these limitations, however, we envision a relatively modest but significant alteration of the basic trendlines which are currently in existence. Presently, the concentration of employment at the metropolitan rim—along circumferential freeways—has reached such thresholds as to foster rapid residential growth in more dispersed nonmetropolitan rimlands. Energy realities, with appropriate public policy actions, present substantial opportunities for significant land use readjustments. Essentially these will be concentrated on intensifying land use in and along the great circumferential bands of development that now ring our central cities. The latter, in turn will not be the scene of great revitalization, certainly in comparison with their past levels of activity and population holding functions. Instead we see in selected areas a much more limited, but nevertheless most meaningful, recycling potential. Most central cities will be but one of a constellation of activity nodes of the post-industrial metropolis; a return to the central city dominance, to a land use pattern of 50 years past, is unlikely. There is a host of lesser adaptive mechanisms which can buffer all but the most acute of energy strictures: carpooling, for example; the rise of much more efficient vehicles; and a multiple of others are well within our grasp. We do not have to invent the future. Its first growth is presently with us.

An Age of Scarcity versus a Latent Reservior

First and foremost in any forecast is appropriate awareness of the new age of scarcity that suddenly is evident, and most particularly, of the housing component of land use development. It is the unparalleled levels of affluence of the American housing consumer that has been one of the great facilitators of dispersed land use arrangements. Will diminished standards of living abort the assumptions of the past?

To put it bluntly, Americans are no longer as rich as we once thought we were. The consumer's shrinking dollar now has to stretch in an increasingly painful fashion to encompass the supermarket and the energy costs of work-related transit. As a result, the resources available for housing will be subjected to increasing constraints. Given appropriate expansion of employment opportunities, more and more the backbone of the market must be the two-worker household. While current statistics indicate soaring labor force participation rates for women in general, and wives in particular (see Table 1), this phenomenon has yet to be exhausted. As of 1977, only 17 percent of all husband/wife households had both members working full

TABLE 1.—*Civilian Labor Force by Sex and Marital Status*
March 1970 and 1978

| | CIVILIAN LABOR FORCE | | | |
| | Number (in thousands) | | Labor force participation rate | |
Sex and marital status	March 1970	March 1978	March 1970	March 1978
Both sexes, total	81,693	98,437	59.1	62.2
Men, total	50,460	57,466	77.6	76.8
Never married	9,421	13,978	60.4	69.2
Married, wife present	38,123	38,507	86.6	81.6
Married, wife absent	1,053	1,703	61.3	77.4
Widowed	672	667	31.9	30.5
Divorced	1,191	2,711	76.0	80.7
Women, total	31,233	40,971	42.6	49.1
Never married	6,965	10,222	53.0	60.5
Married, husband present	18,377	22,789	40.8	47.6
Married, husband absent	1,422	1,802	52.1	56.8
Widowed	2,542	2,269	26.4	22.4
Divorced	1,927	3,888	71.5	74.0

NOTE: Because of rounding, sums of individual items may not equal totals.

SOURCE: Beverly L. Johnson. "Changes in Marital and Family Characteristics of Workers, 1970–78," *Monthly Labor Review.* (April 1979), pp. 49–52.

time, year round.[1] The higher figures conventionally cited in this regard are misleading in that they incorporate part-time workers and those who work for a limited part of the year.

This is an extremely important phenomenon, since the household at the top of the income ladder—as shown in the data of Table 2—is the husband/wife family with the wife in the paid labor force. In a post-shelter era, then, with housing as investment an established convention, the potential for residential mobility will be substantial for select household types.

So, our prognosis starts off with the reality of this still very substantial latent reservoir of housing demand and an assumption that the economic world will be hard—but not come to an end—and that there will be jobs for the able and willing.

The Secular Market Pattern

Within this overall context, what are the areal dimensions of growth going to be? Certainly, the events of recent history provide both the constraints and foundations for future alterations. The long-term patterns of population dispersal and growth are summarized by the data of Table 3, which indicate the tremendous rapidity with which central cities have declined as population loci in the United States. The 31.5 percent share of the nation's population captured by central cities in 1970 diminished sharply to the 28.2 percent level by 1977. This was not simply a consequence of much more rapid growth in suburban and nonmetropolitan territories, but also for the first time, the absolute decline in the population of central cities. Over the seven-year period, the aggregate losses accruing to all central cities approached 2.9 million people, or 4.6 percent of the 1970 base. The bulk of

TABLE 2.—*Income Shifts by Family Type, U.S. Total 1970 to 1977*

Family Type	1970 Income	1977 Income	Change 1970 to 1977 Number	Percent
Total Families	$ 9,867	$16,009	$6,142	62.2%
Male Head Total	10,480	17,517	7,037	67.1
Married, Wife Present	10,516	17,616	7,100	67.5
Wife in Paid Labor Force	12,276	20,268	7,992	65.1
Wife Not in Paid Labor Force	9,304	15,063	5,759	61.9
Other Marital Status	9,012	14,518	5,506	61.1
Female Head	5,093	7,765	2,672	52.5

SOURCE: U.S. Bureau of the Census, *Current Population Reports*, Series P-60, No. 118, "Money Income in 1977 of Families and Persons in the United States," U.S. Government Printing Office, Washington, D.C.: 1979. U.S. Bureau of the Census, *Current Population Reports*, Series P-60, No. 80, "Income in 1970 of Families and Persons in the United States, U.S. Government Printing Office, Washington, D.C.: 1971.

TABLE 3.—*Population by Place of Residence, 1970 and 1977*
(Numbers in Thousands: 1970 Metropolitan Definition)

	1970	1977	Change: 1970 to 1977		Percent Distribution	
			Number	Percent	1970	1977
U.S. Total	199,819	212,566	12,747	6.4	100.0	100.0
Metropolitan Areas	137,058	143,107	6,049	4.4	68.6	67.3
Central Cities	62,876	59,993	-2,883	-4.6	31.5	28.2
Suburban Areas	74,182	83,144	8,932	12.0	37.1	39.1
Nonmetropolitan Areas	62,761	69,459	6,698	10.7	31.4	32.7
Central Cities in Metropolitan Areas of 1 Million or More	34,322	31,898	-2,424	-7.1	17.2	15.0
Central Cities in Metropolitan Areas of Less than 1 million	28,554	28,095	-459	-1.6	14.3	13.2

NOTE: The metropolitan and nonmetropolitan totals differ from Table 1 due to different date of metropolitan delineation (Table 1, 1977; Table 2, 1970).

SOURCE: Center for Urban Policy Research Analysis of Data Presented in: U.S. Department of Commerce, Bureau of the Census, *Current Population Reports*, Special Studies P-23, No. 55, "Social and Economic Characteristics of the Metropolitan and Nonmetropolitan Population: 1977 and 1970," November 1978.

the decline was suffered by the central cities located in metropolitan areas having one million people or more, presumably those with the population thresholds, justifying investment in public transit facilities.

In contrast to the performance of the central cities stands the vigorous growth of metropolitan-suburban and nonmetropolitan territories. By 1977, the two together accounted for 71.8 percent of the nation's populace. Almost 153 million of the nation's 213 million people in 1977 lived outside of central cities.

That this trend has persisted despite the energy shocks of 1974 is evidenced by the data of Table 4, which tabulates migration to and from central cities by families between 1975 and 1978. A net out-migration of 751,000 husband-wife families was experienced over this three-year period, almost 10 percent of the 1978 total. And for the more affluent subset—with incomes $15,000 or above—approximately three central city families migrated to the suburbs for every family that moved from the suburbs to the central city.[2] Clearly, a back-to-the-city movement is difficult to discern, and the inertia of established trendlines is suggested.

A Broader Perspective

But central city population trends are enveloped within a matrix comprising a number of causal dimensions—demographic, regional and metropolitan-nonmetropolitan.[3] The demographic sector is marked by the increasing importance of migration, compared to net natural increase, as a determinant of local growth. The regional axis is evidenced by the high growth rates in the South and West, and a relative stagnation in the aging

TABLE 4.—*Central City Migration by Families, 1975 to 1978*

			MOVERS FROM		
Family Income	*Number of Families*[1]	*Central City to Suburbs*	*Suburbs to Central City*	*Abroad to Central City*	*Central City Net Change*
Under $5,000	295	46	32	20	+6
$5,000 to $9,999	905	175	81	70	−24
$10,000 to $14,999	1,407	244	104	36	−104
$15,000 to $24,999	2,983	692	245	48	−399
$25,000 and over	2,049	423	168	25	−230
Total	7,639	1,580	630	199	−751

[1]Number of husband-wife families with head 14 to 54 years of age, residing in central cities in 1978. (Numbers in thousands)

SOURCE: U.S. Bureau of the Census *Current Population Reports*, Series P-20, No. 331, "Geographic Mobility: March 1975 to March 1978," U.S. Government Printing Office, Washington, D.C.: 1978.

Northeast and North Central states. The metropolitan partition shows a marked resurgence on nonmetropolitan territories, aborting a trendline which had been in effect for over half a century. The data in Table 5 encompass the broader attributes of these three phenomena.

For the United States as a whole, the deceleration of population growth is gauged by an average annual compound growth rate in the 1970-to-1977 period (0.9 percent) significantly less than that (1.3 percent) of the preceding ten years—1960 to 1970. The major determinant of population change in this context is the decline in net natural increase (births minus deaths) over the two periods indicated, while net migration held relatively constant. And it is the increasing relative importance of the latter which translates into special shifts, one dimension of which centers on metropolitan clusters.

The decade of the 1960s was one in which the relative concentration of America's population in metropolitan areas probably reached its pinnacle. While metropolitan areas, for example, experienced average annual increments of 1.6 percent, nonmetropolitan counties lagged considerably (0.4 percent). Within the former, there was only minor variation as a function of size, with the growth rates of the largest metropolitan areas (over 3 million people) generally comparable to metropolitan areas in total. Within nonmetropolitan counties, those increasing in population at the most rapid rate typically were closest to metropolitan centers, as evidenced by the commutation profile indicated in the table.

When the focus shifts to the 1970-to-1977 period, an abrupt change in trendline appears. The annual growth rate of nonmetropolitan counties (1.2 percent) experienced a remarkable upswing to almost twice the level characterizing metropolitan areas (0.7 percent). Within the latter category, it was the largest metropolitan areas (over 3 million people) which were suddenly transformed into virtual no-growth contexts, with a barely discernible growth of 0.1 percent per year. While counties which have the heaviest incidence of commuting to more concentrated areas were at the forefront of the nonmetropolitan resurgence, their growth rates were nearly matched by noncontiguous areas. Even nonmetropolitan counties in which less than 3 percent of workers commuted to metropolitan areas secured gains at ten times the rate of the previous decade.

Even more salient are the net migration data of Table 5. Migration is a telling criterion of location shift by choice, indexing the locational preferences of Americans. Population gains secured via migration are, in effect, immediate gains of economic markets; population growth through net natural increase does not directly produce job holders, homebuyers, or immediate transit users, at least within short-run contexts. Hence migrational patterns can be viewed as signals of market shifts, pointing to loca-

TABLE 5.—*Population and Components of Change for Selected Groups of Metropolitan and Nonmetropolitan Counties, 1960, 1970, and 1977 (Numbers in the thousands)*

Metropolitan areas, nonmetro-politan counties, and regions	POPULATION			AVERAGE ANNUAL PERCENT CHANGE[a]					
				Population		Natural Increase		Net Migration	
	July 1, 1977 (provisional estimate)	April 1, 1970 (Census)[b]	April 1, 1960 (Census)[c]	1970 to 1977	1960 to 1970	1970 to 1977	1960 to 1970	1970 to 1977	1960 to 1970
United States	216,351	203,305	179,311	0.9	1.3	0.7	1.1	0.2	0.2
Metropolitan[d]	158,550	150,291	128,328	0.7	1.6	0.7	1.1	0.1	0.5
Over 3,000,000	53,260	52,864	45,766	0.1	1.4	0.6	1.0	-0.5	0.4
1,000,000 to 3,000,000	42,035	39,341	32,403	0.9	1.9	0.7	1.2	0.3	0.8
500,000 to 1,000,000	24,088	22,548	19,386	0.9	1.5	0.7	1.2	0.2	0.4
250,000 to 500,000	20,051	18,262	15,838	1.3	1.4	0.8	1.2	0.5	0.2
Less than 250,000	19,116	27,276	14,935	1.4	1.5	0.8	1.2	0.6	0.3
Nonmetropolitan counties by commuting to metropolitan areas[e]	57,802	53,014	50,982	1.2	0.4	0.6	0.9	0.6	-0.6
20 percent or more	4,549	4,013	3,663	1.7	0.9	0.5	0.8	1.2	0.1
10 to 19 percent	10,039	9,209	8,607	1.2	0.7	0.5	0.8	0.7	-0.2
3 to 9 percent	14,796	13,644	12,944	1.1	0.5	0.6	0.9	0.5	-0.4
Less than 3 percent	28,418	26,148	25,768	1.1	0.1	0.6	1.0	0.5	-0.9

Northeast	49,299	49,061	44,678	0.1	0.9	0.4	0.9	-0.3	0.1
Metropolitan	42,140	42,481	38,609	-0.1	1.0	0.4	0.9	-0.5	0.1
Nonmetropolitan	7,159	6,580	6,069	1.2	0.8	0.4	0.8	0.8	–
North Central	47,941	56,593	51,619	0.3	0.9	0.6	1.0	-0.3	-0.1
Metropolitan	40,221	39,661	35,073	0.2	1.2	0.7	1.2	-0.5	0.1
Nonmetropolitan	17,719	16,932	16,546	0.6	0.2	0.4	0.8	0.2	-0.6
South	69,849	62,813	54,961	1.5	1.3	0.8	1.2	0.7	0.2
Metropolitan	44,907	40,032	32,755	1.6	2.0	0.8	1.3	0.8	0.8
Nonmetropolitan	24,942	22,782	22,206	1.2	0.3	0.6	1.0	0.6	-0.8
West	39,263	34,838	28,053	1.6	2.2	0.9	1.3	0.8	1.0
Metropolitan	31,281	28,118	21,891	1.5	2.5	0.8	1.3	0.7	1.3
Nonmetropolitan	7,981	6,720	6,162	2.4	0.9	1.0	1.2	1.5	-0.4

[a]Based on the method of exponential change.

[b]Includes officially recognized corrections to 1970 Census counts through 1976.

[c]Adjusted to exclude 12,520 persons erroneously reported in Fairfax County, Va. (Washington, D.C.-Md.-Va. SMSA).

[d]Standard Metropolitan Statistical Areas (SMSAs) or, where defined, Standard Consolidated Statistical Areas (SCSAs) and county equivalents of SMSAs in New England (NECMAs); as defined by the Office of Federal Statistical Policy and Standards, Dec. 31, 1977.

[e]Classification based on 1970 Census data on percent of workers reporting place of work who commuted to metropolitan territory as defined in 1977 (see footnote 4). Of the total 2,455 nonmetropolitan counties, the four groups specified included 178, 331, 479, and 1,467 counties, respectively.

SOURCE: U.S. Bureau of the Census, *Current Population Reports*, Series P-20, No. 336, "Population Profile of the United States: 1978," Washington, D.C.: U.S. Government Printing Office, 1979.

tions of eventual economic vacation (net outmigration) or of expanding support thresholds (net inmigration).

The shifting patterns in this regard are reasonably clearcut. From 1960 to 1970, nonmetropolitan counties lost considerable population through outmigration to areas of greater concentration—the metropolitan nodes. The pattern was most accentuated in those areas in which commuting to the latter was the least significant. In contrast, all the major metropolitan areas benefited from net inmigration. This period may well have represented the terminal point in the shift of population from the land as a function of the final stages of the agricultural revolution.

The reality documented by the 1970–1977 data has rendered obsolete long held spatial conventions. The migration ledgers of metropolitan areas as a whole were in virtual balance. However, the aggregate totals mask the growing variation as a function of size. While the larger metropolitan formations experienced either net outmigration or diminished levels of inmigration, the smaller metropoli (under 500,000 people) actually experienced positive migration gains. Concurrently, nonmetropolitan areas were transformed from origins to destinations in the overall migration process, with the scale of the transition largely correlated with the proportion of workers in the nonmetropolitan region who commute into metropolitan areas (but, as will be noted later, *not* necessarily to the central city).

It is clear that the nation had shifted into a new/phase of growth as the decade of the 1970s reached its end. The emerging growth poles are suburban and nonmetropolitan areas, as well as smaller metropolitan places. Certainly, part of the nonmetropolitan phenomena may be subsumed under the label of exurbanization. One can view this process as merely a continuance of the dispersion from the core city, first to suburbia and subsequently to more peripheral patterns of settlement. From an energy and transportation perspective, however, given the scale of the processes at work, there are a number of issues which are raised. Evident among a wide spectrum of implications is the impact on journey-to-work patterns and trips to the central core.

As shown in the data of Table 6, only 10.5 million workers, out of a total 51.8 million residing in suburban (outside central cities) and nonmetropolitan areas, were employed in the central city. Indeed, 19.3 million out of 28.9 million suburban resident workers were employed in the suburbs.

The central city's diminished pulling power mirrored by this data can be interpreted as a function of the frictions inherent in transportation versus the unique lures and employment opportunities which are available in the city center. To the degree that the data on spatial diffusion suggest longer trips, in the absence of new transportation facilitators, clearly frictions are increased. Secondly, as population expands farther from the historic

TABLE 6.—*Place of Residence by Place of Work, United States: 1975 (Workers 14 years old and over; number of workers in thousands; SMSAs as of the 1970 Census)*

Place of Residence	All workers	REPORTED A FIXED PLACE OF WORK					No fixed place of work	Place of work not reported
		Total	Inside SMSAs					
			Total	Inside central cities	Outside central cities	In nonmetro-politan areas		
All workers	80,125	72,733	51,507	27,116	24,391	21,226	6,724	668
Inside SMSAs	55,418	50,425	49,429	26,119	23,301	1,005	4,512	481
Inside central cities	22,760	20,846	20,568	16,528	4,040	278	1,700	214
Outside central cities	32,658	29,579	28,852	9,592	19,261	727	2,811	267
In nonmetropolitan area	24,707	22,308	2,087	997	1,091	20,221	2,212	187

SOURCE: U.S. Department of Commerce, Bureau of the Census. *Current Population Reports*, Special Studies P-23, No. 99, "The Journey to Work in the United States: 1975," June, 1979.

population concentrations, it reaches critical mass, providing the threshold for the development of alternatives competitive to central city attractions. Indeed this may well intensify the development which has already occurred in terms of regional suburban shopping centers, multicinema units, largescale suburban hospitals, and the like. The data on journey-to-work reflect the growth and impact of the circumferential highways and the thickening of population concentrations in outer metropolitan areas and adjacent territories.

It is also evident from the data shown in Table 5 that the largest metropolitan areas—those which have the greatest absolute potential for intensive means of mass transportation—also have shown the least vigor of growth. At least through 1977, the smaller and more dispersed the metropolitan concentration, the greater the trendline of growth.

The changing regional population parameters intersect the above phenomena and generate an additional axis of variation (see Table 5). The Northeast and North Central Regions shifted to a net outmigration position in the 1970s, with declining net natural increase just sufficient in magnitude to maintain overall population stability. The South, in contrast, secured sharp gains both in migration and total population, while the West retained its position as regional growth leader.

Within this context, the metropolitan areas of the Northeast in the 1970s have lost population while those of the North Central Region are rapidly approaching stability in size. Only in the South and West are there substantial positive annual metropolitan growth rates—in part perhaps as a function of annexation which may obscure the basic centrifugal forces which are at work even in those regions.

Alternative Futures

It is against the backdrop of these established patterns that alternative models of future development must be evaluated. Conceptually there are four major options to be considered.

1) *A Revitalization of the Central City.* The thesis has been advanced that the central city represents an infrastructure which in an age of high energy costs cannot be replicated as casually as it has been done in the past. And further it provides many forms of energy efficiency in terms of housing density, employment centralization and journey-to-work logistics. We would suggest that, despite these potentials, mass central city revitalization is wishful thinking.

There is, nonetheless, a significant residual of potential for *selected* central cities. The key element here is the employment base. With few exceptions, the city's role as a dominant industrial workplace is over. The old smokestack cities will probably not rise again. At the same time there is the development of a very few national cities which pull people with particular attributes and generate unique economies. Particularly striking is the new dominance of consumption functions over those of production in some of the most sucessful settings of core "rebirth." But these new focal points are rare indeed.

The relatively monolithic center-of-the-market housing demand of the last thirty years, characterized by the mass developments of Levittown and the like, have given way to *consumer segmentation*. This in turn generates specific strata of population with quite differentiated tastes. Loft conversion is a meaningful and significant business in New York City, with more than 30,000 units already completed. It does not mean, however, that loft conversion in Youngstown, Ohio would make equivalent sense. Chicago's North Shore development is a thing of beauty, and assuming that the economy doesn't default, it will continue. It does not mean, however, that one can envision a similar scale of rebirth in Cleveland.

Race still plays a very major issue, and the new central city market as a mass phenomenon has yet to meet the test of resales. *The key element that planners must remember is that the housing element of land use must not only provide shelter, but also must provide for resale. Values have to be present not only to extant consumers, but also to those that they expect to sell to—and at a profit.*

Until and unless government policy literally forces employment back into the central city, significant questions must be raised concerning major widespread central city revitalization, subject to the specific cases and their equivalent that we have cited. Few energy savings can be realized by residing in the central city if one is employed in a suburban/exurban location.

2) *The Inner Suburbs.* In the midst of central city stagnation and decline, inadequate attention has been focused on the aging of the older suburbs in America. Some are beginning to replicate the traumas of the central city—declining school systems, rapid white outmigration, tax base erosion and the like. Nonetheless, there is still excellent housing available within them. Small vacant tracts are available and their logistics make reasonably good sense. But many of them are locked into the central city commuting pattern—too distant from new employment bands—and therefore subject to the vagaries of employment in the core. Yet, most strikingly, there is no way the housing values that exist within them could be replicated in terms of new construction. Selective rehabilitation in this context may represent a far larger potential than is presently appreciated. As the scene of major new construction, however, we would have some hesitation. Suburban infill may provide select opportunities for development for those geared to the limita-

tions and possibilities of that demanding field. But it is difficult to see the latter as a mass phenomenon, subject to the employment qualifier presented earlier.

3) *The New Ring City.* These are the areas typically straddling the circumferential freeways. They have evolved into dominant growth bands for jobs and, where zoning is available, housing in our society. We envision these as the real keystones to future residential development. An expansive, modern employment infrastructure has been recently set in place, and will remain whatever energy limitations ensue. Encompassed are the nation's newest and most competitive (in an international sense) industrial activities. The journey-to-work is far from insurmountable—if housing can be provided reasonably close by (and if Detroit would finally provide the kinds of cars that are going to be required).

There is, however, a significant problem in such regions in that residential land availability is restricted because of zoning and subdivision controls. *Workplace and residence must be granted tighter linkages—not the jobs of the past (those of the central city) but the jobs of the here, now and future on the ring highway.* The only way to accomplish this is to institute much more sensible land use planning, tolerating a greater variety of forms and much more intensive housing development than presently holds true in a good many areas. The consequence of the failure to recognize this linkage is indicated by our next area.

4) *The Exurban Spread.* Observers who view this type of spread as a *perversion* of land use (we use strong language here because they do!) fail to comprehend the new job-related facilities of America. *The commute to work to the ring highway for most of these locations is relatively easy. Indeed the journey-to-work to urban locations for central city residents is as long in time as that of suburb-to-suburb commuters.* The extreme level of dispersion to the nonmetropolitan fringes, however, is a tribute to restrictive zoning which has inhibited even greater efficiency of housing allocation to job sites.

Given the level of investment that has been made in the outer regions, it is difficult to believe that their development will abort suddenly. Americans have been sensitized, however, not merely to energy costs, but, through repeated energy shortfalls, to *availability.* The market here, therefore, may be much more subject to irregularities, of boom and bust, of subdivisions that simply do not secure traffic, of holding patterns while the energy crises which will characterize the next decade are lived through. Buying the truck farm and waiting for development to come may require more time—and cost—than used to be the case. Land speculation is always hazardous—but doing so in the farther reaches now may impose even more rigorous strain, and pain.

But this inefficient (in energy terms) market pattern may persist if appropriate policy responses are not forthcoming. Indeed, present casually considered efforts to restrict growth in the burgeoning ring zones does not direct development activity back to the central city, but forces a "spillover" effect into adjacent nonmetropolitan areas, and actually reinforces a land use pattern of greater dispersal.

Conclusion

Thus the decade of the 1980s has far more uncertainties than its predecessors. While the last wave of the baby boom will still generate housing demand through the period, its wherewithal will be much more subject to question.

Greater cognizance will be needed for variations in *housing types*—of party wall construction and of multifamily units—and of *juridical status* —of condominiums and co-ops, either alone or in combination with fee simple holdings. In turn, these will create even greater pressures on conventional control of land use.

From an areal perspective, however, we see the zones of growth which became more and more rigorously defined in the 1970s largely continuing into the decade to come. Energy *costs* will not alter America in our period; the lack of energy *availability* may. There is a time for heroes and a time for caution. The latter is at hand.

The thickening of the new suburban/exurban ring city in the United States will take place with even greater rapidity. Along this bank we envision crucial nodes—now in part nascent, in part becoming obvious—arising as even more significant entities. Their particular centers will vary depending upon opportunity and past levels of commitment. We can envision, for example, older trading centers taking on new vitality, such as White Plains in the New York Region, which has parallels elsewhere. Other forms of aggregative magnets may very well be provided by the regional shopping center, taking advantage of prime locations, significant acreage, the conversion of hitherto sprawling parking lots into more intensive forms of development, while their past function is secured by multistoried or multiuse facilities. There is no rationale for a hundred acre parking lot given the competing values of alternate utilization. Again these formats do not have to be invented; they are presently in the ground.

We can envision with no great stretch of the imagination adjacent intensive office and residential development. The condominium format will play an essential role in our era of post-shelter housing—and afford the occupants of both kinds of accommodation, inflation-proof forms of investment as well as shelter.

The key issue of the next ten years will be the control of land use, moving it away from local parochialism and paranoia about the future and toward the levels of flexibility which we have projected here. As yet we do not see any great wisdom on the part of higher levels of government in terms of land use recommendations which would give us confidence in their participation. The struggle may therefore be much more the continuance and intensification of private entrepreneur versus local zoning community, with the courts increasingly called on to act as adjudicators in the face of legislative incompetence. Standing in the way of a true coming to grips with national land use policy is the specter, and the memory, of the central city. As yet, purposeful, higher level land use policy implementation has been much more dedicated to the cause of things past than of things present and much less concerned with the future.

6

Land-Use Concomitants
of Urban Fiscal Squeeze

Forrest M. Cason*

THE PATTERN of land use in metropolitan areas is intimately related to local government finance; accordingly, changes in urban structure are likely to occur as the fiscal posture of local governments changes. An example is the effect local governments' responses to fiscal pressure may have on the spatial distribution and functional organization of land use in metropolitan areas. It is argued here that, barring substantial horizontal governmental integration, the areal specialization of land use and economic function by jurisdiction now characterizing metropolitan areas will give way to metropolitan complexes composed of communities diversified in their land use because of the fiscal pressures which are forcing local governments to provide relatively similar packages of goods and services.

Conceptual Framework

The developmental model of differentiation and specialization, followed by integration, is commonly used to describe the evolution of metropolitan areas.[1] Areal differentiation and specialization exists to accommodate the locational preferences of individual and firms. Specialization in the public economy is an extension of the preference for areal specialization revealed in the private sector. One influential theory of the imperatives in the allocation and distribution of public goods and services making for the pattern of

*Center for Urban Studies, Wichita State University. The author wishes to acknowledge the financial support of the National Fellowships Fund.

Reprinted from Forrest M. Cason, "Land-Use Concomitants of the Urban Fiscal Squeeze," *Urban Affairs Quarterly*, Vol. 16, No. 3 (March 1981), pp. 337–353, © 1981 Sage Publications, Inc., with permission.

numerous specialized governments in a metropolitan area is summarized in this quote from Bish and Ostrom (1973: 68):

> The large numbers of jurisdictions existing in most metropolitan areas can be viewed as so many different public firms or public enterprises in a public service economy. Some firms are of small size and enable people to meet the service needs that occur within a relatively small neighborhood or community. Other firms are of intermediate size and enable the same people to serve the needs they share with wider communities of interest. Still other jurisdictions and firms give access to capabilities that are related to still larger communities of interest.

Economic integration in the private sector is unimpeded by the arbitrary jurisdictional boundaries which define the market of "public firms" and, thereby, impede horizontal integration. In the public sector, inter-dependence between the constituent jurisdictions of metropolitan areas is clearly recognized, but integrative mechanisms capable of surmounting the political, financial, and social barriers to integration are viable, with few exceptions, only as theoretical abstractions.

The detriments of this pattern of many jurisdictions providing packages of goods and services tailored to meet the special needs of their constituents, and only infrequently cooperating to achieve economies, are very apparent upon examination of the means by which public firms are financed. Excluding from this discussion the so-called paragovernments (authorities and special districts), units of general government rely to a great, although decreasing[2], extent on locally raised revenues to finance their operation. The tax capacity/service needs ratio of a local government is a direct statement of the impact of decisions made in the private sector on the ability of the public sector to perform its mandate. Tax capacity and service needs vary as a function of the use to which the land within a jurisdiction is put. Local governments' revenue bases are as specialized as are the land uses within their territory; their tax structures are designed to optimize the revenue potential of their land use. Because of the locational preferences of individuals and firms, a local government's revenue base may be narrow and identifiably commercial, industrial, or residential, or more rarely, a balance of all three.

Areal specialization of land use, such that jurisdictional boundaries coincide roughly with the areas of specialized land use, that public goods and services provided within each jurisdiction reflect the special needs and preferences of land users, and that the revenue base is tied to continuation of this specialization, makes local governments tremendously vulnerable to change. Governments are not mobile; neither the land nor the infrastructure upon the land can change as rapidly as the locational preferences of individuals and firms. Thus, when individuals and firms migrate, so does the tax base of the local government, leaving behind the capital investments and costs associated with maintaining those capital investments.

Even in the absence of migration, another pitfall of extreme specialization stems from the cost/revenue relationship of various land uses. As a generalization, the only type of residential land use capable of paying its own way is high income. Local governments specializing in high-income residential land use, therefore, are less prone than their middle- and low-income counterparts to have service needs which outstrip tax capacity.

Specialization has been recognized as a contributory factor to the so-called "fiscal crisis" many local governments are now experiencing. Federal incentive programs such as Urban Development Action Grants (UDAG) and Community Development Block Grants (CDBG) designed to help stabilize the fisc of localities have precipitated a surge of new economic development programs. Examination of the policies local governments have formulated, or are in the process of formulating, to take advantage of federal aid reveals a marked effort to broaden their revenue base. Since that base is closely tied to land use, revenue base broadening generally implies land-use diversification.

What this means in a metropolitan context is that, with the exception of high-income residential jurisdictions, the "public firms" are becoming more alike. Williams et al. (1965) noted this tendency toward homogenization in their study of policy differentials between Pennsylvania municipalities. They pointed out that newer suburbs, especially, are diversifying the land use within their community to achieve a more balanced tax base, and that high-income suburbs' increased receptivity to nonresidential land users is linked to the perceived fiscal benefits accruing therefrom.[3]

Land-use patterns resulting from this scramble for tax base are usually less than desirable. Netzer (1962: 193) is graphic on this point:

> In its extreme formulation, the common effort—especially visible just west of the Hudson River where the property tax provides two-thirds of all state-local tax revenues—to attract industry (and, on occasion, shopping centers) but to keep out industrial employees with moderate incomes and large families, finds expression in the grotesque notion that each taxing jurisdiction in a metropolitan area should be a "balanced" community with its own industrial district, commercial area, and zones of upper-middle and upper income housing. One consequence, not surprisingly, is that community A's industrial district which occasionally will be colonized by the hoped-for research and development establishments, is adjacent to community B's high school, hospital, or quarteracre residential area, with bizarre esthetic and circulation effects.

Methodology

In view of the sudden emergence of economic development as a priority program of local governments, research was initiated to discern the extent to which the economic development policies of localities portend increased diversification of land use within and, therefore, decreased specialization among the various jurisdictions of metropolitan areas. The hypothesis of this research is that fiscal pressures are forcing local governments to provide relatively homogeneous packages of goods and services. Interestingly enough, competition for tax base is influencing the move toward more diversified land use, whereas the previous specialization was a result of competition to capture "consumers" with similar preference orderings for public goods and services. This suggests a move away from monopolistic competition to price competition.

Both a mail survey of municipalities with 1970 populations of 50,000 or more, and case studies of the Atlanta and Denver metropolitan areas were conducted. The survey, for which the response rate was 42%, served primarily as a means to comprehend emergent notions of the fiscal impacts of development and to identify the factors influencing the structure of communities' economic development efforts. The survey findings betray the weakness of the above-stated hypothesis as a generalization applied to all cities of 50,000 or more population. However, the findings of the survey also suggest the contexts in which the hypothesis can be supported. In lieu of an elaborate discussion of the research findings overall, the balance of this article is devoted to a description of a setting in which there is support for the hypothesis that fiscal pressures are forcing local governments to provide relatively similar packages of goods and services—metropolitan Denver.

Metropolitan Denver: A Case Study

The Denver SMSA, as defined by the 1970 census, consists of five county areas: Adams, Arapahoe, Boulder, and Jefferson counties, and the City and County of Denver. Like other postindustrial metropolitan areas,[4] in-migration of people and firms to metropolitan Denver has swollen the area in a relatively short period of time. Between 1950 and 1970 the SMSA's population growth rate averaged 4% annually and the population more than doubled. Table 1 breaks down the components of population change in this period; not surprisingly, most of the increase occurred outside the central city.

A brief examination of the fiscal stature of the area reveals that prosperity has not accompanied the rapid growth in population. Between 1957 and 1969, the population of Denver increased by 9% and City expenditures in-

TABLE 1.—Components of Population Change, Selected Areas, 1950–1970

Area	1950–1960					1960–1970				
	Population 1950	Age Adjusted Birth Rate 1950	Age Adjusted Death Rate 1950	Actual Population 1960	Net Migration 1950–60	Population 1960	Age Adjusted Birth Rate 1960	Age Adjusted Death Rate 1960	Actual Population 1970	Net Migration 1960–70
Central City	417,958	117,472	47,180	493,887	5,637 (1.35% increase)	493,887	103,162	53,411	514,678	-28,960 (-5.86% increase)
Ring	194,170	80,405	18,785	435,496	179,706 (25.23% increase)	435,496	122,174	30,605	712,851	185,786 (42.66% increase)
SMSA	612,128	197,877	65,965	929,383	185,343 (30.28% increase)	929,383	225,336	84,016	1,277,539	156,826 (16.87% increase)
U.S. SMSAs	87,581,609			112,885,178		112,885,178			127,417,000	5,280,000 (17.0% increase)

SOURCE: Denver Urban Observatory, 1974.

creased by 106%. Over the same time period the population of Denver's suburbs increased by 96% and suburban governments' expenditures grew by 265%. There was a gap "between expenditure demands and the capacity of county-area revenue sources to meet those demands" between 1972 and 1975 (Table 2) which, according to the Denver Urban Observatory (1972: 49, 39), made it "clearly evident that local governments in the metropolitan region face a fiscal crisis."

The four communities discussed here are believed to be representative of the metropolitan area as a whole. The consolidated City and County of Denver is the central city of the SMSA; Aurora straddles Adams and Arapahoe counties; Commerce City is wholly contained within Adams county, as is Littleton within Arapahoe county (see Figure 1).

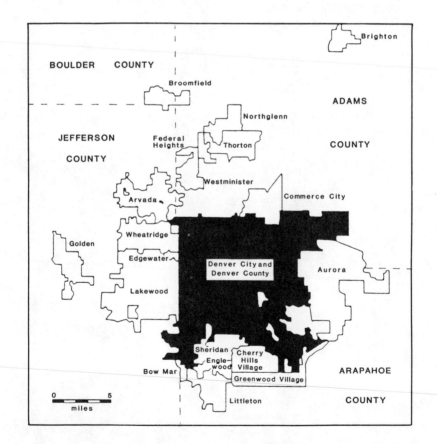

FIGURE 1: *Denver Locality Map*

TABLE 2.—*Estimated Expenditure-Revenue Gaps by County-Area, 1972–1975*

Expenditure-Revenue Gaps (in millions of $)

County-Area	1972	1973	1974	1975
Adams County-Area	3.20	3.24	3.31	3.44
Arapahoe County-Area	15.85	17.05	18.28	19.66
Boulder County-Area	8.18	8.83	9.51	10.28
Denver County-Area	17.42	19.07	20.88	23.08
Jefferson County-Area	8.85	9.46	10.45	10.83
SMSA Total	53.50	57.65	62.43	67.29

SOURCE: Denver Urban Observatory, 1972.

Community Profiles

Table 3 shows the policy emphasis and the principal strategies employed to achieve policy objectives in the four communities. Denver, typical of cities, has the most diversified land use, tax base, and population in the metropolitan area. Not surprisingly, Denver's incipient economic development program emphasizes the need to increase employment opportunities for inner-city residents. To accommodate expansion and retention of firms employing this target population, and to attract new firms into Denver which would create jobs for the target population, the Mayor's staff has recommended granting priority in financial assistance to firms "likely to provide the best potential for employing Denver's unemployed" (Denver, Colorado, Office of Policy Analysis, 1977: 5). This strategy calls for intensification of land use in areas currently zoned industrial and creation of more prime industrial land by rezoning and annexation.[5] Denver has been losing its industrial base. As of 1970 more than half of the total SMSA employment in manufacturing, wholesaling, retailing, and services was

TABLE 3

City	Policy Emphasis
Commerce City	Tax base expansion; community development; annexation
Denver	Job creation
Aurora	Broaden tax base
Littleton	Hold down tax rate; broaden tax base

located in the suburban ring. Thus, the programs recommended to foster job creation would also help the city maintain a broad, diversified revenue base.

Aurora's specialized role in the metropolitan economy is that of bedroom community to Denver. To emphasize that Aurora is not an autonomous unit now advancing along its own development pathway, note that as of 1973, "two-thirds of Aurora's working population commute[d] outside the city to work, and 80 percent of the commuters [had] jobs in Denver" (Aurora, Colorado, Department of Planning and Community Development, 1973: 116). Within the confines of its role as a bedroom community, Aurora houses mainly white-collar workers (65%). The city, however, is not a high-income suburb (median family income, $10,554) and houses a significant number (23%) of blue-collar workers. The telling points about the city's fiscal position are these:

(1) The cost/revenue relationships associated with Aurora's specialization in low-density middle-income housing. For this type of residential development to pay its own way, homeowners would have to be saddled with tremendous tax burdens. Increasing the property tax effort is both politically infeasible and fiscally imprudent, particularly since "over 70 percent of the (property) tax dollar goes to the support of schools" (Aurora, Colorado, Department of Planning and Community Development, 1973:98), the program for which expenditures have risen most dramatically since 1957.

(2) Sales tax reliance. In lieu of property taxation, the city has generated substantial income from the sales tax, first levied in 1964. "It is no wonder that the sales tax is both a powerful and attractive revenue tool. Revenue from the sales tax has increased over 600 percent from 1968 to 1971. It covers a broad base and is tied to the commercial growth of the city" (Aurora, Colorado, Department of Planning and Community Development, 1973: 89).

Although Aurora is not presently straining under the burden of its expenditure requirements, anticipation of strain resulting from too heavy a reliance on one-time revenue sources and a relatively regressive tax structure has prompted the city to embark on a vigorous effort to broaden its tax base. Industrial development and expansion of wholesaling are being pushed through the use of industrial revenue bonds (IRB's), service subsidies (water and sewer, for example), and assorted promotional activities. To accommodate this desired development, between 1972 and 1974 Aurora rezoned nearly 600 acres to industrial usage, bringing its total industrial zoned acreage to 4850 (Aurora, Colorado, Department of Planning and Community Development, 1973: 111). A brochure put out by ECO (Explore Commercial Opportunities) Aurora (1977: 2), the joint city and Chamber of Commerce economic development vehicle, advertises: "There are 5,500 acres for sale and lease, zoned for industry; another 500 zoned and ready for commercial development. Ninety percent have utilities already installed.'' If Aurora's land is developed as zoned, the proportion of the city's land devoted to nonresidential use will swell from the current 3.5% to nearly 18% (4% commercial; 14% industrial).

In summary, Aurora is a satellite city in the metropolitan economy. Over the long haul, the city's specialized role constrains the government's ability to tax equitably and to generate revenues sufficient to cover costs. Increasing industrial and commercial (especially wholesaling) land use will provide the city with a broader revenue base. The city's economic development program spearheads the drive to increase nonresidential land use.

In stark contrast to Aurora, Commerce City's economic base is heavily concentrated in industry and commerce. An estimated 33% of the city's land area was in commercial and industrial use as of 1970. Only 32% of Commerce City's working population are in white-collar occupations, and the median family income was $8,737 in 1970.

Unlike Denver and Aurora, budget projections for Commerce City through the year 2000 forecast increasing surpluses of revenue over expenditures (B.B.C. and Associates, Inc., 1977: 50). With such a rosy fiscal outlook, why does the city perceive the need for an economic development plan? The document which has been adopted as the guideline for the city's economic development program answers this question succinctly: "The financial position of Commerce City is directly dependent on the maintenance of the existing industrial and commercial base of the city in the form of property tax and sales tax revenues. Any erosion of this base could alter the City's position" (B.B.C. and Associates, Inc., 1977: 52).

There is much wariness in Commerce City concerning migration of existing firms and the city's ability to attract new firms because of the poor quality of its environment and the scarcity of developable land. Given these two strikes against future growth and development of the city, the sanguinity of the above budget projections shows through since the projections are tied to future industrial and commercial growth. The major strategies of the city's economic development program, therefore, are (1) increasing the supply of land suitable for nonresidential development, and (2) general upgrading of the community ambience. The first strategy necessitates annexation and land assemblage. The second strategy involves offering more and better quality public goods and services. Quoting from the city's economic development document (B.B.C. and Associates, Inc., 1977: 87):

> Community improvement strategies can help improve one of the most frequently noted problems with Commerce City as a location for new industry: the general undesirable image of the city. Provision of a more pleasant environment is a major step toward the retention of existing firms and residents.

Significant public investment is also a signal to industrial and commercial prospects that the city is committed to providing better living and working conditions.

To this end, 90% of sales tax revenues have been earmarked for street construction and maintenance; park acreage has increased from 9 acres in 1974 to 109 acres as of 1976; acquisition of a greenbelt open space system along floodplains commenced in 1977; a beautification program to "upgrade the aesthetic appearance of the city" is planned; additionally, the development plan recommends housing rehabilitation and revitalization of neighborhood commercial areas. One public official went so far as to suggest the city investigate the possibility of establishing a housing authority which would concentrate on developing *high-income* housing![6]

In the most literal sense, Commerce City can no longer afford its current specialization as low-cost, low-quality dumping ground for the metropolitan area. If the city fails to act, existing firms that have the choice are more likely to leave, nonnoxious firms are less likely to locate there, and an increase in noxious firms is likely to set in motion the flight of those residents with that option. To remain competitive Commerce City feels it must diminish the disparity in environmental quality between itself and competing neighbors.

At the opposite end of the environmental quality spectrum from Commerce City is Littleton. This municipality is ahead of the game now and can remain there unless it loses its water supply or is the target of some immensely unfavorable legislative enactment. Demographically, the city has the fourth highest median family income ($12,740 as of 1970) of the municipalities in the metropolitan area.[7] About the same percentage of the city's total developed land is in residential use (93%) as in Aurora, but, as can be seen from Table 4, Littleton's industrial base in the MTCU industries is more than double that of Aurora's. The tax structure of Littleton and Aurora are similar; both have a 3% sales/use tax, and this tax comprised roughly half of both cities' general fund revenues in 1975 (Littleton, Colorado, Department of Community Development, 1975; Aurora, Colorado, Department of Planning and Community Development, 1973).

The essence of the comparison between Aurora and Littleton is the greater fiscal capacity of Littleton emanating from its industrial base. The benefits accruing to the city from nonresidential development are summarized in a document addressing Littleton's need to evaluate the fiscal impacts of development.

Although commercial/industrial development does not receive the benefits of increased expenditures in most government operation directly, with the possible exception of fire and police protection, they contribute the most in city revenue

TABLE 4.—Employment by Industry

	Aurora,* 1972		Commerce City, 1970		Denver, 1970		Littleton, 1970		SMSA, 1970		USA, 1970
	Workers	%	Workers	%	Workers	%	Workers	%	Workers (000)	%	%
MTCU	2,600	10.6	2,800	40.7	75,070	26.1	2,279	24.5	127.2	23.8	32.7
Trade	6,377	26.0	1,600	23.2	76,324	26.5	2,144	22.9	133.1	24.9	20.1
FIRE	1,000	4.1	100	1.4	25,094	8.7	547	5.8	34.6	6.5	5.0
Services	3,750	15.3	1,100	15.9	56,744	19.7	1,788	19.1	113.2	21.2	26.2
Government	5,220	21.2	400	5.8	34,038	11.3	1,375	14.7	70.5	13.2	5.5
Agriculture & Mining	250	1.0			4,691	1.6	230	2.5			
Construction	5,333	21.7			14,865	5.2	998	10.7			
Other			900	13.0	908	.5			55.6	10.4	10.5
TOTAL	24,539	100.0		100.0	287,734	100.0	9,361	100.0	534.2	100.0	100.0

SOURCES: U.S. Department of Commerce, Bureau of the Census, County Business Patterns, 1970.
*Aurora, Colorado, Planning Department, 1973.

in the form of city sales/use tax. They also contribute almost 50% of all property taxes, while occupying only 7% of the total buildings. . . . From this
summary it is evident that for Littleton to continue to grow commercial/indus-
trial development must be expanded to make up the lag in property tax revenue
[Littleton, Colorado, Department of Community Development, 1976: 24, 27].

Littleton officials emphasize the need to hold down the tax rate and
thereby, presumably, help maintain the high standard of living in their city.
No precipitous measures are contemplated to achieve the commercial/
industrial development deemed necessary, rather the city's strategy employs
selective recruitment of the choice—that is, positive externality—firms. The
land-use mix will change slightly to accommodate this development, but the
city's environmental quality will be affected marginally at most. An example of the activities the Littleton economic development program has undertaken is the city's struggle to annex a major regional shopping center
situated just outside the current city limits on unincorporated land. Higher
income suburbs, such as Littleton, need never get trapped in the fiscal
squeeze which takes away a public firm's alternatives. Denver, Aurora, and
Commerce City, on the other hand, are fated to imperfect alternatives.

Analysis and Conclusion

The brief descriptions above show four very different public firms. Fiscal
productivity is distinctly emphasized in the economic development policies
of the suburbs, whereas officials in Denver stress the need to create jobs.
Two points need to be made about Denver's policy emphasis, however. Erosion of the city's revenue base is a highly salient concern around City Hall.
The desire to combat this erosion is evidenced in the agenda recommended
by the Mayor's Economic Development Policy Advisory Committee which
cites expansion of the city's revenue base, along with job creation, as the
"key sub-goals." Second, rather than passively acceding to the trends
toward specialization in wholesale trade, business services, and headquarters activities (Denver Urban Observatory 1974: 30) the job creation
strategies recommended represent a significant commitment to maintaining
economic diversity. Even though the rationale for job creation is not explicitly fiscal, fiscal productivity is profoundly and inextricably linked to
this goal. The city is not willing to indiscriminately accept into its boundaries any firm which creates jobs for the target population, rather, only
those that do so with neutral or positive fiscal impact.

The economic development policies and programs of the four communities provide information with which we can speculate on change in the
extent of land-use specialization in the metropolitan area. Figure 2 illustrates the position of each of the cities on the Fiscal Productivity-
Environmental Quality substitution plane. Analyzing the trade-off on these

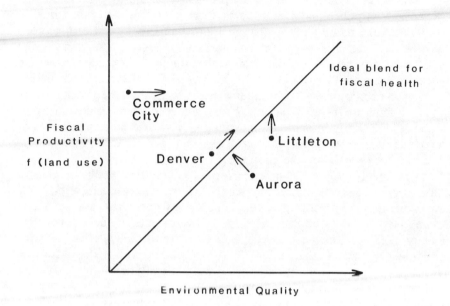

FIGURE 2

dimensions implied in the economic development programs and policies of each city provides insight to the future extent of land-use specialization because fiscal productivity is a function of land use. The assumption here is that fiscally productive land uses diminish environmental quality, and that only high-income residential and nonresidential land uses are fiscally productive.[8] Environmental quality, a public good, is defined in the broadest sense to include amenities such as parks, vista, open space, and the like.

Denver provides the benchmark against which the degree of land-use specialization in the other communities is compared. Along the 45 degree line, consumption of environmental quality is paid for by fiscally productive land uses. Below the line, a city is providing more environmental quality than it can afford unless it is specialized in high-income residential land use. Above the line, a city is paying for its fiscal health with suboptimal environmental quality. The arrows show the direction in which each city's economic development policy aims. Over the long haul, poor environmental quality has the potential to undermine fiscal productivity, given the current locational preferences of individuals and firms.

This analysis suggests that fiscal pressures are influencing all but high income residential jurisdictions in metropolitan Denver to offer similar mixes of environmental quality and fiscally productive land uses. Since basic services such as police and fire protection are not subject to much quality variation,[9] and because the level of environmental quality conferring goods and services such as sewage disposal, curbs and gutters, parks, and the like are reaching parity, the public firms within the metro areas are becoming more like one another. Land use, which had been the principal distinction among the communities, is becoming indiscriminate as the fiscal realities compel land-use diversification. While higher-income residential communities are nearly immune to the situation described here, that does not preclude them from opportunistically recruiting the choicest plums—helping themselves maintain the good life.

Undoubtedly, there are limits to local communities' ability to bolster their revenue base by means of fiscally dictated land use allocation. One must question the practice particularly in regions where land-use demand is slack. Nevertheless, the history of local governments' inducements to industry, predicated on localities' dependence on territorially defined revenue instruments, suggests that so long as there is the possibility that adjusting the land-use mix to meet the perceived needs of fiscally profitable land users will help balance community tax capacity and service needs, the propensity toward land-use homogenization within metropolitan areas will remain.

NOTES

[1] In particular, see Lampard (1968) for a discussion of the utility of the functional-structural process interpretation of urban transformation.

[2] Peterson (1976) describes the magnitude of intergovernmental revenue injected into the local fisc over the period 1965–1973, and identifies leveling of intergovernmental aid after 1973 as one of the key reasons for the current extent of fiscal stress among local governments.

[3] On the topic of convergence among "public firms," Hellmuth (1961) presents data for Cleveland which indicate "growth has created greater similarity of services from local governments in the metropolitan area." Regarding the perception of fiscal benefit flowing from diversification, the following statement by Wightman (1968) can be pointed to as but one example of the carrots reinforcing this perception: "As long as the degree of competition among monopolistic competitors is increasing, those communities which differentiate their services so as to maximize returns of new industry will be most successful in industrial development."

[4] The term "post-industrial" implies a specialization in tertiary or quaternary economic activities.

[5] Denver's annexation plans were in limbo as of December 1977, because of a piece of legislation—the Pound-Stone Amendment—which would require "any annexation by the City and County of Denver . . . to be approved at a general election in the county from which territory is annexed."

[6] This suggestion was made by the City Manager of Commerce City during an interview.

[7] Ranked ahead of Littleton are Cherry Hills ($32,433), Greenwood Village ($22,622), and Broomfield ($13,060).

[8] For an elaboration of this notion see Fischel (1975).

⁹Techniques for measuring the quality of public services have yet to be perfected. Depending on the indicators used, one might effectively argue to the contrary. For discussions of public service quality measurement see Hatry (1974) and Ostrom (1974).

REFERENCES

Aurora, Colorado, Department of Planning and Community Development (1973) "A report on economic analysis in the city of Aurora." (mimeo)

B.B.C. and Associates, Inc. (1977) "Commerce City economic base study and development plan." (mimeo)

Bish, R. L. and V. Ostrom (1973) Understanding Urban Government. Washington, DC: American Enterprise Institute.

Denver, Colorado, Office of Policy Analysis (1977) "Minutes of the Economic Development Policy Advisory Committee." (mimeo)

Denver Urban Observatory (1974) "The economic base of Denver: implications for Denver's fiscal future and administrative policy." (mimeo)

——— (1972) "Local government finance in the Denver metropolitan region, first year report." (mimeo)

Explore Commercial Opportunities (ECO) Aurora (1977) "Fast facts." (mimeo)

Fischel, W. A. (1975) "Fiscal and environmental considerations in the location of firms in suburban communities," pp. 119–173 in E. Mills and W. Oates (eds.) Fiscal Zoning and Land Use Controls Lexington, MA: D. C. Health.

Hatry, H. P. (1974) "Measuring the quality of public services," pp. 39–63 in W. D. Hawley and D. Rogers (eds.) Improving the Quality of Urban Management. Beverly Hills, CA: Sage.

Hellmuth, W. (1961) "Metropolitan finance problems: territories, functions, and growth—a comment," pp. 276–284 in Public Finances: Needs, Sources, and Utilization. Princeton, NJ: National Bureau of Economic Research.

Lampard, E. (1968) "The evolving system of cities in the United States: urbanization and economic development," pp. 81–139 in H. Perloff and L. Wingo (eds.) Issues in Urban Economics. Baltimore: Resources for the Future.

Littleton, Colorado, Department of Community Development (1975) "An economic analysis of Littleton." (mimeo)

Netzer, R. (1962) "The property tax and alternatives in urban development." Papers and Proceedings of Regional Sci. Assn. 9: 191–200.

Ostrom, E. (1974) "Measuring urban output and performance." Social Sci. Q. 54 (March): 691–764.

Peterson, G. (1976) "Finance," pp. 35–118 in W. Gorham and N. Glazer (eds.) The Urban Predicament. Washington, DC: Urban Institute.

Wightman, J. W. (1968) "The impact of state and local fiscal policies on redevelopment areas in the northeast." Research Report 40, Federal Reserve Bank of Boston.

Williams, O. P., H. Herman, C. Liebman, and T. Dye (1965). Suburban Differences and Metropolitan Policies. Philadelphia: Univ. of Pennsylvania Press.

II

Institutional Controls
on the Supply of Land

7

The Public Control
of Land Use

An Anglophile's View

Victor Moore

BEFORE there was any public control over the use and development of land, landowners were free to use their land in any way they wished, subject only to limitations contained in their individual grant and to obligations placed upon them at common law. In essence, therefore, provided an owner acted within the limitations of his estate and committed no nuisance or trespass against his neighbor's property, he was free to use his land for the purpose for which it was economically best-suited. Today, most societies desire, indeed, many require, not only that this freedom should be restricted for the public good, but also that land use in general should be determined by the long-term interests of communities as a whole rather than as a consequence of the incidence or spread of individual land ownership.[1]

In this paper, I shall attempt to look at the legal methods used or proposed to be used to achieve those ends. Although I feel compelled to refer to the British experience as a committed Anglophile, it is not because Britain is regarded by many as the cradle of land-use planning, but rather that the problems of land-use control in societies with mixed economies vary only in

ACKNOWLEDGMENT.—My thanks are due to Professor Robert Freilich for his considerable help in the preparation of this paper and for his guidance which enabled me to focus on some essentials of the American land use system and to those who participated in the seminars on Urbanization and Metropolitan Government at UMKC for their individual (and collective) insight and wisdom.

Reprinted by permission of *The Urban Lawyer*, the National Quarterly Journal of the American Bar Association, Section of Urban, State and Local Government Law, as it appeared in *The Land Use Awakening: Zoning Law in the Seventies*, eds. Robert H. Freilich and Eric O. Stuhler (1981).

degree, and because the solutions to those problems, and, in turn, the problems created by those solutions tend to have a number of common features.

Legal Structure of Land Use Control:
Britain v. United States

Insofar as I pursue a comparative approach, I will highlight the main characteristics of our respective systems. In the United States, the legal perimeters of land-use control are to be found within the tough structure of its written constitution; namely, in the provisions requiring due process of, and equal protection under the law, and that prohibiting the taking of private property for public use without just compensation. Britain, on the other hand, is neither enriched nor enslaved by any similar constitutional document. With one qualification, which for this purpose has no immediate consequence, Parliament is supreme and, in theory at least, this omnipotence would allow it to abolish the Monarchy with the same ease as it could pass or repeal an Act for the Protection of Birds.[2]

The British land use system has been imposed by Parliament. Its twin pillars are a development plan prepared for an area and a prohibition against the carrying out of any development of land unless and until a permit for that development has been granted by the appropriate municipal authority. The development plan may have two parts or tiers: an upper tier "structure plan" which it is compulsory for a county authority to prepare and a lower tier "local plan" which may be prepared either by the county authority or a district authority, the latter being a lesser but autonomous municipality within the geographic area of a county.

The function of each part of the plan and the relationship between them is critical. The upper tier structure plan does not deal with detailed land use. Its purpose is to indicate with a fairly broad brush the long-term strategy for a wide area, in terms of the policies applicable to major land uses in the area, such as industry, housing, transport and communications. In the normally acceptable sense of the word, the structure plan is not a plan at all. As a strategy, its form must inevitably be that of a written document. The lower tier local plan, on the other hand, is concerned with detailed land use. It is prepared in response to development or redevelopment pressure in any area. It will zone land for a particular purpose, but always within the context of the land use policy for the area as set out in the structure plan.[3] As with the American system, the identification of land in a development plan as suitable for a particular use is a guide rather than a guarantee that a permit will be issued to allow an owner to use it for that new purpose. Unlike the American system, there is no later adoption of a zoning ordinance which translates the guide into a guarantee.[4]

At first sight, you may view the British system as arbitrary. It is saved from this label by the requirement of wide citizen participation in the preparation of both tiers of the development plan, the need for a structure plan to be approved by Central Government before it takes effect, the presumption that a permit will be issued for any development in accordance with proposals in the development plan and the power of Central Government to intervene to issue a permit for development if for no valid reason the local authority has refused to do so. The British people have lived with this system for more than thirty years and usually have accepted and supported its terms.

If land-use control in Britain has been imposed from above, in the United States it has sprung from grass roots. Its main mechanisms are the comprehensive plan and the zoning ordinance. The comprehensive plan is a single document, its prime intent being to prevent haphazard or piecemeal zoning. It too is a blueprint which guides municipalities in the exercise of their zoning or subdivision power. The zoning ordinance is a distinctive legislative act which ultimately confers legal rights and the vehicle by which the local municipality determines both the use of land and the type, density and position of buildings within each zoning district. Flexibility is built into the system by the ordinance allowing an owner considerable latitude in the type of development which may be permitted, as for example, by devices such as overlay zones and holding zones; by contract and conditional zoning; and by cluster or planned unit development. This device stands somewhere between zoning and subdivision control and allows an owner of more than one lot who wishes to develop an entire tract of land to have regard to its total area, insuring its comprehensive development as opposed to piecemeal treatment on a lot by lot basis. Furthermore, the whole system is given additional flexibility by the power vested in zoning board of appeals to issue variances and special exceptions from any strict zoning ordinance requirements. How then, one might ask, does the system work in practice?

Traditionally, the application of the police power as seen in the American law of zoning has been used to meet problems associated with health, safety, morality or welfare. Although zoning ordinances which cause reductions in property values are not necessarily invalid[5] their constitutionality as applied to particular land requires that the property restricted be left with a reasonable use. One application of this principle demonstrates that zoning must not be used to give protection to property where to do so leaves adjacent property with no reasonable use. This is seen in *Spaid v. Board of County Commissioners for Prince George's County*,[6] where, for the benefit of residential development on the east side of a turnpike, an attempt was made to create a buffer zone of land lying between industrial development and the west side of the turnpike. In directing reclassification of the buffer zone land to an industrial zoning, the Court of Appeals of Maryland, quoting from *Hoffman v. Mayor and City Council of Baltimore*, said:

> If a residential neighborhood desires protection by a border of unused property, necessarily it must provide its own property, not appropriate its neighbors', for this purpose. . . . Property owners in a residential district cannot create a "no man's land" at the border of their district by forbidding one property owner in an adjoining district from making any use at all of his property, or any use for which it is "peculiarly suitable."[7]

This case can be contrasted with the English case of *RMC Management Services Ltd. v. Secretary of State for the Environment*[8] where a permit was refused for the erection on land of a ready-mixed concrete-batching plant, because it would generate an abnormal level of airborne abrasive dust. It was held that although the level of dust would not amount to even a common law nuisance, it would, nevertheless, affect adversely the operation of four neighboring establishments who had been attracted to the area by the clean air necessary for the high-precision scientific and engineering work in which they were engaged. In refusing to upset the decision, the High Court said. ". . . [the] Minister is entitled to ask himself whether the proposed development is compatible with the proper and desirable use of other land in the area." The risks to four special clean air neighbors, thus, were a consideration properly to be taken into account in restricting the use of the adjacent property.

Contemplating what the decision would have been in the alternate counties if the facts of the cases had been transposed, one would hope that the Maryland Court of Appeals would have held that the continued zoning for agricultural purposes (of the land planned for the concrete-batching plant) did not deprive the owner of any reasonable use of his land and, thereby, amounted to neither an abuse of due process nor a taking without payment of just compensation; and that the Secretary of State for the Environment would have allowed an appeal against the refusal to allow industrial development on the buffer strip on the ground that such restriction was unnecessary in view of the existing buffer which was provided by the turnpike.

There can be no doubt that during the last three decades, in response to changing conditions brought about by increasing urbanization, the scope of the police power in the United States has expanded considerably from the traditional "Euclidian" base. In 1954, in *Berman v. Parker*, the Court said, "It is within the power of the legislature to determine that the community should be beautiful as well as healthy, spacious as well as clean, well-balanced as well as carefully patrolled."[9] More recently, the Supreme Court in the *Village of Belle Terre v. Boraas* upheld a zoning ordinance intended to exclude group student housing from a community, and said, "A quiet place where yards are wide, people few, and motor vehicles restricted are legitimate guidelines in a land use project addressed to family needs. . . . The police power is not confined to the elimination of filth, stench and unhealthy places."[10]

Other areas in which zoning ordinances have been upheld include the preservation of the historic character of a locality,[11] the preservation of a rural environment[12] and the safeguarding from exploitation of a state's water resources.[13] Of recent developments, however, perhaps the most significant is the acceptance by the New York Court of Appeals in *Golden v. Planning Board of Ramapo*,[14] of the legitimacy of the police power to facilitate the sequential control of urban growth. There, in order to overcome the problem of private development outstripping public resource, the ordinances sought to link the former to the provision of the latter. Under the scheme, private development could only take place where a lot could be shown to be within a minimal distance of public services such as roads, parks, drainage, sewers and fire protection facilities. In upholding the validity of the ordinance the Court said:

> [W]here it is clear that the existing physical and financial resources of the community are inadequate to furnish the essential services and facilities which a substantial increase in population requires, there is a rational basis for "phased growth" and hence, the challenged ordinance is not violative of the Federal and State Constitutions.[15]

Having looked at some of the cases in which the police power has been held to be validly exercised, may we find courts holding the reverse? The constitutional principle of equal protection under the law ensures that the police power should not be used to overtly foster or maintain racial discrimination. In the 1975 case of *United States v. City of Black Jack*,[16] the court invalidated an ordinance which rezoned land so as to prevent the construction of federally subsidized low-income multi-family housing in an area. In the more recent case of *Village of Arlington Heights v. Metropolitan Housing Development Corporation*,[17] however, the Supreme Court upheld the refusal of a village to rezone land to allow for multi-family housing where its action was based not on any racial discriminatory intent but upon the preservation of property values and the integrity of the existing zoning pattern. Quite clearly, motivation is to be the yardstick by which future courts will distinguish between "racial" land use regulations which are unconstitutional and "socioeconomic" land use regulations which are not.

Perhaps the more significant fetter on the exercise of police power is that of the Fifth Amendment (as applied to the states through the Fourteenth Amendment), prohibiting the taking of private property for public use without just compensation. The problem here may be summed up in the phrase "take, and you must compensate; regulate, and you need not." Hence, landowners who find that the value of their property has been reduced by the exercise of police power are moved to show that the regulation amounts in fact to a taking and that, accordingly, they should be compensated.

One of the earliest cases to consider the issue was *Pennsylvania Coal Co. v. Mahon*,[18] where the Supreme Court declared unconstitutional as an undue regulation of the company's property Pennsylvania's Kohler Act which was enacted to prevent coal mine subsidence from destroying towns on the surface by regulating the amount of coal which could be mined. Mr. Justice Holmes propounded his much quoted but generalized test, "[T]he general rule at least is, that while property may be regulated to a certain extent, if regulation goes too far it will be recognized as a taking." The case shows that in determining whether the regulation has, in fact, gone too far, the courts will weigh the public benefit flowing from the regulation against the extent of the loss of property value. No doubt there were many who on the facts preferred the dissenting judgment of Mr. Justice Brandeis. He believed that the state only prevented a noxious use of private property and that the Act validly regulated property rights under the aegis of the police power to protect public welfare.

What the conflicting judgments in the Pennsylvania case do presage is the perennial difficulty of determining in any particular situation whether or not a taking can be said to have occurred. Not surprisingly, the courts have struggled constantly with the issue, and their decisions are both confusing and difficult to rationalize.[19] Indeed, until last year the only conclusion that it seemed safe to draw from them was: a regulation does not amount to a taking *merely* because it causes depreciation in the value of the affected property. Now the law has been somewhat clarified as a result of the decision in *Fred F. French Investing Co., Inc. v. City of New York*.[20] There the New York Court of Appeals had to consider whether the rezoning of potential private parks exclusively as parks open to the public constituted a deprivation of property rights without due process of law in violation of constitutional limitations. In possibly the clearest exposition of the demarcation line between the exercise of police power and eminent domain, Chief Judge Breitel said "[a] zoning ordinance is unreasonable if it frustrates the owner in the use of his property, that is, if it renders the property unsuitable for any reasonable income productive or other private use for which it is adapted and thus destroys its economic value, or all but a bare residue of its value."[21]

An Anglophile's View of the Effectiveness of
United States Land Use Controls

Having examined the legal techniques for securing the public control of land use, we may now consider their effectiveness in the light of the concern expressed about them by government agencies, public officials and professional and other expert bodies. In this respect, there seems to be three aspects of land and its use most likely to make an impact on a visitor to the United States from Western Europe. (1) the country's immense vastness, which gives it a range of options not available to most Western European nations; (2) the dereliction in the core of most older industrial cities; and (3) its uncontrolled urban sprawl, an urban sprawl *in excelsis*.

As regards the dereliction of inner cities, the problem in the United States seems more grave than that in Britain, where there has not yet been a significant racial overtone which constitutes a feature of the American scene. Cities have resulted from men's desire to communicate with each other, a communication which is not now always welcome and which has now taken a different form with the growth of the freeway, cheap energy and telecommunications. Occasionally, one sees the view pressed that the rejuvenation of inner cities is as difficult as making the desert bloom—so why do we try? Quite apart from being a philosophy of despair, the view ignores the fact that the problems of inner cities are no longer land use but social problems and that as such they are unlikely to go away without treatment. In Britain, we recently have been taking a fresh look at the inner-city problem. Even if one ignores any social engineering motivation for change, the plain fact which Britain cannot ignore is that its population density is nine times that of the United States and that living as we do, cheek by jowl, all land is a vital commodity. America also faces this problem. We just cannot afford to let any city resemble a doughnut of the variety which has a hole in its middle. The British Government's recent *White Paper*, "Policy for the Inner Cities,"[22] sees the framework of its policy as including the strengthening of the economies of inner areas, improving their physical fabric and environment, alleviating social problems and securing a new balance between inner areas and the rest of the city region in terms of population and jobs. To help achieve these ends, it proposes introducing legislation to enable municipalities to make loans of up to ninety percent to companies for the purchase of land and erection or improvement of industrial buildings. In addition, over the next two years, the Government is making available £100,000,000 for construction work in selected inner-city areas.

Although it must now be clear that wherever they are situated, the regeneration of inner cities requires a long term financial commitment from governments; the speed of regeneration may well depend upon the presence or otherwise of other techniques. In Britain, one of those techniques is central governmental control of industrial development, whereby such development is not allowed to take place unless the developer has been granted an "industrial development certificate." A developer should now be more likely to obtain that certificate if the development proposed is within the inner city. It must also not be forgotten that a land use policy which imposes restrictions on development outside the perimeter of an existing town, is likely to result if universally applied, in the development pressure being transferred to within the perimeter. This is one bonus which can flow from the control of urban sprawl; another is the safeguarding of valuable agricultural land.

On this subject, it is significant that the Department of Agriculture's Economic Research Service has estimated that of the 400 million acres of cropland in the United States, about two million acres are being "irreversibly lost" each year to urban build up and that an additional one million acres are being used for ponds, lakes and reservoirs. The conclusion drawn from these facts and others by the Soil Conservation Service of the Department "is that the days of complacency about America's cropland supply are over."

I would suggest that there are two major hurdles to be overcome before the United States will feel it possesses an acceptable, realistic and effective land-use system. First, there needs to be much greater regional, state and federal involvement in both the determination of land use policy and in securing its implementation, together with public acceptance of their need to do so. One must seriously question whether decisions are being made at the level at which they ought to be made. Second, a solution must be found for dealing with the financial windfalls and wipeouts which are respectively bestowed or inflicted on landowners as a result of land use regulation. Initially, it seems relevant to make a number of observations which, although trite, are often forgotten by many who should know better, in particular, politicians. To begin with, save for the lowest levels of political jurisdiction, land use regulation does not involve the question of whether there should be growth or no growth. It is predominantly a question of whether growth should be controlled, and, if so, how, where and when. In any mixed economy, planners cannot act as Canute. Land use regulation and policies must thus accept both the influence of market forces and an increasing gross national product and accommodate or plan around them. Furthermore, it must be recognized that most land use decisions are concerned with the resolution of conflict. There are many developments necessary for national, state or local well-being which nobody wishes as a neighbor, but which must be located somewhere. Recognition of what is perhaps obvious, has tremendously important implications for citizen participation in the planning process. So, too, does the fact that although some kind of development is fixed as to where it is to take place (e.g., mineral exploration), other developments frequently pose a range of options, all of which may be equally favorable from the state's point of view, but each of which would be distasteful to the community receiving the development.

Greater Regional, State and Federal Involvement

This must inevitably mean a loosening of the iron grip of many of lesser authorities. At the moment, in addition to the federal government and fifty states, there are about 3,000 counties, 18,000 municipalities and 17,000 townships, each of which has the power in some way to plan or regulate land use. That is an average of about 760 per state. Fortunately, there is now a growing recognition that certain aspects of land use must be dealt with on a national or regional basis. Perhaps it may be too much to hope that national involvement will ever extend beyond cooperation between federal agencies and state governments and the use of federal financial assistance to achieve national goals.[23] The states, however, have the constitutional power to regulate their own land use and it must be an encouraging sign for the future that many of them are now beginning to do so.

One of the first examples was the Land Use Law of the state of Hawaii which in 1961 created a comprehensive statewide zoning plan dividing the state into agricultural, conservation, urban and rural districts. Under that legislation, the state determines its overall policy for development, but allows a local input into the administration of the zoning program. Then in 1970, the state of Vermont adopted a comprehensive Environmental Control Law whereby residential subdivision involving lots of more than 10 acres, substantial commercial and industrial development or development exceeding 2,500 feet was to be conditional upon a permit being obtained from the state's Environmental Agency. There are also many states which now exercise control over areas of critical concern such as power plants siting, surface mining, and the management of coastal zones and wetlands. The American Law Institute's Model Land Development Code, which states have been reluctant so far to adopt, while giving to local government the power of zoning and subdivision control allows it to be superceded and exercised by the state in certain key areas.[24]

The British (and indeed the continental) experience suggests that, forward looking though some of these approaches might be, they are not entirely satisfactory, since for land use planning to be effective it must begin with integrated state planning and end with local planning rather than vice versa. I have already made the point that there can be no absolutes in land-use planning and that the detail of land use must be structured upon the choice of options made at some higher level. This makes it imperative, therefore, for that choice to be made democratically. A local community would be bound to feel aggrieved, if, for example, a policy of growth was imposed upon it by the state when it would have preferred one of no-growth and it had been given no opportunity to participate in the decision-making process.[25]

In Britain, we have begun to deal with that problem in this way. Before a county authority submits its structure plan to the Secretary of State for his approval it must have publicized the matters it was proposing to include in the plan and it must alert people who might wish to make representations about those matters to the fact that they may do so and it must give them adequate opportunity to do so. The result is that when the plan is submitted for approval to the Secretary of State it should contain what the county authority believes should be the favored option and one that the majority of the population are prepared to countenance.[26] If the Secretary of State then approves the plan, which he may do so only after considering any objections to it, the district authority's way is then clear to prepare local plans which dovetail into the policies contained in the structure plan. It is significant that most countries on the continent of Europe have also adopted systems for "split-level" development plans (some of which are multi-tiered) as each seeks to translate national economic and social goals into local detailed land-use regulation.

There is another reason for greater state involvement. Land-use regulation is no longer regarded solely as an exercise in physical planning. It is fast becoming part of a jigsaw in which economic, social and environmental policies are coordinated and implemented. It is right that that coordination should begin at the level at which those policies are adumbrated.

How to Deal with the Windfalls Which Accrue to an Owner of Land Allowed to Develop It and the Wipeouts Which Are Suffered by Those Not Allowed to Do So

In Britain since 1947, the policy power has been used to prevent any development of land where central or local government decrees that it should not be developed. In those circumstances, no compensation is generally payable.[27] It is a state of affairs now recognized as a permanent feature of British land use planning. It is accepted by all, and the market generally reflects that acceptance. Attention over the years, thus, has focused on the other side of the coin, namely the windfall profits which accrue to those allowed to develop. These windfalls arise from two major sources: (1) the diversion of the development pressure from the land which is restricted from development to that where it is allowed; and, (2) the presence in the value of developed land of an element which is due to public expenditure or other community action.

Windfall recapture has for long been a political football. Now, after many unsuccessful attempts to deal with the problems, twin legislation has been passed which it is claimed will be a "final solution" to the problem of land values. Under the Development Land Tax Act of 1976, a tax of eighty percent is levied on any development value in land which an owner realizes. The tax is paid by the owner to the national exchequer. Under the Community Land Act of 1975, local authorities are given wider power to acquire land considered suitable for private development (whether by agreement or eminent domain) on special terms. The terms are that the authority pays the seller the net sum he would have received had he sold the land privately and subsequently paid the eighty percent to the state. In short, the local authority *may* now buy undeveloped land cheap and then either sell for the development purpose or develop the land itself and then sell. At some later date, the tax will rise to one hundred percent and local authorities will be *required* to purchase all land needed for major private development before the development takes place.

What is the American position?[28] First, regarding wipeouts: here (as in Britain) no compensation is paid for loss of value where land use regulation prevents an owner from putting his land to its best economic use. The difficulty which has no parallel in Britain occurs where control is exercised in areas where previously there was none, or where existing control is made more severe. The plain fact is that although the legitimacy of land use regulation was originally based upon a nuisance analogy and the protection of private property, from the beginning its effect has often been to provide a public benefit at private cost. It seems quite legitimate that where the police power is used to eliminate filth, stench and unhealthy places, compensation should not be paid to an owner who is unable because of it to put his property to its best economic use. Here, the power is based on reasonably objective criteria and its application is generally universal. It is otherwise, however, where the police power is concerned with land-use regulation such as zoning, since its incidence and effect so often depends upon the making of a choice between a number of options.

No doubt the absence of a general code of compensation for land use regulation may be explained as part of the country's traditional attitude to land ownership as once fostered by those who drove America's frontiers westward to California. Today, however, it can be justified only on the basis that land ownership remains a lottery.[29] This philosophy is most unlikely to persuade those living next to a freeway or those who have bought their property at an enhanced value for later building development, to accept the need for a land use policy which restricts the land to its existing agricultural use. Unfortunately, it seems that before changes can be made in this direction, constitutional obstacles may need to be overcome, namely those provisions to be found in some state constitutions which prohibit the use of public funds for private purpose.

As regards windfall recapture in the United States, there are a number of techniques in current use. They include a special capital gains tax on land (as in Vermont), special assessments, exactions and fees on development permissions, advance eminent domain purchases and transferable development rights, this last technique being one which is capable of avoiding a wipeout whilst at the same time recapturing the windfall. Although the techniques are plentiful in variety, they are regarded either as impracticable or as not taking from the landowner a sufficient percentage of the windfall profit. In Britain, current legislation is geared to eventually taking all the windfall, so removing from the landowner any increment in the value of land which is due to the development process. One suspects that given its constitutional history a similar arrangement would be anathema to the American scene. Nevertheless, no effective and acceptable land use system is likely to be established until the problem of land values has been solved. Fortunately, there is room for optimism.

As Chief Judge Breitel has said:

> The legislative and administrative efforts to solve the zoning and landmark problem in modern society demonstrate the presence of ingenuity. . . . That ingenuity further pursued will in all likelihood achieve the goals without placing an impossible or unsuitable burden on the individual property owner, the public fisc, or the general taxpayer. These efforts are entitled to and will undoubtedly receive every encouragement. The task is difficult but not beyond management. The end is essential but the means must nevertheless conform to constitutional standards.[30]

NOTES

1. *See* RECOMMENDATIONS FOR NATIONAL ACTION, REPORT OF HABIT: UNITED NATIONS CONFERENCE ON HUMAN SETTLEMENTS, VANCOUVER, 1976.

[2]The qualification arises as a result of Britain's adhesion to the European Economic Community by the European Community Act of 1972. In the field of land use, the influence of community legislation on domestic law has been minimal.

[3]The two-tier development plan system described here is the new system introduced in 1968 to gradually replace the single "all-purpose" development plan which has constituted the basic planning document in England since 1948.

[4]In the second major critique of land-use planning and development control in England and Wales within three years (the first being the Review of the Development Control System by George Dobry, Q.C., (H.M.S.O.)) the REPORT OF THE ENVIRONMENT SUB-COMMITTEE OF THE EXPENDITURE COMMITTEE OF THE HOUSE OF COMMONS (Report H.C. 359-1; Session 1976-77),

suggested consideration be given to development plans bestowing a legal right to develop, subject to safeguards.

⁵*See* Euclid v. Ambler Realty Co., 272 U.S. 365 (1926).

⁶259 Md. 369, 269 A.2d 797 (1970).

⁷197 Md. 294, 79 A.2d 367 (1951).

⁸22 E.G. 1593 (1972).

⁹348 U.S. 26, 33 (1954).

¹⁰416 U.S. 1, 9 (1974).

¹¹Maher v. City of New Orleans, 235 So. 2d 403 (La. 1970).

¹²Ybarra v. Town of Los Altos Hills, 503 F.2d 250 (9th Cir. 1974).

¹³Just v. Marinette County, 201 N.W.2d 761 (Wis. 1972).

¹⁴30 N.Y.2d 359, 334 N.Y.S.2d 138, 285 N.E.2d 291 (1972), *appeal dismissed*, 409 U.S. 1003 (1972).

¹⁵*Id.* at 303.

¹⁶508 F.2d 1179 (8th Cir. 1974), *cert. denied*, 422 U.S. 1942 (1975).

¹⁷429 U.S. 257 (1977).

¹⁸260 U.S. 393 (1922).

¹⁹*See* F. Bosselman, D. Callies, & J. Banta, The Taking Issue (1973).

²⁰39 N.Y.2d 587, 385 N.Y.S.2d 5, 350 N.E.2d 381 (1976).

²¹*See also* HFH, Ltd. v. Superior Court of Los Angeles County, 15 Cal. 3d 508, 125 Cal. Rptr. 365, 542 P.2d 237 (1975), where it was held that a mere downzoning gave no constitutional right to compensation. The court left to another day the question of entitlement to compensation if a zoning regulation forbade all use of the land in question. *See* the splendid discussion of the many issues in this case in Hagman, 1976 Land Use Law and Zoning Digest No. 2 at 5.

²²Cmnd. 6845 (H.M.S.O.)

²³The Council of State Governments is beginning to do much encouraging work in this respect.

²⁴Perhaps the closest analogy to the concept of areas of critical concern is the system being adopted in Scotland which varies somewhat from the system in England and Wales. In Scotland, too, legislation provides for integrated structure plans and detailed local plans. In Scotland, however, if the proposed development is one of eleven categories likely to raise nationally important issues, the matter must be referred to Central Government.

²⁵But local democracy can "rule" only in local circumstances. In Britain, for example, a proposal route for a major road to bypass a busy market town may show a number of alternatives alongside the authorities' "preferred route." Local feeling may then persuade the authority to select an alternative route. This is the closest one can get in Britain to the plebiscite situation, as seen in City of Eastlake v. Forest City Enterprises, 426 U.S. 668 (1976), where the charter of the city had been amended to require a change of zoning to be subject to a plebiscite and to be approved by fifty-five percent of the voters, before becoming effective.

²⁶This is the theory, but it has not yet worked in practice. In the first instance the separation of strategic (structure plan) matter from local matters has proved difficult to observe. In the second, there has been a marked reluctance on the part of the public to become involved with structure plan preparation. Interest in development is really generated only when the development is closer to home. *See* 1976 Journal of Planning and Environment 469.

²⁷Compensation is paid for very limited development which is regarded within an owner's "existing-use" rights and for the loss of development value due to planning restrictions where the value existed in 1948. Development value arising after 1948, therefore, is not compensated where that value cannot be realized due to the restrictions.

[28]The text for many years to come for all interested in this area is the work by D. HAGMAN & D. MISCZYNSKI, WINDFALLS FOR WIPEOUTS. The authors give the area a comprehensive treatment and examine many of the techniques used for recapturing windfalls and mitigating wipeouts, both in the United States and other countries.

[29]It may also be justified where the state takes all the development value (*e.g.*, by levying a tax on it at a rate of 100 percent) thus reducing the value of all land to its value for existing use purposes.

[30]Fred F. French Investing Co., Inc. v. City of New York, 39 N.Y.2d 587, 385 N.Y.S.2d 5, 350 N.E.2d 381 (1976).

8

Institutionalizing the Revolution

Judicial Reaction to State Land Use Laws

David E. Hess

SINCE BOSSELMAN AND CALLIES described state land-use laws as a "revolution in land-use controls,"[1] courts have been busily transforming revolutionary ideas into everyday fare.

Judicial reaction to statewide, shoreland and regional land-use programs has been overwhelmingly favorable and supportive. Courts have uniformly upheld state land-use programs as legitimate attempts to control environmental and growth-related problems.

To better understand the breadth of the transformation, it is necessary to look at judicial reaction to key state land-use programs.

Six years have passed since the revolution was first proclaimed and in that time the number of states enacting land-use controls has risen. Ten states now have some form of statewide land-use law.[2] Eleven states have coastal or shoreland management statutes.[3] The four regional agencies continued their land-use control functions.[4]

Gauging judicial reaction to all state land-use programs is not possible for a number of reasons. First of all, the statewide programs in Maryland, Nevada, Oregon and Wyoming are in the early planning or initial regulatory phase, consequently, there has been very little opportunity for a court test; secondly, the shoreland statutes in Michigan, Minnesota, North Carolina and Vermont allowed a long lead time for developing and implementing

Reprinted by permission of The Urban Lawyer, the National Quarterly Journal of the American Bar Association, Section of Urban, State and Local Government Law, as it appeared in *The Land Use Awakening: Zoning Law in the Seventies*, eds. Robert H. Freilich and Eric O. Stuhler (1981).

shoreland regulations. In some instances the deadline for enacting regulations has just passed. As a result, as with the statewide programs, there has
simply not been enough time for issues to arise which require judicial
disposition. For example, Florida recently designated several controversial
areas of critical state concern under its Environmental Land and Water
Management Act. A number of challenges to those designations are making
their way slowly through the courts.[5] In Maine no suits have been filed
against the state's program to regulate critical areas.[6] Minnesota has been
able to gingerly negotiate its way through enforcement problems by settling
disputes out of court.[7]

Statewide Land-Use Management

Statewide land-use laws are victims of many of the difficulties noted
above, but court reaction can be sampled through four programs: Colorado's Land Use Act (1974), Hawaii's Land Use Law (1961), Maine's Site
Location of Development Act (1970) and Vermont's Act 250 (1969). Although Act 250's judicial history is less well known, it is chosen for review
here because it was recently given a clean bill of health by the Vermont
Supreme Court.

Vermont created a system of nine district commissions and a single
statewide Environmental Board. The system was given authority to develop
a State Land Use Plan and to administer a permit program for land uses
over ten acres in size or above 2500 feet in elevation.

Within the permit program, the district commissions are the first to hear
permit applications. The applicant has the option of appealing the district's
decision to the Environmental Board if he is not satisfied. Permits may only
be approved if local governments acquiesce to the project and if the
development is found not to be detrimental to the public's health, safety
and welfare. The Board does not have option to deny permits even if the
local government approves a project.

The Vermont Supreme Court has consistently upheld the Act's constitutionality and the Environmental Board's discretion to administer the Act.[8]
Schuyler Jackson, chairman of the Board, has said that the latest decision,
In re Wildlife Wonderland, Inc.,[9] "shut the door" to future court challenges; provided the Board follows proper procedures.[10] *Wildlife Wonderland* affirmed the Board's authority to enforce the Act so long as it does so
within the Act's guidelines and supports each decision with substantial
evidence. Further, the court held that the permit applicant "has the burden
of showing that his proposal action complies with the Act."[11]

In other cases, the court has insisted that the Board's permit procedure
insure that all interested parties be given an opportunity to participate.[12]

All four stateside land-use laws under consideration have been upheld as valid exercises of the police power.[13] These successes are more significant in view of the variations in purpose and administrative structure among the states. (See Chart 1.)

Shoreland Management

Eleven states have coastal or shoreland management statutes but only four have been judicially reviewed. California's Coastal Zone Conservation Act, Delaware's Coastal Zone Act, Washington's Shoreline Management Act and Wisconsin's Shoreland Zoning Requirement represent the only measure of court reaction to shoreland management laws.[14]

Under California's shoreland statute a series of six regional commissions and a single state-level Coastal Zone Conservation Commission were created by voter initiative in 1972. The initiative gave the commissions planning and permit authority in the state's coastal zone. Permit administration is similar to Vermont's general land-use program. The regional commissions handle the initial application while an option is available to appeal to the state-level commission. The commissions have full authority over land use in a special coastal permit area. To issue a permit, the commissions must find that the development will not have an adverse environmental impact and that it conforms to the enabling Act's policies. Unlike Vermont's program, however, both planning and permit authority will end on January 1, 1977 unless the state legislature approves the coastal plan now before it.

By far the two most important cases upholding the Coastal Zone Conservation Act have been *CEEED v. California Coastal Zone Conservation Commission*[15] and *State v. Superior Court of Orange County.*[16] These two cases approved the Act's purposes, its procedures[17] and the state's right to regulate land use without violating constitutional guarantees of equal protection, due process or the right to travel. *CEEED* also affirmed the state's authority to protect state interests in local home rule jurisdictions.

The issue of exemption from the permit process, either by virtue of the Act's grandfather clause or the vesting of rights, has been a primary issue for review.[18] Oddly enough none of the decisions indicated whether the adoption of the Act by voter initiative had any bearing on the outcome.

The judicial treatment of the other three shoreland management laws is very similar. The laws of Delaware, Washington and Wisconsin were all held to be proper exercises of police power despite the differences in objectives and administrative approaches.[19] (See Chart 2) The key characteristics of the laws were upheld, i.e., discretion of the regulatory agency, the reasonableness of placing the burden on the applicant of proving compliance with the statutes, limiting judicial review to determining if the agency acted within its authority and whether the agency decision was supported by "substantial evidence."

D. E. HESS

CHART 1: *Statewide Land Use Statutes*

	Colorado (critical areas)	Florida (DRIs)[1]	(critical areas)
Date Enacted	1974	1972	
Purposes	Encourages planned orderly development within land's character and adaptability	Protect environmental rights, water resources management	
State plan required	NO	NO	
Special structure created	YES	NO	
Jurisdiction over land uses[1]	Wide	Narrow	Wide
State veto of local approval[2] (without court action)	NO	Possible on appeal	Possible on appeal
State override of local denial[2] (without court action)	NO	Possible on appeal	Possible on appeal
Burden of proof in permit review	Local government	Local or regional agencies	Local
Enforcement of regulations	Local government	Local	Local
# of decisions	1	4 pending	
Major issues	Commission authority to request local hearing and to enjoin development if hearing not held	designation	

[1]This is a general characterization meaning: *wide*—practically no limits on size or location of development coming under the program's jurisdiction; *narrow*—just the opposite.
[2]Approval or denial of land development.

	Hawaii		Maine	Vermont
	(districts)	*(special permit)*	*Maine*	*Vermont*
	1961		1970	1969
	protect agricultural land, control public costs of growth, tax incentives to desired development		Control environmental impact of large developments	Insure land use is compatible with natural capability—especially larger developments
	By amendment		NO	YES
	YES		NO	YES
	Relatively wide		Narrow	Narrow
	(N.A.)	YES	(N.A.)	YES
	(N.A.)	NO	(N.A.)	NO
	Applicant	Regulator	Applicant	Divided—applicant has major burden
	State	Local or state	State	State
	6 major/several pending		4 major/1 pending	7 major
	Classification/ procedural		Grandfather clause/ broadside	Parties to process/ court's role/jurisdiction/broadside

CHART 2: *Shoreland Management Statutes*

	California	Delaware
Date Enacted	1972	1971
Purposes	Protection of natural resources, scenic areas, marine fisheries and delicate ecological balance	Protect an area crucial to the state's quality of life—economic and environmental—encourage recreation and tourism
Coastal plan required	YES	YES
Special structure created	YES	YES
Regulated area	Within 1,000 yards of mean high tide	Varies, about 5,280 yards from mean high tide
Jurisdiction over land uses[1]	Wide	Narrow
State veto of local approval (without court action)[2]	(N.A.)	YES
State override of local denial (without court action)[2]	(N.A.)	NO
Burden of proof in permit review	Applicant	Applicant
Enforcement of regulations	State	State
# of decisions	13 major/100 pending	1
Major issues	Constitutionality/procedures/grandfather clause—vested rights	Purpose/"substantial evidence"

[1]This is a general characterization meaning: *wide*—practically no limits on size or location of development coming under the program's jurisdiction; *narrow*—just the opposite.
[2]Approval or denial of land development.

	Washington	*Wisconsin*
Date Enacted	1971	1965
Purposes	Coastal areas are among most valuable and fragile natural resources—must be managed in the public interest	Control pollution of navigable waters.
Coastal plan required	Local—YES	YES
Special structure created	YES	NO
Regulated area	Within 333 yards of ocean or lake, 100 yards of rivers + associated wetlands	Within 333 yards of lakes or ponds, 100 yards of rivers
Jurisdiction over land uses[1]	Wide	Wide
State veto of local approval (without court action)[2]	Possible on appeal	NO
State override of local denial (without court action)[2]	Possible on appeal	NO
Burden of proof in permit review	Applicant	Local government
Enforcement of regulations	Local/state	Local
# of decisions	11	2
Major issues	Definition of "shoreline" /exemption/procedures	Constitutionality/taking

CHART 3.—*Regional Land-Use Agencies*

	Adirondack Park Agency	*Hackensack Meadowlands Development Comm.*
Date enacted	1971	1968
Purposes	Protect an area of national and international environmental significance	Protect a fragile marshland in the face of development
Plan required	YES	YES
Special structure created	YES	YES
Regulated area	State park with 6,000,000 acres	Marshland—18,000 acres
Jurisdiction over land uses[1]	Wide	Wide
State veto of local approval[2] (without court action)	YES—certain types of development	(N.A.)
State override of local denial[2] (without court action)	YES—certain types of development	(N.A.)
Burden of proof in permit review	Agency	Commission
Enforcement of regulations	Agency/Local	Commission
# of decisions	4 major	10 major
Major issues	Home rule/purposes/ standing in hearings	Constitutionality/interstate commerce/regional issues?

[1]This is a general characterization meaning: *wide*—practically no limits on size or location of development coming under the agency's jurisdiction.
[2]Approval or denial of land development.

	San Francisco Bay Conservation and Development Comm.	Tahoe Regional Planning Agency
Date enacted	1969	1969
Purposes	Planning for the bay as a unit to protect the bay as a valuable natural resource	Protect the Tahoe Basin— its environmental quality and economic productivity
Plan required	YES	YES
Special structure created	YES	YES
Regulated area	Shoreline + 100 foot wide strip on shore	Drainage basin
Jurisdiction over land uses[1]	Wide	Unclear
State veto of local approval[2] (without court action)	YES	NO
State override of local denial[2] (without court action)	YES	NO
Burden of proof in permit review	Commission	Agency
Enforcement of regulations	Commission	Local/Agency
# of decisions	4 major	7 major
Major issues	Taking/grandfather clause/jurisdiction	Taking (inverse condemnation) constitutionality/ regional concerns?

Regional Agencies

Laws creating all four major regional land-use regulatory agencies have been subjected to court tests. The Adirondack Park Agency, Hackensack Meadowlands Development Commission, San Francisco Bay Conservation and Development Commission and the Tahoe Regional Planning Agency have all been regulating land use on a regional basis for some time, and survived judicial attack.[20] While any one of the four agencies would provide a good illustration, the Hackensack Meadowlands Development Commission has withstood the more interesting court challenges.

The Commission has assumed all land-use control functions within its jurisdiction. Local governments may require land-use permits, but developers (and the Commission itself) view the regional agency as the body with statutory authority.[21] In addition to land-use regulation, the Commission is responsible for planning in the region and has authority to manage solid waste and to undertake its own redevelopment and reclamation projects by issuing revenue bonds. It also administers a tax sharing program between municipalities so that they all may benefit from planned growth.

Meadowlands Regional Development Agency v. State[22] represents the first and possibly the strongest affirmation of the Meadowlands Commission's authority by the state supreme court. The Commission was challenged on equal protection and due process levels, as well as an abuse of legislative discretion to designate a region for special attention, and as an intrusion into local affairs to protect regional interests. Each challenge was rejected by the court and the Commission's authority was sustained.

However, the Commission has not enjoyed absolute judicial success. In a case involving the construction of a natural gas plant the Commission's permit authority was held to be an interference with interstate commerce.[23] The staff attorney to the Commission feels the decision does not place a major restriction on granting future permits,[24] because only those facilities coming under the jurisdiction of federal regulatory agencies should be affected.[25]

The court has upheld the Commission's authority to approve or disapprove land uses proposed by other governmental agencies,[26] its tax sharing program,[27] and challenges involving uncompensated taking.[28]

The other three regional agencies closely parallel the Meadowlands Commission's record under judicial review. All have been upheld as legitimate exercises of the police power for the objectives they seek to accomplish; notwithstanding the difference between programs.[29] (See Chart 3) The vital features of each were upheld, i.e. legislative designation of the region for special attention and the discretion of the administrative agency in enforcing permit requirements.

Legal Guidelines

To the state planner involved with existing land-use control programs, or to those considering programs, the courts have produced several legal guidelines which may be summarized briefly:

1. A precisely drafted enabling statute can eliminate litigation on conflicting provisions.[30]

2. A simple, clearly worded grandfather clause can minimize litigation. (Avoiding all litigation on the subject is impossible.)[31]

3. The administering body must develop "substantial evidence" on the record of its proceedings to avoid being overturned upon judicial review.[32]

4. Whatever the procedures, the regulator must follow the provisions of the law in every detail to avoid being reversed by court action.[33]

5. Everyone having a legitimate interest in the outcome of a permit decision must have an opportunity to participate in the permit process.[34]

6. Regulatory agencies following points #3, #4 and #5 will find that the courts, in all but the most extreme factual situations, will not reverse their decisions on the basis of the denial of equal protection, due process or declare an uncompensated taking.

7. It is acceptable to the courts if the burden of proving compliance with the statute is on the applicant rather than the regulator.[35]

8. The courts will approve a wide variety of environmental and aesthetic public objectives and regulatory configurations so long as they are reasonably related.[36]

9. A land-use program enacted by voter referendum seems to be on equal footing with non-referendum based laws in subsequent court tests.[37]

10. State regulation of land uses of state or regional interest does not intrude into municipal affairs; even in home rule jurisdictions.[38]

11. State attempts to regulate federally licensed land uses may be preempted.[39]

It is clear from this review of court reaction that the revolution first identified by Bosselman and Callies in 1971 is rapidly becoming accepted and institutionalized through state and Federal court opinion.

NOTES

[1]F. Bosselman and D. Callies, The Quiet Revolution in Land Use Control (1971).

[2]Colorado—COL. REV. STAT., art. 65; Florida—FLA. STAT. ANN., ch. 380 (1972); Hawaii—H. I. REV. STAT., ch. 205 (1961); Maine—MAINE REV. STAT. ANN., Tit. 38, § 481; MAINE REV. STAT. ANN., Tit. 12, § 685—A; MAINE REV. STAT. ANN., Tit. 5, § 3310 (1970); Maryland—A.C.M., Tit. 8 (1974); Minnesota—MINN. STAT. ANN. § 16.01 (1973); Nevada—NEV. REV. STAT. §321.640 (1973); Oregon—ORE. REV. STAT. § 215.055 (1973); Vermont—VT. STAT. ANN., Tit. 10, ch. 151, § 6001; Wyoming—WYO. STAT. § 9—160.40.

[3]California—West's Public Res. Code § 27000 (1972); Delaware—DEL. CODE ANN. § 7—7000 (1971); Maine—MAINE REV. STAT. ANN., Tit. 12, § 4811 (1971); Michigan—MICH. STAT. ANN. § 13.1831 (1970); Minnesota—MINN. STAT. ANN., § 105.485 (1969); New Jersey—N.J. STAT. ANN., 13:9A-1 (1973); North Carolina G.S.N.C. 113A-100 (1974); Rhode Island—GEN. LAWS 46-23 (1971); Vermont—U.S.A., Tit. 24, ch. 91, § 4301; Washington—R.C.W.A. § 90.54.010 (1971); Wisconsin—WIS. STAT. ANN. 59.971 (1965).

[4]Adirondack Park Agency—E.C.L. 9.0301 (McKinney Supp. 1971); Hackensack Meadowlands Development—N.J.S.A. 13:17-1 (1968); San Francisco Bay Conservation—WEST'S ANN. GOV. CODE § 66600 (1969); Tahoe Regional Planning Agency—WEST'S ANN. GOV. CODE § 66800 (1967).

[5]Telephone interview with Tom Harris and Jim Whisenand, Florida's Attorney General's Office, January 9, 1976.

[6]Telephone interview with Harry Tyler, Maine State Planning Office, January 30, 1976.

[7]Telephone interview with Yo Jouseau, Minnesota State Planning Agency, January 30, 1976.

[8]Great Eastern Building Co., Inc., 326 A.2d 152 (Vt. 1974); In re Quechee Lakes Corporation, 296 A.2d 190 (Vt. 1972).

[9]346 A.2d 645 (Vt. 1975).

[10]Telephone interview with Schuyler Jackson, chairman of Vermont's Environmental Board, January 9, 1976.

[11]This holding concurred with the earlier decision, In re Baker Sargent Corporation, 313 A.2d 669 (Vt. 1973).

[12]Cases involving due process include: In re State Aid Highway No. 1, Peru, Vermont, 328 A.2d 667 (Vt. 1974); In re Quechee Lakes Corp., 296 A.2d 190 (Vt. 1972); In re Preseault 292 A.2d 832 (Vt. 1972).

[13]Colorado—City of Louisville v. District Court in and for County of Boulder, 543 P.2d 67 (Col. 1975); Hawaii—Town v. Land Use Comm'n, 524 P.2d 84 (Hawaii 1974); Maine—In re Spring Valley Dev., 300 A.2d 736 (Me. 1973); Vermont—In re Wildlife Wonderland, Inc., 346 A.2d 645 (Vt. 1975).

[14]See note 3, supra.

[15]118 Cal. Rptr. 315 (Cal. App. 1974).

[16]115 Cal. Rptr. 497, 524 P.2d 1281 (Cal. 1974).

[17]Klitgaard and Jones, Inc. v. San Diego Coast Regional Comm'n. 121 Cal. Rptr. 650 (Cal. App. 1975), agreed here also.

[18]Avco Community Developers, Inc. v. South Coast Regional Comm'n, 122 Cal. Rptr. 810 (Cal. App. 1975); Urban Renewal Agency of the City of Monterey and City v. California Coastal Zone Conservation Comm'n, 121 Cal. Rptr. 446 (Cal. App. 1975); California Central Coast Regional Coastal Zone Conservation Comm'n. v. McKeon Constr., 112 Cal. Rptr. 903 (Cal. App. 1974); Environmental Coalition of Orange County, Inc. v. Avco Community Developers, Inc., 115 Cal. Rptr. 59 (Cal. App. 1974); Transcentury Properties, Inc. v. State, 116 Cal. Rptr. 487 (Cal. App. 1974); County of Orange v. Heim, 106 Cal. Rptr. 825 (Cal. App. 1973); San Diego Coast Regional Comm'n for San Diego County v. See the Sea, Ltd. 109 Cal. Rptr. 377, 513 P.2d 129 (Cal. 1973).

[19]California—CEEED v. California Coastal Zone Conservation Comm'n, 118 Cal. Rptr. 315 (Cal. App. 1971); Delaware—Kreshtool v. Delmarva Power & Light Co., 310 A.2d 649 (Del. 1973); Washington—Department of Ecology v. Ballard Elks Lodge No. 827, 527 P.2d 1121 (Wash. App. 1973); Wisconsin—Just v. Marinette County, 201 N.W.2d 761 (Wis. 1972).

[20]See note 4, supra.

[21]Telephone interview with Jerry Rosenweig, staff attorney for Hackensack Meadowlands Development Commission, February 13, 1976.

²²270 A.2d 418 (N.J. 1970), *appeal dismissed* 414 U.S. 991 (1973).

²³Transcontinental Gas Pipe Line Corp. v. Hackensack Meadowlands Dev. Comm'n, 464 F.2d 1358 (3d Cir. 1972).

²⁴*See* Note 21, *supra*.

²⁵*Id.*: Note: Hackensack Meadowlands Dev. Comm'n, v. Municipal Sanitary Landfill Authority, 348 A.2d 505 (N.J. 1975) also involved an alleged interference in interstate commerce. The Commission banned out of state garbage from landfills within its jurisdiction and the original plaintiffs contended that garbage was an article of commerce. The court disagreed.

²⁶Bergen County Sewer Authority v. Hackensack Meadowlands Dev. Comm'n, 324 A.2d 108 (N.J. 1974).

²⁷Meadowlands Regional Dev. Agency v. State, 304 A.2d 545 (N.J. 1973), *appeal dismissed* 414 U.S. 991 (1973).

²⁸Meadowlands Regional Development Agency v. Hackensack Meadowlands Dev. Comm'n, 293 A.2d 192 (Super. Ct. N.J. 1972), *appeal denied* 229 A.2d 69 (N.J. 1972).

²⁹Adirondack—McCormick v. Lawrence, 372 N.Y.S.2d 156 (1975); Meadowlands Regional Dev. Agency v. State, 270 A.2d 418 (N.J. 1970); Bay Commission—Candlestick Properties Inc. v. San Francisco Bay Conservation and Dev. Comm'n, 89 Cal. Rptr. 897 (Cal. App. 1970); Tahoe—People ex rel Younger v. County of El Dorado, 487 P.2d 1193 (Cal. 1971).

³⁰*In re* Preseault, 292 A.2d 832 (Vt. 1972).

³¹King Resources Co. v. Environmental Improvement Comm'n, 270 A.2d 863 (Me. 1970); San Diego Coast Regional Commission for San Diego County v. See the Sea, Ltd., 109 Cal. Rptr. 377, 513 P.2d 377 (Cal. 1973); Putnam v Carroll, 534 P.2d 132 (Wash. 1975).

³²*In re* Maine Clean Fuels, Inc., 310 A.2d 736 (Me. 1973); *In re* Wildlife Wonderland, Inc., 346 A.2d 645 (Vt. 1975); Kreshtool v. Delmarva Power & Light Co., 310 A.2d 649 (Del. 1973); Department of Ecology v. Ballard Elks Lodge No. 827, 527 P.2d 1121 (Wash. App. 1972).

³³Town v. Land Use Comm'n, 524 P.2d 84 (Hawaii 1974); King Resources Co. v. Environmental Improvement Comm'n, 270 A.2d 863 (Me. 1970); *In re* Quechee Lakes Corp., 296 A.2d 190 (Vt. 1972).

³⁴Town v. Land Use Comm'n, 524 P.2d 84 (Hawaii 1974); Great E. Bldg. Co., Inc. 326 A.2d 152 (Vt. 1974); Klitgaard & Jones, Inc. v. San Diego Coast Regional Comm'n, 121 Cal. Rptr. 650 (Cal. App. 1975); Natural Resources Defense Council, Inc. v. Adirondack Park Agency, 359 N.Y.S. 2d 718 (1974).

³⁵*In re* Maine Clean Fuels, Inc., 310 A.2d 736 (Me. 1973); *In re* Baker Sargent Corp., 313 A.2d 669 (Vt. 1973); *In re* Wildlife Wonderland, Inc., 346 A.2d 645 (Vt. 1975); CEEED v. California Coastal Zone Conservation Comm'n, 118 Cal. Rptr. 315 (Cal. App. 1971).

³⁶City of Louisville v. District Court in and for the County of Boulder, 543 P.2d 67 (Col. 1975); Town v. Land Use Comm'n, 524 P.2d 84 (Hawaii 1974); *In re* Spring Valley Dev., 300 A.2d 736 (Me. 1973); *In re* Wildlife Wonderland, Inc. 346 A.2d 645 (Vt. 1975); CEEED v. California Coastal Zone Conservation Comm'n, 118 Cal. Rptr. 315 (Cal. App. 1971); Kreshtool v. Delmarva Power & Light Co., 310 A.2d 649 (Del. 1973); Department of Ecology v. Ballard Elks Lodge No. 827, 527 P.2d 1121 (Wash. App. 1974); Just v. Marinette County, 201 N.W.2d 761 (Wis. 1972); McCormick v. Lawrence 372 N.Y.S.2d 156 (1975); Meadowlands Regional Dev. Agency v. State, 270 A.2d 418 (N.J. 1970); Candlestick Properties, Inc. v. San Fransisco Bay Conservation and Dev. Comm'n, 89 Cal. Rptr. 897 (Cal. App. 1970); Younger v. County of El Dorado, 487 P.2d 1193 (Cal. 1971).

³⁷CEEED v. California Coastal Zone Conservation Comm'n, 118 Cal. Rptr. 315 (Cal. App. 1974); Eastlake Community Council v. Roanoke Associates Inc., 513 P.2d 36 (Wash. 1973).

³⁸CEEED v. California Coastal Zone Conservation Comm'n, 118 Cal. Rptr. 315 (Cal. App. 1974); Wambat Realty Corp., v. State, 378 N.Y.S.2d 912 (1975); Meadowlands Regional Dev.

Agency v. State, 270 A.2d 418 (N.J. 1970); Younger v. County of El Dorado, 487 P.2d 1193 (Cal. 1971).

[39]Transcontinental Gas Pipe Line Corp. v. Hackensack Meadowlands Development Commission, 464 F.2d 1358 (3d Cir. 1972).

9

The Federal Government and Land Use

Richard H. Jackson

COMPREHENSIVE planning for land use in cities received a great impetus from the Federal government. . . . Such encouragement of planning is only one of many ways in which the federal government affects land use in the United States. In general, the following categories of actions of the federal government can be recognized as affecting land use:

- Public spending as related to transportation and other public facilities.
- Direct land ownership and resultant control.
- Indirect control through programs which may encourage or require land use planning for recipients of federal funds.
- Direct regulatory control through national legislation.

Each of these categories has broad impact on the land resource of the United States. Such impact can be as specific as the decision to locate a post office, as broad as policies affecting building on flood plains throughout the nation, or as explicit as government regulation of land use on federal lands.

The Public Lands

The lands which are owned by the federal government are controlled by nearly 70 separate civilian and military agencies, commissions, corporations, and bureaus, including such diverse agencies as the International Boundary and Water Commission conservation groups, due to overgrazing caused by grazing fees that are too low; by recreational users who are critical of restrictions on the use of the public land; by mining interests who are critical of leasing regulations; and by environmental groups who feel mining regulations are too lenient. The critical federal regulation affecting BLM administered lands is associated with the Federal Land Policy and Management Act of 1976 which requires land use planning for all BLM land. The planning is to include an inventory of public lands and their resource and other values upon which to base plans. Comprehensive plans must be developed for each grazing unit administered by the BLM. As of 1980, only a few have been completed, but BLM is in the process of preparing Environmental Impact statements, designating roadless areas, and evaluating the potential of areas under its jurisdiction. Such planning is threatened by the action of the 1978 Nevada legislature which declared that federal ownership of land within its borders was illegal. Other western states have followed suit, and as of 1980 the legal counsel of western states was challenging the federal government in court in efforts to resolve the issue. It is highly doubtful that the western states will gain control over federal lands in their states, but their action may result in greater state input into the planning for federal lands.

The Fish and Wildlife Service administers less than one-tenth as much land as the BLM. The primary land use is associated with the National Wildlife Refuge System which consists of more than 340 game refugees and national wildlife refugees as well as some 100 fish hatcheries.[5] The lands controlled by the Department of Defense are used for purposes associated with army, navy, and air force bases.

The National Park Service is primarily concerned with recreation land uses although not all of their 23 million acres are available for recreation uses. The Park Service recognizes three general categories of lands: recreation areas, historical areas, and natural areas. In practice, all of the national parks, monuments, recreation areas, seashores, scenic parkways, wildlife, and scenic rivers are used for recreation to a greater or lesser extent. Conflict over land use in areas under the jurisdiction of the National Park Service focuses on issues relating to type of intensity of recreation activity, maintenance of the quality of the natural environment, and provision of services on park land by private concessionaires.

The Water and Power Resources Service (formerly Bureau of Reclamation administers lands and waters associated with various reclamation projects. A significant portion of the 7.5 million acres under their administration is in reservoirs. For example, in Utah the Water and Power Resources Service controls 1.3 million acres, in which 161,390 acres are contained in the Lake Powell reservoir on the Colorado River which is 186 miles long. The land use of their land is primarily related to recreation, fish and wildlife, and water management.

Impact of Federal Ownership

In total, the federal government directly controls one-third of all land of the United States. Although this land is essentially an area of extensive uses, federal land use policies and actions are of significance to the entire populace of the nation. Some of the impact of federal actions is obvious. Decisions limiting visitors to popular parks such as Yellowstone or Yosemite have direct consequence on a potentially large segment of the public. Other decisions may affect only a limited segment of the public, as Forest Service policies concerning leasing of individual or group recreational sites on public lands.[6] Regulation of the national resources on public land potentially affects broad segments of the economy. Controversy over expansion of areas designated as wilderness in the Uinta and Rocky Mountains of the west and in Alaska involves the question of access for potential exploitation of petroleum and other minerals. Restriction on clear cutting of timber poses questions of costs of lumber and lumber related products for the entire public.

The list of impacts of land use actions on federal lands is long, but they can be categorized into three broad, nonexclusive categories:

Type 1:   Impacts on the entire nation.
Type 2:   Impacts on western states because of the interconnected nature of western environments which do not neatly fit the arbitrary land ownership pattern.
Type 3:   Impacts of a local nature related to quasi-land use controls which extend beyond jurisdictional boundaries.

All land use actions on federal land may involve components of each of these three, but generally such actions can be categorized on the basis of dominant impact. Actions affecting recreation use of federal land are perhaps the best example of type 1 effects. Although it can be argued that local residents often are the dominant recreational users on federal lands, the recreational opportunity provided by these lands is a national heritage and thus policies and practices affect all residents.

The effect of federal land use actions on western states such as Utah, Nevada, and Alaska is profound. Normally, the land under federal control is essential for continued use of that land which is in private control. The federal land is often the source of water for urban and agricultural uses, water which is critical for continued occupancy of the land. In addition to critical water needs, the agricultural economy of western states is partially tied to federal land use because of need for summer or winter grazing lands. In the arid and semi-arid west, with its limited biomass production, few ranches have the large expanses of land necessary to support their livestock operations. This is particularly true where the prevalent agriculture system consists of small irrigated farms which also maintain a few livestock, as in Utah and Idaho.[7] In addition, western economies are impacted by federal land use controls which affect recreation use and resource exploration and exploitation. Providing services for recreation users is often the dominant economic activity for towns near national monuments, parks, and historic sites. Additionally, the granting or refusal of permits to operate large developments, such as ski resorts, utilizing federal land can have significant repercussions in the local economy and society. Of particular concern to western states is the impact of federal land use regulations on the development of early resources. Large deposits of coal located on BLM land, for example, are suitable for strip mining, and restrictions which affect their exploitation are viewed as handicapping economic growth in the west.[8]

In addition to the impacts of water and economic relations are those in which the controls on federal lands extend beyond its borders and directly restrict actions on private lands. An example of this is in the Grand Teton National Park area of Wyoming. As the park has expanded through time, it has surrounded "islands" of private land. Since the federal government has the power of eminent domain, it could force the owners of this property to sell. But rather than further alienate westerners who already resent the dominant role of the federal government in land ownership, the government allows owners to continue to use the land, though they are restricted from additional construction on their property. Such restrictions are greeted with hostility, and actions of local managers of federal land may increase tensions. In the case of the Tetons, one owner's cabin burned down and he was prevented from rebuilding. Teton National Park, although eager and willing to purchase the property, is cast in the role of villain and the case has been seized upon as an example of unwarranted harrassment of private landowners by federal agencies.

Federal land use controls which affect more than just a few parcels of private land are associated with the Sawtooth National Recreation Area in Idaho (Fig. 1). The Sawtooth Mountains are a scenic area of south central Idaho. They have been used for scattered mining, lumbering, and ranching activities but retain much of their pristine quality. Some 216,000 acres of the total 754,000 acres of the Recreation Area were originally designated as a wilderness area, but access to the Sawtooth is through a ranching area in the Sawtooth valley. There are 25,200 acres of private land in the valley in the form of scattered ranches, the rural communities of Salmon and Stanley, and several incipient second-home developments.[9] These latter were areas plotted into lots as small as 25 feet wide for trailers. In order to maintain the quality of the recreation experience in the Sawtooth, the

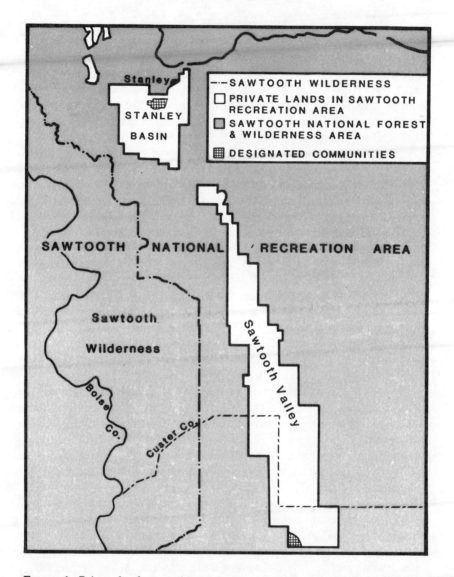

FIGURE 1. *Private land ownership in the Sawtooth National Recreation Area*

management plan controls the use of all of the land in the valley. Existing homes in the summer-home subdivisions have been removed, the lots have been purchased, and Stanley has been designated as the community in which future homes and commercial activity will be permitted. Since it is assumed that visitors to the recreation area have pre-conceived notions of

what a western ranching area should be like, guidelines have been issued
which call for replacing barbwire fence with post and pole fences; use of
"earthy" colors of brown, gray, and tan in buildings; removal of surplus
equipment in ranch yards, and replacement of sheet metal roofs because
they detract from the aesthetic quality of the pastoral ranch scene. The communities and counties involved are under mandate to prepare comprehensive plans, and appropriate zoning ordinances, to insure compliance with
the Sawtooth plan.[10]

Antagonism to such direct federal regulation of private lands is shared by
the private landowners, county governments, and local communities in the
area. The legislation that established the Sawtooth National Recreation
Area which allows a federal agency to impose quasi-zoning controls on
private land is the exception, however. Normally, federal government affects land use on private lands indirectly.[11]

The Power of the Purse:
The Effect of Federal Spending on Land Use

The major indirect land use control of the federal government is
associated with public spending. Some authors have maintained that spending by all levels of government is in fact the single most important land use
control in the United States.[12] Among the indirect controls of federal spending, those associated with transportation, water and sewage, housing and
urban renewal are particularly important.

One of the major examples of the impact of federal spending on land use
is associated with the implementation of the Federal Interstate System in
1956. This began a process affecting land use which continues to the present. Initially, the impact of the interstate system was twofold: direct conversion of land to highway and indirect effect on contiguous land. The land
used by the interstate itself is large, with one mile of interstate requiring up
to 48 acres of land. The interstate and other transport system utilize 26
million acres of rural American land.[13] The second impact is on land adjacent to, or served by, the interstate. The interstate has fostered urban
sprawl, growth of suburbs, and increased commercial and industrial development in the urban-rural transition zone through increased accessibility.

As a consequence of undesirable land use and other detrimental environmental impacts associated with the interstate, subsequent legislation
has fostered planning of land use in conjunction with highway construction.
Most important of these has been the National Environmental Policy Act
(NEPA) of 1969. Control of federal aid for highways was one of the major
programs of NEPA, and subsequently Environmental Impact statements
were required for federally funded highway construction. In 1974, the
Federal Highway Administration issued guidelines for such impact

statements. "Any action that is likely to precipitate significant foreseeable alterations in land use; planned growth; development patterns; traffic patterns, transportation services; including public transportation; and natural and man-made resources . . ." requires preparation of an impact statement.[14] Such impact statements serve as an important part of the planning process affecting land use since they nominally provide data on the land use effects of road construction. Planning for land use is also affected by section 134 of the Federal Aid for Highways Act which requires that after July 1, 1965 the Secretary of Transportation was not to authorize funding for projects in urban areas of over 50,000 population unless "such projects are based on a continuing comprehensive planning process."[15]

Another major federal action which has affected land use is that associated with housing. Section 701 of the Housing Act of 1954 provided funds for small communities to prepare comprehensive plans in anticipation of some day participating in the federally funded urban renewal program. Over time, this has been expanded until no city was eligible for funds unless it had prepared a comprehensive plan upon which urban renewal was based. As the concept of urban renewal also expanded to include provision of low income housing, preservation of historic areas, as well as traditional slum clearance, such requirements have had a significant impact on urban land use.[16] The Department of Housing and Urban Development is presently authorized to fund up to two-thirds of the comprehensive planning process. Amendments of 1974 required that by August 22, 1977 all funded comprehensive plans include a land use element.[17]

The National Environmental Policy Act

Another group of indirect land use controls exercised by the federal government is associated with the National Environmental Policy Act which was signed into law on January 1, 1970 (NEPA). The basic requirements of NEPA focus on the necessity of providing an Environmental Impact Statement (EIS) for any action of a federal agency whose actions significantly affect the quality of the human environment. Although initially directed at federal agencies, this mandate has been expanded to include not only action undertaken directly by the agencies, but also "federal decisions to approve, fund, or license activities which will be carried out by others."[18] The Environmental Protection Agency (EPA) was established to carry out the goals of the NEPA. The impact of the EPA on land use is not restricted to the boundaries of the project under consideration. The courts have ruled that the information provided in an EIS must be such that rational decisions can be made by the public and local governments as well as by the agency involved.[19] The impact of NEPA on land use is diverse. Environmental impact statements are required for reclamation projects; activities of the Forest Service and BLM; licensing and siting of power plants; permits to dredge or fill anywhere within the waters of the United States, and similar actions.

Air Pollution and Land Use

Another action growing out of the environmental concern of the late 1960s and early 1970s in the United States is the Clean Air Act of 1970. The act required that standards of air quality be set for several major air pollutants. The significance of the act for land use is that it required states to develop programs for complying with the national air quality standards. As part of the process involved in encouraging states to reach the national standards, all regions of each state are to be designated as Class I, II, or III air quality, where I is least polluted and III is most polluted.[20] The impact on land use results from attempts to either raise the quality of the air or to prevent degradation of existing high quality air. Under the Clean Air Act, the EPA is required to review all proposed new construction which might lead to further degradation of air quality. Specific types of land uses which might affect air quality are regulated in accordance with the class of air affected. Thus, a 5,000 megawatt power plant might be allowed in Class III regions, but not in Class II. A 1000 megawatt power plant is acceptable in a Class II region, but not a Class I. Designation of air quality regions as I, II, or III will have a significant impact on the land uses which occur within them. The EPA by law designates all of a state's areas with air quality higher than the national standard as Class II air until the state develops its own regional designations and associated plan to upgrade its air quality.[21]

Water Pollution and Land Use

Just as the Clean Air Act has important implications for land use, so the Federal Water Pollution Control Act Amendments of 1972 provided clauses of significant import to land use. The basic purpose of the 1972 amendments was to reduce water pollution by controlling point and non-point sources of pollution. Point sources include sources which are localized in space such as factories and sewage treatment plants, while non-point sources are those which tend to be random, such as storm waters and runoff from an agricultural area. The impact of the amendments on land use is broad since it affects a host of land use activities, but the most important portion of the 1972 amendments in terms of impact on land use is Section 208. Section 208 provides the means for developing the programs necessary to achieve the goal of having the best possible pollution control technology in operation by 1983. Section 208 requires control of point and non-point pollution sources through regulation, including land use regulation and management. To attain the goal of the 1972 water amendments, plans must be established for each area of a state to regulate land use, provide adequate sewage treatment, and control activities which affect pollution of water. Central to the requirements are the need for each state to have a continuing planning process, and the necessity of a state agency to oversee Section 208 planning since ultimately the state is responsible for all 208 planning within its boundaries. In terms of land use control, this is significant since it requires state agencies to assess existing state and local regulations to determine how well they provide for water management programs as well as establish what additional regulatory programs are needed.[22]

Land Use and the Coastal Zone

The coastal areas of North America are among the most intensively used lands of the continent. Geographically, they provide advantageous locations for many of man's activities, including cities, industries, and recreation. The same geographic characteristics which make coastal locations useful to man also result in environments which are highly susceptible to degradation by those activities. To minimize damage to critical coastal locations useful to man also results in environments which are highly susceptible to degradation by those activities. To minimize damage to critical coastal environments, the Coastal Zone Management Act of 1972 (CZMA) was passed by Congress. The act makes federal funds available to states to help them prepare and implement comprehensive plans to control land use in the coastal zone.[23] The critical portions of the CZMA are Section 305, which provides two-thirds of the funds for the planning process, and Section 306, which provides similar funding for the implementation of the plans. Participation of the states under the CZMA is voluntary, but all 34 states which have coastal zones (including those adjacent to the Great Lakes) have applied for funds.[24] As of 1979, 13 states had received approval for their plans, and an additional 7 anticipated approval by the end of the year.[25] Only two states seemed in danger of loosing funding for lack of progress in planning for land use in the coastal zone. Illinois was denied further funding in 1979 because its legislature failed to pass the necessary legislation to establish a control zone management program in the state.[26] Texas has the seventh largest coastline in the U.S., but public opposition to the concept of strict regulation of the coastal zone through quasi-zoning regulations has handicapped efforts to develop a coastal zone management program and the state may lose funding by the end of 1979.[27] But even in these two states, federal funds from the CZMA have been used for planning purposes for the past 6 years.

The CZMA defines the coastal zone as the coastal waters (including the zone of transition zone between land and water occupied by marshes, tidal flats, beaches, and wetlands) and an indeterminate amount of the adjacent land. The inland limit of the coastal zone is defined as that necessary "to control shorelands, the users of which have a direct and significant impact on the coastal waters."[28] Planning for the area which is ultimately designated as the coastal zone in each state must include the following in order for the state to receive federal funding for the planning:

1. Identification of the coastal zone boundaries.
2. An inventory and designation of areas of particular concern.
3. Guidelines establishing priority of land use in particular areas.
4. A definition of what shall constitute permissible land and water uses within the coastal zone which have a direct and significant impact on the coastal waters.
5. An identification of the means by which a state intends to control the land uses within the coastal zone.
6. The organizational structure that would implement the management program, including state, regional, and local aspects.[29]

Once a state has prepared a management plan, it must be approved by the National Oceanic and Atmospheric Administration, Office of Coastal Zone Management, which administers the CZMA.

Of central importance to land use controls are the provisions of the 1972 act which require control of land use in the coastal zone. The act provides for three alternative types of control, but all are indirect forms of federal control of land use. States may opt for direct state regulation of coastal lands, local regulation in accordance with state standards, or local regulation subject to state review. Whichever option of control the states select, the land use regulations must be administered according to the management plan approved by the Office of Coastal Zone Management (OCZM).

It is too early to critically assess the full impact of the CZMA fo 1972 on land use, but the following general statements can be made. The act does not include any means of enforcing preparation of an acceptable management plan. The fact that all 34 eligible states are participating should not be construed as evidence of state control of land in the coastal zone in all. These states are receiving funds for the planning and implementation process, but should either plan or management program fail to meet OCZM standards the only thing OCZM can do is withhold future funding.

Federal Control of the Flood Plain

Floodplains, like coastal zones, are areas with geographic characteristics which have led to concentrations of man's activities. Accessibility provided by rivers, level land, and abundant water has contributed to development of cities, towns, and suburbs on the floodplain. Land use activities associated with urban and suburban use of the floodplain create problems when floods destroy life and property. Since the floodplain is a part of the dynamic system of a river it will flood inevitably, and historically, residents of such flood prone areas were unable to obtain any insurance to protect them against loss. When floods occurred, the federal government became responsible for providing millions of dollars in assistance to residents of the flooded areas in the form of aid to victims of a natural disaster. In response to the damages and associated costs of flooding, the government has funded massive flood control programs whose dams, levees, and assorted structural components were designed to protect against all but the worst floods. Unfortunately, the net effect of these structural solutions has resulted in the potential for even greater flood related damage and destruction. Construction of a dam has been viewed as a panacea for flooding, and the floodplains below dams have consequently received even more urban-related development. The illusion of permanent protection afforded by flood control structures, and associated development of floodplains, has meant increasing destruction and greater costs to the federal government. In response to increasing costs, Congress passed the National Flood Plain Insurance Program in 1968. This program provided flood insurance which was subsidized by the government and encouraged regulation of land use to minimize flood damage.

Since few flood-prone communities volunteered to participate in the program, Congress passed stronger regulation in the form of the Flood Disaster Protection Act of 1973. This act provides important regulations affecting land use in the floodplain. Specifically, it states that no federal assistance can be granted for the acquisition or construction of property in identified flood hazard zones after July 1, 1975 unless the community involved is participating in the National Flood Insurance Program. This action requires communities to adopt land use regulations for their floodplains which meet the federal criteria in order to participate in the program. In addition, the act requires that federal agencies which "supervise, approve, regulate, or insure banks, savings and loan institutions, or similar institutions" must prohibit loaning money on real estate in identified flood hazard zones unless they participate in the National Flood Insurance Program.[30]

The potential impact on land use regulation of such sanctions is evident. In essence, they prevent any bank or savings and loan institution from loaning money for construction in floodplains unless the community regulates the land use to prevent damage from floods. When fully implemented, the Flood Insurance Program will significantly affect land use in floodplains which are prone to flooding. It should be noted that the extent of the floodplain designated as flood-prone is the part subject to what is known as the "100 year flood." The "100 year flood" is a misnomer since it is actually simply a probability measurement, i.e., the area designated as flood prone is that area which lies below the water level which has a 1 in 100 chance of being equalled or exceeded in any given year.

Other Federal Regulations

A number of other programs of the federal government affect the American land. There are over 850 federal programs which provide some type of assistance or regulation for state and local governments, and over 130 of them have a direct impact on land use.[31] One of the more important is Section 404 of the 1972 Federal Water Pollution Control Act which charges the U.S. Army Corps of Engineers with the responsibility for controlling dredging and filling activities as they affect the waters of the United States. The act requires an impact statement before permits will be issued for such activities when they affect navigable waterways, freshwater wetlands adjacent to navigable rivers, and coastal wetlands affected by periodic flooding that are contiguous to navigable waterways.[32] As a result of court actions by environmental groups, the 1972 Act has been extended to all waters of the United States. In practice, this means the Corps of Engineers will regulate dredge and fill operations of all types except those associated with normal agricultural and silvicultural activities.[33] Thus the Corps becomes an important regulator of land use activities in wetlands and land adjacent to other water bodies.

Another important act which affects land use in certain areas is the Wild and Scenic Rivers Act of 1968. This originally designated all or portions of eight rivers and adjacent lands as part of a National Wild and Scenic Rivers System (Table 1). An additional 27 rivers were designated as possible additions to this system. Subsequently, 16 other rivers have been designated part of the system (including some of those originally considered for possible addition) and an additional 43 have been added to the potential list. The act provides for protection of the rivers and their immediate environments through funding acquisition of land along the system rivers, prevention of construction on the river, and guidelines for zoning regulations of communities along the designated rivers. The latter point specifies that zoning ordinances in communities along the rivers in the system must prohibit new commercial or industrial uses along the banks and protect the river bank lands through setback, acreage, and frontage requirements.[34]

The federal role is somewhat restricted in that the government is not allowed to purchase more than an average of 100 acres of land per mile of river. The federal government may not take land by eminent domain if 50% or more of the acreage along the river is privately owned, or in any existing town and city with zoning which protects the river. The federal government is authorized to purchase scenic easements, allowing them to regulate subdivision, removal of vegetation adjacent to the river, distance of new dwellings from the river, and industrial and commercial development.

TABLE 1. *Rivers of the National Wild and Scenic Rivers System*

Name	Date
Clearwater, Middle Fork, Idaho	1968
Eleven Point, Missouri	1968
Feather, California	1968
Rio Grande, New Mexico	1968
Rogue, Oregon	1968
Saint Croix, Minnesota and Wisconsin	1968
Salmon, Middle Fork, Idaho	1968
Wolf, Wisconsin	1968
Lower Saint Croix, Minnesota	1972
Chattooga, North Carolina, South Carolina, and Georgia	1974
Rapid, Idaho	1975
Upper Middle Snake, Idaho and Oregon	1975
Allagash Wilderness Waterway, Maine	1970
Little Miami, Ohio	1973
Little Beaver, Ohio	1975
New River, North Carolina	1976
Middle Delaware, Pennsylvania and New Jersey	1978
Pere Marguette, Michigan	1978
Rio Grande, Texas	1978
North Fork American	1978
Upper Delaware, New York and Pennsylvania	1978
Missouri, South Dakota and Nebraska	1978
Skagit, Washington	1978
St. Joe, Idaho	1978

SOURCE: American Rivers Conservation Council, July 1978, p. 1–5; Oct., 1978, p. 1–2.

It would be impossible to list all of the federal activities and agencies which have some impact on land use, but other important ones affecting restricted areas include the Bureau of Outdoor Recreation, The Wilderness Act, the National Scenic Trails Act, Regulations Governing Use of Off-Road Vehicles, and the Land and Water Conservation Fund Act. Of necessity, this listing is fragmentary, but it is indicative of the broad range of land use activities affected by various federal activities.

Conclusion

Taken together, the extent of federal control over land use in the United States is of fundamental importance. In general, these controls can be characterized as indirect. With the exception of lands actually owned and administered by federal agencies, the federal impact on land use is essentially carried out through programs which provide incentives to state and local governments to plan. Funds for water and air quality, protection of coastal zones, open space preservation, etc. encourage land use regulation but do not mandate compliance with federal guidelines unless the state or local units accept the funding. Because of the importance of such funding to local communities, however, the regulations upon which funding is contingent have a near universal impact in the United States.

The importance of the federal role in land use control continues to increase. As states proceed in the process of complying with the various provisions of the NEPA and associated acts, the impacts on land use are increasingly affecting each individual in the country. The logical conclusion of increasing control would be a national land use act of some type, but it is questionable whether such legislation will be proposed in the near future. There was great interest in such an act in the early 1970s, but 1975 was the last year in which national land use legislation was actually proposed. With increasing resentment of federal government and federal regulation in the late 1970s, it is doubtful whether new legislation which is perceived to have such a broad societal impact as a national land use act can be passed. For the time being, therefore, the role of the federal government will probably continue to be indirect.

NOTES

[1] *Public Land Statistics, 1976* (Washington, D.C.: Government Printing Office, 1977), pp. 14–30.

[2] Elaine Moss, editor, *Land Use Controls in the United States* (New York: Dial Press for Natural Resources Defense Council, Inc., 1977), p. 225.

[3] U.S. Code, Vol. 16, Sec. 528–531.

[4] Daniel R. Barney, *The Last Stand* (New York: Grossman Publishers, 1974). Report on the National Forests prepared by the Ralph Nader Study Group. *The Last Stand* provides a detailed and critical analysis of the management practices of the Forest Service.

[5] Moss, op. cit. p. 229.

[6] Jon A. Kusler, *A Perspective on Flood Plain Regulation for Flood Plain Management* (Washington, D.C.: Department of the Army, 1974), pp. 12–21.

[7] Charles Peterson, *Look to the Mountains* (Provo, Utah: Brigham Young University Press, 1977) discusses the impact on small farms of increasingly restrictive land use controls on federal lands in Utah.

[8] *Environmental Quality, 1977. Council on Environmental Quality* (Washington, D.C.: Government Printing Office, 1977), pp. 23–24.

[9] "Sawtooth National Recreation Area," Hearings Before the Subcommittee on Parks and Recreation, 92nd Congress, S. 1407 and H.R. 6957 (Washington, D.C.: Government Printing Office, 1972), p. 16.

[10] Ibid.

[11] "Federal Land Planning: The Indirect Approach." (Washington, D.C.: Resources for the Future, 1976), pp. 17–18.

[12] Marion Clawson and Burnell Held, *The Federal Lands: Their Use and Management* (Lincoln: University of Nebraska Press, 1957), p. 34.

[13] *Environmental Quality, 1974,* Council on Environmental Quality (Washington, D.C.: Government Printing Office, 1974), p. 39.

[14]Moss, op. cit., p. 177.

[15]Ibid., p. 184.

[16]William I. Goodman and Eric C. Freund, *Principles and Practices of Urban Planning* (Washington, D.C.: International City Manager's Association, 1968), pp. 485-506.

[17]Moss, op. cit.

[18]Ibid., p. 19.

[19]*Guidelines for Air Quality Maintenance Planning and Analysis*, Environmental Protection Agency (Research Triangle Park, N.C.: Office of Air Quality Planning and Standards, 1974-1975), 13 volumes, Vol. 1, *Designation of Air Quality Maintenance Areas.*

[20]Moss, op. cit., p. 58.

[21]Ibid., pp. 71-75.

[22]U.S. Code, Vol. 16, Sec. 1451.

[23]Bradley E. Spicer, De Witt H. Braud, and John M. Bordolon, "States' Interest in Land Use," in *Land Use: Tough Choices in Today's World* (Ankeny, Iowa: Soil Conservation Society of America, 1977), p. 409.

[24]U.S. Code, Vol. 16, Sec. 1453 (a).

[25]Moss, op. cit., pp. 101-102; Spicer et al., op. cit., p. 410.

[26]*The Christian Science Monitor*, March 2, 1979, p. 6.

[27]*Planning*, April 1979, p. 9.

[28]*The Christian Science Monitor*, op. cit.

[29]Moss, op. cit., pp. 121-122.

[30]Spicer et al., op. cit., p. 406. A good overview of federal actions affecting land use can be obtained by reading Elaine Moss. editor, *Land Use Controls in the United States* (New York: Dial Press for National Resources Defense Council, 1977); Arnold W. Reitze, Jr. *Environmental Planning: Law of Land and Resources* (Washington, D.C.: North American International, 1974), and Mary Robinson Swe, editor, *Environmental Legislation* (New York: Praeger Publishers, 1976).

[31]Spicer et al., op. cit., pp. 408-409.

[32]Moss, op. cit., p. 86.

[33]*Flowing Free: A Citizen's Guide for Protecting Wild and Scenic Rivers* (Washington, D.C.: The River Conservation Fund, 1977), pp. 64-76 for the entire act.

[34]Ibid., pp. 10-12.

10

Regulating Sensitive Lands

An Overview of Programs

Jon A. Kusler

W HILE REGULATION of sensitive lands is relatively new, state and local natural resource management dates from the last century when park, wildlife, and forestry programs were established for lands in the public domain. Until the 1920s and 1930s, little effort was made to control the private use of land without outright acquisition. During this period, states authorized local units of government—cities, towns and counties—to adopt zoning and subdivision regulations.

In the 1950s, it became clear that the marketplace and exclusive local control of lands would not meet long-term state and national needs. The demand for land resulted in construction in flood plains, wetlands, slopes, and other areas traditionally considered unsuitable for development. Natural hazard losses mounted despite massive federal expenditures for protective works.[1] Areas needed for science, wildlife, and recreation uses were being destroyed at an alarming rate. Prime agricultural lands, forestry lands, and mineral resource areas were quickly subdivided for residential and second home use in both urbanizing and rural areas.

Local governments often did little to control these trends due to a combination of inadequate natural resource data, lack of expertise, inadequate budgets, inadequate geographical scope, and narrow interests.

These abuses led to the "*quiet revolution*" in land use control.[2] State legislatures during the 1965-1977 period adopted 94 statutes promulgating minimum development control standards for sensitive areas. These statutes usually directed local units of government to adopt and administer regulations meeting or exceeding state standards within a specified period of time.

If the local units failed to adopt the regulations, the state agency was itself authorized to administer and enforce regulations. Only two-fifths of the statutes authorized direct state regulation without local administration and enforcement. Thus the quiet revolution primarily involved a shift to cooperative state and local control. In response to federal and state initiatives and their own concern for dwindling resources, local governments adopted more than 1,000 wetland and 1,400 inland lake and stream protection programs. More than 17,000 local governments adopted, or indicated an intent to adopt, flood plain regulations as part of the national flood insurance program. Thousands of others adopted regulations for coastal areas, erosion control, seismic areas, steep slopes, prime agricultural lands, forestry areas, and mineral resource areas.

Since 1965, many state legislatures also considered more sweeping state planning and land use regulation statutes.[3] Comprehensive land use legislation was adopted in a few states, but failed to gain widespread support. In the Congress, a National Land Use Policy Act was considered and rejected in four separate sessions. Two types of programs were consistently adopted by state legislatures during this period. The first, sensitive land programs, usually emphasized the regulation of a single type of resource area.[4] The second, regulatory permit programs, governed special uses such as strip mining, large scale development, and utility plants.[5]

The success of sensitive land programs compared to broader proposals has sometimes been dismissed as opposition by conservatives to too much state or federal power. This factor played an important role, but more basic forces were at work.

First, comprehensive statewide planning and regulation pose complex data gathering, planning, standard-setting, and implementation issues not easily understood by legislators or the public. They suspect this complexity and the hidden value judgments implicit in most planning approaches. In contrast, an emphasis on resources focuses land use policies on basic, understandable issues. Performance-oriented controls linked to natural resource values and hazards have an obvious logic.

Second, sound comprehensive planning and regulation are time-consuming and expensive. Lacking money, manpower, and time, planning efforts are superficial and of little value. In contrast, a focus on resource areas establishes clear priorities for data gathering, planning, and implementation and also provides a rational basis for later planning. The term "critical" has commonly been applied to these areas to indicate their importance to society and their need for immediate attention through allocation of scarce manpower and monies.

Third, comprehensive planning and regulation at the state level threaten local home rule. Resource programs are less a threat where they address selected sensitive areas with clear regional and statewide interest. Further, sensitive areas are precisely the areas where local governments lack the expertise or motivation for adequate control. State regulation can be linked to traditional state resource protection roles, such as the protection of the public trust in navigable waters.[6] These interests have visibility and strong public support in many instances.

The merits of state or local land use programs which focus on sensitive lands alone can be overemphasized. Transportation, economic development, and housing needs, for example, cannot be resolved with a sensitive area focus. But it is clear that all needs of man depend upon land, water, and mineral resources. Serious shortages will occur without careful utilization of renewable and nonrenewable resources.

Motivation for Programs

A major motivation for adopting sensitive area programs has been the protection and management of state waters and aquatic life. These concerns have resulted in shoreland, wetland, coastal, flood plain, and some broader comprehensive critical area programs. They form the majority of existing sensitive area efforts. For example, the threat of water pollution led to the adoption of lake and stream shore zoning programs in Wisconsin and Maine; fills in lakes led to the enactment of the Washington shoreline zoning statute; erosion problems along Lake Michigan prompted the adoption of the Michigan shoreland program; a water shortage led to adoption of the Florida state planning and critical area act; destruction of spawning grounds prompted coastal wetland protection in Georgia; and severe floods prompted flood plain legislation in Nebraska and Minnesota.

Federal legislation has proved another major motivating factor. The National Flood Insurance Act, requiring the regulation of the 100-year flood plain, was a direct motivation for adoption of state flood plain programs in New York, Texas, Alabama, and other states. Similarly, the Coastal Zone Management Act, requiring the definition of coastal areas of "particular concern," prompted coastal legislation in North Carolina. National scenic and wild rivers legislation has encouraged many state scenic and wild river programs.

In a broader sense, sensitive area programs reflect deep public concern with natural resources and the environment. A variety of statutes evidence this concern. They require environmental impact statements, authorize citizen suits for environmental degradation, regulate large-scale development, control air, water, and noise pollution, and establish statewide land resource inventories and planning.

Overview of Regulatory Approaches

Areas with special natural resource values and hazards are found on both public and private lands. Regulations may be adopted at federal, state, or local levels, for both types of lands, although most efforts to date have focused on private lands.

The federal government is playing an increasingly important role in protecting sensitive areas on the one-third of the nation's land which is federally owned.[7] This includes more than 755 million acres of land managed by the Bureau of Land Management, the U.S. Forest Service, the Department of Defense, the Army Corps of Engineers, the Bureau of Sport Fisheries and Wildlife, the Bureau of Reclamation, the Tennessee Valley Authority, and the National Park Service. Protection takes the form of resource inventories, management planning, and, in some instances, regulation of private activities such as grazing, mining, and recreation.

States and local units of government also plan and manage public lands such as parks and forests. Private activities other than outdoor recreation are tightly regulated.

State regulation of privately owned sensitive areas takes two forms: direct state regulation and state standard-setting for local regulation. Approximately two-fifths of the state regulatory statutes authorize some direct state control of uses. These include most of the wetland, some floodway, and several coastal statutes. Statutes authorizing direct state regulation generally require permits from a state regulatory agency for proposed structural uses and some nonstructural uses such as dams and fills in navigable waters. States usually map sensitive areas and adopt specific administrative regulations controlling particular uses.

Administrative regulations, like their statutory counterparts, usually contain a statement of goals and policies. They often include more precise critical area definition along with minimum standards pertaining to lot sizes, building setbacks from roads and waters, use of septic tanks, and flood protection elevations. Administrative regulations usually apply to all lands of a particular type within the state. For example, general standards are adopted for all flood plains requiring protection of structures to the 100-year flood elevation and preserving floodway areas. However, some agencies have established several sets of standards with varying degrees of restrictiveness for a particular type of area. In Minnesota, the shoreland and zoning program classifies lakes and establishes different shoreland use restrictions for each category.

Most state critical area enabling statutes authorize state standard-setting for local regulation rather than direct state control. The state regulatory agency typically adopts administrative regulations establishing minimum standards for local zoning, subdivision controls, and, less frequently, minimum standards for building codes, sanitary codes, or other types of regulations. Local governments are usually required to adopt regulations that meet or exceed state standards within a specific time period. This period generally begins when the state agency formally maps the sensitive area. The state regulatory agency is authorized to regulate development in the event local units fail to adopt and enforce satisfactory controls.

Prior to 1972, sensitive area statutes were adopted solely on an individual area basis for particular types of areas such as flood plains. Since then Florida, Minnesota, Wyoming, Oregon, Maine, North Carolina, Virginia, Maryland, Nevada, and Colorado have authorized a single agency to define and map several types of areas. However, these statutes place primary regulatory responsibility at the local level.[8]

Local regulations continue to play a dominant role in controlling sensitive area development. They are typically adopted pursuant to broader zoning, subdivision control, and building code enabling statutes. Statutes authorize cities to adopt zoning and subdivision regulations in all states except Hawaii and Alaska, where counties and boroughs have zoning powers.[9] Counties are authorized to zone and adopt subdivision regulations in all but a few states. Towns and townships are authorized to zone and exercise subdivision control powers in most states. Cities, counties, towns, and townships are authorized to adopt building codes in many states. A number of these general enabling acts contain specific resource protection provisions.

In addition, special enabling acts authorize local sensitive area regulations in some states.[10] Special statutes authorizing flood plain regulations have been adopted in Alabama, Texas, and Kansas; shoreland regulations have been authorized in Minnesota, Wisconsin, Maine, and Vermont; and wetland regulations have been authorized in Connecticut, Virginia, and Massachusetts. These acts, while more abbreviated, contain the same general types of provisions as zoning, subdivision control, and building code enabling statutes.

Some local sensitive area regulations are adopted pursuant to constitutional or statutory home rule provisions.[11] However, general or special statutory enabling powers usually suffice without resort to home rule powers.

A brief look at the principal local regulatory techniques follows:

Zoning

Zoning is the most widespread sensitive area implementation technique at the local level. Traditional zoning, as opposed to sensitive area zoning, has been adopted by most larger cities in the country and by many towns and counties. Zoning divides communities into districts on a zoning map and applies varying use standards to the districts through a written text. Zoning often contains a wide variety of provisions specifying permitted and prohibited uses within particular areas and minimum standards governing lot sizes, building heights, and setback from roads.

Sensitive area zones are mapped either as primary zones or as "overlay" districts. Sensitive area zoning restrictions include:

A. Restrictions upon the *types of uses* permitted in critical zones and subzones such as prohibition of fills in wetlands.

B. Bulk restrictions establishing *minimum size, location, and density specifications for uses* including building setbacks, building heights, side yard requirements, and lot sizes.

C. *Performance standards* defining the maximum permissible impact of specific uses on resources such as removal or disturbance of vegetation, alteration of flood flows, alteration of drainage, and so forth.[12] Performance standards are usually applied through special permit requirements. New uses require special permits. To obtain a permit, the applicant must demonstrate that use impacts will not exceed permissible levels.

While local zoning is a broad sensitive area management tool, it is also subject to many limitations including limited data base, lack of administrative expertise, inadequate geographical perspective, and failure to take into account the unique features of each site. Other limitations include statutory exemptions for agricultural uses, nonconforming uses, and public utilities. In addition, courts have generally held that zoning is not applicable to public uses.[13]

Subdivision Regulations

Subdivision regulations are also adopted at the local level to meet broad land-use control objectives. They are less common and less effective for sensitive area protection since they do not control the type of land use or subsequent development. Subdividers are required to prepare detailed maps (called plats) prior to sale of lots or prior to building. Plats must be reviewed and approved by the planning commission. The commission determines whether lands are suitable for their intended purposes and whether the plats are in compliance with zoning and other regulations. Typically, subdivisions are required to install roads, sewers, water, and sometimes park areas to meet the needs of subdivision residents.

While subdivision regulations affect limited aspects of land use, they have been well received by the courts and do have several useful features in minimizing development impact upon sensitive areas. First, they require case-by-case consideration of each proposed development to permit an evaluation of project impact and the attachment of conditions to minimize impact. Communities usually have considerable bargaining power in this process. Second, subdividers may be in a better position to undertake detailed fact-finding than private landowners. They employ surveyors and other specialists in preparation of the plat and may be able to pass costs on to subsequent purchasers.

Building Codes

Building codes are a more limited tool for sensitive area protection than subdivision regulations. They do not determine the types or locations of uses allowed in particular areas. However, they may impose either inflexible design standards or more generalized performance standards for flood, seismic disturbance, or other natural hazards protection. In some instances they also influence the location of buildings. For example, a code requiring very expensive flood proofing in a flood hazard area may practically preclude development in the area. Special types of building codes such as architectural controls and historic building preservation codes are sometimes used to preserve scenic beauty and protect historic sites.

Special Codes

In addition to conventional regulations, a variety of special codes are adopted to reduce the impact of particular uses. These include air, water, and noise pollution controls, sanitary codes, regulations for junkyards and other nuisance uses, sign regulations, strip-mining controls, regulation of filling and grading, dune protection regulations, beach setbacks, encroachment lines, and tree-cutting regulations. Special codes generally require that developers seek permits which conform to the ordinance standards.

Common Denominators in Implementing Programs

State and local regulatory programs for sensitive areas reveal striking similarities in basic issues and implementation approaches. In part, these similarities are due to the technical and scientific problems of determining the impact of various uses upon natural resources and establishing standards to minimize these impacts. They are also due to budgetary, legal, political, and administrative constraints common to all programs. There are eight major areas of agreement:

A. With few exceptions, regulatory efforts balance preservation and development needs through the establishment of *performance standards* rather than prohibition of all uses. The approach reflects a genuine effort to promote multiple land uses and minimize the impact of development upon important resources.

B. Programs are generally shaped by similar *constitutional, political,* and *financial restraints.* All programs have been faced with state and federal constitutional guarantees of due process, including prohibitions against discrimination and the taking of private property without just compensation. This has favored the use of performance standards and special permit approaches. Programs have been required to cope with traditional home rule and strong concepts of private property, favoring local involvement in most state programs. Other problems have included limited budgets and staff for definition of areas, standard-setting, and administration. Limited budgets and staffs have resulted in the phased, area-by-area approaches and the application of money-saving techniques as discussed below.

C. The adequacy of the data base is a principal issue in all programs. The mapping of areas and evaluation of individual permits is complicated by (1) *the diversity in resource values and hazards* typically found in a single critical area as in flood plains where varying soils, slopes, and vegetation affect the severity of height of flooding; (2) *the varying impact of the design, construction, and operation of any single new use* on site-specific resource values and hazards; and (3) *the cumulative effect* of the proposed use, ancillary and adjacent uses, and future uses on the specific site and on the resource area as a whole. Often minor variations in the location or design of a proposed use substantially affect impact.

D. Due to these technical problems and the lack of detailed data, state and local programs *make widespread use of "special permit" procedures* whereby a board of experts (1) evaluates the impact of each proposed use at a particular site through case-by-case data gathering; (2) determines acceptable levels of impact through application of statutory, administrative rule, or ordinance quantified standards, or more often, through application of generalized guidelines and policies as applied to that site; and (3) denies, permits, or conditionally permits the proposed use. This approach tailors project restrictions to the natural resource values found at particular sites but requires expertise in evaluation of the cumulative impact of future development.

E. Limited budgets have resulted in *a wide range of money-saving techniques.* (1) Developers are required to prepare environmental impact statements or supply other types of data. (2) Data gathering and regulation of areas under development pressure are carried out on a priority basis for areas with special values and hazards. (3) Nomination procedures,[14] workshops, public hearings, and other public involvement techniques are used to solicit information from local units of government, other agencies, and interested citizens. They are used to locate potential critical areas with special values or hazards, such as habits of rare and endangered species. (4) Permit issuance is partially or wholly delegated to local units of government who must carry out necessary data gathering and conduct public hearings.

The latter requirement reduces state program costs where necessary data is available at the local level or can be gathered inexpensively by experts living near the sites.

F. *Successful programs* often combine several characteristics: (1) strong local involvement in program administration and enforcement; (2) strong state technical assistance and data gathering; (3) clear and specific minimum state standards for local controls; (4) flexibility and options built into standards for local regulatory efforts; (5) an enabling statute which expresses clear program goals and contains specific definition criteria; (6) adequate program funding; (7) a cost-conscious approach to all phases of program implementation so that funds are not all allocated to one program phase such as sensitive area mapping; (8) dynamic program leadership; (9) expert and imaginative agency staff; (10) strong public involvement and education through workshops, hearing, guidebooks, and newspaper releases; (11) a genuine attempt to balance public and private interests and a willingness to negotiate where nonessential values and hazards are involved; (12) careful monitoring and enforcement efforts; and (13) a fact-conscious approach to the evaluation of individual development permits. The latter should emphasize relatively accurate maps and air photos at reasonable scales— 1:24,000 or larger—combined with case-by-case date gathering to resolve boundary disputes and evaluate individual permits.

G. Major *impediments* to successful efforts include: (1) inadequate funding or a defeatist attitude held by the program staff; (2) inadequate leadership; (3) failure to involve local units of government; (4) inexperienced and unimaginative program staff; (5) uncooperative and inflexible attitudes in state program administration such as "let landowners and local governments be damned;" (6) poor public education and public involvement; (7) enabling statutes with weak definition criteria and vague outlines of agency or local government responsibilities; (8) expenditures of scarce funds on small scale maps or other data of little use in program implementation; (9) inability or unwillingness to carefully evaluate development permits; (10) failure to promulgate rules and guidelines for the processing of individual development permits; and (11) political pressures which result in policies or development permits inconsistent with natural resource values and hazards.

H. Even programs functioning with fair success concede the *need for improvements* such as: (1) increased funding for all phases of program development and implementation; (2) improved land suitability and land capability methodologies to provide systematic documentation of natural values and hazards at particular sites; (3) improved project impact evaluation methodologies; (4) studies to indicate threshold disturbance levels for natural systems; (5) statutory amendments, in some cases, to clarify authority and definition criteria; (6) formulation of sensitive area policies within a broader context of population growth limits and resource utilization policies; (7) improved public education; (8) improved monitoring and enforcement of regulations; and (9) improved techniques for dealing with the cumulative impact of uses.

Programs for Particular Types of Areas

Considerable similarity exists in the definition criteria, data, and development standards applied to each type of area at state and local levels and from state to state. The following discussion highlights these similarities.[15]

Flood Plains

At least twenty-four states either directly regulate floodways or floodway and flood fringe areas or establish standards for local regulation.[16] More than 17,000 local units of government have adopted or indicated an intent to adopt flood plain zoning, subdivision controls, building codes, or special codes in order to qualify for federal flood insurance. As such, flood plain regulations are the most extensive and the oldest of the sensitive area controls.

The 100-year flood (flood of the magnitude likely to occur once each 100 years) serves as the basis for mapping and regulation in most programs. This standard has been adopted for the National Flood Insurance Program and by federal agencies.

Flood plain areas are primarily mapped by the federal government through the National Flood Insurance Program, the flood control efforts of the U.S. Army Corps of Engineers, and the natural resource data gathering efforts of the U.S. Geological Survey and Soil Conservation Service. A flood profile—a graph showing flood elevations along a stretch of stream—and flood boundary maps based upon engineering calculations are usually prepared. Sometimes soil maps, historic flood records, air photos of flooding, and even "eye-balling" techniques are included on a preliminary basis. Where more detailed federal data is available, many flood plain regulatory programs distinguish inner flood conveyance areas adjacent to a stream, called floodways, from outer areas subject to lower flood depths and velocities called flood fringe areas. Floodways are usually mapped through engineering calculations designed to prevent damaging retardation of flood flows.

Usually, state and local flood plain programs prohibit permanent buildings and fills in floodway areas but permit a wide range of structural uses in flood fringe areas if elevated or structurally flood-proofed to a flood protection elevation.

Special permit approaches are often applied to all structures and fills where floodway and flood fringe areas are not mapped in advance of regulation. Case-by-case data gathering is carried out for each special permit to determine whether the proposed use is located within the floodway or flood fringe portion of the hazard area and establish flood protection elevations. Such an approach requires considerable technical expertise and data gathering capability.

Due to widespread adoption, flood plain regulations have been the most extensively litigated of the sensitive area controls. Courts have strongly endorsed the objective of flood loss reduction,[17] but sometimes have found deficiencies in specific regulations as applied to particular property. Several cases have invalidated restrictions as unreasonable;[18] one case found regulations discriminatory;[19] and a fair number of cases have invalidated tight regulations for a broad flood plain area as a taking when all economic use of the land was prevented.[20]

Lake and Stream Shores

Six states have adopted special legislation for the protection of inland shoreland areas: Maine, Vermont, Washington, Minnesota, and Michigan.[21] In addition, California and Nevada have created a joint Lake Tahoe Agency. The acts of Maine and Washington apply both to inland and ocean shorelines and the acts of Wisconsin and Minnesota apply to the Great Lakes as well as inland lake and stream areas.

All six states define shorelands in relationship to the high water mark: areas within 1,000 feet in Michigan and Vermont; 250 feet in Maine; and 200 feet in Washington. Wisconsin and Minnesota regulate river as well as lake shorelands for up to 300 feet from the high water mark or to the landward side of the flood plain. Maine controls a 250-foot river shoreland area. Washington regulates a 200-foot strip. These shoreland definition criteria reflect political and administrative considerations rather than precise resource characteristics.

In general, shoreland programs do not actually map definition boundaries. They rely upon field surveys to determine whether a use is within the resource area. However, programs often map more discrete subzones such as wetlands, flood plains, erosion areas, wildlife habitats, and recreational development zones.

Two approaches have been used to classify shoreland areas more specifically. The first approach, applied in Wisconsin, identifies individual subzones such as wetland areas around individual lakes. A second approach, used in Minnesota, classifies lakes in their entirety for "natural environment, recreational development," and other uses. Varying shoreland use standards apply to lot size, water frontage, building setbacks, and other matters in each class.

All shoreland regulatory programs apply state standard-setting for local adoption of zoning, subdivision controls, and, in some cases, sanitary codes. State minimum standards serve multiple goals which include pollution control, protection of wildlife, prevention of land use conflicts, protection of scenic beauty, and protection and enhancement of recreation values. In general, standards permit low density residential and recreational uses in shoreland areas. However, they place tight restrictions on wetland areas and floodways.

The shoreland zoning programs of all states make extensive use of special permit procedures. Generally, a special permit is required for any use with a substantial potential impact upon adjacent uses, water quality, or scenic beauty. Case-by-case evaluations are carried out by the zoning boards of adjustment or planning commissions. Typical special permit uses include marinas, apartments, restaurants, filling in wetlands, substantial tree-cutting, and heavy grading. The Minnesota, Maine, and Wisconsin model shoreland ordinances establish detailed but unquantified standards for evaluation of special permit uses.

Only a few court cases have considered the validity of traditional zoning for shoreland areas or special shoreland area regulations. A landmark Wisconsin case, *Just v. Marinette County*,[22] strongly endorsed cooperative state/local shoreland zoning. This case upheld very tight wetland protection controls and stated that a landowner has no inherent right to destroy the natural suitability of the land.

Coastal Zone Programs

All coastal and Great Lake states exercise some control over coastal zone uses. Regulations range from minimal beach setbacks, as in Florida and Hawaii, and wetland regulation in 15 states to comprehensive coastal zone acts, as in North Carolina and California where uses are regulated within a broad coastal zone. Many wetland and some broader programs involve direct state control.[23] However, the Washington, North Carolina, California, Maine, Wisconsin, and Minnesota programs rely primarily upon local control within a framework of state standards. State and local coastal zone regulatory programs have been stimulated by the National Coastal Zone Program although many state programs predate the national legislation.

Regulatory acts generally define the coastal zone to include lands within a specified distance of the highwater mark. Coastal zone boundaries include a narrow shoreline area in Washington, 250 feet in Maine, 1,000 feet in Wisconsin, Minnesota, and Michigan, and 1,000 yards in California and coastal counties in North Carolina. The Delaware and New Jersey coastal zone acts, directed to industrial development, define coastal zone boundaries in relationship to particular roads. The distances selected have reflected political realities and the need to form mappable and measurable boundaries.

Implementation of broad coastal zone programs has required the definition of more discrete coastal subzones such as wetlands, erosion areas, flood areas, and recreation areas. The National Coastal Zone Management Act and the basic enabling acts of several states require the identification of such subzones of "particular concern." They may include virtually all other types of resource areas. Many of the standards applied to coastal zone mineral resource areas, flood plains, erosion areas, and wetlands resemble those for individual resource areas.

Courts have been receptive to coastal zone regulations, particularly where they relate to protection of public waters. For example, courts have approved minimum five-acre lot zoning for an area of special scenic beauty and historic interest along the Maryland shore,[24] control of fill in San Francisco Bay,[25] a statute affirming the public use of beaches in Oregon,[26] a statute prohibiting the removal of stones from beaches in Massachusetts,[27] open space zoning for a beach area in California,[28] flood hazard regulation in New Jersey,[29] an oil refinery siting act in Maine,[30] and coastal wetland regulations in many states.[31]

Wetlands

At least fifteen states regulate or establish standards for local regulation of coastal wetlands. Six states exercise some control over inland wetlands.[32] More than 1,000 local communities have adopted wetland protection regulations pursuant to these acts or other standards contained in broader shoreland or coastal zone acts.[33] For example, 49 Wisconsin counties apply conservancy zoning to wetland areas as part of shoreland zoning. The expanded jurisdiction of the U.S. Army Corps of Engineers under the "404" permit law requires Corps' permission for fills in waters of the U.S. and adjacent wetlands, and is a stimulus for state and local programs. Federal permits will not be issued where a state or local permit is denied.

Coastal wetlands are usually defined in reference to vegetation and high-water marks. Air photos, high-water records, and field surveys are used to prepare maps.

The definition of inland wetlands has been more difficult. The wide variation in vegetation types, fluctuating water levels, and the importance of particular wetland types for flood storage, wildlife, and other purposes have caused disagreement. Inland wetlands are usually defined in reference to specific vegetation, flooding, and, in the case of Connecticut, soil type. Air photos, soil maps, and field surveys are used for mapping.

Wetland regulatory objectives vary depending upon the program. They include protection of fish spawning and duck nesting areas, flood storage, pollution control functions, hunting areas, aquifer recharge areas, rare plants and animals, scientific study areas, scenic beauty, and the function of wetlands as nutrient and sediment traps for the protection of lakes, streams, and ponds. Development may be regulated to reduce flood damages, prevent water pollution from on-site waste disposal, and prevent threats to safety from construction on peaty soils with inadequate support.

State and local regulatory efforts often tightly control all fill, excavation, and structural development in wetlands. Open space uses such as wildlife preserves, harvesting of marsh hay, and outdoor recreation are permitted. State programs rely primarily on a permit approach, sometimes combined[34] with protective orders for particular wetland areas. Local programs make less use of special permit approaches and often prohibit fill and development.

Supreme court decisions in Wisconsin,[35] Maryland,[36] New Hampshire,[37] and other states[38] support tight wetland controls. Nevertheless, courts in New Jersey,[39] Massachusetts,[40] and Maine[41] have held or warned that wetland regulations which prevent all economic uses are unconstitutional.

While adverse decisions suggest caution in wetland control, the Wisconsin *Just v. Marinette County*[42] case took an interesting approach to the taking issue which may be followed by many states. It held that a landowner has no inherent right and cannot claim a taking for uses which threaten public waters or destroy the natural suitability of the land.

Scenic and Wild Rivers

Twenty-four states have adopted legislation for the protection of wild, scenic, or recreation rivers.[43] State programs have been stimulated by the National Scenic and Wild River program, which now applies to 19 rivers. State designated rivers may be included in the national program, subject to the approval of the Secretary of the Interior. Inclusion in the national program protects the rivers from federal water resources projects.

States such as Oklahoma, California, Virginia, and Maryland impose particularly tight controls on dams or other structures in designated rivers but do not regulate shoreland areas. In contrast, Oregon directly regulates a quarter-mile corridor along scenic and wild rivers. Minnesota and Michigan authorize state standard-setting for local regulation in corridors of up to 1,320 feet and 400 feet, respectively. Maryland authorizes direct state regulation for the Youghiogheny River and Wisconsin authorizes state standard-setting for local regulation along the lower St. Croix.

Scenic and wild river acts generally define several classes of rivers, although the Wisconsin act refers only to "wild rivers." The Maryland act addresses "scenic" and "wild" rivers. The Minnesota act addresses "wild," "scenic," and "recreation" rivers. Michigan has developed administrative guidelines for designating "wilderness," "wild scenic," and "country scenic" rivers. In general, acts provide that wild, scenic, and recreation rivers are to be distinguished from other waters based upon their "extraordinary," "unusual," or particular "water conservation, scenic, recreational, or wildlife values."

Most enabling statutes directly designate certain rivers or stretches of rivers for regulatory control. However, the administering agency is usually authorized to study and designate other rivers. Detailed advance data gathering rarely precedes statutory designation of rivers. However, data gathering often precedes adoption of regulatory guidelines. Maryland, Virginia, and Ohio, which have largely nonregulatory programs, have also carried out detailed inventory efforts.

Principal regulatory objectives include preserving water quality and free-flowing river conditions and protecting natural scenic beauty, vegetation, wildlife, and recreation values. Secondary objectives include minimizing conflicts between uses, controlling access to areas, protecting health and safety, and reducing possible flood losses.

Programs generally prohibit all new dams, fills, or obstructions in waters and other major sources of water pollution. Land use regulations include: (a) use restrictions with most areas limited to conservancy and light residential uses; (b) controls on fills and grading, tree-cutting, and mineral extraction; and (c) specifications for permitted uses such as minimum lot sizes and building setbacks from the water. General guidelines have usually been prepared and then tailored to specific rivers.

All programs regulating dams and other waterway obstructions require state special permits. Oregon has administered a state permit system for shoreland areas for seven rivers involving 520 river miles since 1971. Most permits involve residential uses. Only about one-quarter of the permits requested have been refused. Other programs also make widespread use of special permit techniques for land uses.

Several federal and state court cases have sustained regulations prohibiting dams in rivers with special scenic and recreation values.[44] The Oregon Supreme Court sustained shoreland regulations for a one-fourth mile wide corridor along the Rogue River.[45]

Areas of Scientific Interest

Land acquisition, rather than regulation, has been used to protect or preserve areas of unique scientific interest (except wetlands) in most instances. However, Maine has adopted a special "Register of Critical Areas" Act which authorizes an agency to prepare a register of natural areas and exercise interim regulatory controls. Local conservancy zoning has been applied in some states to protect areas of special flora, fauna, and geologic or ecologic interest.

Despite the limited present use of regulations in the U.S., experience in the British Isles suggests that regulations can effectively protect areas of scientific interest, if combined with public education, tax incentives, and, in some instances, easement acquisition.[46] In the British Isles, the Nature Conservancy, a statutory body, is responsible for identifying and preserving areas of special scientific interest, including sites of special flora, fauna, and geologic interest. Preservation is achieved in part through the creation of natural reserves, land acquisition, or voluntary agreements with landowners. Nevertheless, local government controls provide the major protection for scientific areas.

To begin, the Nature Conservancy maps areas. Local land use control agencies must consult with the Conservancy before granting permission for development impacting the mapped sites. The Conservancy may appear on its own or as an expert at public hearings on proposed development. The approach has worked with considerable success.

Like the English approach, regulations adopted to date in this country (Maine, Florida) make extensive use of special permits. Landowner education and the use of incentives to gain landowner cooperation is essential. The landowner has the power to destroy the values at the site despite the existence of controls. Further, without education and incentives, landowners may raise constitutional challenges to the plans and regulations.

As one might expect, regulations designed to preserve areas of special scientific interest have not been widely litigated in the U.S., although many courts have sanctioned land use regulations designed to protect wildlife.[47] In contrast, some cases have struck down special hunting restrictions imposed on lands adjacent to game preserves[48] and highly restrictive wetland regulations.[49]

Areas Adjacent to Parks

Areas adjacent to local, state, and federal parks are of environmental concern for two reasons.[50] Many of these areas are, in their own right, of special scenic beauty or scientific interest. In addition, uses located within such areas may impact upon adjacent parks through water pollution, air pollution, increased traffic, noise, destruction of wildlife, or destruction of scenery.

Conflicting adjacent land uses are now a major problem for many state and federal parks. The problem becomes more severe with increased park use. Conflicting uses often include motels, restaurants, campgrounds, grocery stores, camping suppliers, gasoline stations, drive-in theaters, souvenir shops, and other types of development along park boundaries, on private land within parks, and along park access roads.

To date, only a small number of state and local regulations have been adopted solely to protect park areas. One joint state/federal/local park protection plan was prepared for the Gettysburg National Military Park. State and local planning efforts are underway for Voyageurs National Lakeshore in Minnesota and a special Adirondack Park Commission has been created in New York. A model parkway protection ordinance was prepared for lands adjacent to the Blue Ridge Parkway.

Precedent for park protection regulations is also found in the experiences of Cape Cod and other national recreation areas applying the "Cape Cod formula." This approach involves the adoption of federal standards for private lands within park boundaries. The federal government suspends its condemnation powers for those lands as long as the local governments regulate in accordance with federal standards.

Finally, the English have had extensive experience with park protection controls. The English national park system consists almost entirely of private land subject to tight development control.[51]

The regulation of lands adjacent to parks may have multiple and somewhat contradictory objectives: (1) protecting park values and amenities; (2) providing basic accommodations and services to meet the needs of park visitors; and (3) accomplishing local community goals for growth and increased tax base. Other specific objectives may include preventing air and water pollution, controlling water extraction that interferes with water supply within the park, protecting wetland and wildlife areas related to the park area, protecting scenic beauty, controlling vegetation removal and tree-cutting, controlling uses that disrupt the flow of traffic, and separating incompatible uses.

Courts have sustained a number of regulations that protect parks including control of signboards along parkways[52] and access controls for parks and boulevards.[53] Courts have held that diminution in land value caused by regulations is not a "taking" where part of the value was created by adjacent public uses.[54] However, attempts to prohibit all private development may encounter arguments similar to those used to defeat coastal wetland regulations. Private landowners may contend they are prevented from all private economic uses in order to bestow an uncompensated benefit upon the public.

Forestry Areas

Many states, such as Wisconsin, Minnesota, and Oregon, encourage and assist private tree farms and sustained yield timber operations through tax incentives and fire prevention efforts.[55] A smaller number regulate private forestry practices to achieve these objectives.[56] Washington, Maryland, Minnesota, and other states have adopted state tree-cutting regulations. State shoreland zoning regulations in Wisconsin and Maine also incorporate tree-cutting regulations. Hawaii has mapped and tightly regulated special forest protection zones.

Local tree-cutting restrictions are more common.[57] Zoning enabling acts specifically authorize forest protection in Wisconsin, Minnesota, and a number of other states. Many cities, towns, and counties have adopted tree-cutting regulations using either this broad zoning enabling authority or special enabling acts. Regulations typically require a permit for the cutting of trees in residential, conservancy, wetland, or other districts.

Tree-cutting regulations serve one or two principal objectives: (1) protecting sustaining yield forest base and (2) preserving amenities such as scenic beauty or wildlife. Ancillary objectives include protecting watershed areas, controlling erosion, and preventing forest fires.

Generally, regulations do not prohibit all tree-cutting. They control harvesting practices and, in some instances, require replanting. Most tree-cutting regulations operate entirely on a special permit basis with general performance standards related to tree-planting, erosion, and scenic beauty. Forest recreation zones adopted by Wisconsin counties in the 1920s and 1930s prevent most structural uses in forest districts.

Judicial reaction has been favorable to tree-cutting regulations although their validity has not been extensively litigated. In *State v. Dexter*,[58] the U.S. Supreme Court upheld a Washington statute requiring permits for tree-cutting and landowner participation in a state reforestation program. In *Perely v. North Carolina*,[59] the Court upheld North Carolina's tree-cutting and slash disposal regulations for watershed areas.

Whether or not courts will uphold restrictive forest district regulations, especially those preventing all structural uses not associated with forest operations, remains to be seen. Favorable judicial reaction is likely where forestry is an economically viable use, land values are low, land is presently in large lot forest uses, and tax incentives are available.

Despite the limited adoption of forest protection regulations, more programs are likely as conversion of forestry land to second homes, agriculture, and active recreation land produces shortages in wood and wood products.

Prime Agricultural Land

Only Hawaii has adopted state zoning for prime agricultural lands.[60] The 1955 statewide zoning law created agricultural districts and placed all lands in one of four zones: (1) conservancy, (2) agricultural, (3) rural, and (4) urban. The agricultural districts were designed to preserve the pineapple and sugar cane industries. District maps were based upon soils, existing use of land, acreage, and other factors. Vermont also provides limited regulatory protection for prime agricultural lands through provisions in its large-scale development site review act.

Despite the limited regulation of agricultural lands at state level, many counties and towns have adopted exclusive agricultural districts or, more commonly, agricultural-residential districts permitting low density uses. Some local agricultural zone regulations and state controls in Hawaii prohibit virtually all nonagricultural uses or activities. However, many local regulations permit low density uses on five to 100 acre lots. The latter approach is more acceptable politically but opens a wedge for nonagricultural development.

Agricultural regulations are adopted to preserve existing production areas and prime agricultural soils of sufficient size for economical agricultural operations. Secondary objectives include preventing incompatible uses, preserving open space, protecting flood plains, minimizing public service costs, and protecting the local tax and economic base.

Despite the widespread adoption of local agricultural zones, few courts have considered their validity. A 1968 Utah decision sustained a grazing district classification that limited the market value of certain road frontage land to $20-30 per acre where the free market value was $10,000 per acre.[61] The court held that the landowner had purchased the land with full knowledge of restrictions and could not claim hardship. Some indirect support for agricultural zoning may also be found in the rationale of the Wisconsin wetland case cited above[62] which held that a landowner has no absolute right to destroy the natural suitability of his land. On the other hand, a Wisconsin case held an agricultural zoning classification invalid when it was applied to lands clearly unsuitable for agriculture.[63]

Although state-level agricultural protection laws have been adopted in only a few states, at least 45 states provide property tax incentives for agricultural and open-space uses.[64] The laws generally authorize a "roll back" tax which requires landowners to pay all or a substantial portion of the unassessed tax if the land is subsequently developed. The California effort, the Williamson Act, required several changes in the California constitution and numerous statutory modifications. Nevertheless, the program has been only partially successful. Farmers have failed to utilize the program fully while subdividers gain speculative benefits.

Mineral and Energy Resource Lands

The environmental and energy crises have focused attention on energy resource areas containing coal, oil, gas, and oil shale; metal deposits such as iron, zinc, lead, copper, aluminum, manganese, and rare metals; and deposits of aggregates such as sand, gravel, clay, and granite. Apparently, only Colorado[65] has mapped mineral deposits expressly for regulatory purposes. However, many state geological surveys and the United States Geologic Survey have surveyed mineral deposits. In addition, 37 states have adopted mine reclamation laws to meet a wide range of objectives.[66] Some communities have adopted regulations controlling or preventing gravel extraction, mining, and oil and gas extraction in residential and commercial areas.[67] Some communities have adopted special resource protection districts for sand and gravel deposits.

Regulatory objectives include: (1) protecting mineral and energy resource areas from encroachment by incompatible uses; (2) preventing waste; (3) preventing nuisances from mineral operations; and (4) reclaiming mined areas.

The degree of restrictiveness required depends on the type of area, mode of anticipated extraction, specific objectives, and other factors. Very tight control of subdivision and adjacent uses is needed to protect surface deposits mined through open pit methods. In contrast, residential, commercial, and industrial developments may be permitted closer to areas where deep shaft mining is used to extract metal ores.

Both state and local regulations typically require special permits for all mineral, oil, and gas extraction. Each proposal is evaluated on its merits for compatibility with adjacent uses, adequacy of the reclamation plan, impact upon roads, and other factors. Development conditions are often attached, and require particular methods of operation, fencing and screening, and reclamation.

Local zoning regulations which prevent or tightly control extraction of early products in residential districts have been widely litigated.[68] Courts usually uphold these controls despite severe economic impact because of threatened nuisances.

The U.S. Supreme Court and state courts have upheld state regulation of oil and gas operations to prevent waste.[69] These cases provide conceptual precedent for mineral resource protection districts to achieve the same objectives. In addition, the Colorado supreme court specifically upheld a local mineral protection district.[70]

The fixed supply of mineral resources provides a strong incentive for future regulatory programs despite the variety of difficult issues raised. Assuming that minerals should be preserved for future use, what consumption rates are acceptable? What assumptions should be made concerning technological advances in mining or energy production? Or what of the development of substitutes for metals and other materials? To what extent should the state overrule local zoning that prohibits mineral extraction?

Erosion Areas

Coastal erosion is a major concern in Florida, California, Hawaii, Michigan, and other states.[71] Hawaii and Florida establish 50-foot coastal setbacks to minimize erosion and flood damages and serve resource protection goals. The Michigan shoreland program has defined and regulated erosion areas along Lake Michigan based on air photos and site surveys. Time sequence photos define setback lines representing a 30-year protection period.

Broader soil and water conservation surveys have been carried out to identify inland erosion areas in many states. Regulations have been adopted in some instances to control subdividing and building on highly erosive soils.

Courts have sustained a variety of state and local regulations for beach erosion areas.[72] A Colorado court sustained local soil conservation regulations to reduce wind erosion.[73]

Scenic Areas

Vermont bases special control over large-scale development for areas above 2,500 feet primarily on scenic values. Wild and scenic rivers are defined, to a considerable extent, by the natural beauty of adjacent shorelands. Maine strongly considers aesthetic factors in its review of large-scale development. However, fixed criteria are not used for evaluating scenery in each of these programs. Air photos and field surveys have been used to identify areas with special topographic and vegetative qualities. Many courts have afforded increased weight to protection of aesthetics,[74] although this was not traditionally considered a valid sole police power objective.[75]

Comprehensive Sensitive Area Acts

In addition to the regulatory programs for individual areas, comprehensive sensitive area regulatory programs authorize the regulation of many types of areas by a single state agency. They have been adopted in Florida and Minnesota, and partial elements have appeared in Oregon and Colorado. All programs are in early stages of implementation. All involve state standard-setting for local regulation of areas and direct state regulation only in the event of local inaction.

These comprehensive sensitive-area programs depend primarily on "nomination and screening" procedures for initial identification of areas. In the nomination process, local units of government, other agencies, and interest groups suggest areas in need of special protection. Using this approach, the Florida program has designated three areas: Big Cypress, Green

Swamp, and the Florida Keys. Other areas are under consideration. The Minnesota program has designated the St. Croix wild riverway.

To date, comprehensive critical area efforts have focused on water-oriented natural areas. Regulatory standards have been performance-orientated. Apparently no state supreme court has considered the validity of these regulations.

Other efforts to define sensitive areas comprehensively are underway in Maine, North Carolina, Maryland, Colorado, Nevada, Virginia, California, and Wyoming. In addition, Missouri and Wisconsin have developed criteria for defining areas, although both states lack implementing legislation.

NOTES

[1]A 1966 Task Force on Federal Flood Control Policy estimated that more than 7 billion dollars had been spent by the federal government alone on flood control work since 1936 and, despite these expenditures, flood losses continue to mount.

[2]See F. Bosselman and D. Callies, *The Quiet Revolution in Land Use Control.* Council on Environmental Quality, U.S. Government Printing Office (1971); N. Rosenbaum, *Land Use and the Legislatures, the Politics of State Innovation.* The Urban Institute, Washington, D.C. (1976).

[3]See N. Rosenbaum, *Land Use and the Legislatures, the Politics of State Innovation*, The Urban Institute, Washington, D.C. (1976) for a listing and analysis of these efforts. Dr. Rosenbaum notes on page 3: During their 1974 session, seven state legislatures—Idaho, Iowa, Michigan, New Hampshire, Ohio, South Dakota, and Wisconsin rejected proposals to expand state land use authority. In four states, Colorado, Maine, Maryland, and North Carolina, where new land use legislation was passed in 1974, the powers given state governments were far weaker than those provided in the legislation of the pioneering states. At the present time only Hawaii has adopted statewide zoning.

[Note omitted.]

[5]See N. Rosenbaum, *Land Use and the Legislatures, the Politics of State Innovation.* The Urban Institute, Washington, D.C. (1976). A number of states also required local units of government to adopt zoning and subdivision controls during this period although most established no mechanism for direct state regulation in the event local units of government failed to adopt and enforce adequate regulations.

[6]See Sax. "The Public Trust Doctrine in Natural Resource Law: Effective Judicial Intervention," 68 Michigan Law Review 491 (1971).

[7]A strong federal resource assessment and land management role was recommended by the Public Land Law Review Commission, *One Third of the Nation's Lands*, U.S. Government Printing Office (1970).

[8]State regulation is authorized only where local units fail to adopt and administer satisfactory controls. Florida, Nevada, Oregon, and Minnesota authorize quite broad state regulation in these circumstances. Maine and Colorado authorize very limited state regulation. Wyoming, North Carolina, Virginia, and Maryland do not authorize state regulation.

[9]See E. Strauss and J. Kusler, *Statutory Land Use Control Enabling Authority in the Fifty States*, U.S. Department of Housing and Urban Development, Federal Insurance Administration (1976).

[10]*Id.*

[11]Thirty-four states authorize municipal or county exercise of home rule powers. *See* table 4 in E. Strauss and J. Kusler, *Statutory Land Use Control Enabling Authority in the Fifty States*, U.S. Department of Housing and Urban Development, Federal Insurance Administration (1976), for a listing of relevant statutory and constitutional provisions.

[12]Performance standards relate to protection from natural hazards (100-year floods) and the use impact upon natural systems. In other words, emphasis is upon the end result, rather than use type or design. *See* C. Thurow, W. Toner, and D. Erley, *Performance Controls for Sensitive Lands*, American Society of Planning Officials, Report Nos. 307, 308 (1975), for an excellent description of local programs and examples of ordinance provisions.

[13]*See, e.g.,* Ann Arbor Twp. v. United States, 93 F. Supp. 341 (D.C. Mich., 1950) (federal uses exempted); Town of Bloomfield v. New Jersey Authority, 18 N.J. Highway Authority, 18 N.J. 237, 113 A.2d 658 (1955) (state use exempted); Town of Oronoco v. City of Rochester, 293 Minn. 468, 197 N.W.2d 426 (1972) (local governmental uses generally exempted).

[14]Individuals, organizations, or local governments are asked to "nominate" or suggest areas with special resource values or hazards needing protection or management.

[15]This discussion addresses major types of sensitive area programs. For example, flood hazard programs are examined, but not seismic area programs.

[16]*See* . . . J. Kusler, *A Perspective on Flood Plain Regulation for Flood Plain Management*, Chapter 6, Department of the Army, Office of the Chief of Engineers, Washington, D.C. (1976).

[17]*See, e.g.,* Turner v. County of Del Norte, 24 C.A. 3d 311, 101 Cal. Rptr. 93 (1972); Vartelas v. Water Resources Comm'n, 146 Conn. 650, 153 A.2d 822 (1959); Iowa Natural Resources Council v. Van Zee, 261 Iowa 1287, 158 N.W. 2d 111 (1968); Turnpike Realty Co. v. Town of Dedham, 284 N.E. 2d 891 (Mass., 1972).

[18]*See, e.g.,* Kessoring v. Wakefield Realty Co., Inc. 306 Ky. 725, 209 S.W. 2d 63 (1948); Sturdy Homes, Inc. v. Township of Redford, 30 Mich. App. 53, 186 N.W. 2d 43 (1971).

[19]City of Welch v. Mitchell, 95 W. Va. 377, 121 S.E. 165 (1924).

[20]*See, e.g.,* Dooley v. Town Plan and Zoning Comm'n, 151 Conn. 304, 197 A.2d 770 (1964); Baker v. Planning Board, 353 Mass. 141, 228 N.E.2d 831 (1967); Morris County Land Twp. Co., v. Parsippany-Troy Hills Tp., 40 N.J. 539, 193 A.2d 232 (1963).

[21] . . . For a more detailed description of state shoreland programs, *see* B. Berger, J. Kusler, and S. Klinginer, *Lake-Shoreland Management Programs: Selected Papers*, Univ. of Mass. Water Resources Research Center, Publ. No. 69, Technical Report, Amherst, Mass. (1976).

[22]56 Wis. 2d 7, 201 N.W.2d 761 (1972).

[23]*E.g.,* The coastal wetland program of Georgia and Rhode Island: the broader coastal zone programs of Rhode Island (certain uses) and Delaware (industrial uses).

[24]County Commissioners v. Miles, 246 Md. 355, 228 A.2d 450 (1967).

[25]Candlestick Properties, Inc. v. San Francisco Bay Conservation Development Commission, 11 Cal. App. 3d 557, 89 Cal. Rptr. 897 (1970).

[26]Thorton v. Hay, 462 P.2d 671 (Oreg., 1969).

[27]Commonwealth v. Tewsbury, 11 Met. 55 (Mass., 1946).

[28]McCarthy v. Manhattan Beach, 41 Cal. 2d 879, 264 P.2d 932 (1953).

[29]Spiegel v. Beach Haven, 46 N.J. 479, 218 A.2d 129 (1966).

[30]In the Matter of Maine Clean Fuels, Inc. 310 A.2d 736 (Me., 1973).

[31]*E.g.,* Potomac Sand and Gravel Co. v. Governor of Maryland *et al.*, 266 Md. 358, 293 A.2d 241 (Md. Ct. of Appeals 1972), *cert. denied*, 409 U.S. 1040; Sibson v. State, 336 A.2d 239 (N.H. 1975). . . .

[32] . . . In most instances, statutes are primarily designed to protect wetlands. In some instances, wetland protection is a component of broader coastal regulation (*e.g.,* Washington,

California. For a more detailed analysis of state wetland statutes and programs *see* J. Kusler, Draft, *Strengthening State Wetland Regulation*, Environmental Law Institute, produced for the Office of Biological Services, U.S. Fish and Wildlife Service, Washington, D.C. (1978).

[33]*See* J. Kusler, C. Harwood, and R. Newton, Draft, *Our National Wetland Heritage, A Protection Handbook*, Environmental Law Institute, produced for the Office of Biological Services, U.S. Fish and Wildlife Service, Washington, D.C., (1971) for analysis of local programs.

[34]Protective orders are authorized by the coastal wetlands statutes of Maine, Massachusetts, North Carolina, and Rhode Island and the inland wetland statute for Massachusetts. Protective orders establish detailed written standards for particular wetlands and include both a text and map.

[35]Just v. Marinette Co., 56 Wis. 2d 7, 201 N.W. 2d 761 (1972).

[36]Potomac Sand and Gravel Co. v. Governor of Maryland *et al.*, 266 Md. 358, 293 A.2d 241 (1972).

[37]Sibson v. State, 336 A.2d 239 (N.H., 1975).

[38][Footnote omitted.]

[39]Morris County Land Improvement Co. v. Parsippany-Troy Hills, 40 N.J. 539, 193 A.2d 232 (1963).

[40]Commissioner of Natural Resources v. S. Volpe and Co., 349 Mass. 104, 206 N.E. 2d 666 (1965) (Court remanded decision for further findings): MacGibbon v. Board of Appeals of Duxbury, 356 Mass. 635, 255 N.E. 2d 347 (1970).

[41]State v. Johnson, 264 A.2d 711 (Me., 1970).

[42]56 Wis. 2d 7, 201 N.W. 2d 761 (1972). See note 58 in Part 8, *infra*.

[43]*See* Bureau of Outdoor Recreation, "Outdoor Recreation," Spring 1977, Report No. 43, Washington, D.C. for a complete listing. The entire report is devoted to description and analysis of scenic and wild rivers.

[44]*See* Namekagon Hydro Co. v. Federal Power Comm'n, 216 F.2d 509 (1954) in which the court upheld an order of the Federal Power Commission denying a license for the construction of a dam and hydroelectric project on the Namekagon River in northern Wisconsin. *See also* note 45 *infra*. Application of Hemco. Inc., 283 A.2d 246 (1971) in which the Maine Supreme Court upheld state denial of a dam permit to protect "sport fishing, undamaged stream bed and white water canoeing."

[45]Scott v. State *ex rel*. State Highway Comm'n., 23 Oreg. App. 99, 541 P.2d 516 (1975).

[46]*See* Part 4, J. Kusler, *Public/Private Parks and Management of Private Lands for Park Protection*, University of Wisconsin, Institute for Environmental Studies, Madison (1974).

[47]*See* the wetland cases cited above. *See also* Geer v. Connecticut, 161 U.S. 519 (1895) in which the U.S. Supreme Court sustained regulations on the taking of wildlife.

[48]*E.g.*, State v. Becker, 215 Wis. 564, 255 N.W. 144 (1943).

[49]*E.g.*, Morris County Land Improvement Co. v. Parsippany-Troy Hills Tp., 40 N.J. 539, 193 A.2d 232 (1963).

[50]*See* J. Kusler, *Public/Private Parks and Management of Private Lands for Park Protection*, University of Wisconsin, Institute for Environmental Studies, Report 16 (1974), for a discussion of threats to parks and techniques for reducing threats.

[51]*Id.*, Part 4.

[52]*See, e.g.*, General Outdoor Adv. Co. v. City of Indianapolis, 202 Ind. 85, 172 N.E. 309, 72 A.L.R. 453 (1930) (Court upheld regulation of signs within 500 feet of park): People v. Sterling, 267 App. Div. 9, 45 N.Y.S. 2d 39 (1943) *reh.* and *app. den.* 267 App. Div. 852, 47 N.Y.S. 2d 285 (Court upheld park commission's ban of signs in Adirondack area.)

[53]*See* Annot., "Power of Park Commission to Directly Regulate or Prohibit Abutter's Ac-

cess to Street or Highway," 73 A.L.R. 2d 671 (1960); Burke v. Metropolitan District Commission, 262 Mass. 70, 159 N.W. 739 (1928) (Court upheld park commission's restrictions of abutter's access to one driveway along a park): State v. City of Toledo, 75 Ohio App. 378, 31 Ohio Ops. 144, 62 N.E. 2d 256 (1944) (Court held that municipality can limit the ingress and egress of an owner of land abutting a park or boulevard.)

⁵⁴*See, e.g.*, Kelbro v. Myrick, 113 Vt. 64, 30 A.2d 572 (1943), in which the Vermont Supreme Court upheld the regulation of signs in part on the theory that display of signs was a privilege, not a right, and that the value of the property for signboard use derived from the public thoroughfare from which signs could be seen. *See also* New York State Thruway A. v. Ashley Motor Court, 10 N.Y.S. 2d 640 (1961).

⁵⁵*See* E. Solbert, *New Laws for New Forests*, University of Wisconsin Press, Madison, Wis. (1961) for a description of the Wisconsin effort.

⁵⁶*E.g.*, Idaho, Washington, Massachusetts.

⁵⁷*See* C. Bingham, *Trees in the City*, American Society of Planning Officials, Planning Report No. 236 (1968).

⁵⁸32 Wash. 2d 51, 202 P.2d 906, *aff'd*. 338 U.S. 863 (1949).

⁵⁹249 U.S. 510 (1919).

⁶⁰*See* R. Poirier, *State Zoning: A Case Study of the Concept Administration, and Possible Application of the State of Hawaii Land Use Law*, M.A. Thesis, Urban and Regional Planning, University of Wisconsin, Madison (1967).

⁶¹Chevron Oil Co. v. Beaver Co., 22 Utah 2d 143, 449 P.2d 989 (1969).

⁶²Just v. Marinette Co., 56 Wis. 2d 7, 201 N.W. 2d 761 (1972).

⁶³Kimee v. Town of Spider Lake, 60 Wis. 2d 640, 211, N.W. 2d 471 (1973).

⁶⁴*See* J. Keene *et al.*, *Untaxing Open Space*, Prepared by the Council on Environmental Quality, U.S. Government Printing Office, Washington, D.C. (1976).

⁶⁵*See* S.D. Schochow, R.R. Shroba, and P.C. Wicklein, *Sand, Gravel, and Quarry Aggregate Resources, Colorado Front Range Counties*, Colorado Geological Survey, Department of Natural Resources, Denver, Colorado (1974).

⁶⁶*See* E. Imhoff, T. Friz, and J. LaFevers, *A Guide to State Programs for the Reclamation of Surface Mined Areas*. U.S. Geological Survey Circular 731, Washington, D.C. (1976) for a listing, description and analysis of these laws.

⁶⁷*See* "Annot.: Prohibiting or Regulating Removal or Exploitation of Oil and Gas, Minerals, Soil, or Other Natural Products Within Municipal Limits," 10 A.L.R. 3d 1226 (1966) for a discussion of cases contesting these restrictions.

⁶⁸*Id.*

⁶⁹*See, e.g.*, Bandini Petroleum Co. v. Superior Court, 284 U.S. 8 (1931); Lindsley v. Natural Carbonic Gas Co., 220 U.S. 61 (1911); Champlin Refining Co. v. Corp. Comm. of Oklahoma, 286 U.S. 210 (1932).

⁷⁰*See* Famularo v. Board of County Commissioners, 505 P.2d 958 (1973).

⁷¹For a discussion of erosion problems in coastal areas, *see* Department of the Army Corps of Engineers, *Report on the National Shoreline Study*, U.S. Army Corps of Engineers, Washington, D.C. (1971). For a discussion of techniques to calculate recession rates, *see* Great Lakes Basin Commission, *Proceedings of the Recession Rate Workshop* (Dec. 5-6, 1974), Great Lakes Basin Comm'n, Ann Arbor, Mich. (1975).

⁷²*See, e.g.*, Commonwealth v. Tewksbury, 11 Met. 55 (Mass., 1846) in which the court upheld a statute prohibiting removal of sand and gravel from beaches to protect natural storm and erosion protective barriers; Spiegle v. Beach Haven, 46 N.J. 479, 218 A.2d 129 (1966) in which the court upheld building setback and fence ordinances for coastal flood and erosion area.

[73]Oberst v. Mays, 148 Colo. 285, 365 P. 2d 902 (1961).

[74]*See, e.g.*, People v. Stover, 12 N.Y.S. 2d 462, 191 N.E. 2d 272 (1963), *appeal dism.*, 375 U.S. 42 (1963).

[75]See, e.g., Barney and Casey Co. v. Milton, 324 Mass. 87 N.E. 2d 9 (1949) and cases cited therein.

11

Developing a National Water Policy

Problems and Perspectives on Reform

John J. Rhodes*

C OUNTLESS LAWS, administrative procedures and regulations, administered by various regulatory institutions, allocate this nation's waters. Many of these mechanisms were devised to resolve local disputes and, at the time of their design, were adequate for the tasks for which they were created. Unfortunately, the slow, uncoordinated, and narrowly focused process which produced our hodgepodge national water policy has, in itself, generated conflicts and imposed constraints on water development. Consequently, we are still grappling with yesterday's problems, while many of today's critical issues remain unattended. The time for reform is clearly at hand. However, the nature of the necessary reforms and the process for their adoption are solutions not so easily identified. The complexity of this problem is compounded by the fact that its most controversial aspects are wedded to long-standing social customs and regional biases. Local practices and customs are not easily changed, but unless they are immediately and objectively addressed, water crises of staggering and enduring scale may result.

The Need for a National Water Policy

Our national "water policy," if in fact there is one, might be extracted from a plethora of federal statutes, regulations, and administrative decisions. The Reclamation Act of 1902,[1] the 1909 Rivers and Harbors Act,[2] the Flood Control Acts of 1917,[3] 1936,[4] and 1944,[5] the Water Resources

ACKNOWLEDGMENT.—The author wishes to thank Doug Smith and Warren Viessman, Jr., for their assistance in preparing this article. Mary M. Mertens, *Journal of Legislation* staff member, served as research assistant for this article.

Volume 8, *Journal of Legislation*, Issue 1, pages 1-15 (1981). Reprinted with permission. © 1981 by the *Journal of Legislation*, University of Notre Dame.

Planning Act of 1965,[6] the Federal Water Pollution Control Act Amendments of 1972,[7] and the Inland Waterways Revenue Act of 1978[8] are products of the uncoordinated legislative process that has been mapping our water course over the years. The most recent trends in this development can be traced to the recommendations of the National Water Commission (NWC) in 1973,[9] Congressional requests in the 1974 Water Resources Development Act for an Executive Branch study of national water policy,[10] and the Water Policy Initiatives set forth by President Carter in 1978.[11] The NWC's report urged that users share more heavily in payments for water projects; it also stressed a need for greater emphasis on the environmental impact of water resources development and emphasized concerns about restoring the quality of the nation's waters. The Executive Branch study of the Water Resources Development Act was never transmitted to Congress. As a result of Western States' fears of inadequate representation and the Carter Administration's policies, the Administration's initiative to develop a national water policy never got off to a favorable start.

Though recent programs have emphasized environmental concerns and conservation, it must be stated that conservation alone will not solve the national water problem. The need for development of new water resources still persists. Many regions in the United States are experiencing rapid growth, which demands that additional quantities of water be made available. Implementing conservation strategies may stretch present water supplies, but population growth cannot be sustained by demand reduction alone.[12] Future water developments will take advantage of more efficient water-use practices, but efficient use will only reduce demand incrementally. It cannot eliminate water supply requirements.[13] To accommodate increased supplies, additional storage capacity will have to be developed, and plans to replace aging urban water systems must be made, especially in the Northeast. In short, conservation's role in federally supported water resources programs must be placed in context with other proposed solutions to the water-supply problem.[14]

As a possible result of overemphasizing conservation, the last four years have witnessed little progress in development of the nation's water resources. Presidential initiatives have spurred some changes in water policy, but studies and regulations have been produced in far greater quantities than has water for cities, agriculture, industry, or energy. During this period, water policy debates between the executive and legislative branches of government generally have resulted in stalemates. Nearly every energy and water development appropriations bill in the last four years has been embroiled in controversy, including the Carter Administration's 1977 "hit list,"[15] the Presidential veto in 1978,[16] and the snail darter (Tellico Dam) issue in 1979.[17] The only significant water resource legislation in that period appears to be the authorization of Locks and Dam 26 and its accompanying waterway-user charge. At a time when water problems are escalating, the fact that no other major water resources development legislation has been enacted underscores the need for a revitalized approach to national water policy.

Physical and Institutional Restraints on the Development of Water Resource Policies

Discussions of national policy generally focus on perceived shortages in water supply or on degradation of water quality. Yet, the real problem often lies with the various institutions charged with solving water-related problems. These institutions have been created by state and federal legislation, local customs, agency directives, and court actions. In some cases they have outlived their usefulness and now restrain, rather than facilitate, efficient water management. Reassessing the utility of these organizations is certain to involve legislative disputes on a state and national level, considerable cost in time and money, and assumption of some political risk. Unless reforms are made, however, future water supplies may be insufficient to meet growing regional demands.

Water Allocation among Competing Uses

The drought of 1976-77 intensified the nation's emerging water allocation problems. At issue is the distribution of scarce water resources for recreation, environmental enhancement, food and energy production, and municipal and industrial supplies. From a nationwide perspective, there is sufficient water to meet projected needs well beyond 1985.[18] This projection should be tempered, however, by a realization that national totals do not reflect geographic or seasonal variations; in fact, some severe local and regional problems can be expected. The most significant water supply problems exist or are anticipated in Southern California, the Great Basin,[19] the Lower Colorado River Basin, the Rio Grande Basin, the High Plains of Texas, and the South-Central portion of the Missouri River Basin.[20] The agricultural irrigation necessary in these areas requires consumption of great quantities of water. The possibility for water shortages increases in those regions in which mining and processing of coal and oil-shale deposits is expanding. Unless the allocation of water resources is improved, scarcity of water supplies may soon limit economic growth in these critical areas.[21]

The avenue of relief ought to include development of additional resources, reduction in the quantities of water used, and more efficient management of water-allocation plans. Implementation, however, of every option available to ease the severity of water resource problems will be a difficult task. As noted by the Senate Committee on Agriculture, Nutrition, and Forestry, obstacles to development of optimal water policy and use include:

—the prevailing body of variant and constraining water law;
—the failure to recognize the interdependency of surface and ground waters;
—the artificial separation of water quality from water quantity management;
—the belief that per-capita water use must continually increase to maintain a high standard of living; and
—the failure to establish a price for water which is commensurate with the value of its use.[22]

Although a shift towards "total water management" has been urged by some as a solution to these problems, such a shift may not be attainable, unless there is greater cooperation among institutional entities.[23] A sound federal-state partnership has been recommended by many as the foundation for efficient water management, but it has yet to become a reality.

Water Quality

According to the tenth annual report of the President's Council on Environmental Quality (CEQ),[24] pollution and misuse continue to damage our water resources.[25] The report cites water problems throughout the country and notes that improvements in water quality and supply are lagging due to sewer overflows, urban and agricultural runoff, overloaded sewage treatment plants, and toxic-waste disposal. Nationwide measurements of five key pollutants—fecal coliform bacteria, dissolved oxygen, phosphorous, mercury, and lead—have shown little change in concentration during the period of 1975 to 1978, the last period for which complete pollution data exist.[26] In particular, the CEQ criticized the slow progress of the municipal sewage treatment construction grants program. Although Congress has appropriated over twenty-eight billion dollars for the massive cleanup effort, only two and one-half billion dollars were spent on completed projects by December 1979.[27]

To date, most of the effort to improve water quality has focused on point-sources of pollution and on particular pollutants.[28] The dimension of the non-point source pollution[29] problem, however, is such that many experts believe little new progress in cleaning up rivers and streams is attainable unless a major effort to control these diffuse sources is mounted. Non-point pollution is tied to large regional systems that are not amenable to conventional water pollution controls. For example, the CEQ reported that sediment flows from non-point sources were 360 times greater than those from municipal and industrial outlets.[30]

The trend in water quality management has focused on centralization of water management through imposition of federal uniform rules. The Water

Quality Act Amendments of 1965[31] attempted an individualized description of the nation's water courses with regard to composite water quality. This approach was abandoned in favor of a "uniform technology program" that ignores the water quality problems of different geographical areas. The development of regional institutions, which can confront individual issues and manage them accordingly, must be reconsidered as part of a national water policy.

In light of the problems identified, we must undertake a careful legislative reexamination of the Clean Water Act.[32] Establishing realistic clean water goals, reducing the high costs of sewage treatment works, and determining the proper role of advanced waste treatment are issues that should be addressed. In addition, innovative options should be encouraged and implemented, including land applications of effluents and wastewater reuse. Overriding these issues is the need to clarify the roles of private industry and government at all levels, and the need to determine how realistic water quality goals may be achieved at reasonable cost to taxpayers.

Hydroelectric Development

The energy crisis has rekindled interest in the development of new hydroelectric facilities and the improvement of existing ones. In particular, the idea of installing small units on minor rivers and tributaries has become increasingly popular. With the escalating costs of other energy sources, many abandoned hydroelectric facilities now offer attractive possibilities for augmenting electrical energy needs.[33] Moreover, hydroelectric projects are not fuel consumptive and do not create air or water pollution problems.

In 1979 hydroelectric power was providing approximately 64,000 megawatts (MW) of electrical energy from 1,251 facilities. This was approximately thirteen percent of the country's electric generating capacity. Hydroelectric potential from existing, additions to existing, and undeveloped sites is now estimated at more than 512,000 MW.[34] Preliminary estimates of the National Hydroelectric Power Resources Study by the United States Army Corps of Engineers suggest that additional development of 4,500 feasible, undeveloped sites could raise the nation's generating capacity by approximately 354,000 MW. This would be in addition to the increase in hydroeletric power which could be generated at approximately 5,400 existing locations. Although as much as fifty percent of this potential might be difficult to realize, the remainder is significant and warrants rapid development.

Constraints on achieving the projected potential are mainly economic, environmental, and institutional, rather than technical.[35] The inadequacy of federal criteria and procedures for licensing new hydroelectric facilities, the continuing standoff between the Administration and the Congress over water project development, the difficulties encountered by small dam owners in attempting to market the energy they produce, and the uncertainty of payoff from retrofitting existing generating systems or installing new units at existing dams have acted to slow the movement toward capitalizing on this readily avialable and generally noncontroversial energy source.

Instream-flow Use of Water

"Instream-flow use" is the amount of water flowing through a natural channel which sustains the supply of water needed for the channel's various uses; these uses may include fish and wildlife population maintenance, outdoor recreational activities, navigation, hydroelectric generation, waste assimilation, ecosystem maintenance, and conveyance to downstream points of diversion. Water that must be maintained for instream-flow uses cannot be withdrawn for alternative purposes.

The United States Fish and Wildlife Service was given the task of quantifying instream-flow requirements for the Water Resources Council's 1975 National Assessment. Their estimates were not completely accurate or scientific, but they show that instream-flow reservations could be considerable and create major impingements on water uses.[36] The impact of proposed instream flow reservations on energy development and expanded irrigated agriculture in the West is a case in point.

Determination of reasonable estimates of instream-flow needs and delineation of the federal government's role in resolution of regional issues present policy questions which must be answered. Another question of concern to policymakers is who should set national and regional priorities for instream-flow reservations; in this regard, the role of the Fish and Wildlife Service needs careful scrutiny. In addition, fair and practical mechanisms that maximize the compatibility of instream and offstream uses of the nation's waters must be implemented.

Ground Water Depletion

Ground water resources in some regions are being rapidly depleted due to inadequate regulation of withdrawals. In many states, the water rights system fails to recognize that ground water is related to surface water and that stream flows can be affected by ground water pumping.

Ground water management is of national importance. It is complicated by poorly devised laws, spotty regulations, lack of data, and political sensitivity. Some developments are oblivious to critical ground water-surface water interrelationships.[37] The President's water policy of 1978 recognized the problem and directed the Departments of Agriculture and Interior, through a variety of approaches, to encourage conservation and discourage ground water depletion in agricultural assistance programs which affect water consumption in water-short areas.[38]

Federal and state government should seek to develop a comprehensive program of incentives and penalties which will facilitate the wise use of groundwater resources.

Additional Factors Affecting Water Resources Policies

State Water Law

Water policies in the Western States must focus attention on the need for improvement in state water law. The federal government should not be permitted to preempt or countermand state water laws. The states and the federal government, however, must achieve a level of uniformity and understanding so that critical issues of water allocation can be resolved with a minimum of conflict.

According to Emery N. Castle, western water law can best serve those holding water rights ". . . if existing rights can be defined and quantified, if the extent of third party interests can be specified, and if water rights can be transferred through the payment of compensation."[39] The trouble is that there are no mechanisms to facilitate the sale, lease, or transfer of water rights in many states. In the East, common law water rights doctrines often forbid the transfer of ground water from overlying land, and states that regulate water by means of permit systems generally prohibit transfers. In theory, many Western States can accommodate water rights transfers, but these can be difficult to effect in practice.[40] Adding to the difficulty is the uncertainty about possible adverse affects on third parties, an uncertainty which often inhibits water rights transfers that are otherwise legal.

Federal Reserved Water Rights Determination

Few water issues have caused more friction in state-federal relations than that of the "federal reserved right." This right interferes with state laws governing the acquisition, control, and distribution of water. It also permits the federal government to circumvent the states' appropriation procedures.[41] The impact of these federal reserved water rights is significant in public land states because considerable amounts of water originate on or flow through federal lands. To date, adjudication of federal reserved rights has been minimal.

In attempting to strike a water-allocation balance, special consideration must be given to the integration of federal reserved water rights into existing state water rights systems. Thereafter, these rights could be subject to court decrees, interstate compacts, or other institutional developments affecting the source of water involved.

Indian Water Rights Determination

The competition between Indian and non-Indian claims to water rights poses extraordinary problems.[42] Most Indian reservations predate the extensive water development projects in the Western United States. The use of water by Indians in significant quantities, however, has developed only in recent years.

The resource potential of Indian reservations is enormous. In the Northern Great Plains, for example, large reserves of coal and other valuable minerals lie under most Indian lands. In addition, many reservations have outstanding recreational features, and several contain large areas suitable for agricultural development.[43] In keeping with these potentials, preliminary surveys indicate that Indian water requirements may absorb a significant portion of the annual flows of the Missouri River and its tributaries.[44] The tribes are concerned that water used for energy and other non-Indian development will adversely affect their water rights by causing depletion of supplies critical for sustaining future economic developments on their reservations. They seek assurances from the federal government that their water requirements will be properly considered in development of water resources policy.

The federal government has embarked on a ten-year plan to evaluate Indian claims to water.[45] In the meantime, important issues must be addressed. Indian claims must be coordinated with other water uses. To accommodate non-Indian developments, such as those associated with energy, mechanisms for sale, lease, or other transfer must be devised.

Rational water planning requires eventual quantification of all existing water rights and proposed water uses, including Indian claims. Until consensus on this issue is reached, estimates of future demands on water resources will be inaccurate, and decisions on tradeoffs with other uses will be difficult.

Technical Solutions to Regional Problems

Inter-basin Transfers of Water

Inter-basin transfers of water offer technical solutions to regional water problems. The concept of inter-basin transfers is not new. In a report published in the *Geographical Review*,[46] Frank Quinn surveyed 146 inter-basin transfers in the Western United States that as of 1965 totalled more than eighteen million acre-feet of water per year. Attitudes toward such undertakings range from approval to strong condemnation, especially on environmental grounds.

Many large-scale inter-basin transfer schemes have been proposed. The best known are the Pacific Southwest Plan,[47] the North American Water and Power Alliance (NAWAPA),[48] the Texas Water Plan,[49] and California's large intrastate project.[50] These projects would transport up to 110 million acre-feet of water annually.[51] Many existing and anticipated water shortages could be resolved in this manner, but the necessary tradeoffs deserve careful attention.

The concept of water importation has always sounded good, especially to the receiving region, and from a regional development viewpoint there is no doubt that significant benefits might be derived. It is apparent, however, that the unit costs of imported water would be extremely high and that even if funds for construction were available, few states would be willing to sell their "birthright" without rewards so high as to preclude economic feasibility.[52] On the other hand, international water transfers might be effected, if the benefit from water development in the exporting country (Canada) could be made high enough, and if the water for export flowed north into the Arctic unused. However, environmental disruptions could be large, and solutions for such ecological problems would have to be found.

Inter-basin transfers are viewed more favorably, if the imported water is to be used for oil shale or coal development to alleviate the energy crisis.[53] In a recent study of the Upper Colorado River Basin,[54] the Colorado Department of Natural Resources found that a program for production of oil from shale and coal, yielding the equivalent of one and one-half million barrels of oil per day, could be developed in that region without significantly affecting other water uses through the year 2000.[55] If Mideast oil crises and national energy requirements necessitate greater production of energy by 2000, then water importation into the Upper Colorado Basin could be essential. Thus, large water-import schemes may be necessary for development of such energy projects.

Conflicts in Interests and Efforts: The Institutional Quandry

As waters are designated for special uses, the potential for conflicts among environmentalists, ranchers, irrigators, adjacent well-users, energy firms, cities, and industries escalates. For example, agricultural development in the Western United States has advanced to the point where it must compete for water supplies with the demands made by energy production; this competition signals dry years for farmers. Water is often available but locked out of use due to regulations, laws, institutions, and fear.[56] As Governor Scott M. Matheson of Utah has commented, "The key to an effective water resources policy for the United States is in the institutions we build to manage this resource."[57]

Cost of Law Enforcement

During recent years a formidable body of laws and regulations has been enacted, most of which pertains to environmental controls; however, it impacts on water use and development as well. These laws and regulations have been monitored to assure compliance. Strict interpretation by federal agencies and courts has hampered subsequent water development. In several instances, the construction of major water projects has been foreclosed.[58]

These disjointed actions by various arms of government produce indecisiveness in the policymaking process. This uncertainty must be reduced. Environmental goals and objectives must be specified, and the means for achieving them, stabilized, for decisionmaking in the private sector responds to incentives and adjusts to regulation. Private sector performance is hampered if rules constantly shift and agencies apply regulations in an erratic manner. Furthermore, if the public sector makes dilatory determinations of permissible activities, the private sector functions at a less efficient and more costly level. According to Castle,[59] the economic cost of improving environmental quality may not be excessive, if the cost of rulemaking, enforcement, and intervention is ignored.[60] Nevertheless, these costs cannot be ignored and, therefore, such regulation must be made more consistent and predictable.

In addition, environmental laws and regulations have been used inappropriately to impede development of water and other resources. Many activities of special interest groups, including the formation of coalitions, aid the development and application of legal, economic, and social constraints to the use and acquisition of water. Calling for an end to the misuse of environmental laws, R. Keith Higginson, former Commissioner of the Water and Power Resource Service, has said:

> Congress ought to seriously consider requiring those who bring suits under NEPA or the other environmental laws to post bonds sufficient to offset the increased costs of projects when their objections are overruled. . . . The Rare and Endangered Species Act should be used to protect significant plants and animals —not as a tool to stop projects.[61]

To the extent that state water laws are exempted from proposed "fast-track" procedures for energy development, water acquisition will become a focal point for opposition to development projects. Experience has shown that social and political resistance to a project can transform what are otherwise procedural steps into major obstacles.

Legislative Delays

Congressional initiatives to protect, develop, or manage national water resources are often subject to delays and stoppages due to overlaps in committee jurisdiction in the House and to a lesser degree in the Senate.[62] For example, programs of the Corps of Engineers are under the jurisdiction of the House and Senate Public Works Committees, while those of the Water and Power Resources Service are under the jurisdiction of both the House Interior Committee and the Senate Committee on Energy and Natural Resources. The related issues of water-quality management and water supply are placed within the jurisdiction of different subcommittees, exacerbating the separatism problem. Herein lies a fundamental weakness in developing a comprehensive water policy.

Alternative Mechanisms for Charting Reform

One possibility for reform lies in Congressional restraint from detailed decisionmaking, in favor of a more programmatic approach to water rights policy.[63] With regard to small, non-controversial projects that require a minor commitment of federal funds, Congress has been willing to let federal agencies make decisions.[64] This practice could be extended. Constituency relationships at the local level would still need to be monitored, since such a change could actually decrease the level of Congressional support for water projects. Nevertheless, delays in authorizations and reductions in appropriations would probably be reduced by such a process. Congress would also be free to set priorities more carefully and assess the merits of major programs and projects, using this more general approach to water policy.

As previously noted, Congress needs a more unified and efficient system for developing water policy. Committee assignments are not based upon subject matter of the proposal but upon the identity of the sponsoring agency. To deal more directly with river basin planning, therefore, Congressional practices must be modified through incremental changes in jurisdiction. Concerned committees could also hold joint hearings on comprehensive river plans.

The United States Senate recognized this need in April of 1959, when it created a Select Committee on National Water Resources.[65] The authorizing resolution directed the Committee

[to] make exhaustive studies of the extent to which water resources activities in the United States are related to the national interest, and the extent and character of water resources activities, both governmental and nongovernmental, that can be expected . . . to provide the quantity and quality of water for use by the population, agriculture, and industry between the present time and 1980, along with suitable provision for related recreational and fish and wildlife values.[66]

In its report, the Committee defined water resources in the United States in terms of gross water supply and water use for the entire country and in terms of twenty-four water-resources regions into which the contiguous United States had been divided. It made five general recommendations for action deemed necessary to permit the nation to meet the future demands on its water resources.

Although the report of the Senate Select Committee contained relatively few recommendations,[67] it provided the basis for legislative action. Out of that study emerged the Water Resources Council, the Office of Water Research and Technology, and the existing national assessment process. The Senate Select Committee effected progressive reforms, for it was composed of members of the Congress who believed in their findings and were instrumental in seeing them implemented.

Conclusion: Proposal for Congressional Action

The many complex issues reviewed in this paper demand the development of an effective strategy for their resolution. This strategy must be implemented on a broad scale, taking into account federal, state, and local governments and all facets of water policy. To effect such a change, Congress must become directly involved in this process, as it was in the late 1950s during the existence of the Senate Select Committee.

In order to avoid massive shortages of water and resulting economic disruptions, we must devise a sound water policy posthaste. This policy must take into consideration competing water uses, social custom, environmental quality, and the development of new sources of energy. Moreover, it is the Congress which must initiate the process by eliminating the current bottlenecks in its committee system and procedure that currently stymie efforts at reform.

To this end, I propose a joint committee whose members represent the key water resources committees of Congress. This joint committee would be charged with the task of producing a water strategy capable of being implemented within the shortest time frame possible. It would call for participation of state agencies in a determined effort to provide a plentiful supply of water in all parts of America, a supply adequate to meet the needs of every reasonable use.

It is time for us to realize that we do not have to choose between economic growth and environmental quality or between extreme individualism and collective paralysis. Rather, what is needed is a marshalling of our talents to provide for a coordinated effort to further all of our legitimate concerns. This is the task that lies before the architects of our nation's water policy. The time for action is now. I believe that if the task is to be done, the most knowledgeable and influential members of Congress must be at the vanguard.

NOTES

[1]Reclamation Act of 1902, Pub. L. No. 161, ch. 1093, 32 Stat. 388 (codified at 43 U.S.C. § 371 *et seq.* (1976).

[2]Rivers and Harbors Act of 1909, Pub. L. No. 317, ch. 264, 35 Stat. 815.

[3]Flood Control Act of 1917, Pub. L. No. 367, ch. 144, 39 Stat. 948 (codified at 33 U.S.C. §§ 702, 702h, 703 (1976).

[4]Flood Control Act of 1936, Pub. L. No. 738, ch. 688, 49 Stat. 1570 (codified at 33 U.S.C. § 701 *et seq.* (1976).

[5]Flood Control Act of 1944, Pub. L. No. 534, ch. 665, 58 Stat. 887 (codified at 16 U.S.C. §§ 460d, 825s, 43 U.S.C. § 390 (1976).

[6]Water Resources Planning Act of 1965, Pub. L. No. 89-80, 79 Stat. 244 (codified at 42 U.S.C. § 1962 *et seq.* (1976).

[7]Federal Water Pollution Control Act Amendment of 1972, Pub. L. No. 92-500, 86 Stat. § 16 (codified at 33 U.S.C. § 1251 *et seq.* (1976).

[8]Inland Waterways Revenue Act of 1978, Pub. L. No. 95-902, 92 Stat. 1693, Title II (codified at 26 U.S.C. §§ 513, 527, 4042, 4293 (1976).

[9]NATIONAL WATER COMMISSION, FINAL REPORT TO THE PRESIDENT AND TO THE CONGRESS OF THE NATIONAL WATER COMMISSION, WATER POLICIES FOR THE FUTURE (1973).

[10]Water Resources Development Act of 1974, Pub. L. No. 93-251, 88 Stat. 12, Title I (codified in scattered sections of 16, 22, 33, 42 U.S.C.).

[11]ENVIRONMENT AND NATURAL RESOURCES POLICY DIVISION OF SENATE COMMITTEE ON ENERGY AND NATURAL RESOURCES, 95TH CONG., 2D SESS., AN ANALYSIS OF THE PRESIDENT'S WATER POLICY INITIATIVES (Appendix) (Comm. Print 1978) [hereinafter cited as ANALYSIS].

[12]URBAN WATER RESOURCES RESEARCH COUNCIL, AMERICAN SOCIETY OF CIVIL ENGINEERS, *et al.*, PROCEEDINGS OF THE CONFERENCE ON WATER CONSERVATION: NEEDS AND IMPLEMENTING STRATEGIES 117-18 (1979).

[13]W. Viessman, Jr. & C. DeMoncada, Water Policy Issues Before the 96th Congress 18 (April 1979) (report published by Library of Congress, Congressional Research Service).

[14]*See* Federal Water Pollution Control Act Amendments of 1972, Pub. L. No. 92-500, ch. 26, 86 Stat. 816 (codified in scattered sections of 33 U.S.C.).

[15]President's Message to Congress Recommending Deletion of Funds for 19 Projects from the 1978 Fiscal Year Budget. 13 WEEKLY COMP. OF PRES. DOC. 234 (Feb. 21, 1977).

[16]H.R. 12928, the Energy and Water Development Appropriation bill, funding several dams and water projects, passed the Congress in September, 1978 and was vetoed by President Carter October 5, 1978. The House refused to override the veto. (The vote was 223-179: 276 votes were needed to override.) Later, Carter signed a version of the bill modified to meet his objections (H.R.J. Res. 1139). 124 CONG. REC. H11, 599 (daily ed. Oct. 5, 1978).

[17]The long-running controversy over the Tennessee Valley Authority's Tellico Dam began when Congress ordered completion of the dam, the Endangered Species Act notwithstanding, and the flood gates were finally closed on November 30, 1979. *See* Energy and Water Development Appropriation Act of 1980, Pub. L. No. 96-69, 93 Stat. 437 (Sept. 25, 1979).

The Supreme Court halted construction of the dam in 1978, arguing that it violated the act because it would destroy the habitat of the snail darter, a tiny endangered fish. Congress then amended the law, setting up a special board with the power to grant exemptions. But in January the panel refused to exempt Tellico.

In June, still angered by the decision, Sen. Howard H. Baker Jr., R-Tenn. tried to get Congress to grant an exemption for Tellico. But the Senate refused to go along, and voted 43-52 against an exemption amendment offered by Baker to the Endangered Species Act re-authorization (S. 1143).

However, proponents of the dam persisted in the House and successfully slipped an exemption for Tellico into the fiscal 1980 energy and water development appropriations bill (H.R. 4388).

When the appropriations bill reached the Senate, members again turned down a Tellico exemption. But on Sept. 19, when it became clear House conferees would not budge, the senators reversed themselves, 48-44, and gave the go-ahead to Tellico.

President Carter signed the bill Sept. 26 over the strenuous objections of environmentalists but apparently in exchange for a promise from congressional leaders that the Endangered Species Act would be reauthorized without substantive changes.

37 CONG. Q. 2888 (1979).

[18]U.S. WATER RESOURCES COUNCIL, 1 THE NATION'S WATER RESOURCES: 1975-2000 2 (Dec. 1978).

[19]The Great Basin refers to the northern part of the Basin and Range Province of West-Central United States:

Great Basin, the northern part of the Basin and Range Province of west central United States. It is roughly a heart-shaped area about 800 miles long, and in the north 500 miles wide. The northern boundary is formed by the Snake River district of the Columbia Plateau, and the eastern margin is the Wasatch Range and the Colorado Plateau. The narrow southern end is bordered by the Lower Colorado Basin and the Arizona Highlands, while the western boundary is the Sierra Nevada Range. This district coincides with the state of Nevada, and a small part of western Utah, southeastern Oregon, southwestern Idaho, and the extreme southeastern border of California.

11 COLLIER'S ENCYCLOPEDIA 340 (1977).

[20]SENATE COMM. ON AGRICULTURE, NUTRITION AND FORESTRY, 96TH CONG., 1ST SESS., RENEWABLE NATURAL RESOURCES: SOME EMERGING ISSUES (Comm. Print April 9, 1979) [hereinafter cited as RENEWABLE NATURAL RESOURCES.]

[21]Id.

[22]Id. at 42-43.

[23]Id. at 43.

[24]PRESIDENT'S COUNCIL ON ENVIRONMENTAL QUALITY, TENTH ANNUAL ENVIRONMENTAL QUALITY REPORT (1979) [hereinafter cited as TENTH ANNUAL REPORT].

[25]See id. at 75-155.

[26]Id. at 78.

[27]TENTH ANNUAL REPORT, supra note 24, at 112.

[28]Kneese, Better Use of Water Management Tools, in WESTERN WATER RESOURCES: COMING PROBLEMS AND THE POLICY ALTERNATIVES 96 (1979) (symposium sponsored by the Federal Reserve Bank of Kansas City, Sept. 27-28, 1979) [hereinafter cited as WESTERN WATER RESOURCES].

[29]An Environmental Protection Agency report defines non-point sources as the effects from urban run-off, construction, hydrologic modification, silviculture, mining, agriculture, irrigation return flows, solid waste disposal, and individual sewage disposal. Supra note 27, at 86, citing U.S. ENVIRONMENTAL PROTECTION AGENCY, NATIONAL WATER QUALITY INVENTORY-1977 REPORT TO CONGRESS, EPA-440/4-78-001, 9-15 (1978).

[30]Well-stocked, undisturbed southern pine forests of the Coastal Plain may be expected to yield 200 to 300 tons of sediment per square mile per year. WATER RESOURCES RESEARCH INSTITUTE, NON-POINT SOURCES OF WATER POLLUTION 10 (July 1976) (seminar conducted by Water Resources Research Institute, Oregon State University).

[31]Water Quality Act of 1965, Pub. L. No. 89-234, 79 Stat. 903 (codified at 33 U.S.C. § 1151 et seq. (1970).

[32]Clean Water Act of 1977, Pub. L. No. 95-217, 91 Stat. 1566 (codified at 33 U.S.C. § 1251 et seq. (1976).

[33]J. GLADWELL & C. WARNICK, LOW-HEAD HYDRO: AN EXAMINATION OF AN ALTERNATIVE ENERGY SOURCE (September 1978) (published by the Idaho Water Resources Research Institute) [hereinafter cited as ALTERNATIVE ENERGY SOURCE].

[34]W. Viessman, Jr. & C. DeMoncada, Water Resources: Small-scale Hydroelectric Development 1 (Feb. 14, 1978, updated Jan. 9, 1981) (report published by Library of Congress, Congressional Research Service).

[35]Id. at 4.

[36]ALTERNATIVE ENERGY SOURCE, supra note 33, at 34.

[37]RENEWABLE NATURAL RESOURCES, supra note 20, at 44.

[38]ANALYSIS, supra note 11, at 44.

[39]Castle, Keynote Address, in WESTERN WATER RESOURCES, supra note 28, at 9.

[40]Trelease, Water Law, Policies, and Politics: Institutions for Decision Making, id. at 205-06.

[41]Federal reserved water rights refers to the right to sufficient water for public lands such as national parks, military posts, national forests, and wildlife refuges.

[42]For a concise treatment of some of these problems, see NATIONAL WATER COMMISSION, WATER POLICIES FOR THE FUTURE, FINAL REPORT 473-83 (1973).

[43]SUBCOMM. ON ENERGY RESOURCES AND WATER RESOURCES OF THE SENATE COMM. ON INTERIOR AND INSULAR AFFAIRS, 94TH CONG., 2D SESS. WATER RESOURCES OF THE MISSOURI RIVER BASIN at x (Comm. Print 1976).

[44]Id.

[45]U.S. DEPARTMENT OF INTERIOR, OFFICE OF THE SECRETARY, FINAL REPORT ON PHASE OF WATER POLICY IMPLEMENTATION 20 (1980).

[46]Quinn, Water Transfers, 58 GEOGRAPHICAL REV. 108-32 (1968).

[47]Warnick, Historical Background and Philosophical Basis of Regional Water Transfer, in ARID LANDS IN PERSPECTIVE 345 (1969), citing U.S. BUREAU OF RECLAMATION, PACIFIC SOUTHWEST WATER PLAN, DEPARTMENT TASK FORCE REPORT (1963).

[48]Id. at 345, citing Ralph M. Parsons Company, North American Water and Power Alliance. Brochure 606-2934-19 (1963).

[49]Id. at 346, citing Schorr, Fetching a Water Plan, Texas Style, Wall St. J., Sept. 23, 1968, at 12; U.S. BUREAU OF RECLAMATION, REGION 5, U.S. DEP'T OF INTERIOR, PROGRESS REPORT ON WEST TEXAS AND EASTERN NEW MEXICO IMPORT PROJECT INVESTIGATIONS (1968).

[50]Id. at 345, citing Cal. Dep't of Water Resources, The California Water Plan, Bull. No. 3 (1957).

[51]Id. (Figures represent summation of figures in last column of table 1, pp. 345-46.)

[52]Schad, Western Water Resources, WESTERN WATER RESOURCES supra note 28, at 120.

[53]K. Kauffman, Guns, Courts and Compromise 10 (unpublished report on file at Journal of Legislation office).

[54]COLO. DEP'T OF NATURAL RESOURCES, DRAFT REPORT: AVAILABILITY OF WATER FOR OIL SHALE AND COAL GASIFICATION DEVELOPMENT IN THE UPPER COLORADO RIVER BASIN (1979).

[55]See K. Kauffman, supra note 53, at 10.

[56]Baumann & Boland, Urban Water Supply Planning, WATER SPECTRUM 35 (Fall 1980).

[57]Matheson, A Western Governor Looks at Water Policy, in WESTERN WATER RESOURCES, supra note 28, at 103.

[58]K. Kauffman, supra note 53, at 7.

[59]Dr. Emery N. Castle is President of Resources for the Future, Inc., a leading natural resources research organization. Dr. Castle has been associated with Oregon State University, Department of Agricultural Economics.

[60]Castle, Keynote Address, in WESTERN WATER RESOURCES, supra note 28, at 11.

[61]National Water Line (Oct. 31, 1980) (available from the Nat'l Water Resources Ass'n).

[62] *Water Resources Development Act of 1979: Hearings before the Subcomm. on Water Resources of the Senate Comm. on Environment and Public Works*, 96th Cong., 1st Sess., pt. 5, at 37 (1980).

[63] *Id.* at 39.

[64] *Id.* at 40.

[65] S. Res. 48, 86th Cong., 1st Sess., 105 CONG. REC. 6302 (1959).

[66] *Id.*

[67] S. Rep. No. 29, 87th Cong., 1st Sess., 17–19 (1961).

III

Modifying
Land Use Regulation

12

Reducing the Cost Effects
of Local Land Use Controls

David E. Dowall

INFLATION of housing costs and its causes have become the focus of enormous concern and debate. While housing inflation is the result of many demand-pull and cost-push factors, numerous studies now claim that government regulations are major factors contributing to the cost-push spiral (U.S. Department of Housing and Urban Development 1978; Seidel 1978; Urban Land Institute et al. 1977). In May 1978 the U.S. Department of Housing and Urban Development released its housing cost task force report. While stopping short of recommending national standards for land use regulation and imposing federal sanctions on communities employing restrictive land use and environmental regulations, the report suggested that over-regulation of land development by many communities was a major factor restricting the supply of land for new development. Although it is unlikely that the federal government will impose federal standards for local land use and environmental control, pressure to revaluate current local land-use policy seems likely.

To date, little systematic effort has been made to make land use regulations more efficient and cost effective. Most research assessing the effects of regulation attempts to show the correlation between housing-price inflation and "environmental restrictions."[1] Most studies do not rigorously evaluate specific land use control devices nor do they consider the benefits produced

ACKNOWLEDGMENT.—A version of this paper was presented at the American Planning Association Conference, March 6, 1979, Miami Beach. The author would like to thank Bernard J. Frieden and an anonymous reviewer for helpful comment.

by them. Such incomplete assessments do not provide a basis for improving the effectiveness of land use controls—such suggestions must be based on detailed determinations of how to increase the benefits and decrease the costs produced by land use control mechanisms. This article attempts to aid efforts to improve the effectiveness of land use regulation by outlining a land market monitoring program that can be used for designing and evaluating the performance of local land use control systems.

How Land Use and Environmental Regulations Affect Land and Housing Costs

Communities use a variety of regulations to control residential development. Traditionally, community-wide land use plans, zoning and subdivision ordinances, and building codes have been used to regulate development. As more sophisticated regulations evolved, communities augmented traditional programs with impact assessment procedures, multiple permit systems. growth management timing ordinances, impact fees and taxes, and urban limit line designations. Not only have these additions made the process more complex, they have introduced numerous effects which can lead directly or indirectly to housing cost inflation.

Local land use controls directly affect the cost of land and new housing. By restricting the supply of developable land through the use of open space acquisition and agricultural zoning, or by limiting the extension of public facilities, land prices and new housing costs rise. Local regulations can also affect housing costs by placing onerous subdivision requirements on builders. Extensive review procedures, subdivision requirements, and limited land supplies may greatly affect the operation of many communities' land and housing markets. Table 1 presents the various ways land use controls can affect land and housing markets.

These effects can have considerable impacts on the operation of housing markets. The degree of magnitude of impact depends on the demand for land and housing and on the way that local policy affects the supply of residential land and housing. However, most local planning agencies do not have accurate measures of land supply and residential development potential. Without such information, land use controls are developed and implemented with little understanding of the potential impacts they have on land and housing markets. In this article the author proposes that land planners monitor the performance of land and housing markets. Such monitoring can help gauge the performance of land use regulatory systems and anticipate effects on land and housing markets.

Reductions in the supply of land are most often created by zoning ordinances that limit the amount of land available for residential development by placing lands in agriculture or open-space zones or by overzoning other

TABLE 1. *Effects of land use controls on land and housing markets*

Effect	Land Use and Environmental Controls Most Responsible for Effect
Reduction in the supply of raw land	Zoning; urban limit lines; capital budgeting and timing ordinances; siting and environmental review and permit processes.
Limitations on the level of development intensity	Zoning; height and bulk regulations.
Qualitative changes in residential lots, housing, or development	Capital budgeting and timing ordinances; siting and permitting procedures; subdivision regulations.
Shifting development costs from public to project	Capital budgeting and timing ordinances; service pricing and development charges; siting and permitting procedures; subdivision regulations.
Administrative and delay costs	All to various degrees, but most prevalent with siting and permitting procedures and subdivision regulation compliance.

SOURCE: Dowall (1979), and Dowall and Mingilton (1979).

land uses (particularly industrial and commercial uses in urban "enclave" municipalities). With the widespread adoption of growth management controls, many communities have created urban limit lines (Salem, Oregon), or have tied capital budgeting programs to development timing ordinances (Ramapo, New York; Boulder, Colorado; Petaluma, California). Urban limit lines restrict development to areas inside the designated boundary. If strictly adhered to, all land outside the line is eliminated from the supply of potentially developable land. Capital budgeting and timing ordinances can also have the same impact; they restrict development to areas in a community that have local services. Siting and permitting procedures, to the extent that they operate to restrict development to areas that will generate a minimum of fiscal and environmental impacts, can limit the supply of developable residential land. Also, since the development review process is often lengthy, the supply of land available for development can be restricted by bottlenecks in the siting and permitting program.

Besides regulating the physical stock on residential land, zoning ordinances directly affect the number of residential lots. Density and lot size requirements implicitly determine the supply of developable lots. Changes in local zoning ordinances, minimum lot size requirements, and other policies which affect the density of residential development, translate directly into lot supply changes.

In recent years, many growing communities have changed subdivision ordinances to require developers to provide more and more public facilities. Due to more sophisticated fiscal impact assessment models and higher development charges and fees, development is shifting to areas with existing public services. While such shifts are desirable for controlling urban sprawl, they can limit the supply of residential land.

The proliferation of sophisticated land use control and growth management systems has made development review processes more lengthy and costly. For example, in a telephone survey of home builders Seidel (1978) found that the time required for development approval had increased dramatically between 1970 and 1975 (see Table 2). A nationwide study of development review process time completed by Derkowski (1975) for Canadian cities is presented in Table 3. Both surveys show that the development review process can be lengthy. Delays can cause bottlenecks and inhibit housing and land supplies from meeting market demand.

These are the ways that land use and environmental regulations can affect land and housing supply and cost. While the control of land development is desirable and necessary for avoiding excessive adverse environmental and fiscal impacts, control measures often greatly constrain land and housing markets and contribute to high housing prices. As land use and growth management control systems become more sophisticated, their impacts on land and housing markets will grow in magnitude.

Many of the unanticipated and undesirable land and housing market effects discussed above can be largely avoided or lessened. If the supplies of developable residential land and new and existing housing units are monitored over time, and matched with anticipated land and housing demand, land and housing price inflation effects can be avoided. The next section of this article outlines a method for developing a local land and housing supply monitoring system.

TABLE 2. *Developers' Estimates of the Time Required to Obtain Approval to Develop*

| | Percent of Developer Responses | |
Time required	1970	1975
Less than 7 months	72.2	14.5
7–12 months	25.0	27.5
13–24 months	2.4	47.0
More than 24 months	0.4	11.0
	100.0	100.0

NOTE: Sample size is 346 for 1970 responses and 350 for 1975.
SOURCE: S. Seidel (1978).

TABLE 3. *Number of Agencies Involved and the Minimum Time Necessary for the Subdivision Review Process for "Routine" Projects—1974*

Area	Number of Agencies Involved in Review	Minimum Time (in months) Required for Subdivision Review
Calgary	20	3
Edmonton	20	6
Halifax	8	6
Montreal	5–8	2
Ottawa		
Ontario Portion	40–50	18
Quebec Portion	~ 5	2
Regina	10	3
Saskatoon	8	2
Toronto	40	18
Vancouver	25	8
Winnipeg	15	6

SOURCE: Derkowski (1975).

Monitoring Land and Housing Supply

A program for developing a land and housing supply monitoring system is outlined in this section. The program described is based on several simplifying assumptions to make the presentation less complicated. First, it is assumed that the community for which the system might be used is of medium population size (about 75,000) and not located in the sphere of influence of other cities. Therefore, the demand for housing and land is easy to determine since it is the result of household formation and increased housing demand generated by employment growth in the town. After a simple hypothetical example has been presented, this assumption will be relaxed to consider developing a monitoring system for interdependent communities in metropolitan areas.

Assessing land supply should begin with a complete inventory of land uses in the community. Raw land and vacant parcels should be identified. Physical constraints to development such as excessive slopes, flood plains, and environmentally sensitive areas should be identified. Raw land should be categorized as developable or undevelopable according to these criteria. Next, the number of acres of developable land should be classified according to the availability of public services. Land prices of raw land at various locations within the community should be determined by annually sampling land transactions.

Map overlays of zoning and density regulations should be used to determine the potential supply of developable residential lots or building sites. The supply of lots should be categorized by the availability of services. Using local capital budgeting projections, the number of lots that can be serviced each year should be estimated for at least five years. Local developers should be interviewed to determine the cost of lot preparation. Spot prices for finished lots should be obtained. A measure of the administrative performance is needed to assess the likelihood on land policy compliance and efficiency. The length of the approval process and the ratio of the number of lots in approved projects to the total number of units contained in all proposed projects can be used to estimate the potential supply of lots likely to be approved for development per year. Table 4 summarizes these indicators.

Comparable measures for the housing markets should be assembled. The total housing stock should be inventoried and categorized by location and type of unit. Housing prices by type and location should be monitored for both new and existing units. Building permits should be monitored and used to calculate future additions to the housing supply. The turnover rate of the stock should be estimated; this can be computed by dividing the total number of sales in a year by the number of total stock. Finally, vacancy rates for housing units should be estimated by type and location. (These data are often obtainable from the U.S. Postal Service or from utilities.) Table 5 summarizes these indicators.

So far reference has been made to classifying information by location of land parcels and housing units and by the types of the housing units. Ideal-

TABLE 4. *Land Market Attributes to Be Monitored*

Acres of existing land uses by category and location

Inventory of raw and vacant land by location

Determination of developable land in jurisdiction categorized by the availability of services

Prices of raw land by location and service availability

Based on zoning or intensity constraints, the potential number of residential lots, classified by service availability

Estimate of the expansion of public services per year and the number of lots added to supply

Annual estimate of lot-preparation costs

Lot price estimates for finished lots by location

Estimate of the time required to obtain development permission (subdivision review)

Estimate of an approval rate based on dividing the total number of units contained in applications for development approval, divided into the total number of units contained in projects receiving approval, categorized by location

TABLE 5. *Housing Market Attributes to be Monitored*

Total housing-stock inventory categorized by type and location

Sale prices of units by type and location, both new and existing units

Building permits issued by type of structure and location

Turnover rate of the housing stock (sales/total stock)

Vacancy rate by type and location of unit

ly, the monitoring of land and housing markets should be spatially disaggregated according to distinct land or housing submarkets. Since the concern is with anticipating potential inflationary effects of land use and environmental policy, the demand for and supply of both land and housing within each submarket must be known. The problem with identifying precise submarkets for land and housing is that submarkets are multidemensional; that is, they vary by location, lot type, housing unit type, and the socio-economic characteristics of the neighborhood. Since land policy has effects that can only be meaningfully assessed along spatial lines, the submarket designations must by spatial.

One of the important findings of research on the effects of land use and environmental controls on land and housing market operations is the role that controls have in segmenting land markets. Regulations act to differentiate land into submarkets based on the degree of development restriction. The effect of land use controls on housing markets depends on how each submarket within a jurisdiction is affected. If the imposition of land use controls is not uniform over a region, the excess demand created by excessive controls in one submarket will shift to other submarkets as consumers search out substitute housing. To the extent that other unrestricted submarkets provide altervative development opportunities, the aggregate price effects of land use restrictions may be minimized. To determine whether these substitutions can and do occur, land and housing markets must be monitored on a spatially disaggregated basis.

Data availability should be given primary consideration when developing submarkets. In communities over 50,000 in population, census tracts should serve as the basic building blocks for submarkets. Clustering tracts can be accomplished by two methods, judgmental and empirical. Based on intuitive grounds, community tracts can be aggregated into groups judged to be relatively homogeneous. Discussions with knowledgeable real estate brokers will prove very valuable. Empirically, using census data, tracts can be combined into submarkets by using multivariate analytical techniques (cluster analysis, numerical taxonomy, etc.). Another promising approach is using telephone directories to trace household movements by spotting address changes from previous years' directories. The movement data can serve as the basis for grouping tracts when coupled with socioeconomic data. This approach has been used by Adams in the Twin Cities area (Adams 1978).

Tracts can usually be categorized into broad types. A research project studying land and housing markets in Alameda and Contra Costa Counties, California, has identified twenty-two central-city, seventy inner-urban, one-hundred suburban, and ten exurban submarkets. While these categories are purely locational, they differentiate between housing types well: single-family in suburban and exurban areas; mixed single-family and multifamily in inner urban areas; and multifamily units in central-city locations (Dowall 1979). Also, these categories do a good job of isolating types of development pressures, such as infill pressures in central cities and inner urban areas, and large-scale development pressures in suburban and exurban areas. As a consequence, because land use and environmental policies are quite different in each area, these broad distinctions are useful for assessing policy impacts.

The data outlined in Tables 4 and 5 would be collected and disaggregated according to these submarket designations. If collected annually, the data can be used to monitor land development and land policy for the community. In a manner analogous to the preparation of a housing element, planners can use the data to generate a land element to assess the state of land market operation for the jurisdiction. Such information can be used to determine the likely impacts of changes in local land policy (e.g., a down-zoning, or the rezoning of an area to industrial or open space) and to monitor land supply to identify bottlenecks likely to force land prices up (Dowall 1980).

Assessing Land Policy:
A Hypothetical Example

Suppose that a community has four submarkets: central-city, inner-urban, suburban, and exurban. Based on existing land policy, the number of lots available for development during the next year (those not requiring costly service extensions) are presented in Table 6. Recent lot prices in each submarket are $2,500, $5,000, $6,000, and $3,000 for central-city, inner-urban, suburban, and exurban residential parcels respectively.

TABLE 6. *Hypothetical Supply of Residential Lots*

Central-city	150
Inner-urban	250
Suburban	350
Exurban	150

Based on estimated of household formation and of the rate of net in-migration, aggregate housing demand can be approximated. Suppose that total expected demand for housing will be 600 units. Allocating this demand to submarkets is difficult if not impossible to do precisely. As an approximation, demand can be classified by income, and households allocated to submarkets on the basis of purchasing power. Furthermore, it can be assumed that households will purchase the most expensive unit affordable. Therefore, the allocation of would-be purchasers to submarkets is based on the price of the units in each submarket, with the higher-income purchasers outbidding lower-income purchasers. To make the analysis less complex, demand can be restricted to new units. Demand for new housing per area is presented in Table 7.

TABLE 7. *Demand for New Housing by Submarket Expected for Next Year*

Central-city	100
Inner-urban	50
Suburban	300
Exurban	150

Suppose that the community wants to alter its land policy to stop urban sprawl and encourage infill development. Since it does not want to restrict growth, the community does not limit the number of developable lots, it merely shifts the distribution of lots from suburban to central-city locations. By changing its land use restrictions, the community will alter the location of lots developable during the next year. The new supply is presented in Table 8.

If the approximations are reasonably accurate, there will be an excess demand for new housing of 100 units in both the suburban and exurban sub-

TABLE 8. *Supply of Lots Available Assuming the Shift in Land Policy to Promote Compact Development*

Central-city	250
Inner-urban	400
Suburban	200
Exurban	50

markets. If it is assumed that developers have the same information as presented here, the demand for residential lots will be similar to the demand for housing. One can expect the excess demand for lots to force up prices. If Witte's estimate of the price elasticity of the derived demand for lots of -0.7 is applied (Witte 1977), and if it is assumed that the market adjusts through price and not quantity movements (which is a reasonable assumption in the short run and given the degree of constraint exerted by the land policy), the price of residential lots should increase by 46 percent for suburban lots and 95 percent for exurban lots, implying lot prices of $8,760 and $5,850 for suburban and exurban lots respectively. The degree to which these lot prices will increase to these levels depends on the price elasticity of demand for lots. Because the demand for these lots is derived from the demand for housing, the extent to which other submarkets are viewed as suitable substitutes by housing purchasers will act to increase the elasticity and reduce the potential increase in price.

Since the land price effects of a particular land use control system depend on the degree to which the demand that has been cut off in restricted submarkets can be satisfied by other submarkets, the implications of alternative spatial patterns promoted by land use policies are very important. For example, a policy that attempts to stop sprawl by restricting suburban growth and encouraging central-city infill development may have more inflationary price effects than a policy trying to stop sprawl by channelling growth into satellite communities. This is because there is considerable difference between central city infill parcels and suburban ones. Therefore, the price of the fewer unrestricted suburban parcels will have to rise considerably for the market to readjust to infill lots. On the other hand, the restriction of suburban land development to satellite communities will generate less price effects because the restricted suburban land submarkets are similar to those submarkets in the satellite towns. Prices will not rise appreciably since demand will shift to developable areas quickly.

Projections of demand and supply for land and housing by submarket can be used to assess the potential spatial and price effects of various land use policies. Policies that restrict the supply of land for development, so that excess demand is created in all comparable submarkets, are likely to generate significant inflationary pressures. On the other hand, spatial development policies that shift the supply of developable land from one set of similar submarkets to others are not likely to generate significant inflationary tendencies.

If submarkets are readily substitutable within their broad categories (central-city, inner-urban, suburban, exurban), estimates of demand need not be broken down by more than these broad categories; land policies by submarkets can be assessed to determine whether they are adequate to meet aggregate demand. Efforts to shift development from, say, suburban to inner-urban submarkets may be difficult due to the limited substitutability perceived by housing consumers. In situations where land policy attempts to achieve this objective, the land and housing supply and price data should be monitored closely to determine whether market forces are being redirected, or whether considerable land price inflation is occurring.

The land and housing monitoring system can be used to develop an offset or tradeoff policy for land use and environmental regulation. The systematic monitoring of land and housing supply and prices can serve as the basis for designing land use control programs that are less inflationary than those that limit land development in some submarkets without encouraging it in others. The intent of the land and housing monitoring system is not to equalize land prices between submarkets (inner city and suburban ones, for example) or to alter the relative prices of land in a city's land markets. Rather, the system is intended to help land use planners design land use control programs that do not cause massive price inflation in land markets by providing land market information that can be used to develop tradeoffs between restricted and growth targeted submarkets. The land supply monitoring system will not eliminate the windfall and wipeout problem. Unlucky landowners holding land that is restricted from development will still be wiped out. However, windfalls will be much less concentrated on landowners in particular submarkets, if the monitoring system is used to develop a program that opens other submarkets to development.

The land monitoring system is supply oriented because it does not attempt to affect the level of demand for land. In outlining the hypothetical example it was assumed that the community does not want to limit its growth, but to merely channel it into particular areas. The advantage of the land monitoring system is that it can tell planners how much land is available where, and whether it is sufficient to meet anticipated demand. If the supply of land is limited below that which is necessary to meet demand, the price of land will rise. The land monitoring system can be expanded to determine how much demand for growth should be restricted so that the level of housing demand will match the desired supply of developable residential land. Instead of applying land use policies that restrict growth by limiting housing supply, the monitoring system can be used to determine the amount of employment growth that can be accommodated given the desired level of land supply. This approach would generate much less land and housing price inflation than traditional growth management approaches.

The above outline and hypothetical example of a land monitoring system was based on the simplifying assumption of independence from other communities. In settings where other communities are in close proximity, such as in suburban portions of metropolitan areas, the land use policies and employment growth of other communities can greatly affect both the demand for land and housing, and the delineation and performance of land and housing submarkets. These spillover effects have important implications for the design of a land use monitoring system.

In communities that are in close proximity to one another, a single land use monitoring system must be developed for all interdependent communities. Housing and land submarkets should be identified as suggested above. In some instances the submarkets may straddle several comunities. It would be futile for one community to develop a land monitoring system that was based only on submarkets that were coterminous with community political boundaries since the land use and economic development policies of other communities could greatly affect the supply of and demand for land and housing. However it does not seem necessary that the land use monitoring system be developed exclusively at the regional level. While the Association of Bay Area Governments could competently develop a regional land monitoring system, it would be reasonable and perhaps more efficient for Santa Clara or Marin County to each develop its own system. Each system could be tied into the efforts of both counties to restrict development in unincorporated areas, and could be used by the cities included to balance employment and housing growth. The only limitation on developing mulitjurisdiction land monitoring systems is that the communities together constitute a land and housing market area that is relatively unaffected by other communities.

Setting a land monitoring system in operation will require a substantial commitment from local planners and elected officials. In instances where the monitoring system is best developed at a multijurisdictional scale, much coordination and cooperation between local governments will be needed. In some cases, if the monitoring system is to serve as the basis for an areawide land use planning program, formal compacts between communities will be necessary, or if adopted by regional government, a formal resolution or perhaps binding legislation will be needed. Obviously, the obstacles to implementation are much greater than in the independent, single community example.

Possible Directions for Future Land Use Policy

While the monitoring of land and housing supply and prices may prove valuable for evaluating local land use policy, it provides no incentive for communities to balance the supply of developable land with demand. A possible way of balancing land supply and demand is to use the land use monitoring system to develop land use plans and policies that equalize the supply of and demand for land. The demand for housing and land would be estimated annually and housing approval targets established. Land policy would be formulated to meet environmental objectives, but would provide for an adequate supply of land to meet housing demand over time. The review of development proposals would proceed as is now the case, except that the process would be required to approve enough projects to meet targeted housing production goals. These targets would be classified according to price range and type. Establishment of a required number of approvals would eliminate the tendency of organized special interest groups to oppose all development projects. Since a minimum number of units would be guaranteed approval each year, projects would be scrutinized as to their relative costs and benefits; those projects with the best benefit/cost ratios in terms of environmental, fiscal, and social attributes within each price range and category would be given development permission.

While this housing target system may seem similar to the popular growth management schemes of Ramapo, Petaluma, and Boulder, there are several fundamental differences. First, the targets are minimums, not maximums. There is no reason why the target cannot be exceeded. Secondly, unlike the situation in Petaluma, where the maximum quota of annual housing production is often not met (O'Donnell 1978), the proposed minimum automatically guarantees that as long as projects are proposed, they will be granted permits. In this case developers can operate under a greater certainty, and hence are more likely to propose projects. Third, unlike many growth control quotas (Boulder, Petaluma, Davis) the target is not set arbitrarily; it is based on demand projections and is subject to change. As projections of demand are altered by employment growth and net inmigration, the target will change. Fourth, unlike current growth control programs where only residential development is regulated, the proposed target system would increase housing quotas as new growth increases housing demand.[2] Finally, the target system encourages the approval of development, while other growth management programs do not reduce the tendency to reject development because of citizen opposition to development. While Petaluma and Boulder can advocate compact development or the development of designated areas, their systems of growth management offer no guarantee that actual development will occur. Stopping sprawl, or as in the case of Petaluma shifting development from the east side to the west side of town, does not guarantee that development will occur. While the policy proposed here does not provide for explicit incentives to encourage development, given the automatic guarantee of a certain level of development *regardless of location*, the system will implicitly encourage planners to promote growth in the "right" areas.

This last feature seems to be particularly important, given the increasing advocacy of infill development to offset the containment of sprawl. As Frieden has pointed out, environmental groups ostensibly in favor of such policies have frequently attempted to block infill development in several areas of the San Francisco Bay Area (Frieden 1979). While planners can promote compact development (infill instead of sprawl), given the present design of land use and environmental regulations, it seems likely that sprawl will be contained but that infill will not occur to offset restrictions of outward metropolitan expansion. By guaranteeing development, a land use policy attempting to promote compact development is likely to facilitate infill development actively if it is required to offset containment restrictions. Whether this will generate substantial adverse housing market effects is another issue, but at least the targeting approach guarantees that suburban restrictions be offset with development in vacant and underutilized urban areas on a one-for-one basis.

The proposed land use policy guarantees the production of a minimum number of housing units in local areas. As suggested it will reduce the consistent tendency of citizen opposition to all development proposals. Instead, a given development project would be evaluated on its environmental merit relative to other projects. By guaranteeing the production of a minimum number of units, land policy that attempts to restrict sprawl would be required to promote offsetting development in other locations. Although significant housing market impacts are still likely to exist under this approach, the price effects of such a policy may be less, depending on the substitutability of the offset housing for the unrestricted units.

Why Would Local Communities Be Willing to Use the Monitoring System?

An obvious question is why a local community would consider use of the monitoring system outlined above. The answer depends in part on the type of community and where it is located. The simplest case is that of the isolated community with its own self-contained land and housing market. Very few communities of this type actually are engaged in growth management.[3] Those that are tend to be resort towns concerned with maintaining their environmental "endowment." Taken up with the growth management movement of the 1970s, many of those communities are beginning to experience substantial side effects from limiting growth. In Vail and Aspen, Colorado, two prime examples, local businesses have begun to feel the pinch. They are having increasing difficulty attracting labor at the going wage rate. These highly labor-intensive, service-oriented businesses have historically relied on young "ski bums" for work. The flow of workers has been down recently. Many attribute this to the extremely high cost of living (primarily housing expenses) and low wages. The term "ski bum" has become a misnomer; in order to meet expenses, "bums" are increasingly forced to work fifty to sixty hours per week, eliminating the leisure time that attracted them to these resorts in the first place. Another visible result is the increasing development of the Roaring Fork Creek Valley beyond Aspen and Pitkin County. Many workers are forced to commute great distances because they are not able to afford housing. Thus the impact of environmental regulation yields perverse results—more auto travel, congestion, and pollution. A similar story can be told for Vail and other resorts. It is in Aspen's best interest to expand the housing market. Development policy based on the principles outlines above would seem appropriate for reducing worker housing shortages while still maintaining moderate, environmentally acceptable levels of growth.

Communities of another type are located in metropolitan areas. The incentives for adopting a land use policy such as the one outlined above are different. Land and housing markets of this type of community are connected with those of other towns. Local policies, particularly policies that restrict development, tend to shift demand to neighboring towns (Alonso 1973). For example, rapid growth in the Silicon Valley, coupled with the lack of affordable housing, is hampering the efforts of electronics firms to attract workers. Industry concern spawned the Santa Clara County Manufacturing Group and efforts to identify housing bottlenecks. The group's recent study of the jobs–housing imbalance clearly illustrates that local land use controls are the cause of the problem (SCCMG 1980). Recently, after release of the study and several public hearings, Sunnyvale, Santa Clara, and San Jose have rezoned industrial land to residential use. While not all communities may be willing to make changes like Sunnyvale, Santa Clara, and San Jose did, it is clear that land supply information was a crucial ingredient for drawing attention to the Silicon Valley's housing problem.

In some instances, regional or state legislation may be needed to make communities consider the regional housing implications of local land use controls. California has passed legislation requiring communities to consider regional housing demand (California 1980). The California bill (AB2853) requires that communities complete land availability inventories and that local general land use plans consider regional housing needs. The California bill could be largely implemented with a land use monitoring system as outlined above. With proper enforcement the bill could make the implementation of a regional land use monitoring system possible.

Several other approaches seem promising and warrant consideration. The first is that local communities' housing elements be expanded to include land supply and development potential, and an assessment of whether local land policy is consistent with expected local housing demand. At the regional level, estimates of "expected to reside" projections could be compared with local land and housing supply potential. Finally, evaluations could be used to set priorities for local applications for federal funds through the A-95 review process. With the use of one or a combination of these approaches, a land use monitoring system can indeed become a viable technique.

Conclusion

The potential of land use monitoring systems to help balance housing supply and demand is great. The technique presented here can be used to better plan for residential development, and in communities operating growth management programs, help to mitigate land price inflation. The land use monitoring system can increase the effectiveness of land use and growth management programs.

NOTES

[1]Examples include: Orange County Cost of Housing Committee (March 1975) and Lincoln et al.(April 1976).

[2]Most growth management programs focus entirely on residential development. Construction of housing requires a special permit, and the application for the permit starts the growth management system. Requests for other types of uses are not subjected to this review process.

[3]For an analysis of 230 growth management communities, see Dowall (forthcoming).

REFERENCES

Adams, John. 1978. The definition of areal submarkets for housing in Minneapolis and suburban areas, Working Paper No. 1 in the Project on Monitoring Growth Management Systems. Minneapolis, Minnesota: University of Minnesota, Hubert H. Humphrey Institute.

Alonso, William, 1973. Urban zero population growth. *Daedalus* 102: 191–206.

California, State of. Assembly Bill No. 2853, (Local Planning: mobile home parks and housing elements), 1979–80 Regular Legislative session.

Dowall, David. 1979. *Assessing the effects of environmental controls on land and housing markets; a report to the California Air Resources Board.* San Francisco: Public Interest Economics.

———. 1980. Effects of land use and environmental regulations on housing costs. *Policy Studies Journal* 8, 2: 227–288.

———. forthcoming. An examination of population-growth-managing communities. *Policy Studies Journal.*

———, and Mingilton, Jessie. *The effects of land-use control on housing costs: a literature review.* Chicago: Council of Planning Librarians, Bibliography No. 6, May 1979.

Derkowski, A. 1975. *Costs in the land development process.* Toronto: Housing and Urban Development Association of Canada.

Frieden, Bernard J. 1979. *The environmental protection hustle.* Cambridge: MIT Press.

Lincoln, James R., Jr., et al. April 1976. *An analysis of the impact of state and local government intervention on the home building process in Colorado, 1970–1975.* Denver: Bickert, Brown, Coddington and Associates.

O'Donnell, Macky. 1978. *An evaluation of Petaluma's growth management system.* MCP Professional Report. Berkeley: University of California, Department of City and Regional Planning.

Ohls, James; Weisberg, Richard; and White, Michelle. 1974. The effects of zoning on land value. *Journal of Urban Economics* 1:428–444.

Orange County Cost of Housing Committee. 1975. *The Cost of Housing in Orange County (Cal.).* mimeograph. Anaheim, California: The Committee.

Santa Clara County Manufacturing Group (SCCMG). 1980. *Vacant land in Santa Clara County: implications for job growth and housing in the 1980s.* Sunnyvale, California: SCCMG.

Seidel, S. 1978. *Housing costs and government regulation.* New Brunswick, N.J.: Center for Urban Policy Research.

Urban Land Institute and Gruen, Gruen and Associates. 1977. *Effects of regulation of housing costs: two case studies.* Washington, D.C.: Urban Land Institute.

U.S. Department of Housing and Urban Development. 1978. *Final report of the task force on housing costs.* Washington, D.C.: the Department.

Witte, Ann. 1977. An examination of various elasticities for residential sites. *Land Economics* 53, 4.

13

Procedural Reform of
Local Land-Use Regulation

Charles Thurow and John Vranicar

A S LONG AS there are regulations, basic tensions will exist between the regulated and the regulators. The proliferation of government regulation in the past decade, however, has even the government worried. Planners, developers, public officials and concerned citizens are dissatisfied with the current "system" of land-use regulation, a system which straddles local, regional, State, and Federal jurisdictions. Not only do the overlapping and frequently conflicting controls operate inefficiently, they also do not guarantee that resulting land use is of high quality. Although residential development has not been subject to the same pro-liferation of permits that other forms of development, such as energy facilities, have experienced, housing, like other development, is subject to greater regulation now than it was in the past. This increased regulation has been held to be at least partially responsible by some critics for increases in housing costs. Critics point to both the requirements in the regulations themselves—the substantive issues—and the way in which they are ad-ministered—the procedural aspects.

In this paper we will focus on the procedural aspects of regulation at the local level, summarizing what we feel are some central issues, and then take a look at the most promising techniques available to local practitioners to reform their systems. We will also consider some ways in which the States can enhance, encourage, or even direct local regulatory reforms and im-prove intergovernmental coordination. . . .

Reprinted from *Reducing the Development Costs of Housing: Actions for State and Local Governments.* Proceedings of the HUD National Conference on Housing Costs, August 2, 1979, by the U.S. Department of Housing and Urban Development.

The Debate over Procedural Reform

Land use controls are one of many cases where it is difficult to distinguish between the regulated and the regulator—industry and government. The development community and related industries which supply it have played a central role in the evolution of land regulations, both through frequent representation on planning commissions and boards and in strong leadership in promoting new styles of regulation. This has been particularly true for residential development.

Government is obviously not the monolithic entity that editorials rail against, but a loosely connected collection of agencies from the local to the Federal level. This ad hoc "system" has little or no vertical or horizontal integration. Land-use controls are extremely decentralized, and by no means uniformly practiced. While the regulation of any single jurisdiction may impose only moderate processing requirements, the cumulative effect may be a true problem.

There are two ways to tackle this: the first is for each level to clean up its own act; the second is for the State and local governments and special districts to cooperate to integrate their procedures. The first is a relatively easy task, but the results may be somewhat disappointing. The city or county that eliminates a public hearing and cuts two months from its review process may find to its dismay that the developer is still cooling his heels six months later, waiting for a State permit or review by another agency. This is a classic case of "hurry—lack of local expertise and parochial politics, convinced that the real bottlenecks are at the county or municipal level." Buck-passing results in standoffs. Someone needs to take the initiative, and it is the State that seems to be the logical choice. Serious questions remain, however, as to the extent and effectiveness of State action.

When we turn our attention to the housing industry, we encounter an anomaly in this age of conglomerates and mass production. Highly competitive and decentralized, subject to cycles, at the mercy of labor and material shortages, dependent upon a fickle consumer, and always mindful of the weather, residential development is a high-risk business. The typical contractor builds on a small scale, for a highly localized market. Just as the responses of local governments vary depending on size, rate of growth, and economic resources, so too do the demands of developers upon governments differ. Depending on relative market position, some developers may want to beef up regulations at the expenses of speed to protect projects from surrounding developments. Some may want more discretion while others are asking for less.

The developer is acutely aware that the meter is ticking while the regulatory process chugs on. Carrying costs include such items as interest on loans, insurance, property taxes, inflation, office overhead, and capital tie-up. Wasted time means higher housing prices without increased quality of product. It is not delay, however, as much as it is *unexpected* delay that presents problems for homebuilders. The more basic problem is uncertainty. Uncertainty translates into risk, and risk is reflected in price. Also of serious concern is how the perception of risk may influence industry behavior in choosing "safe" styles of housing and subdivisions, searching out fringe areas with more relaxed standards, instead of attempting innovations that could lead to cost savings.

The relationship between public decision-makers and developers is symbiotic. Each is highly dependent upon the other in shaping the future environment. But the fundamental differences between the two create many inherent tensions. Perhaps the most central of these—and the one which can never be satisfactory resolved—is the tension arising from a desire to lay down rational and dependable rules in advance of land development, on the one hand, and the need for leeway to respond to changing demands or to maximize potential of individual sites, on the other. This have-your-cake-and-eat-it-too wish is expressed by both industry and government. Although traditional land regulations were intended to be self-administering, clearly they cannot possibly cover all cases, or be designed to anticipate economic and social changes. In this respect, land use regulation does not seem to be much different than any other aspect of the American democratic process, from the Constitution down to traffic court. As one more political arena where conflicting interests hammer out compromises, the local land regulatory system, ad hoc and decentralized as it is, may still be our best bet. It represents a balancing of the conflicting desires for certainty and flexibility, differently weighted in each community, and thus, inherently messy.

Challenges to the Regulatory System

Since understanding problems in local land use regulation is essential in working towards solutions, we will briefly review the major charges that have been leveled at regulatory administration. We should make it clear that these criticisms do not, in our opinion, characterize most communities. At the same time, they have been raised so persistently over the years that they must be taken seriously. No one knows how frequently these charges are accurate, but as long as the system holds the potential for them, the system should be reexamined when criticisms recur.

Overly Complicated Ordinances

Regulations tend to be overly complicated, outmoded, and in some cases, unnecessary. Zoning and subdivision regulations are often unintelligible, a jumble of conflicting standards and procedures that do not mesh with community development practices. Many ordinances have been put together by committee, cutting and pasting from model ordinances or examples from other communities. Once drafted, even the cleanest and best conceived ordinance goes through revisions during the process of adoption that may muddy its original purity. Likewise, amendment and subsequent changes after adoption can add to the problem.

Innovation Increases Risk

Flexible development regulations are too risky for the developer and the local government. Innovative land controls, particularly PUD ordinances, were instituted, in part, to find new ways to lower housing costs. Inherent in them, however, is greater administrative complexity. While procedures and criteria are established by ordinance, the techniques still require a case-by-case reivew. There are disputes about how much extra time it takes to process these types of devclopments, but there is no argument that they tend to front-load costs, making the project more risky. The local government also takes a risk on future maintenance of the project when traditional standards are departed from. Consequently, the municipal departments which provide basic services act cautiously and conservatively during the review process.

Red Tape

Land use regulations are plagued by red tape which leads to unnecessary, prolonged delay or inaction. Chief offenders are as follows: mechanical adherence to regulations; needless duplication of reports and publications; lack of coordination among various reviewing bodies; timing problems when one agency may wait for another to sign off before it acts; and the requiring of excessive amounts of extraneous information.

Administrative Incompetency

Administration suffers from governmental incompetency and is often designed to mask it. While government may be competitive in hiring at the entry level, the experienced technician knows he or she can almost always be hired away by the private sector. Most public promotion ladders move technical staff into managerial positions for which they are often untrained and unsuited. Thus, it is not surprising to hear charges that the planning departments are staffed with bright but green young planners and older "lifers" who could not make it in private practice. Developers complain that one of the bigger problems is a basic lack of understanding on the part of public planners as to what goes into a private venture in terms of risk management and the overall development process.

Unqualified Lay Reviewers

Lay review of technical issues is of dubious value. Perhaps one of the most serious charges against the regulatory system is that lay boards and commissions are not qualified to review development proposals. This is actually two seperate charges. On the one hand, boards are accused of being controlled by the development community, through heavy member representation by architects, builders, real estate brokers, and planning consultants. Serious conflicts of interest may be present. On the other hand, critics charge that boards are filled with "housewives and ministers" who know little about land use regulations and even less about construction and development practices. Further study would probably find that both situations frequently co-exist.

Corruption

The present system offers opportunities for cronyism and corruption. Accusations that zoning and subdivision approvals are bought and sold have been made since the system's inception. The outright criminal acts of bribery or extortion are less central to this discussion than is the large, grey area of personal influence in zoning and subdivision administration. Having merely one friend—or enemy—on a board can make or break a developer in a particular community. Another weakness in the system is its susceptibility to community groups that have packed public meetings.

These problems are generally laid at the feet of discretionary powers, or, to put it another way, to the lack of due process and accountability in the system. In fact, the real problem is probably not discretion, per se, but rather how it is exercised. Rezonings, for example, are particularly troublesome; one reason is that the distinction between the proper legislative and administrative roles is blurred. The processing of applications frequently has no standards for record keeping. Just as frequently, there are no rules for the admission of evidence, the accessibility of documents consulted by decision-makers, or for the "finding of fact."

Hidden Agendas

Land use administration is used to implement hidden agendas or mask illegal acts. Of the many techniques communities have used to keep out new residents, and one of the more underhanded, is to make the development process so impossibly fraught with difficulties that no developer would attempt to use it. When the intent is to keep out low- and moderate-income households, it is a clear-cut case of exclusionary practice. Less clear-cut is the concern about whether a community can handle the level of services new developments will require. In either case, procedural foot dragging can be an extra obstacle to growth. Multiple public hearings offer opportunities for no-growth advocates to block developments by raising environmental issues, spurious or otherwise. Finally, negotiation can be used by local officials to shift the entire costs of expansion onto the newcomers through the developer, even when the community as a whole benefits from the growth. Not only does this keep property taxes low for the current residents, it can raise housing costs to the point where "undesirables" are priced out.

Reform Techniques in Local Regulation

We feel that the best response to the criticisms leveled at local land use regulation is not to mount defenses or make counter-charges, but to take a good look at the systems and go to work cutting out unnecessary delay, uncertainty, dishonesty, or incompetence. With this in mind, we offer a list of the most promising techniques in use by local governments, and what we believe States can be doing to facilitate these efforts. This is not by any means an all-inclusive catalogue. We expect the results of our field work will lead us to revise our opinions on some of these measures. What follows represents our best thinking on the subject to date.

We will consider what can be done at the local level first. For the purposes of this discussion, we have broken down the regulatory process into four steps: (a) Application phase: (b) Staff review phase; (c) Public review phase; and (d) Official action. We have done this in an attempt to find some commonality in the bewildering variety of local processes.

Two other observations: First, we are stressing measures directly connected to land use controls. The wise administrator is already aware of basic techniques in effective personnel supervision and office management. Secondly, with a couple of exceptions, these techniques cannot achieve their full potential standing by themselves. Most are mutually reinforcing and work best when combined for a cumulative effect.

Application Phase

The initial point of contact between the applicant and the local government should realistically describe the process, including submission requirements, give a reasonably accurate estimate of time lines, clarify the applicant's legal rights, and suggest how to avoid common pitfalls. In short, it should address the applicant's reasonable expectations about public action so that he or she can assess the risk and determine whether or not to go ahead with the project. The following techniques have been used to remove some uncertainty or delay in the application phase:

Permit Register. This may consist of a directory of all permits required, information about departments and regulations and/or a manual or instruction sheet(s) on steps for obtaining approvals. The idea is to demystify the permitting process. This is a baseline service, one which no community can justifiably lack.

Clear, Concise Regulations. As we discussed, many communities are due for some major overhauling of old, over-amended ordinances, not only to remove conflicts and ambiguities, but to cut down on time-consuming variances and rezonings amending obsolete provisions.

Preliminary Informal Conferences. This practice is already an element in many subdivision regulations, either as an option or as a requirement. Pre-application meetings provide an opportunity to iron out difficulties with the planning or other staffs before the developer has prepared expensive technical materials. The developer and staff are alerted to potential obstacles ahead. Early problem identification makes public hearings and commission meetings more productive, and may reduce the need for continuances.

Consolidation or Standardization of Forms. Despite the fact that everyone complains about them, good forms are tools for increasing efficiency. They settle questions of format and content and may even help guide decision-making. For example, in the variance procedure, forms could be designed to focus attention on the requirements, with space for the applicant to enter the nature of the hardship, why the applicant believes it is unique, and the basis for asserting that the variance, if granted, will not alter the character of the neighborhood. Since any information other than this is, strictly speaking, irrelevant, the form would not provide space for it. The form on which the board records its decision could require a statement of the findings under the same three headings.

Dual Track System. Found in many subdivision regulations, a dual track separates projects with very minor impacts and processes them through an abbreviated approval process. In the past "minor" has been rather narrowly defined, but there is no reason why it cannot be expanded to include a variety of noncontroversial, routine applications of limited size—within the bounds of the State-enabling legislation.

Assistance in Preparation of Development Plans. Some communities see their role as enabling rather than prohibiting. A service-oriented staff works with the developer in modifying his plans to conform to standards rather than simply rejecting them as not in compliance. This service can be expensive, and end by doing the developer's work for him. At the same time, it is one of the few opportunities a community has to act positively to shape development. It may be particularly effective in communities welcoming a certain kind of growth or redevelopment. One specific application of this approach is in States with stringent environmental regulations. Local governments can help developers in three ways:

(a) Offer technical assistance at the preapplication stage in modifying the proposal so as to obtain a negative declaration, thus sidestepping preparation of a full environmental impact report;

(b) Generate an areawide impact statement applicable to most proposals of a given type, eliminating the need for individual reports to go over duplicative material. This exercise may also help communities better assess the cumulative impact of several developments, rather than being forced to consider impacts in piecemeal way; and,

(c) Create an area-wide data base from which developers may freely draw in the preparation of environmental impact reports.

One-Stop Permitting. This concept, so appealing in theory, has generated a great deal of attention and has come to refer to several different approaches. However, "one-stop" is no panacea, and may promise much more than it can deliver. Many communities that snapped up the idea at first have now abandoned it as a disappointing gimmick. They claim it is either needless counter-shuffling or adding another layer to the process. Others have found that it turned out to be a convenience, but did little to really make a dent in delay or uncertainty—an expensive accommodation to the client. Common problems include: insulating customers from personnel who review applications; interruptions in staff tasks; access to records; and simply finding floor space.

Of course, there are some sound ideas contained in the concept of one-stop permitting. The more promising applications of which we are aware:

(a) A centralized department or office which actually accepts and processes applications and maintains central files. Personnel coordinate and track applications through the departmental reviews, schedule hearing dates and meetings, and act as a single contact for the applicant.

(b) Public information center. This can be a glorified reception desk where applicants could obtain materials explaining procedures, or be referred to appropriate departments. If detailed questions are to be fielded by personnel at the information center, then specialized staff must be assigned to the work space. Otherwise generalists can be cross-trained to deal with most questions.

(c) Reorganizing floor plans to put all permitting on one floor.

One last thought on "one-stop": It may be that some ambitious agencies have carried the concept one logical step too far in attempting a single centralized office. Perhaps "two-stop" or "three-stop" is a more sensible alternative and certainly one which is preferable to "eight-stop" or "ten-stop."

Permit Expeditor. This idea relates very closely to one-stop permitting in that it makes one individual accountable for an application as it moves through the system. The assignment of an expeditor may be especially useful if a community is anxious to encourage a particular development. Because this can be an expensive measure, it might be used selectively.

Staff Review Phase

The staff review phase entails checking for conformity with regulations along with review of less concrete qualitative factors which are apt to be elements in final approval. Technical aspects require review by specialized staff; therefore, several individuals generally participate. In some instances staff review may end in official action; more commonly, staff review ends in recommendations to decision-makers.

Joint Review Committee. Typically, applications are routed through departments separately, with individual sign-offs or comments assembled at the end by the planning department or another lead agency. A commonly used alternative is to institute a project review committee to meet regularly to discuss proposals. The many advantages to this practice stem from the fact that decisions are not made in departmental vacuums, but can be modified in light of the total context of the application. Because group meetings are no substitute for careful study beforehand, this practice may not reduce time as much as it opens the door for constructive input by staff, and provide a group dynamic for working out problems before they are brought before the planning commission or the public.

Simultaneous Permit Processing. When one permit is a prerequisite for the rest, reviews must follow sequentially. In many cases this is logical and efficient for both developer and agency staff, but there are areas that lend themselves to simultaneous consideration. One example might be applications for rezoning and plat approval.

Deadlines. Many phases of the approval process are legislatively mandated, some at the State level. However, overruns are common. One widespread practice, frequently an abuse, is for communities to "ask" developers to waive adherence to deadlines. On the positive side, deadlines should be assigned to procedures which lack them. One approach is for staff to estimate a realistic processing schedule for each project; the estimate becomes a set of nonbinding milestones against which staff can measure performance. The developer, of course, benefits from a solid projection of time required.

Staff Training. This includes (a) continuing education for professional staff; (b) courses to upgrade skills of paraprofessional or clerical staff to increase their scope of responsibility; (c) simple information sessions among department staffs; and (d) more formal cross-training of staffs. Improved education would certainly help alleviate some of the criticisms regarding the competence of public employees.

Revamped Recordkeeping. This can run the gamut from computerized on-line terminals which track application through the approval process to simple centralization of files. Solutions will depend on local problems.

Use of Consultants. Some planning departments have begun to make a practice of bringing in consultants to help regular staff review applications when a backlog occurs. This can be expensive, of course, and is probably more effective in large, high-volume planning departments.

Public Review and Participation Phase

Due process considerations make some degree of public involvement both necessary and desirable. But local practice often makes public hearings frustrating and unproductive exercises for developers, citizens and staff. Not only is public opinion unpredictable and volatile, the notification process is time-consuming. When more than one hearing is held, the developer may be justified in wondering what legitimate purpose is being served. Some things can be done to make the process not only less painful, but even constructive.

Timing of Public Hearings. In general, the earlier in the process the public can be involved, the better. Citizen groups resent being put in the position of reacting to already completed plans and feel input is more meaningful at the concept stage. Developers, too, prefer knowing what kinds of changes will be required before time and money have been spent in detailed plans. At the same time, if final plans differ too greatly from those commented upon by the public, then the purpose of early review is defeated. Another possible drawback is that citizen groups feel that they are unofficial consultants and continue to tinker with plans throughout the process. Some balance must be achieved here. Generally this can be achieved through a hearing at the preliminary plat stage.

Informal Public Meetings. Public meetings—as differentiated from formal hearings—can help the developer to identify problems early and calm suspicions of neighbors. It makes sense for local government to encourage informal neighborhood meetings, and even to assist the developer in setting them up. This type of meeting is not a reliable vehicle for eliciting binding promises from the developer, but it can serve to focus issues for the formal hearing and eliminate surprises.

Eliminate or Consolidate Multiple Public Hearings. Unless required by State law or dictated by major revisions in development plans, in general, one public hearing per project should suffice. This is especially true if the other measures we are suggesting are followed.

Standardized Notification Procedures. Frequently overamended ordinances have incorporated two or even three different methods for public notification, depending on the type of action involved. This adds needless confusion to the system for the developer, the administrator, and the public. Where possible under state legislation, notification procedures should be standardized.

Public Education. It may be difficult, if not impossible, to change basic public attitudes about growth and about making provisions for low-and moderate-income housing. However, it may be possible over time to alleviate some suspicions about innovative types of development or higher density housing with presentations, slide shows, etc., at club luncheons and other public forums. Pamphlets which explain the development process and public hearing procedures may aid in guiding public input along constructive channels—e.g., complaints and criticism should be expressed as specific recommendations for changes in the plans.

Official Action

The issuance of permits can be administrative (quasi-judicial) or legislative—requiring a vote by elected officials. The typical application may encounter several varieties of official action. We have already covered what we view as the major issues in official action. Here we are suggesting some measures to improve the process.

Consolidate or Eliminate Commission Reviews. Frequently, planning commissions spend a disproportionate amount of their time on day-to-day details at the expense of larger policy issues. One way to free time for policy making is to eliminate redundant reviews of pending proposals. If the staff has done its homework, usually one review at the preliminary plat state should suffice. More radically, commission review of some applications can be eliminated altogether. Simple variances or minor subdivisions, among others, may fit this category.

Consolidate or Eliminate City Council or County Board Reviews. As is the case with commissions, many decisions now made by elected officials are not truly legislative in nature, but administrative. Thus, review by these bodies may add more steps to the approval process without substantially improving its effectiveness or accountability.

Dual Planning Commission. In order to free up time for consideration of policy-related issues, in a few places commissions have set up committees to review all specific land use applications. An even more progressive version of this idea is to institute two separate commissions, one for policy and one for projects.

Applications on Agendas. Infrequent board meetings in communities with a high volume of development mean that sometimes it takes two or three months simply to get onto the agenda. The obvious solution is to hold more frequent meetings. This may be the most straightforward suggestion offered in this paper, and the most difficult to put into effect, given the fact that commissioners volunteer their time.

Improve the Caliber of Commissioners. This measure relates to our earlier discussion on the role of lay decision-makers. Commissioners have too great an impact on the quality of the future environment for their selection to be taken lightly. Communities should set policies on qualifications for individual membership and on the occupational make-up of the board. Another way to improve the judgment of lay decision-makers is to provide on-the-job training during their tenure.

Strengthen or Institute an Appeals Process. Far too many local decisions finally end up in the courtroom; often this is the only recourse for a developer. Other developers have discovered that a reputation for using the courts routinely improves their chances of initial approval by the local board. In any case, the judge who renders the final decisions frequently lacks the requisite expertise or sensitivity to local land use disputes. The courts are slow and expensive, and ultimately remove decision-making from the local arena. A good local appeal procedure could cut down on use of the courts and contribute to fairer procedures by building up a body of precedent, establishing consistent standards and directing the attention of the commission to issues, inconsistencies or problems that may have been overlooked earlier.

Zoning Administrator or Hearing Examiner. Of the many techniques discussed here, the hearing examiner goes the farthest towards tackling directly the problem of lay review and the problems arising from the lack of due process. A hearing examiner is an appointed official who conducts quasi-judicial hearing on applications for one or more flexible devices—parcel rezoning, special use permits, or variances—and enters written findings based on the record established at the hearing. The outcome may be a recommendation to the city council or county board, or, in some cases, the hearing examiner decides upon the application himself. This means that some of the review functions traditionally performed by the board of adjustment, city council, or planning commission shift to the hearing examiner. Generally, however, parcel and major rezonings and frequently PUDs are considered to be legislative decisions and continue to undergo a final vote by the council or board. Instituting a hearing examiner may not reduce the actual time required in reviewing an application. But it impacts directly on the fairness, consistency and predictability of the decisions rendered.

Other Techniques

Two other measures which do not lend themselves to cataloging in the four-phase process are worth consideration.

The Development Permit System. This approach is a departure from traditional zoning, in that it consolidates all permits into a single permit, which is issued if an application satisfies a point system. The point system quantifies trade-offs in policies regarding such items as densities, public amenities and environmental quality. Its advocates claim that it is simple, straightforward, and relatively easy to administer; and that it decreases delay and uncertainty for the homebuilder.

Mediation. Although utilized only rarely at this time, and for very large projects, the use of an official arbitrator to resolve stand-offs appears to hold promise. There are several studies underway to evaluate the potential of this technique.

Role of State Government in Aiding Local Reform

We have been focusing on what local governments can do unilaterally to improve efficiency. Turning now to the States, we see ways in which they, too, can undertake reforms. The relatively plentiful literature on State regulatory procedures has covered innovative legislation in such States as Vermont, California, Florida, Washington, Hawaii, and Oregon. Other basic materials on State reform include the American Law Institute's *Model Land Development Code*, Bosselman's *The Permit Explosion*, and a soon-to-be-published collection of papers presented at an Urban Land Institute Seminar on Regulatory Simplification, held in South Carolina, in February, 1978.

Here we will limit our discussion to some specific suggestions on what States can be doing to enhance, encourage, and even require local streamlining. We borrow heavily from Bosselman, and ALI, and especially from an article by Burchell and Listokin in ULI Research Report No. 29 entitled, "The Impact of Local Governmental Regulations on Housing Costs and Potential Avenues for State Meliorative Measures."

States can modify their enabling legislation to allow more latitude in local streamlining. In some cases State-enabling legislation may present obstacles to one or more of the techniques we have suggested. In others, where State legislation is simply silent on a given point, local governments may be unwilling to go out on a legal limb. Revised enabling legislation is admittedly a passive form of State involvement, but is a necessary first step.

States can provide technical assistance, proposing model ordinances and procedures, or act as a clearinghouse for information. Information dissemination is an important function, as our preliminary study has indicated; and one which cannot be accomplished satisfactorily on a national basis, since local practice may depend on the peculiarities of State legislation.

There are a number of initiatives available to State government that have imposed a heavy overlay of regulation on top of local or regional controls. *The Permit Explosion* summarizes several of these. One suggestion is to provide the option for representatives from local governments to sit on State agency review panels at public hearings on local projects, as is done in Washington under the Environmental Coordination Procedures Act (ECPA). Duplicative permit requirements can be addressed in several ways. One is to establish the functional equivalence of environmental impact reports required at different levels. Another is for the State or region to surrender its authority to issue permits to the local government under certain special conditions. A third related idea is to statutorily authorize an agency to presume, on the basis of an approval acquired from another agency, that certain conditions will be met by the development. A permit at one level could serve as a rebuttable presumption that criteria for a given permit are being met at the other level.

An often overlooked opportunity to encourage local reform is for States to use their A-95 review function to report negatively on Federal funding proposals from communities that do not meet minimum standards for efficiency. But first, such standards must be developed by the States.

The strongest avenue for State action is in the form of legislation which requires local procedural reform. Traditionally this has been done in areas of substance rather than procedure, a good example being uniform State-wide building codes. Another much discussed strategy is to require local regulations and developments to conform to comprehensive plans, thus tying land control more effectively to planning.

Additional legislation could address directly problems of delay and uncertainty. A "grandfather clause" statute could remedy the problem of developers being forced to comply with regulations that were not in effect at the time of the initial application. Deadlines can also be legislatively mandated. A third suggestion is to provide statutory assurance to the developer that third party appeals will not be heard in the courts after a specific time period, thus mitigating the risk of a retracted approval.

The State which has gone farthest in mandating procedural reform is California in its recent legislation, AB 884, as amended by AB 2825. Briefly, the law is designed to simplify and speed up permitting by both State and local agencies. While it substantially modifies the California Environmental Quality Act (CEQA) and procedures for State agencies, what is particularly remarkable about AB 884 is that it reaches deep into local agency practice. It requires that local agencies:

(1) Determine the completeness of an application within set time limits;

(2) Develop lists and criteria for determining the completeness of application;

(3) Require no subsequent information after an application has been accepted as complete;

(4) Complete all decisions within set time limits or the proposal will be deemed automatically approved.

AB 884 also set up an Office of Permit Assistance for ensuring compliance with the law and to give assistance to developers.

It is too soon to measure the success of AB 884; early returns are mixed, and as usual, depend on the perspective of the reviewer. On the local level, the intrusion of the State is meeting some resentment. Some local administrators are claiming that the Office of Permit Assistance simply adds another layer to the process. Others observe that the provisions are forcing them to require more information early in the process than had been their practice, since subsequent requests were no longer allowed. This has the effect of adding to the developer's front-end costs. How major or minor these problems are is not known, but they serve to suggest that troubleshooting is still necessary to make AB 884 successful.

We would suggest that legislation of this kind is only passed in response to what is perceived as a serious problem. If local communities in other States are concerned about similar legislation at home, their best defense is to take the initiative themselves in streamlining their systems, thus eliminating the need for State intervention.

Conclusion

The purpose of this paper has been to provide an overview of the problems and possibilities in procedural reform in land use regulation at the local level. Based on our exposure to local public practitioners, we believe that they are concerned about their systems and ready and willing to make changes. We are also aware that in some communities, land use regulations are always the subject of controversy. Poorly conceived reforms, enacted for the wrong reasons, may waste time in random tinkering or do far more harm. It is essential that the local regulatory system be carefully evaluated before changes are made. . . .

The focus of reform may be efficiency, but other equally important goals of the regulatory system must be considered. First, and most important, is whether the system is effective; that is, whether the process guides development to conform to policies regarding land use. Secondly, the process must be fair, consistent, and predictable. Lastly, the system should be equitable —public costs should be borne proportionately by those who benefit from new development.

At some point these goals may be mutually reinforcing; at others they will conflict. Minimum standards must be established which are not open to compromise, and opportunities for trade-offs should be made explicit. In the last analysis, there may be no final "product," but rather the beginning of an on-going process where the land use regulatory system is continually monitored for its responsiveness to changing local needs.

SELECTED BIBLIOGRAPHY
ON STATE AND LOCAL TECHNIQUES
TO
IMPROVE REGULATORY EFFICIENCY
IN LAND USE CONTROLS

American Law Institute. *A Model Land Development Code.* Proposed Official Draft. May 21, 1975. Philadelphia, The American Law Institute.

Bosselman, Fred, et. al. *The Permit Explosion: Coordination of the Proliferation.* Urban Land Institute, Washington, D.C. 1976.

Burchell, Robert W. and Listokin, David. "The Impact of Local Governmental Regulations on Housing Costs and Potential Avenues for State Meliorative Measures." *Thirteen Perspectives on Regulatory Simplification*, ULI Research Report No. 29. Urban Land Institute, Washington, D.C. 1979.

Einsweiler, Robert C. *State/Local Options in Regulatory Reform* (unpublished paper). Urban Land Institute, Washington, D.C. 1978.

Finigan, David G. "Walnut Creek's Development Review Program—It's Self-Supporting." *Western City.* September, 1978.

Hawaii Coastal Zone Management Program. *Red Tape vs. Green Light: Proceedings of a Workshop on Government Permit Simplification, Coordination and Streamlining.* Honolulu. July, 1978.

Harty, Harry, et. al. *Program Analysis for State and Local Governments*. The Urban Land Institute, Washington, D.C. 1976.

Healy, Robert C. *Environmentalists and Developers: Can They Agree on Anything?* The Conservation Foundation, Washington, D.C. 1977.

International City Management Association. "Measuring Effectiveness of Municipal Services." *Management Information Service*, Vol. 2, No. LS-S, August, 1970.

"The Permit Application Center: Time, Money Saved." *Municipal Management Innovation*, Series No. 25, Spring, 1978.

Jarret, J. and Hicks, Jr. *Untangling the Permit Web: Washington's Environmental Coordination Procedures Action*. The Council of State Governments, Lexington, Ky. June, 1978.

Lauber, Daniel. *The Hearing Examiner in Zoning Administration*. PAS Report No. 312. ASPO, Chicago, Ill. 60637. 1975.

Longhini, Gregory. "Steamlined Permitting Procedures." *Planning Advisory Service Memo, No. 78-9*. ASPO, Chicago, Ill. September, 1978.

May, James W. "Regulatory Simplification: The Florida Experience" (Unpublished paper). Urban Land Institute, Washington, D.C., 1978.

International City Management Association. "Measuring Government Effectiveness." *Governmental Finance*, (entire issue). November 1973.

O'Mara, Paul. "Regulation: Where Do We Go From Here?" *Urban Land*, Vol. 37, No. 5. May, 1978.

Rice Center for Community Design and Research. *The Delay Cost of Government Regulation in the Houston Market*. May, 1978.

Sagalyn, Lynne B. and Sternlieb, George. *Zoning and Housing Costs*. Center for Urban Policy Research, Rutgers University. 1973.

San Mateo County. *Final Report on the Study of the Development Review Process*. Redwood City, Ca. February, 1978.

Seattle Land Use Administration Task Force: Report. April 1978.

Senecal, Kenneth E. "Regulatory Coordination in Vermont" (unpublished paper). Urban Land Institute, Washington, D.C. 1978.

So, Frank S. "Tips on Cutting the Delays of Regulation," *Planning*, No. 44, No. 9., pp. 16-20. October, 1978.

Starnes, Earl, et al. "Is One-Stop Permitting a Good Idea?" (Unpublished article). University of Florida, Department of Urban and Regional Planning. July 18, 1978.

Styles, Frederick G. "Sacramento County's Dual Planning Commission—Improving the Local Planning Process." *Environmental Comment*, September, 1978.

Urban Land Institute. *Environmental Comment*, entire issue. May, 1976.

U.S. Department of Housing and Urban Development. *Final Report of the Task Force on Housing Costs*. May 25, 1978.

Vitt, Joseph E. "Developing in a Cooperative Environment," *Urban Land*, November, 1978.

Wickersham, Kirk, Jr. "A Lot More than Just an Ordinance: The Breckenridge Development Code." *Urban Land*. January, 1979.

Wright, Laurie K. "Streamlining the Permit Process," *OPR Journal*, Vol. 1, No. 2. State of California, Office of Planning and Research. October, 1978.

14

Modifying Land Use Regulations for Economic Development

Cheryl Farr

LAND USE and development regulation activities at the local government level include zoning, building codes, and subdivision regulations. Because they affect both the community's future and the individual's fortunes, they are the focus of many meetings, elections, and press articles. Yet a majority of local officials would probably agree that their communities' land use regulations and development permit processes are overwhelming. In places the regulations appear to have been written in Sanskrit. Trying to change them, however, can stir up trouble. Everyone has a war story about the time he tried and failed.

Reforms have been attempted for good reasons, though, and recent studies indicate that these reasons are not going away. They exist more than ever. When a developer or builder has to hold onto land for several months while the subdivision approval process grinds along ever so slowly, he has to pay interest on money that has been borrowed for the project. This ends up costing the home buyer thousands of dollars, which can shut some buyers out of the market. The result is that many developers can only afford to build very expensive housing. The prices developers are paying for raw land, building materials, and labor are so high that delays can push costs for a moderate income housing project too high for them to make a reasonable return on investment.

Local regulations also hurt local job development programs. Many communities search for ways to cut development costs by cutting land costs, providing infrastructure, and seeking federal funding sources. For small and medium sized communities interested in encouraging the development or retention of local industrial and commercial enterprises, untangling local regulatory requirements and procedures has proven to be an effective and low-cost incentive.

Background

Business location decisions are based on the availability of land, a labor force, a market for goods, raw materials for industrial processes, and capital for development financing and operating costs. Cutting regulatory delay is just one of many approaches in influencing business location decisions. It has the effect of making land relatively more "available" by reducing the risk that the project will fail. And it reduces development costs by shortening the time between the developer's first look at the property and the day the doors open for business, thereby reducing the costs of financing the project's development.

Many communities seek to encourage development by cutting businesses' fixed costs through tax abatements, which reduce property taxes for a specified number of years. Tax incentives often cost the city more than the revenues they produce, and have little if any effect on business location decisions, according to much recent research. Taxes are a small percentage of a business's total costs; most firms claim that they pick a location based on transportation, market, and labor force concerns and would not have changed their decision if the tax incentive was not offered.[1]

If the desired result of a local economic development strategy is to reduce development costs, finding ways to cut regulatory delay can be a tool which does not have a negative, long-term impact on revenue in the community. Rising interest costs make delay and uncertainty increasingly expensive for developers and builders. When money has to be borrowed at close to 18 percent interest, every wasted day can cost hundreds of dollars even on a project that is not terribly large. One recent study showed that each month of delay adds one percent to two percent to the selling price of a house. At that rate, four months of delay would tack $3,600 onto the price of a $45,000 home.[2]

Regulations at the state and local level are frequently amended over the years to address timely concerns. The confusing result can often cause the city staff, local boards, and elected officials to waste uncounted hours re-reviewing projects. Regulatory reform can save your city time and money (in the form of staff salary hours). Some regulatory changes may actually result in a net increase in staff hours spent on development projects, but it is hoped that this will only happen because local economic development objectives are being met.

This report will look at regulatory reform and local economic development through the programs of several communities. The lesson from their experience is succinct: figure out what's most important to you in development and try to find a way to expedite projects that further that goal. With a sluggish economy, there is less growth. At the same time there is increasing interest among local governments in capturing the jobs and tax revenues that commercial and industrial growth can bring. Developers and builders will tell you that what they most want from city hall is to see a positive attitude toward growth. This does not mean handouts. It means that you say directly that you want to see the project happen, and help it go forward as expeditiously as possible. Every approach must be a personalized one, because the regulatory stumbling blocks to development are different depending on local land characteristics, state requirements, and staff and board personalities.

The report examines where and how regulations can cost time and money, and provides some suggestions on ways to streamline your own regulations. It describes some approaches communities have used to reduce regulatory confusion. The approach of Danvers, Massachusetts, is examined in depth because it accomplishes the key goal in local regulatory reform: creating a program that can gain local support. The report concludes with a look at the common approaches leading to regulatory solutions that support local economic development goals.

Land Use Regulation: Whose Job Is It?

Land use regulation has a lot in common with the fashion industry. Trends come in and out of style, and some designs are meant to restrict movement, others to encourage it. And one thing never changes. Regardless of the current trend and its popularity (or lack of popularity), there is, in almost every case, a minimum amount of regulation (or clothing) that is considered necessary for health, safety, and the general welfare. However, unlike the needs and styles of clothing, the debate will probably never be resolved concerning which regulations are critical and who ought to be doing the regulating.

The seventies was a decade in which land use regulations gained new notoriety. The rapid development in the fifties and sixties of rural areas had caused problems which some observers felt were the result of ineffective local control. Concern over environmental degradation and the protection of "critical areas" which crossed local jurisdictional boundaries led to a movement to encourage greater regulation of land use at state and regional levels of government. Today that movement boasts some successes, particularly in programs developed under the Coastal Zone Management Act of 1972 and in state land use planning and control programs in Oregon, Hawaii, and Florida. But recent years have seen few new state programs enacted. In addition, court decisions have recently invalidated some state regulations of critical areas on the grounds that they constituted a taking of private land without just compensation due to their restriction of the use of land.[3]

One of the main causes identified for the slow acceptance of state and regional attempts at land use regulation has been resistance at the local level, some of which is clearly the result of turf battles. Much of this is caused by the justifiable belief that land use regulation belongs at the local level. Robert G. Healy, in his work, *Land Use and the States*, puts it this way:

> It is important to separate the failure of specific local controls from the shortcomings of the concept of "local control." If local zoning has failed, the fault may lie with the tool rather than with the level of government that wields it. Given new policy instruments, new property tax systems, and tough conflict-of-interest laws and prodded by an environmentally aware citizenry, local government can go far toward improving the quality of their land use. A record of local government failure in dealing with land use conflicts does not in itself mean that the state could do a more effective job.

Our working presumption here will be that local control of land use is, other things equal, the most desirable arrangement. In judging the merits of most land use changes, local authorities are not only better informed about the facts of the situation but are also (at least ideally) more responsive to the interests affected. When higher levels of government deal with such problems, they typically must create layers of bureaucracy simply to channel the appropriate information to decision-makers. The decision-makers, moreover, are responsible to a constituency which is probably far larger than the group of citizens affected by most land use decisions. Thus, by virtue not only of tradition, but of efficiency and political responsiveness, there is a strong case for local control of land use.[4]

Zoning of land is a power delegated by states to local governments. This relationship was first upheld in court in 1926 in the case, Village of Euclid vs. Ambler Realty. The court found that a municipal zoning ordinance bore a substantial relationship to the public welfare and inflicted no irreparable injury on the landowner.

The right of cities to regulate land use was challenged earlier this year in the Supreme Court in the case, Agins vs. Tiburon. The court's decision, in

June 1980, that open space zoning laws do not automatically involve a taking of property was unanimous in favor of the city. The court said, in part:

> . . . the zoning ordinances substantially advance legitimate governmental goals. The State of California has determined that the development of local open space plans will discourage the 'premature and unnecessary conversion of open space land to urban uses.' The specific zoning regulations at issue are exercises of the city's police power to protect the residents of Tiburon from the ill-effects of urbanization. . . . The zoning ordinances benefit the appellants as well as the public by serving the city's interest in assuring careful and orderly development of residential property with the provision for open space areas. In assessing the fairness of the zoning ordinance, these benefits must be considered along with any diminution in market value that the appellants might suffer.[5]

While the decision did not answer the question of when such ordinances require compensation to the landowner, it did reaffirm the right of cities to control land use.

As surely as pressure will continue from developers and landowners to protect the market value of their land, so will pressure come from various interest groups to modify, strengthen, and increase regulations to protect the environment, to provide housing for people of all income levels, to accommodate growth within the fiscal constraints of the community's ability to provide services, and to create a built environment that is safe, sanitary, and enhances the quality of life. Some of the regulations will be tested through court battles and lost for going beyond the boundaries of providing for health, safety, and general welfare; others will be upheld. Meanwhile, the pressure for state or regional land use controls will also continue because of the different needs and concerns of other interest groups. The events of recent years, however, suggest that much of the responsibility will remain at the local level.

Land use regulation serves many good purposes. But it also affects the development cost of building by restricting the supply of buildable land, by requiring the use of specific materials and on- and off-site improvements, and by causing delay through lengthy procedural requirements. The goals of some local government regulations have, over time, become lost in the project-by-project world of development. It is important for local government to step back and look at the effects of existing development regulations, and the relationship of these regulations to local needs.

Effects of Local Ordinances:
Housing vs. Business Development

Local governments tend to regulate housing development more strictly than other forms of development, primarily because of concern over revenues and expenditures. As most local officials know, industries and commercial establishments generally produce more local tax revenues than they demand in services. Housing developments, on the other hand, generally do not. They can result in the need for new schools, parks, and other community facilities, and social services which are expensive to both establish and maintain. So, many communities have sought to pass on at least a portion of these residential growth costs to the developer by requiring on- and off-site improvements which are then passed on to the consumer through higher purchase prices.

Even when businesses are required to make on- and off-site improvements when developing a tract of land, the costs of complying with specific regulations are not usually a source of complaint from the developer. There are two primary reasons for this. First, the revenue producing status of businesses makes their development projects subject to different financing criteria. Second, as a percentage of total project costs, a small, *well-defined* cost for certain improvements to the property is relatively unimportant.

From the perspective of the non-residential developer, it appears that the major concern is over the costs (in time and money) of delays which cannot be anticipated. These delays are associated with the regulatory procedures rather than the requirements themselves. The message from developers of commercial and industrial properties is quite clear: be specific about what documentation you want, what type of building and site development requirements will be allowed, and how long the regulatory process will take. Forewarning prospective developers and businesses about problems and producing what you promise are effective ways of showing that your city has a positive attitude toward development.

How Developers View Local Regulations

A 1976 survey of the home builders' industry documents the aspects of regulation that are most frustrating and costly to the private sector. Because many of the survey respondents were land developers, and not builders of houses, the responses of commercial/industrial developers and of home builders are assumed to be comparable. As a group, the land developers ranked local discretion (34.0%) and delay (30.0%) slightly higher than those involved only in building the houses (see *Table 1*). Firms which did both land development and building "overwhelmingly sided with the land developers and chose local discretion (28.6%) and delay (27.7%) as the most burdensome aspect of their experiences."[6]

Table 1 shows that the regional differences are small. Discretion and delay are by far the most burdensome aspects of regulations, even for home builders who generally are subject to stronger limitations on what can be built than commercial property developers.

TABLE 1.—*Most Burdensome Aspects of Government Regulations by Region (Percent*)*

Aspects of Regulations	Northeast (n = 386)	South (n = 887)	North Central (n = 502)	West (n = 375)	National Average (n = 2150)
Local administrative discretion	33.9	22.0	28.3	24.5	25.9
Unnecessary delays	21.8	27.5	21.3	30.1	25.7
Costs of paperwork, filing permits, etc.	10.9	17.6	21.3	14.1	16.8
Limitations on what can be built	13.7	10.0	11.8	8.0	10.7
Lack of coordination among government agencies	14.5	17.6	14.3	19.5	16.3
Other	5.2	5.3	3.0	3.7	4.6
Total	100.0	100.0	100.0	100.0	100.0

*May not add to 100.0% due to rounding.

Perhaps even more interesting are the responses of development firms to the question of whether or not regulations affect their choices of development locations (see *Table 2*). In all regions of the country the majority said that government regulations were an "important consideration" in their choice of location for development.[7]

These tables only suggest how the development industry views local government land use regulations. To know that regulations do affect developers' location decisions does not simplify decision making locally. Too little regulation can cause a variety of problems: downstream storm runoff, dangerous street designs which reduce fire protection capability and cause driving hazards, and monotonous or ugly development to name a few.

How can you decide if your city's regulations are protecting your community or hurting it by driving the cost of housing out of sight and discouraging the development of business? There is no one answer or a right set of regulations. Model regulations are not always useful because they require too much change too fast. The next section will offer some actions your city can take to evaluate local regulations and permit processes and to see where changes can be made.

Evaluating Your Ordinance: Trouble Spots and Solutions

The following is a step-by-step process to help you identify critical spots in your city's regulations that might be causing trouble. Some solutions that have been suggested for each of the trouble spots are also provided.[8]

Step One: Jot Down Your Community's Goals

Before sitting down to your local zoning ordinances, jot down your community's goals for commercial and industrial development. They may already be available in a local growth plan, development proposal, or council resolution. Try to come up with the most specific list possible, and *be realistic*. Identify goals that are possible to meet and that address community needs. Below are two examples of possible goals.

Priority One. Small assembly plants are needed for six parcels of the City Industrial Park. The plants should provide at least 40 percent low-skill jobs paying no less than _____ per hour, because unemployment among semi-skilled workers is high.

Priority Two. Some specialty shops (selling perhaps ceramics or designer merchandise) and restaurants would help the Town Center Commercial District. We know there is a potential market for such items because local income levels could support it and the competition from other businesses is over 25 minutes driving distance away.

TABLE 2.—*Importance of Government Regulations in Deciding Where to Develop by Region (Percent*)*

Size of Firm* (units)	Number of Municipalities	Not Considered	Considered Somewhat	Important Consideration	Total
Northeast	(405)	9.6	18.8	71.6	100.0
South	(971)	11.8	22.9	65.3	100.0
North Central	(521)	10.6	24.2	65.2	100.0
West	(384)	6.3	17.2	76.6	100.0
Average	(2239)	10.2	21.7	68.2	100.0

*May not add to 100.0% due to rounding.

Ask private sector people (developers, bankers, business persons) what they would change in your local ordinance. Use all this material to draw up a "wish list" of what you want to do.

Step Two: Review Your Equipment Specifications and Submission Criteria

Equipment Specifications. Many local regulations specify the use of certain building practices or materials for structures and/or site improvements. Some of these standards have been criticized for preventing innovation and driving up development costs by requiring overly expensive materials and construction practices. The most important things to look for in reviewing these specifications are: (a) how specific or vague they are about the use of certain designs or materials, and (b) the requirements for frontage, setbacks, lot size, road widths, etc.

As far as building practices and materials go, it is important to try to keep up with design advances and to use as models up-to-date building codes, such as recent revisions by the Building Officials Conference of America. In the case of roads, sewer lines, and other infrastructure charges it is important to compare who benefits from their development against who pays for their costs. If a substantial portion of the benefit goes to a larger population (including future residents) than the one covering the costs, alternative ways of financing the investment such as local bond issues should be considered.

Submission Criteria. The criteria which local boards use to decide whether to permit a project to be built as proposed, to permit a project to be built with modifications, or to deny permission for building a project are worth looking at very carefully. Submission criteria come into play when a project is only a possibility, and require a developer to tie up both time and money with a sometimes less-than-even chance of reaping any benefits.

Ambiguous criteria can make the local planning board's decision rather arbitrary. Watch out for phrases like "reasonable number of parking spaces," "pleasing landscape design," or "adequate outdoor lighting." You may not want to change these phrases to numbers, but it will help developers if you have some idea of what was "reasonable" or "pleasing" in the last few projects that came up. Recognize that if the criteria for decision making are too general, the lack of guidance can cause lengthy negotiations with local boards. If they are too exacting, the developer may have to spend a lot of money on maps, surveys, and design drawings while running the risk that the project will be rejected. A development project is an expensive risk, and if attractive alternative sites are available elsewhere, the developer will probably try the alternative first.

Where submission criteria are concerned, try to be specific about what is required and why it is needed. At the very least, do not force developers to guess. Write a list of what information is needed in an information sheet. . . . If possible, arrange for a pre-application conference to allow the presentation of proposals without formal design drawings. Scheduling this meeting in the early stages to discuss what will and will not be acceptable can make for an easier negotiation process at a later stage. This pre-application step is used by two of the cities discussed later in this report (Danvers, Massachusetts, and Rockville, Maryland).

Step Three: Place Responsibility for Proposal Decisions with One Board

The processing of applications with their requirements for notice and public hearings can cause long delays between the conception of a project and its completion. Developers have complained that decision makers unfamiliar with the development process and its costs make excessive demands or do not judge the project by the standards set in the zoning ordinances. An additional problem is the practice of shuttling proposals through a number of boards and departments, with different and often conflicting requirements.

The first step in processing applications is to create submission criteria which limit the discretion of boards by providing clear standards to be used in judging projects. Where possible, responsibility should be placed with one board for all proposal decisions, with other relevant boards and departments required to submit their comments to that board within a specified time frame. Both developers and planners have encouraged the use of hearing examiners who understand development, rather than laymen. All those involved in a hearing should have a purpose for being there and should understand their role in making comments and decisions.

Step Four: Inform Council about Ongoing Projects

Local follow-through on projects can be a real problem when one administration makes promises, leaves office, and then successors overturn its decisions. Developers make it their business to become familiar with the local political climate. When it sways from growth to no-growth, developers for good reason are wary about starting a project which will be completed in phases over a number of years. The manager can help acquaint new council members with ongoing projects, and plays an important role in maintaining continuity between administrations.

On another level, the ability of the staff to make and keep promises is particularly important. One of the most important roles managers with community/economic development staffs play is providing their staffs with credibility by making it clear that the city will deliver what the staff promises. To do this effectively managers must make it their business to be aware of (and keep councils informed about) ongoing negotiations between staff and private sector representatives.

Economic growth resolutions passed by the council can provide a base for local actions. One suggestion is to require all amendments to local ordinances to be evaluated for their impact on local economic development plans.

Step Five: Develop Informal Methods to Accomplish Your Goals

In some cases it is going to be impossible to make all or even some of the changes you might like to make in the local ordinances to overcome procedural or substantive impediments to your goals. Because land use regulation mechanisms become familiar to and accepted by local citizens and officials, they are difficult to change radically. Try to think of ways to make changes outside your formal regulatory process. For example, use an informal preliminary review team of key staffers for major projects you want to have happen in the city, as Rockville, Maryland, has done. This informal review does not make any binding commitments between the city and the developer, but it does give the developer a chance to see how well an idea will work before submitting complete design plans for approval. Another idea is to try out a proposed process change on a developer before trying to get it adopted as law, as Danvers, Massachusetts, has done. (See the case studies which follow for other informal approaches.)

This section has suggested a framework for evaluating your development regulations and permit processes and strengthening spots in the process that might be causing problems. Unless your city is a lot different than the average city, the initial list of goals will probably be longer on "dreams" than on "do-ables." To accomplish a realistic goal, it is worthwhile to start by looking for a way to change one or two of the impediments to meeting that goal. Focused change may gain more support among local boards and from the city council, and if successful in helping the city meet its goals, can engender support for future changes. The next section highlights the land use regulation changes that three cities focused on to foster their economic development goals.

Cutting Regulatory Delay on Higher Quality Development: Danvers, Massachusetts

Danvers, Massachusetts, a community of roughly 25,000 persons, is located about a half hour's drive north of downtown Boston. Danvers has had a town manager government since 1949. The manager is appointed by a five-member board of selectmen.

The community's location, enhanced by good access to major highways, a small port facility, and the availability of rail, freight, and commuter lines, has made Danvers an attractive development choice. However, not all of the development that has come to Danvers has had a positive impact on the community. When Danvers began to feel the budget squeeze of the late 1970s, the town leaders looked at what previous development had brought to the community. Local leaders were trying to determine what kind of development would help increase local tax revenues, but not hurt the quality of life.

Choosing Industrial Development

Residential development boomed in the fifties and sixties. But the revenue over expenditure contribution was small because of the new demand housing generated for roads, sewers, water, and social services. The growth had caused serious drainage problems in some areas, and available residential sites with sewer service were few. Actively encouraging such growth did not promise to provide significant revenues over expenditures. Still, housing needs were not ignored. A HUD grant for rehabilitation of dilapidated housing was helping low to moderate income and elderly homeowners repair their houses, and some small housing developments were under way.

Danvers's location near the crossroads of several state and local routes and in the midst of many "bedroom communities" had made it an ideal site for commercial development. But the town already had a much larger percentage of its workforce in commercial businesses than the regional average, and market studies showed little potential for additional commercial growth. Even if there was that potential, a program to revitalize the downtown commercial area was taking form, and creating additional competition for that project was not desirable.

Industrial development seemed to be the most likely candidate for new development which would generate revenues. Danvers's undeveloped industrial land included two large parcels with good access to major roads and owners interested in selling. Industrial growth had been weak in New England for some time, but state and regional analyses showed that the market had improved. Office space and high-tech manufacturing development was rapidly occurring in communities on Route 128, the road that loops through Boston's suburbs, and land costs had risen as a result. Route 95, the interstate running north-south, had recently been extended into the area and development was following it towards New Hampshire. Danvers' location made it a prime candidate to attract industry or office space in the burgeoning market. Area statistics show that there is a large labor force available, and costs of wages and benefits are slightly lower than in towns closer to Boston. Danvers's tax rate is also lower than many nearby communities with industrial land.

Some industrial development had taken place in Danvers in recent years, but much of it was considered by town officials to be of poor design, attracting companies with small growth potential and jobs that offered few opportunities for advancement. A study of growth industries regionally showed that Danvers was not attracting many of the higher quality industries (in terms of wages, projected growth, and industrial process side effects like noise and air pollution) that nearby communities had attracted. Town officials believed that the regional growth industries such as computer parts and scientific and research instruments ought to be encouraged to locate in Danvers. The question was how to do it.

Studying Industrial Zoning Requirements

The town's community development division, which was given responsibility for local economic development in 1978, began to gather information about the business community's attitude toward the town. Community Development Director John Mahoney met with several area developers to find out their perceptions about Danvers's future growth and how Danvers could encourage attractive development. The division conducted a mail survey of local manufacturing firms to see what the town could do to encourage them to grow. The responses were straightforward: the procedures required to get permission to build were long and confusing, and the results were never certain. A few respondents complained that the town gave industries too low a priority on snow plowing routes, but otherwise there appeared to be general satisfaction with services.

The town manager requested the community development division to review the current zoning regulations for industrial land. The review found that they were extremely lenient, but vague. In 1961, when the regulations were written, industrial growth was only a future possibility. The concern was to reserve land for future use rather than to develop realistic regulations for an industrial zone. The only industrial zoning requirements were that no more than 50 percent of the lot be covered with buildings, that there be adequate setbacks, and that there be off-street loading and parking facilities. The community development division recognized one additional existing regulation as a stymie to development: almost half of each of the two largest industrial sites available was overlain by an Inland Floodplain Zone. Within this area, the building of roads and parking areas would require an Order of Conditions from the conservation commission, as well as a special permit from the board of appeals. The building of any structure in an Inland Floodplain Zone requires, in addition to a special permit, a variance. Subdivision plans also required a separate process, with additional submission criteria and restrictions.

As this review of the current regulations was beginning, the planning board, with the aid of a consultant, was completing a revision of the town zoning bylaws for adoption by town meeting. (Town meeting is the forum through which system changes are implemented in Massachusetts communities like Danvers.) The proposed zoning bylaws included substantial modifications to the industrial regulations. The revisions were much more strict than the regulations in force because the planning board members believed that the old regulations had encouraged haphazard, unattractive development to occur on sites bordering residential neighborhoods.

The proposed changes of the planning board would make the development of the major available sites subject to two separate, special permit processes: one for subdivision of the land, and one for crossing over wetlands with roads. Frontage requirements jumped from 20 feet to 200 feet, and setbacks were also extended. Because no lot would be allowed to have more than one-third coverage of buildings and accessory structures, and remaining open space could not be more than 50 percent wetlands, the proposed regulations would effectively preclude almost all development on the two most attractively located large sites.

The planning board had received little direction from town officials in setting land use policy. For the most part it initiated zoning reform ideas on its own, employing outside consultants for technical assistance. Discussions with the town manager, the planning board, and the community development division helped clarify the problems that this lack of communication had caused. The planning board agreed to not request adoption of its proposed changes for one year and to consider alternative proposals which would be developed by the community development division.

The community development division began to tackle the problem of finding a way to reconcile industrial growth and environmental protection. The first major decision was to focus the division's efforts on solving the development problems of having wetlands on the large available sites because of the larger impact their development would have on the town, and because of the sites' development potential.

Reform of all the local regulations and development procedures was not likely to succeed in the short run. The basic reason for the continuation of the old system was obvious: the current legal and administrative processes were the status quo. In the old system a variety of town departments, local boards, and citizen groups would concentrate on specific issues and rarely consider the overall question of how development affects the public welfare. That system was accepted and understood by the town meeting members. Any proposal for a more integrated process would require a base of support from the individuals whose influence over development could be undermined by the change. Major modifications could not gain that support.

The approach which the community development division took was to create a special permit process for large industrial parcels that would streamline the permit process and involve town staff early in the procedure. Developers are given the option of using the planned industrial area special permit process for any industrial development on a parcel over 50 acres in size.

Developing the Planned Industrial Area Special Permit

There were three goals in using the new permit:

- Protecting wetlands within the parcels
- Finding a way to interest some of the state's best developers and companies in the sites
- Allowing developers a reasonable rate of return on their investments, while requiring an attractively designed industrial area.

An overriding concern was to *decrease* the red tape that was associated with the development process, as it was believed that this was the key to interesting potential developers in designing an attractive area.

The planned industrial area (PIA) special permit process allows industrial development at a greater density than would normally be allowed in an area substantially overlain by Inland Floodplain Districts (wetlands). One condition is that the developer must place conservation restrictions on critical wetlands and adhere to strict site design requirements. More important than the density bonus, according to area developers interested in using the PIA permit, it ties in key local government officials and boards early in the process, and seeks to cut delay in the permit process by consolidating the decision-making powers into one authority.

The objectives of the special permit process are broad, but the process includes specific criteria which are used to judge whether a proposal meets these goals.

Wetlands Protection. The intent of the PIA process is not to allow continued modification to the Inland Floodplain District, but to encourage quality development. Without this special permit process, in areas where there are substantial wetlands problems developers would be encouraged to create lower quality and less attractive industrial development in order to maximize profit from a site constrained by regulations.

The PIA is an approach which looks at the overall impact of the development. The developer has an incentive to increase the number of buildings through the modification of wetlands, but in exchange must place permanent conservation restrictions on a percentage of the remaining open space, and must show that the development will not increase the rate of storm water runoff from the property. The town suggests the development of water retention ponds for this purpose, as well as for their aesthetic value. The conservation commission believes that the conservation restriction serves as a much greater protection for wetlands than does the inland floodplain map, which is subject to modification.

Reducing Red Tape. The PIA concept, in its attempt to manage growth, has been written to be administratively less complicated and more practical than the present or proposed zoning regulations. It consolidates the powers of control of the subdivision process and wetlands regulation into one special permit, under one board, to prevent shuttling the developer between boards for lengthy and confusing negotiations. It requires *all* the key individuals in the development process to meet for a pre-application conference so that the developer can present a tenative proposal without spending a lot a money on plans, surveys, and purchase agreements.

The following individuals must attend: the applicant, town manager, manager of community development, planning board chair or a representative, board of selectmen chair or a representative, conservation commission chair or a representative, board of appeals chair or a representative, director of public works, town counsel, building inspector, fire chief, electric light superintendent, and industrial development commission chair or a representative. The pre-application conference must be held within ten days of an applicant's request.

Before the PIA bylaw was adopted it was tested through a pre-submission of plans conference with a developer. (The developer had bought a 96 acre parcel and hoped to develop it under the PIA regulations. This land had been subdivided into six lots by a previous owner, and would have been built under the old regulations if the PIA zoning had not been passed. It could not have been built as six lots if the proposed planning board amendments were in effect, but the six lot subdivision would have been "grandfathered," and therefore allowed.) Before drafting building and lot design plans for approval by the planning board the developer met with the pre-application conference team listed above to discuss his plans. In effect, he went through the process before it was adopted by the town so that its effect could be roughly evaluated. This preliminary test suggested that the PIA process would shorten the permit process for such a development from approximately eighteen months to six months. The developer, at a public hearing on the proposed special permit, commented, "It's the best process I've been through."

Interest in the PIA process also came from a developer who planned to buy a 120 acre parcel and create a park for computer parts assembly plants. The developer said that what generated his interest was the fact that the process involves the staff.

"Attractive Design": Letting Developers Know What It Means. An attempt has been made throughout the PIA permit process to specify criteria for judging whether or not the project meets the requirements. This has been done to provide the special permit authority with some clear-cut items when evaluating a proposal. Perhaps the best examples are the site design criteria. Individual lots are evaluated based on the following criteria.

- The building or structure should contribute to the overall area's character and design. Scale, proportion, texture, color or materials, and landscaping are considered.
- Exterior lighting should illuminate a building and its grounds for safety purposes, and not in a manner that draws more attention to the building or grounds at night than in the day.
- Landscape design and planning should be part of the overall area design.
- Parking areas should include a minimum of 10 percent of their gross area as landscaping, low lights of a human scale, and safety lighting to emphasize barriers, entrances, and exits. (Off-street loading areas need not conform to parking area requirements, so long as they are adequately screened from public view, and from the view of adjacent properties.)

Landscaping according to the approved site plan must be completed, or a cash bond posted for its estimated cost, before the building inspector can issue an occupancy permit.

While the town attorney is wary of "aesthetic zoning" and has not encouraged the use of the types of criteria mentioned above in the town's overall site design review process, he has not rejected them for the special permit process. Site design criteria for projects other than those under the PIA special permit process cover only off-street parking and trash receptacle areas. By allowing density bonuses when site design criteria are addressed, and by offering a fast-track permit process, the town of Danvers encourages acceptance of the PIA site design requirements.

Summary

Danvers adopted the PIA permit process in June 1980 as a town bylaw. It does not incorporate any revolutionary ideas. It is simply a recombination of several well known land use mechanisms to fit this town's needs. The concept of allowing individual lots to have joint parking areas and driveways and encouraging clustering of open space and buildings is taken from cluster zoning mechanisms. Incentive zoning concepts fed the idea for site design and amenity requirements in exchange for the development of non-critical wetlands (provided that overall stormwater runoff is not increased by their development). The process represents Danvers's attempt to reduce red tape and encourage attractive design within the constraints of the town's existing political, legal, and administrative practices.

Even before the bylaw was adopted the PIA had an impact on Danvers' economic development: it interested new developers in the community and changed the way some town officials looked at development. In the short run, the awakened interest in Danvers by businesses and developers has shown that a positive attitude toward growth can generate good development. And Danvers's experience suggests that a negative attitude (particularly in a strong market) only discourages developers who are interested in, and recognize the financial benefits of, high quality industrial area development. In addition, the teamwork that was required to adopt the ordinance has smoothed the road for partnership in future projects between the town staff and boards.

The community development staff's ability to convince the planning board and town meeting members that the regulatory changes were important to the town's business development goals helped the reforms gain the support they needed. Limiting the fast track program to major industrial parcels meant that department and board heads would not get involved in every project. This helped the changes gain acceptance among the staff persons involved in land use and development. Finally, because attractive design is encouraged and wetlands are protected by conservation restrictions, the support of other important individuals was garnered.

The town manager plays an important role in Danvers's pro-industrial strategy, particularly in two areas. Town Manager Wayne Marquis drops in briefly to meet developers and business prospects who are discussing locating in Danvers with the community development director. Director John Mahoney says that this provides him with the credibility he needs to negotiate effectively. And to help keep all the town's development-related staff and boards involved in the town's active business development program, Marquis and key local officials get together every few weeks to discuss problems and issues relating to development.

Below are brief examples of two other local programs designed to cut regulatory delay. They suggest alternative business development strategies.

Removing Development Obstacles: Simi Valley, California

The city of Simi Valley, California (population: 70,000), began a comprehensive strategy to encourage business development in 1977 with three separate approaches to cutting regulatory irritants out of the development process. The city developed a program that would confront physical, procedural, and attitudinal obstacles to business development.

First, the city council directed the city's planning commission and staff to give higher priority to reviewing and processing commercial and industrial applications than to residential applications. The result was that business

applicants experienced two-thirds less processing time than residential
building applicants. The city council also made it possible for the planning
director to give approval to commercial development proposed for areas
with specified development criteria. This shortened review time by cutting
out planning commission review.

Second, the city council adopted a blanket environment impact review
(EIR) covering 425 acres of land in three major industrial and commercial
areas. Because the EIR was completed by the city, it saves time and money
for new developers in the three areas while maintaining the integrity of the
environmental review process. This is particularly important in California,
where environmental regulations and reviews are more stringent than in
many states.

Third, for a period of one year permit fees for industrial and commercial
projects were cut to $1.00 per permit. Normally, planned development and
special use permits run over $300.00, and sign permits are $50.00. While the
savings on a project may have been small as a percentage of total costs, the
action said a lot about the city's interest in business growth.

The bargain permit fees were only in effect for one year, but Simi Valley
is still giving priority to business development applications and is making
use of its blanket environmental impact review data. The city also updates
its general plan every five years to keep it current with local needs and concerns, and is currently creating an effective promotion strategy for the
community.

Encouraging Downtown Revitalization:
Rockville, Maryland

The city of Rockville, Maryland (population: 45,000), wants to encourage commercial and office space development in the town center. Rockville, a suburban city located north of Washington, D.C., and the county
seat for Montgomery County, has experienced significant growth in housing development over the last decade. The city decided several years ago
that a concerted effort would be necessary to help its town center commercial district come back to life and compete with new commercial growth in
other areas.

One of the city's approaches to meeting its redevelopment goals was to
reduce development processing time by offering a one-stop service. The
goal was process developer's plans faster than they can draw them. In the
surrounding county's unincorporated areas it takes roughly 1,000 days for a
large project to go from raw land to breaking ground; a similar project in
Rockville takes about nine months.

Recently, the city created a development coordination team to help expedite major project proposals. The team is composed of the director of

public works, the director of finance, the director of planning, and the director of community development and housing assistance. Developers considering a large project (e.g., from 200,000 to 500,000 square feet of mixed use) may request an informal meeting with the development coordination team, which will preview the plans if team members think the project is an important one.

Developers like the process because they do not have to make a large commitment for project design and surveys before they have a sense of the level of local government support for the project. The city staff likes it because it allows it to let a developer know early if there is a problem with the concept. The staff may encourage the developer to go ahead as planned, offer suggestions for ways to make the project more acceptable, or tell the developer that it will not support the project. The developer is then able to decide what to do next with an awareness of the sort of objections that could be raised by the staff.

An urban design scheme and innovative zoning requirements are also part of the city's program to interest developers in the central business district. The city's pro-development activities, put in high gear about five years ago, have had positive results for local commercial/residential property tax ratios. Historically, commercial properties have made up approximately 24 percent of Rockville's assessed value. Today, the figure is up to 31 percent.

Conclusion

Because the costs imposed on a developer are passed on to the home buyer or the consumer of goods and services, in the end we all pay a high price for excessive regulation. As the clamor over the high cost of regulation grows louder, pressure to cut regulation inevitably increases. In addition, many communities have realized that some land use regulations and procedures are working against efforts to provide jobs, tax relief, and reasonably priced housing for local residents. Communities which recognize the costs of regulation for both developers and consumers must seek individual solutions to meet their needs.

The examples of Danvers, Simi Valley, and Rockville have common threads which were woven into overall programs that are uniquely their own. The common threads are:

- An economic development goal or project which addresses specific sites and/or job development needs in the community, and an approach to cutting regulations that gives priority to that goal or project.
- Recognition by local officials that the city staff could be instrumental in streamlining the permit process and in helping developers and business prospects reduce the costs of delay.

- A willingness to be flexible in cutting red tape, and to use both formal and informal methods to change the regulations and processes.

All three communities identified their economic development goals, and part of their strategy was to identify and "fast track" those projects or sites that would help them reach their goals. This is not an ideal solution for a planner or a developer who feels that all development delay should be minimized, but it is not an ideal world. Local officials who desire effective change might do well to think a little smaller at the start.

NOTES

[1] Jerry Jacobs, *Bidding for Business: Corporate Auctions and the Fifty Disunited States* (Washington, D.C.: Public Interest Research Group, 1979), pp. 8–10.

[2] Stephen R. Seidel, *Housing Costs and Government Regulation: Confronting the Regulatory Maze* (New Brunswick, New Jersey: Center for Urban Policy Research, 1978), p. 31.

[3] Daniel Mandelker, "The Quiet Revolution Reconsidered," *Land Use Law and Zoning Digest*, Vol. 31, No. 8, August 1979, pp. 4–7.

[4] Robert G. Healy, *Land Use and the States* (Baltimore: Johns Hopkins University Press, 1976), p. 6.

[5] Excerpted from the opinion delivered by Mr. Justice Powell on June 10, 1980 in the case of Donald W. Agins et. ux., Appellants, v. City of Tiburon, on appeal from the Supreme Court of California.

[6] Seidel, *Housing Costs and Government Regulation*, p. 31.

[7] Ibid., p. 36.

[8] This section is indebted to a variety of articles and papers on the topic of streamlining regulations published by the Urban Land Institute and the American Planning Association. Particularly useful was Annette Kolis, ed., "Thirteen Perspectives on Regulatory Simplification," *ULI Research Report #29*, 1979. Another key source was Paul O'Mara, "Regulation: Where Do We Go From Here?" *Urban Land*, May 1978, pp. 9–15.

[9] Most of the material in this section comes from Richard Kaplan and Robert Kovitz, "Business Developers: Simi Valley Wants You," *Western City*, November 1978, p. 10. It has been updated where necessary.

15

The Role of the Planner
in a Deregulated World

Douglas W. Kmiec*

L AND USE controls have proliferated within the last 50 years. Complex
land use problems have generated a host of equally complex solutions. Indeed, the progression from the common law of nuisance to
detailed building and housing codes, zoning laws, subdivision controls, and
environmental impact regulations has been a staggeringly rapid one. Not
surprisingly, many of these controls duplicate—or worse, contradict—each
other, thus increasing the cost of development. While the justification and
cost of public regulation have frequently been challenged, land use controls
are primarily local in origin, and hence, the challenges themselves have been
individual or piecemeal in nature. There have been occasional calls for the
total repeal of public controls;[1] more commonly, however, efforts like the
ALI Model Land Development Code have been directed at streamlining or
unifying the existing development control process.

Both approaches are inadequate. So long as land use decisions have
spillover or external effects that cannot be internalized through private
bargaining, some form of public control is necessary. To the extent that the
manifold existing controls invade areas more properly reserved for private
decision making, the streamlining of control addresses merely the cosmetic,
rather than the substantive, difficulties of the existing system. Thus, land
use reforms have often taken all-or-nothing positions.

---

*Editor's Note: *This commentary is an adaptation of a more comprehensive examina-
tion by the author of an alternative land use management system,* Deregulating Land Use: An
Alternative Free Enterprise Development System, *in* 130 U. PA. L. REV. 28 (1981).

Reprinted from Douglas W. Kmiec. "The Role of the Planner in a Deregulated World."
Land Use Law & Zoning Digest (June 1982). Copyright © 1982, American Planning Association. Reprinted by permission.

This article suggests an alternative system that is not at the extremes. The proposed system would retain public control, but only where private decisions—because of inadequate information, transaction costs, or resources —would not reach an optimal result in terms of an articulated community policy and the maximization of economic resources.

The Shortcomings of Zoning and Subdivision Regulation

The collective foundation of the existing system is its greatest shortcoming.[2] Basically, the system is designed to supersede individual decision making and the logical dimensions of the concept of private property in favor of the undefinable "general welfare." While such displacement may be well justified in the presence of a nuisancelike interference, it is without justification otherwise. Nevertheless, such unjustified interference with property and the individual is largely tolerated by the Supreme Court; however, even accepting that, one can still ask the question of how well the existing system accomplishes the values and preference it has been allowed to impose on others. Specifically, does the existing system allocate land with fairness, efficiency, flexibility, and certainty? The brief answer is: No, it does not.

In particular, the existing system is procedurally unfair because it unjustifiably accords substantial weight to self-selected samples of neighbors to the detriment of the landowner and the consumers he represents; distributionally unfair because it arbitrarily favors some landowners while burdening others; inefficient as a mechanism for internalizing spillovers because it relies upon a system of specific deterrence; inefficient as a mechanism of public control because it is fractured among numerous agencies and legislative bodies; inflexible because it is founded upon predetermined, crude categories of permitted uses unable to accommodate new development techniques; and uncertain because it is subject to changes granted without standards or without adherence to announced standards and without sufficient or consistent regard for investments made in reliance thereon.

An Outline of an Alternative System

To clean the slate, zoning and subdivision controls as presently applied to undeveloped land should be repealed and replaced by an alternative free enterprise development system ("alternative system") that would allow private decisions to determine the desired use, location, and design of land development.

To illustrate, the alternative system can be set out in a step-by-step format using as an example a landowner who voluntarily decides to develop his land into a mixed residential/commercial project.

Step 1. All undeveloped land is reclassified agricultural/open space.

Step 2. The local legislative body, after consultation with planners and the public, specifies the maximum permissible land use intensity (LUI) in each of four separate schedules for residential, commercial, industrial, and mixed-use projects.

Step 3. The landowner notifies an administrative Land Use Control Agency (LUCA) of his decision to build a residential/commercial project at or below the density permitted under the mixed-use schedule.

Step 4. An appraiser determines the difference in land value (the unearned increment) between the agricultural/open-space use and the selected mixed use.

Step 5. On the basis of the landowner's private improvement plans, LUCA specifies in the Public Improvement Contract the nature of the public improvements to be constructed with the recaptured unearned increment. (If private improvement plans materially change thereafter, the landowner is required to negotiate an Intensity Modification Contract to reflect corresponding changes in public improvements.)

Step 6. The landowner constructs private improvements as desired and public improvements as required by the Public Improvement Contract.

Step 7. The subdivision plat is recorded for the purpose of accurate title description.

This outline covers the whole of the alternative system. What follows is a closer look at some of its parts. First, the proposal to reclassify all undeveloped land to agricultural/open space will be evaluated in light of recent Supreme Court decisions dealing with land use regulation and the constitutional requirement that property not be taken for public use without the payment of just compensation. Second, the scope of public land use control is narrowed to issues of land use intensity. Third, the treatment of, and objections to, contractual land use agreements under both the existing and alternative systems are examined. Fourth, the role of the neighbor under the existing system will be explored. Suggestions will be made for redirecting neighbor participation toward policy making, rather than toward policy application.

Finally, methods of financing public improvements under the existing system are examined in relation to the alternative system's proposal to recapture the unearned increment and apply it to the cost of public improvement.

Uniform Reclassification of Undeveloped Land

The radical step of reclassifying all undeveloped land to agriculture/open space serves three primary purposes: (1) it generally vests a reasonable beneficial or economically viable minimum use in the landowner; (2) it avoids the classification of land into preestablished categories and the inevitable legislative, judicial, and administrative challenges to such classification; and (3) it establishes a base land value for later use of the unearned increment of land value attributable to adjacent public and private improvement.

The taking issue has proven to be a source of considerable divergence for land use scholars[3] and a source of considerable confusion for the courts. Nevertheless, the Supreme Court's contemporary analysis in *Penn Central Transportation Co. v. City of New York*, 438 U.S. 104 (1978), 28 ZD 545, and *Agins v. City of Tiburon*, 447 U.S. 255 (1980), 32 ZD 256, suggests that, while it is possible for a governmental unit to take property by regulation, it will be considered to have done so only under the harshest of circumstances—for example, where the property is rendered economically nonviable. The agricultural/open space classification proposed here should generally avoid the finding of a regulatory taking. If the land is unsuitable for agricultural uses, the freedom of the landowner to select any other use at the densities available under any of the LUI schedules more than satisfies the constitutional requirement.

Affording more development opportunities for the landowner than are constitutionally required ensures that the regulatory process itself is not used as an impediment to rational development, as it often is under the existing system. This does not mean that a community cannot decide to slow its growth. It does mean that any such policy must be either explicitly reflected in the LUI schedule or bargained for under an Intensity Modification Contract, both of which are radical departures from the existing system. Under the existing system, a no-growth attitude is often hidden in numerous and expensive requirements, such as minimum lot and dwelling sizes.

A second reason for the uniform agricultural/open space reclassification is the avoidance of the pretense that such preestablished categories have any rational basis or, if they do, that such categorization is a necessary precondition to rational land use. In spite of what courts may believe, most zoning of undeveloped land is not a realistic appraisal of what land use is planned, likely, or even compatible with surrounding existing uses. Rather, zoning often is used as a device for deterring these difficult decisions. Undeveloped land is either underzoned in unintensive, and generally uneconomic, uses or overzoned in economic, but unrealistic uses. For example, substantial undeveloped land is zoned agricultural, not because the land is adequate, or even suitable, for farming, but because the classification represents a nondecision—a choice less controversial than a classification favoring housing over the environment or vice versa. Similarly, undeveloped land may be zoned industrial. To be sure, industrial development would enhance the locality's tax base or employment opportunities, but in fact the land will not be developed industrially because it is located too far from transportation centers or water resources.

Even when a non-holding zone category is applied to underdeveloped land, its "rational" basis is likely to be related to exclusion rather than orderly growth. In this regard, zoning ordinances impose minimum lot or building sizes or restrict apartment and manufactured home developments, not because they are legitimate nuisances, but because these protect neighbor expectations of property appreciation—expectations premised upon restricting the entrance and competition of comparable land uses in the market. Nevertheless, in view of the presumed validity of legislative acts, a court finds itself in the awkward position of articulating and accepting patently ridiculous justifications for zoning enactments.

When land use classification under the existing system is neither irrational nor exclusionary, it probably is unneeded. While zoning may reduce nuisance costs by segregating incompatible uses, the available research indicates that the operation of the land market itself would have accomplished a similar segregation without the corresponding administrative costs.[4]

The third primary reason for the reclassification relates to the recapture of unearned land value; that is, the uniform reclassification will facilitate the calculation of the amount to be expended by the landowner on public improvements.

Several ancillary benefits may also flow from the reclassification. First, by reducing the gain from speculating in farmland, the pressure on farm owners to sell land into development will also be reduced. Specifically, the reclassification should defer property tax reassessment and developer acquisition to a point closer to actual development. Second, the reclassification should generally depress land values, thereby reducing the developed cost to the consumer (assuming the recaptured unearned increment is both less than the present speculation value cost and not entirely passed on) and to the government, which may then be encouraged to acquire environmentally sensitive areas not by regulation but by the purchase of development rights and fee interests.

The Retention of Public Control over Land Use Intensity

Fundamentally, the alternative system assumes that public regulation should not define how land is to be used specifically, but should instead articulate general standards ensuring that land will be used—without regard to its specific use—in a manner that is safe and healthful. From the land development standpoint, safety and health issues relate to matters of population density and the quantity and quality of public improvements. The alternative system articulates safety and health standards through the determination of land use intensity (LUI) schedules and the supervision and specification of public improvements. Thus, the alternative system establishes a general framework for guiding private development and a mechanism for supplying complementary public improvement.

Density would be regulated by the LUI system originally devised by the Federal Housing Administration. Under the LUI system, floor area ratio (FAR) is related to five other ratios, each expressing a ratio of some open space use to total floor area. The open space ratio (OSR) is the relationship between total floor space on a parcel and the total area left open, including parking. The OSR is then divided into four sub-types of open space, each of which expresses a ratio between floor space and the minimum requirements for living space (open space less parking), recreational space (open space less living space), and occupant car space (total car space less nonresidential car space).

Under the alternative system, the local legislative body, with extensive public participation, will periodically devise four separate schedules of available LUI ratings. These schedules will apply to residential, commercial, industrial, or mixed-use projects. The LUI schedules will not apply to a limited number of uses that historically have been treated as special exceptions because of their unusual character—for example, airports and churches. These uses will continue to be treated as special exceptions.

The ratio of open space ratios to FAR for each of the four land use schedules can be fixed, and all six of the ratios can be expressed as a single number or LUI rating. It is important to realize that the fixing of this "ratio of ratios" is an expression of public policy—a decision, for example, that a given floor area of residential use calls for a given area of occupant parking, a given area of recreational space, and so forth. The LUI rating will differ among uses simply because a given FAR will generate different use densities in commercial and residential use. Further, the different uses will mandate different allocations of open space. In addition, a community may decide that certain of the ratios are inapplicable to commercial and industrial projects. For example, the occupant car and recreational space ratios probably could be excluded for commercial and industrial projects without residential elements. It can be assumed that the LUI ratings will reflect successful existing projects as well as the community's conception of normal or adequate development.

The LUI schedules would form the basis of the community's land use policy. A landowner may select a LUI rating from any of these schedules, and public improvements would be constructed at the time of LUI selection. In this regard, while an unimproved, agriculturally classified lot of any size may be sold, the community would be likely to establish a minimum parcel size—say 10 acres—for LUI selection in order to encourage "project" rather than lot-by-lot development. Of course, LUI selection need not immediately trigger private improvement since the landowner may wish to subdivide the now publicly improved lots into smaller parcels for sale rather than development. In that event, the buyers of the smaller lots would be able to develop the property subsequently in any manner consistent with both the original LUI selection and the public improvements installed by the original landowner at the time of LUI selection.

Thus, a private decision, not public control, determines what type of use will be made and where the use will be located. This is not meant to suggest that private decisions will always result in the "correct" choice or location of use. Imperfect knowledge or incentives may result in harmful externalities if land use decisions are made on a totally laissez-faire basis. Nevertheless, this possibility does not justify highly collectivized public control. The alternative system recognizes that some private decisions may result in harmful externalities and that some public control may therefore be justified. Public control must, however, be carefully structured to protect individual liberty and to create greater economic efficiency by minimizing needless prevention and administrative costs.

The LUI system can successfully meet these requirements. What constitutes a harmful externality is largely defined by a community's conception of normalcy. The alternative system assumes that the community will translate its normalcy standard into the LUI rating schedules. Because normalcy standards may change over time, as community demographics change or housing and employment needs are fulfilled, the alternative system provides for the periodic revision of the LUI rating schedule.

The LUI system can also fail. For example, LUI ratings can be intentionally designed to exclude through the imposition of unreasonable open space requirements. But failure can be minimized or avoided under the alternative system by adopting generalized LUI policies and letting the individual apply them to specific parcels. The LUI choices available to the individual can be maximized by tying the recapture of the unearned increment to the LUI rating actually chosen.

Beyond the initial collectivized statement of normalcy (in the form of an overall limit on density), the alternative system favors individual freedom and less collectivized methods of control. For example, the individual landowner selects the type and location of use. In addition, the landowner determines, in reference to market demand, unit size and building and site design. This freedom opens up possibilities for architectural competition and supplies flexibility to meet changing consumer preferences for units of different sizes.

Bargained-for Land Use Control under the Alternative System

The alternative system involves bargaining at two junctures. First, the public improvements to be provided by the developer will be incorporated into a Public Improvement Contract. Second, an increase or decrease from the LUI selected by the landowner or a change in one of the ratios making up the LUI can be accomplished only through an Intensity Modification Contract.

For the most part, the arguments made against contract zoning seem inapposite to the contract devices of the alternative system. Because zoning itself has been eliminated, neither contract can constitute spot zoning. Similarly, because the comprehensive planning requirement found in existing enabling legislation will not be incorporated into the enabling legislation for the alternative system, this objection also becomes irrelevant.

Both contract devices are incorporated into the alternative system, notwithstanding the fact that the discretion inherent in contract negotiation may be abused by an improperly motivated official or landowner. An attempt has been made to limit the number of opportunities for corrupt behavior by requiring that both contracts be made matters of public record. Beyond this, it is hoped that LUCA's internal monitoring and management control, together with the criminal process, would adequately deter corruption.

Perhaps the most serious objection to contractual land use agreements is that they constitute the improper contracting away of the police power. This objection concerns the limitations placed on a state's exercise of its police power by the federal contract clause prohibiting the impairment of obligations, or what has become known as the reserved power doctrine. Until the Supreme Court decided *U.S. Trust Co. v. New Jersey*, 431 U.S. 1 (1977), the contractual devices of the alternative system were probably unattainable because of the reserved power doctrine—that any contract concerning the exercise of the police power—but not the spending or taxing powers—would be invalid *ab initio*. Although still open to interpretation, the *U.S. Trust* opinion appears to do away with formalistic distinctions between state powers.

We may speculate as to the effect of the newly interpreted reserved power doctrine on the alternative system. Our speculation is aided by distinguishing Public Improvement Contracts from Intensity Modification Contracts. Public Improvement Contracts should not run afoul of any conception of the reserved power doctrine. Because the Public Improvement Contract merely defines the quantity and quality of the public improvement to be constructed with public money, the contract can be characterized as an exercise of the spending power. Thus, if, contrary to the analysis suggested here, past formalism survives *U.S. Trust*, the Public Improvement Contract should survive an initial determination of validity. Whether or not LUCA or the local legislative body could subsequently modify or repeal a Public Improvement Contract would depend upon the impairment's reasonableness and necessity. While there may be cases in which necessity might justify impairment, the burden of that justification would be with the community, as it was in *U.S. Trust*.

Intensity Modification Contracts clearly run contrary to the formalistic application of the reserved power doctrine. The subject matter of such a contract, as the name indicates, may relate to the intensity of development and the public's role, if any, in defining permitted uses, height, size, and overall design of the private improvements. Under the existing system, all of these matters are traditional police power concerns; hence, a court that insists on confining *U.S. Trust* to its facts would be likely to find an Intensity Modification Contract to be void *ab initio* and the state would be free to modify unilaterally any agreement entered into with a developer. This analysis would be an impediment to the alternative system; it would also represent the substitution of simpleminded categories for substantive analysis.

Redirecting Public Participation toward Land Use Policy Issues

Surprisingly little thought has been given to the role and scope of public participation in the land use process. The role of the neighbor has been assumed to be indispensable since the Standard State Zoning Enabling Act provided that "any person aggrieved" could appeal to, and any person aggrieved or any taxpayer could appeal from, the administrative determinations of the board of adjustment. The SZEA also accorded significant deference to the views of neighbors, and occasionally all taxpayers, with respect to local legislative action. Moreover, to the extent that land use decisions may be the subject of initiatives or referendums, the neighbor's role in policy application under the existing system is superior to that of the legislative body.

A recent study by Professor Robert Nelson[5] concludes that, despite zoning's contrived nuisance-prevention justification, it is really a tool employed by some property owners to control the property of others. To protect their interests, individual property owners use zoning and the zoning litigation to stop development or slow the development process. Individual property owners know all too well that inhibiting development constricts supply and enhances the market value of their property.

If one accepts the argument that neighbors have used zoning to foster their individual interests rather than public policy, two alternatives present themselves: either expressly authorize neighbor control or expressly eliminate it. Professor Nelson has chosen the first alternative; the second is adopted here.

Within the context of the alternative system, the individual property interests of neighbors are dealt with in a policy-making, rather than a policy-applying, process. The neighbor is afforded an opportunity to advocate public policy that coincides with his individual interest at legislative hearings held periodically to determine the community's LUI policy. Because the LUI policy is legislatively determined, constitutional doctrine premised on the type of proceeding involved would not appear to mandate procedural due process. Nevertheless, because neighbor input at this stage is considered important, notice and an opportunity to be heard would be afforded neighbors expressly under the alternative system's enabling legislation.

The alternative system does not encompass any governmental proceeding of the traditional quasi-judicial type; thus, it might seem as if the structure of the alternative system avoids this constitutional issue. The negotiation of Public Improvement and Intensity Modification Contracts, however, involves the exercise of judgment and the careful balancing of conflicting interests, which are the hallmarks of adjudication. These contractual negotiations may affect individual property interests; if the interests are significant and substantially threatened, constitutional objections can be anticipated if notice and an opportunity to be heard are not provided.

Because the landowner is a party to both negotiations, his interests are adequately protected. The alternative system, however, excludes the neighbor from this part of the land use process on the assumption that his interests will be well protected by market forces, nuisance remedies, and LUCA's pervasive control of the public improvements to be provided.

If the contractual arrangements are analogous to adjudication, can the alternative system constitutionally exclude the neighbor? In those jurisdictions that have recognized the neighbor's property rights, the answer is probably no. However, most jurisdictions merely weigh the neighbor's rights as one factor to be considered. Some courts have found no due process implications when the neighbor's aesthetic or more subjective values were offended or when the threatened harm amounted to something less than a taking.

The Recapture and Use of the Unearned Increments

In any decision to purchase undeveloped land, land value will be calculated not only in reference to the land's current use, but also with respect to any possible future use. The value of agricultural land will be the present value of the agricultural production as well as the discounted present value of the land's future developed use. Thus, the price of agricultural land is equal to the sum of the capitalized value of the current use plus the capitalized value of any future use discounted to the present. The value of any future use will depend upon the intensity of future development, the time of development, and the property's holding costs—principally interest and taxes.

The alternative system recaptures the difference between the future use value, represented by the voluntarily selected LUI rating, and the value of the land's current agricultural/open space use. The recaptured amount is termed the unearned increment, and it will be used primarily to fund any public improvements required by the Public Improvement Contract. Any portion of the unearned increment not used by the developer for public improvements will be paid to the community as general revenue.

The recapture of the unearned increment and its application to public improvement under the alternative system is a workable and fair method for imposing infrastructure costs on the developer. Unlike impact fees or exactions, which are justified on the basis of vague judicial standards, the unearned increment could be objectively determined by an appraiser mutually acceptable to the community and the developer. Unlike the construction or business license taxes that have been imposed without legal limitation, the amount of unearned increment recoverable from any given landowner under the alternative system will be expressly limited to the amount determined by the appraiser.

Land value taxation schemes, like the unearned increment recapture suggested here, have been found objectionable by landowners for a number of reasons. First, as a matter of historical equity, landowners may point out that, to the extent the community's infrastructure was financed with the property tax that they (or a predecessor in title) paid, the unearned increment recapture constitutes double taxation. While such an argument is historically accurate and theoretically valid, it loses sight of the present-day reality that inflation and the general cost of money have made today's infrastructure more costly than yesterday's and that statutory limits and political pressure have kept the property tax from keeping pace. Nevertheless, the argument has current validity to the extent that property tax is still being used to finance the capital construction of new or replacement public improvements that benefit the existing community. Clearly, there would be an inequity, as some court have recognized with regard to school facilities, "if new construction alone were to bear the capital cost of new schools while also being charged [through property taxes] with the capital costs of schools serving other portions of the school district."[6]

The alternative system proposes to eliminate this potential inequity, not by refusing to recapture the unearned increment from the developer, but by also recapturing it from landowners in the existing community. Specifically, when a landowner in the existing community is specially benefited by capital construction, that unearned increment will be recaptured by means of a special assessment. In this way, the developer's property tax should be reduced—because that source of revenue will no longer bear the liability of capital construction for the existing community—and the alleged inequity of prospective double taxation will be eliminated.

A second reason land value tax programs have been politically unpopular can be traced to the fact that the tax has been imposed to recapture the land value windfall without providing any corresponding benefit to the landowner. Specifically, the landowner has been asked to forfeit all, or most, of the land value while being left to face an increasingly deficient existing system of public land use control.

One can seriously question whether a system of public regulation that results in extensive delay and downside losses should be perpetuated. To paraphrase Donald Hagman, the alternative system suggests that it is better to eliminate, rather than mitigate, wipeouts. Once wipeouts are eliminated, the recapture of unearned increment windfalls is highly equitable.[7]

The Planner's Role

Planners have done a great deal to secure their role under the existing system. The profession is assured of work by the increasing number of states that either mandate planning as a prerequisite to land use control or require consistency or do both.[8] It would be entirely naive to assume that the profession or the collective views it occasionally propagates will wither away.

Indeed, the deregulation proposal outlined here suggests that planning ought not to fall into desuetude. However, the alternative system does require a reformulation of the planner's role from public commander of requirements to private advocate of suggestions. Like the existing system, the alternative system envisions that planners will continue to advise both local legislators in the fashioning of a community's growth policy and administrators in the implementation of that policy. Contrary to the modern trends of the existing system, however, the planner's advice need not be followed as a matter of law. Moreover, it can be assumed that planners will continue to offer to assist private landowners in the design and layout of private land use plans.

The removal of the coercive force from planning pronouncements is overdue. While planning is often perceived as a way of cutting market imperfections, it has seldom been shown to have this effect. Rather, planning "is based upon the assumption that the planner's redistributive values are superior to those of the market and will result in a net gain to the aggregate welfare. . . . [P]lanner's choices . . . , however, risk being arbitrary since planners bear little responsibility for distribution of the costs or benefits of their activity."[9] In addition, even if the redistributive values of the planner are accepted without question, planners themselves disagree as to the appropriate method for determining those values and whether those values, once identified, can be projected into the future for any significant time period. In this regard, planners have employed a great variety of styles over time, from end-state master plans to policy and advocate plans to today's emphasis on strategic incrementalism—that is, concern with short-range strategies and special purpose plans.

No matter what name is given to the process, muddling through is still muddling through. Given the planner's own recognition of the dynamic nature of land use decisions, there is certainly no reason to pepper the statutes with end-state planning requirements, such as those found in most mandatory plan elements. Nor should it be concluded that mandatory dynamic planning is the answer because such is still antithetical to a logically consistent view of private property and just as likely to be used as a prop for the perpetuation of the unfair, inefficient, uncertain, and inflexible existing system as more conventional planning methodology.

In short, if the underlying existing system of land use control is rotten, there's no point in trying to salvage it with decent planning.

NOTES

[1]See, e.g., B. SIEGAN, LAND USE WITHOUT ZONING (1972); Note *Land Use Control in Metropolitan Areas: The Failure of Zoning and a Proposed Alternative*, 45 S. CAL., L. REV. 335 (1972).

[2]Tarlock, *Euclid Revisited*, 34 LAND USE L. & ZONING DIGEST NO. 1 at 4 (1982).

[3]See generally, Kmiec, *Regulatory Takings: The Supreme Court Runs Out of Gas in San Diego*, 57 IND. L. J. _____(forthcoming, 1982).

[4]Siegan, *Regulating the Use of Land*, in THE INTERACTION OF ECONOMICS AND THE LAW 159 (B. Siegan, ed. 1977).

[5]R. NELSON, ZONING AND PROPERTY RIGHTS (1977); See also, Kmiec, *Private Control of Collective Property Rights*, 13 VAL. U. L. REV. 589 (1979).

[6]West Park Ave., Inc. v. Township of Ocean, 48 N.J. 122, 126–27, 224 A.2d 1, 4 (1966).

[7]D. HAGMAN & D. MISCZYNSKI (eds.), WINDFALLS FOR WIPEOUTS (1978) at 24.

[8]See generally, Mandelker & Netter, *A New Role for the Comprehensive Plan*, 33 LAND USE L. & ZONING DIGEST NO. 9 at 5 (1981).

[9]Tarlock, *Consistency with Adopted Land Use Plans as a Standard of Judicial Review: The Case Against*, 9 URB. L. ANN. 69, 76 (1975).

16

The Market's Place
in Land Policy

George Lefcoe

W E ARE ALL influenced by our national experience when we approach the question of whether land policy should be primarily a matter of government decision or whether land policy should in the main reflect market forces. Haim Darin-Drabkin, a leading advocate of public land ownership, articulates a land policy view quite understandable in the Israeli context. Nations often engage in centralized land planning in bellicose times. But in Israel the link between the land and the concept of political sovereignty has been forged by more then expediency. The land *is* the state in a fundamental way. The Hebrew phrase *Eretz Yisroale* refers both to the land or earth of Israel and also to the state of Israel. In the United States we romanticize our wilderness areas. We celebrate our cities with pop tunes. But we have no phrase which equates territory with sovereignty.

The Market's Role in Southern California Land Development

In sunny Los Angeles county centralized land planning would be bound to fail. Our only war is with the limits of our environment. Our demands as consumers are so varied as to defy containment within the cognizable channels of a rigidly planned economy. We are over 7 million residents. Our gross product, if we were a nation, would place Los Angeles county among the 20 wealthiest countries in the world, and our per capita income in 1977 would put us fourth in the world (just behind Switzerland, just ahead of Sweden). We have untold hundreds of thousands of recent immigrants from

Reprinted from George Lefcoe. "The Market's Place in Land Policy." *Urban Law and Policy* 3 (1980): 205–216. Copyright © 1980, North-Holland Publishing Company. Reprinted by permission.

Mexico, Asia, and elsewhere, whose numbers we cannot even assess accurately.

We depend on a system of market pricing to measure what people want and are willing to trade their labor to buy. We depend on the incentives of a market economy to encourage initiative and effort. No planning system yet invented offers techniques for assessing consumer wants better than those of the market. As for the market's incentive-function, I cannot imagine a planning substitute short of the public spiritedness evidenced in times of war or other crisis.

To see what a market-driven land policy produces for us in Southern California, consider two development areas that have come into their own over the past ten to twenty years: Valencia New Town and the Marina del Rey. Valencia, about 60–90 minutes from downtown Los Angeles by freeway, is being built on a 5,000 acre portion of a 44,000 acre private land holding. The Marina, 30 minutes from downtown, possibly 45 on a busy freeway, lies on 804 acres, half land, half water.

They both have the appearance of "planned" spaces. Professional planners might characterize the Marina as "infill." It is part of a wetland on the Southern California coast, surrounded by built urban areas. The Marina is a medium-to-high density project of apartments, restaurants, and small boat craft harbor. It was made possible by considerable dredging and filling. Valencia is representative of the Valingby-type of new town development, mostly one-family homes, low-to-medium density, not so far from the city as to make commuting impossible but far enough to provide an incentive for establishing a strong local job market. At both projects engineering has been carefully performed. Parking is more than ample for residents though a bit short for visitors at the Marina. Design controls are stringent and diligently administered at both.

Both offer recreational opportunities of all types from tennis courts and swimming pools, used mostly by residents, to region-attracting amusements. Valencia has Magic Mountain. The Marina has Fisherman's Village, boat docking for 5,800 small craft, and 35 restaurants, the most profitable and busy in the United States, I am told. Both projects abound with open space. Most of the communal open space at the Marina—swimming pools and patios—lies in the central courtyards of apartment buildings. Valencia offers neighborhood parks and community "rec" centers. Its crowning innovation is a network of pedestrian walkways—the paseos—linking houses to schools and shops.

Valencia and the Marina offer rather different types of living environments. The Marina is a "swingers" paradise; bars and restaurants are always full, chance meetings in apartment elevators lead to new acquaintances and romances. Valencia is a more relaxed, quiet place where a stroll on a neighborhood land or a dip in the community swimming pool on a warm summer night might be followed by an evening of TV-watching. Both cater to younger households, in the 25–45 age range. The Valencia project is family-oriented, a home-owning group. Only 12 percent of the housing at Valencia is in apartments. All of the Marina's housing is in luxury apartments—5,000 garden, 800 high-rise, and children are barred from most of them.

Both developments house about 10,000 people and contain jobs for 6,000. While not everyone who lives in these developments works there, employment opportunities do exist for principal wage-earners, and for part-time help in the shops, restaurants and amusement facilities.

There is no low-income housing in the Marina, and only about 100 units of subsidized housing for the elderly at Valencia. Both are inhabited predominantly by Caucasians. While overt racial discrimination is barred at both sites, the percentage of blacks, Chicanos, Asians and other non-Anglos is negligible at both locations.

Is it possible to tell whether these projects were undertaken by governments acting as land developers or by private land subdividers? Those familiar with the efforts of the Urban Development Corporation, organized by the state of New York to build new towns, may observe that in the UDC's projects, a much larger percentage of low- and moderate-income families were served. For instance, in UDC's Lysander New Town—12 miles north of Syracuse—fully 50 percent of the housing was reserved for low- and moderate-income people. This raised the ire of the people living nearby who felt that the crime, lower educational standards, and poor housekeeping practices suffered by Syracuse's low-income population would emerge at Lysander.

Without subsidies the poor cannot outbid the middle class for prime land and newly built housing. California taxpayers are as generous as any in the United States. Our welfare entitlements for the elderly, the handicapped, the unemployed, the sick and for dependent children are among the highest in the nation. We spend four billion dollars a year on medical subsidies alone. But even Californians feel there are limits to the contributions we can make to those in need. Most of our tax dollars are collected from people for whom the $500–$1,000 per month Marina apartments or the $100,000 houses in Valencia are beyond reach. In any event, housing subsidies, which are primarily national grants, were cut back sharply in the last of the Nixon administration and have not been much expanded since then by the Carter administration. (Because of the cutbacks in these programs, the UDC, which had relied heavily on them, defaulted on its bonds in the early 1970s and had to be reorganized.)

Although the Marina and Valencia compete in the sense that they offer

Southern Californians a choice of habitats, they cannot be cited as examples of unfettered capitalism. Marina del Rey was developed and is owned by Los Angeles county, having been originally conceived as a small craft harbor. Because the costs of dredging the harbor and securing it against ocean storms exceeded revenue estimates from boat docking, the county government decided to develop a "mixed" use instead of a boating-only project.[1] In this way the county's share of the land development costs could be met out of revenues from the project itself.

The judgment that the Marina venture could be self-financing was not made by government planners alone. Private financiers provided guidance, and more. About a third of the Marina land development cost was met through the issuance of revenue bonds. Since these were to be repaid solely from the leasing of land and water, the successful sale of these bonds evidenced a measure of private market confidence. The Marina has been a financial success. From a total land development cost of $36 million, the county realizes $6 million dollars a year in leasehold revenues from apartment, hotel and restaurant ground leases. These facilities were built entirely by private ground lessees who invested $150 million in buildings at the Marina. The Marina is a worthy example of public enterprise capitalism.

A key difference between public and private capitalism is that when contests arise in a purely private market setting among competing users of scarce resources, the ultimate victory usually belongs to the highest bidder. For publicly owned properties the rules of market competition are subject to political hedging. At the Marina 55 private developers enjoy 60-year ground leases which promise them a fair return on their investments. County officials have construed "fair return" to mean not just a return on invested dollars but on the much higher current fair market value of those properties. This interpretation has justified rent hikes for apartment tenants and higher docking fees for boaters. It has also encouraged intensive development of the Marina. Public open spaces—public boat docks, beaches and parks—are seen as carrying a very high opportunity cost in terms of public and private revenue loss. Consequently, there is little public open space at the Marina. Public land ownership has thus far resulted in much the same development pattern as private ownership would have yielded. Nonetheless, the fact of public ownership converts every major financial move at the Marina into a political event with the outcome as uncertain as political outcomes usually are.

Can Valencia be called a purely private enterprise? It was the inspiration of the head of a family which owned the 44,000 acre Newhall Land and Farming Company in the Santa Clarita Valley and who wanted to see a better quality of development than that which had preceded the completion of the Golden State Freeway connecting Valencia with the rest of Los Angeles.

Had the state not extended the freeway to the site, the project would not have been possible. Had the Newhall Land and Farming Company been free of all development controls, Valencia might have been different. It might not have provided as much open space, guest parking facilities, school sites at the developer's expense, as elaborate an interior road system, and as active a program of attracting jobs. Even its 100 or so low-income housing units might not be there but for government pressure. Without government planning controls, Valencia's home-buyers would have no assurance that the entire region would be built to a comparable standard.

Such protection has ever been one of the primary purposes of public planning in the U.S.—to make sure that once market bets are down, "free loaders" do not crowd in to take advantage of the amenities while overshadowing them with cut-rate work. One consequence of "protectionist" planning standards is that governments may impose greater development amenities than housing consumers want to buy. Free marketeers might prefer that private developers and home-owners be left on their own in safeguarding themselves against lower priced, lower quality competition. There are very few places in the Western world where the owners of luxury housing do not insist on some level of planning protection against intrusive land uses. The question is seldom whether there shall be such controls but rather how stringent the minimum development standard shall be.

Valencia's residents, joined by others in the Santa Clarita Valley, are staging a campaign now to secure government protection for the valley's oak trees, threatened with demolition by development. Those trees cannot withstand the earth moving cut-and-fill operations of subdividers, and the trees are expensive to replant—about $30,000 a tree. The current market value of a sound oak is only $10,000, so without public intervention few of the valley's oaks would survive urbanization. Yet the trees provide shade in the valley's hot, dry climate and because they retain pools of water beneath them they also serve as a fire break in a high fire-risk area. This is a typical "tragedy of the commons" problem. Let my neighbor save his trees while I eliminate mine so that I may enjoy them from my efficiently constructed homesite. County planning authorities are intervening to make sure that the oaks are preserved where feasible. Presumably, in the quest for a "feasible" oak preservation program, we will need to find an efficient way of deciding which oaks to protect and which to sacrifice in order to facilitate sensible and sensitive land development.

Understandably, some property-owners are astounded that we would prohibit them from cutting trees on their own land. But we are not at all prepared to revert to a model of unrestrained competition in land development because we are not prepared to suffer its side effects. If Valencia and the Marina are taken as two acceptable models of land development, we may conclude that our choice is not between perfect competition and public land ownership, but rather between private enterprise socialism and public enterprise capitalism.

The thrust of planning in the U.S. in recent years has gone even farther than this. Not content to secure common resources and to protect land-owners from the harmful impact of neighboring development, planning now strives for a sort of comprehensiveness which would displace this market almost entirely in the allocation of land. It is time we examined the wider implications of this drift towards activist planning.

The Market Place as a Restraint on Planning Excesses

Three planning policies that would pre-empt market decision-making are the following: (1) the socialization of land ownership so that the public sector might reap the gains which would otherwise accrue to private individuals from the sale of pre-developed land; (2) the realization of national decentralization policy to free crowded cities of "excess" population and provide economic growth for declining regions; and (3) urban growth boundary controls.

Land Profit

The notion that gains from the sale of undeveloped land are undeserved is traceable to the fact that land is not to be subject to market forces. No matter how high it is priced, new production of land is seldom possible, the supply of land being relatively fixed. However, while the amount of land may be fixed in supply, innovation is still possible in its efficient use, evidenced by both the Marina and Valencia projects. Although land may be relatively fixed in supply, development on the land is not. Gains from land are often important as a potential source of cross-subsidization for home-builders and other land developers.

Land is far from unique in not being subject to the rules of perfect competition. Labor unions, cartels, and government regulation all mitigate against conditions of perfect competition throughout our economy. By allowing consumers to bid against each other for land we allow the allocation of land to flow to that user who can make the most efficient use of it. Assuming our planning controls set acceptable limits on the exploitation of land resources and limit the discomfort one owner may inflict upon another, the highest bidder is likely to be the one who can put the land to its optimal use.

If we substitute the government for the market-place as the allocator of land resources, a decision must be made whether to release publicly owned land at market prices, or not. If governments sell land or housing at below market prices, then government officials are subject to the temptation of selling bargains to friends, relatives, and political allies. If governments sell land at market, consumers pay at least what they would have paid but because public bureaucracies would be involved, the costs of land development and marketing might be higher. If studies of government-run enterprises can be trusted, a very large share of the price will go towards the wages of public employees since publicly run enterprises are notoriously inefficient in their use of labor. Capitalists will substitute other factors of production for labor. Governments mechanize only reluctantly; government employees offer politicians votes, loyalty, and the performance of favors for constitutents.

Regional Policy

One of the often-cited achievements of European policy has been the decentralization effort undertaken in England, Sweden, and France. So long as the capital cities—Paris, London and Stockholm—seemed bound to grow indefinitely, a policy of subsidizing industry to locate in less populated places seemed efficient. The problem with this as with most planning mechanisms is that, unlike the market-place, it has no ready way to self-adjust when public sentiment and market trends mitigate towards relaxation of the policy.

James L. Sundquist reported that when Stockholm during the 1960s was making plans to serve double their population by 2000, city officials welcomed the central government subsidizing firms to locate in the north.[2] An urban agglomeration six times the land mass of Stockholm *circa* 1950 was not a future which Stockholm's officials wanted. But as Mr. Sundquist observed: "[A] slowing of growth is one thing, and an absolute decline in population quite another" (p. 230). In the early 1970s, with a general economic downturn and an out-migration of foreign workers, Stockholm's population was decreasing. Subsidies to firms locating in the north might be tolerable; more stringent controls would not be universally applauded. A similar shift has occurred in England where London is now threatened with a steady decline, and planners are wondering whether they had gone too far in trying to curtail development in London.

When governments interfere with the market choices of firms, they may do so in several ways. At the far extreme they can absolutely prohibit development by a permit system rigorously administered. In addition to the costs of implementing such a program, a nation can damage its economic base this way if firms were seeking efficient locations. Government policy may inadvertently restrict industrial growth to sites extremely costly in terms of transporting raw materials to them, and finished products to intended markets. Especially for firms that must meet international competition, the wrong regional policy can be ruinous.

Subsidies are a less intrusive form of intervention than outright prohibitions, depending on how great the subsidy. But they are likely to be either too generous or too stingy to achieve their stated goals. It is heroically difficult to design systems which bar those firms from capturing subsidies for moving which would have moved anyway. More difficult still would be adjusting the subsidy level to exactly offset the "externalities" costs of firms trying to crowd themselves into already over-burdened urban places. None of the location subsidies in place has come close to matching the last increment of subsidy payment to the marginal benefit of the relocation decision.

In the United States we can offer one hideous and one hopeful model for handling the problem of regional dispersal. On the hideous side, communities that do not want growth have adopted the practice of limiting housing supply by restricting the sites on which housing can be built, and curbing the densities of development on those sites that are left open to development. There are no direct controls over the location decisions of major employers. As a consequence it is possible for firms to move into a region from which all moderate and middle income housing has been excluded. Employees must then commute from the nearest housing they can afford.

We have had a better, though controversial, experience with the only emergent form of industrial location policy in the United States—our national air pollution laws. A national air quality standard has been set which some areas have attained, and other areas have not. Major power and other industrial plants may be located in attainment areas if they use the best available technology for controlling emissions. In the nonattainment areas, like Los Angeles county, we are debating a plan under which a new major polluter will only be allowed if it can "buy" the reduction of pollution from an existing firm so that after the new industry is in, the aggregate emission levels will not have increased above the current level.[3]

Industrial firms argue that the costs of environment protection may be too great. How may government agencies determine how much of society's resources are properly spent on environmental quality? Recently, the Environmental Protection Agency has pioneered various market-based techniques for estimating how much people in Southern California value air pollution control. Researchers compared property values in 12 paired neighborhoods where smog levels were approximately 30 percent different, and double checked the differences in property values with a "bidding game" they constructed with residents of the area, asking them, essentially, what they are willing to pay for lowered air pollution levels. Roughly the same numbers showed up as had appeared in property value studies. A 30 percent difference in smog levels accounted for $650–950 million difference in property values.[4] The study is primitive in some respects. We do not

know what the relative values of property would be if there were little air
pollution in the LA basin. But it is a start.

Urban Growth Boundary Controls

The public demand for planning limits to growth is understandable. If
projects are built well beyond the line of present urbanization, governments
may be expected to extend roads and utility services, to make police and fire
protection available, and to open and maintain new schools. If development
comes to an already built-up area, it will inconvenience the neighbors, make
roadways more congested and, possibly, block views or access to air cur-
rents and open spaces. But if no new developments are allowed in an urban
region, business firms and housing consumers will be forced to bid against
each other for a fixed supply.

Allocating the costs of the various inconveniences which new development creates is, at its root, a policy issue. But it is far better public policy to
estimate and allocate these costs than to bar new development entirely from
previously unbuilt areas. Communities will seldom be able to determine
how much land should sensibly be open to development. In Sweden the
socialist regime mandated in the late 1960s and early 1970s that all localities
purchase ten years' land for expansion; the city of Orebro, as I recall, was
among the most eager to follow that instruction. But they overestimated demand and expended taxpayer kroner to purchase what might well have been
a 20-year supply, contributing to a precipitous rise in local tax rates, much
to the consternation of the local electorate. Planners have no crystal balls
which guarantee that their visions of the future will come true. In Sweden
the consequence is simply that the taxpayer pays for these miscalculations.
In Southern California we are faced with a worse fate.

Our regional planning agencies are required by federal law to estimate
population growth in order that the federal authorities may allocate funds
for sewage treatment plants on some intelligent basis, and so that air pollution control regulators in Washington may better appraise our efforts to attain national air quality standards. Once these projections have been made,
pressure is then brought to bear against local governments to utilize its land-
use controls so that they do not exceed their growth projections. Restrictive
land-use controls, in turn, have the consequence of increasing the price of
developable land by reducing its availability for building. This is always the
danger in comprehensive planning, *i.e.* that to save the planners' estimates
from being proved wrong individuals will be coerced into behaving in ways
they do not want to behave. Instead of planning for people, people are
manipulated for the benefit of the plan and the planners.

An alternative to outright prohibition against all development or government's supplanting the market as the prime allocators of land is simply to

establish politically the community costs that new development must pay, and to assess those upon new development.

For facilities that require massive public improvements that must be amortized over many more users than any single developer is likely to bring, instead of this "leapfrog" risk falling to the public sector, we could require the developer to provide the initial funding, with recoupment from later developers.[5] At present we might regard such a development as "premature" if it is far outside our urban growth boundary line. But that line is arbitrary, having been drawn from fallible statistics about population trends and not from market research on effective demand updated periodically. A developer who believes that a remote area will attract sufficient population to amortize the capital costs of, say, a sewage treatment plant, can provide the funding and be reimbursed by later arrivals. He bears the loss if he is wrong, not the taxpayers.

There has been a steady trend towards requiring development to pay its own way in California. In new subdivisions developers have for decades had to provide interior roads at their own expense. In some jurisdictions they are now being asked to alleviate overcrowding on roads many miles from their tracts if traffic engineers determine that their developments will cause congestion at those intersections. Developers in California have had to provide land within their projects for school sites if the local school board requests it. Now they are being asked to contribute toward the cost of constructing those schools. Before long I would not be surprised if they were asked to fund some portion of the ongoing operating costs. They must provide a certain amount of parkland, varying with project density. They are now being asked to fund the maintenance costs for those parklands. The capital and operating costs of libraries, police and fire service could come next.

This trend has unhappy implications for the price of land and housing. In this respect planners have something of a bias at times. They can claim credit for having procured public goods at no visible cost to the public. As Bruce Johnson explains:

> Assume that the [planning] agency directs that a particular parcel be left as open space for the public instead of developed into a residential community, and assume that no compensation is paid to the property owner for the decrease in the capital value of the property. The agency's output will increase outside the budget process, the costs will be localized on a given property owner, the special interest group among the general public will receive the benefits of the open space free of charge, and the agency will receive the praise of its legislative sponsors.[6]

Elected officials have a similar bias, compounded by the fact that in our localized, pluralist politics, only those presently residing in a community exert much influence over local officials. Lacking the party discipline of the English and Swedes we have no centralized authority which adequately represents consumer interests in local affairs unless those consumers are also registered voters in the locality.

If we are to hold land developers accountable for the harmful effects of their activities, we should certainly consider ways of crediting them for the benefits they confer on others.[7] One of the strengths of large-scale development like the Marina and Valencia is that much of the benefit of quality planning shows up in higher property values on the developer's own land. Still, Valencia and the Marina have enriched owners at their peripheries. I doubt that we are ready to allow private developers the rights of eminent domain to enable them to capture "positive" externalities.

Incentive zoning can work as a form of compensation for the developer who offers public goods. Here again planning mechanisms err since they are not customarily constructed with a market pricing model in hand. In New York City developers were awarded the right to exceed prevailing building densities (measured by floor-area-ratios) in exchange for plazas, arcades, and theatres. Developers availed themselves of these opportunities and built bigger buildings. From 1963 to 1975, over 8 million square feet of bonus floor area was built under the plaza and arcade incentive zoning ordinance. At $25 a square foot, this added space was worth $182,000,000. Most observers will have to conclude that New York City would have been able to purchase far more plaza and arcade space for $182,000,000 than it got. This added footage contributed to an oversupply of office space and mounting vacancy rates which resulted in a devaluation of all office space in New York City. This, in turn, led to a reduction in the value of all of Manhattan's office space, and a consequent loss to the city in property tax revenues of $8,000,000 in a single tax year, 1973–74.[8] Incentive zoning, because it had not been cast in a market mold, exacerbated New York City's financial crisis.

In sum, when planning tools are utilized which absolutely bar development from nonurban areas, they have the same effect as if the social cost of this unwanted development had been assessed as infinite. When there are no public controls on urban expansion, the community is valuing the public costs of urban expansion at zero—a doubtful assumption—unless the extension of urban services happens to be self-financing. Assessing the costs of growth against land developers or the buyers of new suburban homes offers a sensible alternative to either approach. But costing urban growth is far from easy. In addition to deciding what public costs are properly paid by private parties, there are the problems of estimating these costs. Moreover, we have yet to identify sensible mechanisms for crediting land developers with the benefits of their efforts not otherwise reflected in their sales prices.

Conclusion

A false dichotomy can be drawn between public and private sector land development. Private developers can misjudge the market just as planners may. We have no shortage of examples of major private firms turning to governments to bail them out of poor management policies, declining markets, and inefficient use of labor and capital. Conversely, there are few large-scale land development projects anywhere in the world more successful than the British new towns. If governments acting as land developers can build more efficiently than private entrepreneurs, they should be encouraged to do so. But their efforts should not be subsidized unless the amount of the subsidy is made clear in advance, and elected officials have a chance to judge whether what the subsidy buys is worth the price. Very seldom do public sector land projects meet that test. The Marina does and in this respect it can be recommended as a model which planners in several other countries are presently studying.

We should avoid the false juxtaposition of planning and the market-place. The market-place cannot determine where the "externalities" of development ought to fall—how much to the consumer of new housing and how much on residents already living in the neighborhood. This is a political choice. But planners and politicians have yet to invent better tools than the pricing system for determining consumer demand, and encouraging productivity. The market is perfectly capable of setting efficiency limits to urban growth by compelling new development to pay its own way. Far better use could be made of the market in helping elected officials decide how much money is justifiably spent on such programs as regional decentralization and pollution abatement. To this extent the market is needed and ought to prevail in the formulation of land policy.

NOTES

[1] Now that the Marina has met the test of market acceptability, the owner of the adjoining undeveloped Ballona wetlands is proposing a development of comparable scale, to the consternation of environmental advocates who fear the loss of Southern California's last wetland.

[2] J.L. Sundquist, Dispersing Population: What America Can Learn from Europe (1975).

[3] R.E. Becker, Jr., *Land-Use Implications of the Clean Air Act for the Mountain West: The Utah Example*, 5 J. Contemp. L. 127 (1979).

[4] P. Houston, *L.A. Smog: Cleanup Could Save Millions; 30% Cut Would Net $650 to $950 Million a Year*, EPA Rep., 5 May 1979, pt. II, at 1, col. 1.

[5] R.E. Emmerson, *Fiscal Accountability for New Development in L.A. County*.

[6] B. Johnson, *A Discussion of Land Use Regulation Without Compensation*, in Planning Without Prices 63 (B.H. Siegan ed. 1978).

[7] Note, *Efficient Land Use and the Internationalization of Beneficial Spillovers: An Economic and Legal Analysis*, 31 Stan. L. Rev. 457 (1979).

[8] J.S. Kayden, Incentive Zoning in New York City: A Cost-Benefit Analysis (1978).

17

Controlling Urban Growth
via Tax Policy

Curtis J. Berger

FOR NEARLY TWO CENTURIES, America extolled "growth for growth's sake." In this spirit, municipalities proudly boasted—often simultaneously—of being "the fastest growing city (or county) in the nation." A seemingly endless supply of land and natural resources, the still-burning embers of a pioneering zeal, and a sturdy belief in the power and versatility of unchained capitalism all contributed to this growth dynamic.

Today, Americans seem less convinced of the *per se* benefits of growth than they were only a few years ago.[1] A wave of environmental self-consciousness has driven us to consider urbanization with a new mindset: will further growth harm our air and water, upset a fragile ecological balance, or scar the landscape's natural beauty? An awareness that we have squandered energy, land, older housing, and governmental revenue has led to many new concerns: how do we plan growth so as to conserve fuel, farm acreage, inner city neighborhoods, and municipal budgets? A finer appreciation for non-material values—the pleasure of leisure time, the healthfulness of recreation, the comfort of tradition—evokes a new challenge: how do we manage growth to reduce the travel to work, provide places to play and browse, and preserve our historical landmarks?

This changing attitude toward unrestrained growth can be seen everywhere. Some communities have placed annual quotas on newly built dwelling units.[2] Other communities have sought to bar any development in ecologically sensitive water basins.[3] Several states have placed stringent controls on construction within such critical areas as shorelines, forest lands, or

Reprinted from Curtis J. Berger. "Controlling Urban Growth via Tax Policy." *Urban Law and Policy* 2 (1979): 295–314, Copyright © 1979, North-Holland Publishing Company. Reprinted by permission.

the vicinity of regional airports.[4] Since the enactment of the National Environmental Policy Act of 1969[5] and many similar state laws,[6] large-scale developers must routinely prepare an environmental impact statement before starting an activity that may significantly affect the quality of the environment; this statement must satisfy the agencies that will decide whether or not to approve the activity. Tough new federal laws have been aimed at setting nationwide air quality standards.[7] Hundreds of cities now seek to protect landmark buildings and historic districts.[8]

The measures described above reflect the use of regulation, the so-called police power, to advance a societal goal. In each case, the community has intervened, in the interest of a better environment or the conservation of scarce resources, to *curb* the developer's normal urge to maximize his profits. Regulation is government's usual method to impress its will upon private land use decisions: zoning, building codes, subdivision approval, demolition permits, rent control, are all common forms of regulation. Because these methods impinge directly upon the private decision, and because they are widespread and highly visible, they have received close attention from legal writers. Moreover, landowners seeking to shake off these controls often turn to litigation when other forms of advocacy fail. This has spawned a huge mass of reported decision which, in turn, breeds an equally massive commentary.

This article focuses on another aspect of urban development—the role of *tax* policy, as distinguished from *regulatory* policy, in promoting or discouraging the nation's growth. Compared with regulation, taxation has not seemed to be as clearly related to decisions that shape urban development. Thus, it was possible, as recently as 1975, for someone to write a fairly original article entitled "Exploring the Role of Taxation in the Land Use Planning Process."[9] We have moved slowly on this front for several reasons: many purists believe that a tax system must discharge its primary function—the raising of government revenue—in a way that deals neutrally with private economic decisions. In any event, taxpayers ought not to believe that there are other taxpayers better off than themselves because of some advantage built into the law or, worse still, into its administration. Thus, we are only beginning to have frank discussion about the inequities and preferences that pervade the system. Paradoxically, however, as we become more candid in conceding that advantages do exist, we become more willing, not less, to use tax advantages openly to gain non-fiscal, societal goals. As we have become more conscious of environmental issues, getting a handle on urban growth has become a paramount national concern. We are learning to see that tax policy, as well as regulation and other forms of government action (*e.g.*, capital expenditure), has a role to play (potentially useful, sometimes harmful) in the shaping of urban development. This article deals with that role.

Some Basic Background on American Tax Policy

Tax policies in the United States are a product of both federal and local laws. Each of the fifty states (and to some degree, the District of Columbia) has its own statutory and decisional law which operates concurrently with the body of national law that the federal Congress, agencies, and courts generate. Adding further complexity, especially when the focus is upon urban development, are the powers given to local units of government—cities, villages, towns, and counties[10]—to regulate land use and to levy taxes upon land ownership.

Two principal modes of taxation concern us here—the local *property*[11] tax and the federal and state *income* tax. Property taxes remain, as they have been for over two centuries, a key source of revenue for local government. In 1975-1976, all units of local government raised over 54 billion dollars from property taxes, more than 80 per cent of their total *tax* revenue.[12]

As a federal and state revenue source, the income tax replaces the property tax in first importance. Individual and corporate income taxes still provide nearly 60 per cent of all federal receipts and have now become, at 32 per cent, the largest source of state tax receipts as well.[13]

One can readily see, therefore, that property and income taxes involve huge sums. Our attention lies, however, not on the taxes' overall impact upon the nation's economy, but on their separate impact upon individual taxpayers. The mere existence of taxes shapes individual investment decisions even if government has not deliberately sought to calibrate the decision one way or another. For example, the property tax levy represents for the owner an annual out-of-pocket expense that can absorb a sizable part of his operating income (upwards from ten per cent). That levy may mean the difference between a profit and a loss, controlling the original decision whether or not to buy, hurrying a later decision to sell or abandon, and in all cases requiring that market prices reflect the tax incidence.[14] Similarly, the federal income tax may extract almost as much as 30 per cent of a landowner's profit should he sell to a developer[15] (most states will also tax this gain). By retaining the land, however, until his death and letting his estate make the sale, the taxpayer can avoid much of the tax.[16] While not unique to land, this tax avoidance option may mean the difference between a sale now or later, and almost certainly affects the availability of land that developers can acquire. If, while ostensibly "neutral" *vis-à-vis* land development, these two taxes are a key factor in investment decisions, if follows, *a fortiori*, that government may use its taxing power purposefully to favor some decisions over others. As we shall see, this, indeed, occurs.

In using the tax system to regulate urban development, government might approach its goals from polar directions. It might move to encourage preferred forms of activity—for example, the building of housing for the poor, or home ownership rather than rental—by creating tax "stimuli" that will divert investment in favor of these activities.[17] Alternatively, government might discourage undesirable forms of activity—for example, the destruction of historic landmarks—by imposing tax "deterrents" that will make these activities more costly. Although our policy makers have moved in both directions, they seem more inclined to the "carrot" approach than to the "stick."

This sets the necessary stage for the rest of the article. We will examine, in turn, the property tax and the income tax and the "manipulation" of each to influence urban growth. We will deal with our topic functionally; thus, we will group our discussion around the various activities that government seeks to control.

The Property Tax

The Construction of "Subsidized" Housing

In 1937, when President Franklin Roosevelt spoke of the nation's one-third who were "ill-housed,"[18] he called upon government to remedy that condition. Before the year was out, Congress had enacted the Housing Act of 1937;[19] this would become the standard vehicle for the construction of low-rent housing for the next generation.

It should be at once apparent that the poor tenant usually cannot afford decent housing if he must pay the full market rent. Quite simply, his landlord must charge more for the shelter than the tenant can reasonably spare from his limited income.[20] Two of the chief items of housing expense are the real estate taxes and the debt service (interest and principal) on the building's mortgage; together they often comprise more than half of the total shelter cost. Although debt service is by far the larger of the two items, real estate taxes will consume between 10 and 20 per cent of the market rent.[21]

In designing the low-rent housing program, Congress agreed to pay the entire debt service on any construction bonds that local authorities might issue to build public housing. This would sharply reduce the monthly rents because neither the local authority landlord, nor ultimately, the low-income tenant would carry the debt service burden. But Congress doubted that this subsidy alone would sufficiently lower shelter costs. Accordingly, Congress conditioned the federal subsidy on local community agreements to forego any real estate tax levy on the subsidized units. In effect, Congress was coupling its direct subsidy with an indirect local subsidy—the tax revenue foregone. To the low-income tenant, this meant a shelter rent that would reflect only the bare essentials of maintenance and utilities.[22]

The federal public housing program, therefore, became an early exemplar of property tax abatement directed toward a social goal. By 1975, the program had yielded about 1.1 million newly built units nationwide.[23] Despite its apparent success, the program has not been popular among the local communities, and while the causes are varied and complex, they include local unhappiness about the loss of tax revenue. Aggravating this concern is the belief that public housing tenants demand far more than their fair share of the community services—schools, welfare and protection—which the property tax helps to finance. Since the federal program depended upon *local* initiative, communities that remained active began to turn much of their public housing output into the construction of units for the elderly;[24] senior citizens would cause fewer social disturbances and, without school-age children, would cost the community far less per capita to service.

Faced with a growing pressure from restive communities, Congress since 1968 has made key changes in the subsidy formulae for sheltering the poor. In summary, these changes involve shifting the burden of tax abatement from the community to either the federal government (in the form of a larger per unit subsidy) or the tenants themselves (in the form of a higher per unit rental). We are likely to see in the immediate years ahead, relatively little new housing that receives local tax abatement built for the poor.

Yet, even as communities resist giving tax abatement to the poor, in some instances, they are expanding their programs of tax relief for the middle classes and even the well-to-do. New York State's programs have clearly been the most extensive. The archetype has been the Limited Profit Housing Program, better known as Mitchell-Lama after its two legislative sponsors.[25] Introduced in 1956, Mitchell-Lama was intended to reduce shelter costs for families having incomes that were above those qualifying for occupancy of public housing units. The State provides subsidies in two forms. One involves reduced interest rates and thus lower debt service on the project mortgage. The second involves local property tax abatement. State law enables the local legislature to exempt a Mitchell-Lama project from all property taxes (other than special assessments) to the extent that the assessed value of the project exceeds the assessed value of the property it replaces. To illustrate: if Mitchell-Lama units replaced a block of slum tenements having a $1.0 million assessment, the new units would enjoy, regardless of their market value, an assessment ceiling of $1.0 million. This ceiling would continue for as long as 30 years. Throughout the decade of the 1960s, the heyday of Mitchell-Lama, local approval was given almost automatically to requests for maximum tax abatement. Because Mitchell-Lama families typically had incomes at or slightly above the city-wide median, the community was quite ready to offer incentives to keep them in town.

One might expect tax abatement to end with middle-income housing but New York City, in order to spur new construction and retain its higher income residents, has now extended the concept to benefit luxury housing as well. By the early 1970s, inflation had driven shelter costs so far skyward that even the well-to-do found it difficult to pay market rental for newly built apartments. Faced with the unwelcome prospect of a virtual halt to the construction of unsubsidized units—and a further loss of upper-income residents—the City created yet another tax abatement subsidy. This program offers tenants (in the form of rent reduction) the benefit of a ten-year schedule of tax abatement on new apartments. There are no income eligibility limits for this benefit; in some cases, the beneficiaries are among the City's wealthiest residents. Moreover, cooperative and condominium, *i.e., owner*-occupied, apartments also qualify. The units receive full tax exemption for the first two years after completion. Thereafter, at two year intervals, the exemption declines 20 per cent until, after a ten year phase-in period, the project becomes fully taxable.[26]

The Renovation of Older Housing

In the last section, we illustrated the use of property tax abatement as an indirect rental subsidy to the occupants of newly built housing. Renovation presents a related problem for the community that is concerned about its housing stock. Often, older units, while still structurally sound, have become so run down that their continued vitality is uncertain. Sometimes, even well-maintained buildings will suffer from technological obsolescence. The present owner might be ready to invest heavily in renovation, but that investment, which the community should welcome, may penalize both the owner and his tenants. Since property tax assessments are tied to the value of building improvements, a $100,000 renovation may cause a corresponding rise in assessed value and tax levy. Insofar as the owner absorbs the tax increase, modernization cuts down his profits; and, insofar as he passes on the tax increase, the tenants pay higher rents. Either alternative, or even the threat that they will occur, is undesirable.

Another New York City program, known as J-51,[27] illustrates not only how to meet this problem but also how to offer a positive incentive for renovation. J-51 offers both a tax abatement *and* a tax credit. The law was originally designed to encourage outlays to eliminate unhealthy or unsafe conditions, but its scope has widened gradually to encompass general upgrading as well. J-51 imposes a 12-year freeze on any increase in assessed value resulting from a qualifying renovation. In this respect, the law offers tax abatement similar to that found in the Mitchell-Lama program (although for much shorter periods). But the J-51 program goes much further. In addition to the freeze on valuation, the owner receives a further abatement in the form of an annual credit against his tax bill on the frozen assessment. This annual credit comes to as much as 8.33 per cent of the certified reasonable cost of the renovation, and it may continue for as long as 20 years, returning to the owner 90 per cent of his renovation outlay. In short, J-51 is an indirect form of rehabilitation grant.

Since 1961, when the program began, more than 11,000 buildings (totaling nearly 300,000 dwelling units) have participated in the J-51 program. The dollar value of certified costs has averaged $5,500 per unit. Although all New York City rents are subject to rent control, landlords have managed to greatly increase their rental income from J-51 buildings despite the tax subsidies. This suggests that J-51 has been far more successful in spurring landlords than in sparing tenants.[28]

The Preservation of Farmland and Open Space

The real estate developer is nearly always a capitalist who will build whatever and wherever the market will buy. He has little regard—nor can we expect him to—for the loss of a fruit orchard or rich farmland or a natural vista.

In acquiring his building sites, the developer must deal with other capitalists—farmers, speculators, landed gentry—who must decide whether to hold or sell. There is strong reason to believe that the property tax system innocently stacks the deck against those who might prefer to keep the land out of development.

Undeveloped land has two components of value—its present use (or income capitalization) value and its *situs* (or development) value. *Situs* value represents the increment over, let us say, farm use value that a developer would be ready to pay to convert the farm into a residential, shopping center or some other urbanizing use. In rural areas in the vicinity of large cities, a parcel's *situs* value may be considerable. Its magnitude depends largely upon the growth prospects in the area and upon the land's legally permissible uses.

A strong presumption exists, embodied in the United States Constitution, that every landowner is free to develop his parcel as he chooses. Zoning laws designate the permitted building uses. Accordingly, a zoning law that would preserve land in its natural or cultivated state by denying the owner the right to improve the site seldom survives a court challenge;[29] judges regard such zoning restrictions as impermissible deprivations of property without due process.[30] To satisfy the Constitution, in most circumstances, the zoning law must indicate a minimum developmental use for each parcel. Where a potential market for such use exists, the land then carries a *situs value* (based on the expectation that someone will wish to develop the parcel) that may far exceed the land's *present use value*.

The real estate tax has traditionally captured both the present use and the *situs* values of land. This results from the reliance upon market value, which reflects *situs* value, as the standard for property tax assessment. To the farmer, however, who would prefer to cultivate his land rather than to sell out to developers, the inflated tax levy based on market value becomes an unrelated cost of staying in business whose burden may precipitate an unwanted sale. Recognizing this tax bias against non-intensive land uses, many states have modified their taxation of farm and other "open space" properties so as to reach only the land's present use value.[31]

California's statute, the Land Conservation Act of 1965 (Williamson Act),[32] is fairly representative. Because of the state's preeminence both as an agricultural and high-growth community, we will examine the law and the ensuing experience.

The Williamson Act permits "preferential assessment contracts" between landowners and local taxing authorities. The owner agrees to restrict his land, regardless of zoning, to farming or some other open space use. The authority agrees to assess the land at present use and not at market value. The contract continues indefinitely unless the landowner decides to end it but only after serving a *ten* years' notice! When the notice expires, the property is once again assessed at full market value.[33]

The effectiveness of the Williamson Act has become a hotly debated issue. Proponents insist that the scheme has furthered its goals of preserving an agricultural economy and reducing the loss of open space. Opponents make the following criticisms:

—Communities have not administered the Act with close attention to planning goals. Local planning boards, prone to political pressures, tend to treat all farmland as equally deserving regardless of location. Thus, a great deal of land not imminently threatened by development and too remotely situated for use as open space has obtained tax preferences.

—The program has become a windfall for large corporate landowners. The ten largest beneficiaries hold 20 per cent of the tax-preferred land. One landowner alone has received an $18.6 million reduction in tax assessment.

—Studies have not demonstrated a slowdown in the conversion of farmland into suburban development.

Two unresolved issues underlie this dispute: does market value assessment, in fact, speed the loss of prime farmland and open space: and how should such land be included in a tax preferential program? Critics insist that few farmers ultimately sell out because of high property taxes; rather, the incentive of a high profit—which is lightly taxed—and the presence of cheap land elsewhere to reinvest tax dollars explain more accurately why prime acreage disappears. Critics also assert that planning, not political factors, must govern local decisions whether to admit land into the program before open space tax exemptions can begin to work.[34]

Historic Preservation

Americans have begun to value their architectural heritage. Every community has buildings, block-fronts, and entire districts whose historic or structural significance warrant preservation. Yet, like prime farmland, these "landmarks" often occupy parcels that the market would like to redevelop far more intensively—a multistory office of apartment building in lieu of a row of nineteenth century town houses. Once again, the conventional property tax has worked against preservation. Where assessed values reflect a site's "highest and best" use, the landmark owner whose actual use may be far more limited pays a tax penalty; this may hasten his decision to demolish and rebuild. Where assessed values reflect the market or replacement costs of the renovated building, the landmark owner who chooses to restore and preserve his structure also faces a tax penalty in the form of an assessment increase.

Nearly every state and many cities have now legislated to protect buildings and areas of historic value.[35] Property tax abatement has become an integral part of such laws. Three examples follow: Connecticut cities may abate taxes on landmark properties where the current level of taxation threatens the structure's survival. An owner who then demolishes the landmark, however, must repay all of the monies saved because of abatement.[36] Similarly, the New York City law authorizes tax abatement in order to yield the landmark owner a minimum six per cent return on his investment.[37] The New Mexico Cultural Properties Act of 1969 exempts landmark properties (those on the Official Register) from local taxes for the full amount of approved restoration, preservation, and maintenance expenses.[38] In effect, the owner receives a tax credit making his preservation outlays cost-free.

Miscellaneous Activities

We have already indicated the principal ways in which property tax abatement relates to urban activities. But the stimulant of tax abatement does not stop here. Special interest groups from every part of the spectrum have sought and often gained tax preference. Indeed, statutes like New York's are so riddled with preferences that one wonders whether any properties are assessed and taxed at full market value. Below is an *incomplete* list of activities enjoying partial or full tax relief under state law:[39]

(1) Performing arts buildings;
(2) Cemeteries;
(3) Railroad passenger stations;
(4) Industrial waste treatment facilities;
(5) Reforested lands;
(6) Air pollution control facilities;
(7) Business facilities that generate new jobs;
(8) Infant homes;
(9) Structures essential to the operation of agricultural and horticultural lands;
(10) Structures owned by nonprofit groups such as churches, hospitals, schools, charities, bar associations, and fraternal orders.

"Proposition 13" and the "Taxpayers' Revolt"

In June, 1978, California voters unexpectedly approved an amendment to the State Constitution that would limit the annual real property tax to one per cent of a property's "full cash value."[40] This amendment, known as Proposition 13, has inspired a "taxpayers' revolt" of nationwide dimension. In the November, 1978 general elections, voters in 12 other states approved measures to curb government spending either directly (by tying spending increases to economic growth) or indirectly (by curtailing tax-generated revenues).[41] As in California, local property taxes bore the brunt of voter dissatisfaction.[42] Anti-tax activism continues today, unabated and encouraged; one can foresee many more initiatives to curb government spending before the present fervor finally crests. What implications do we see for the interplay between taxes and urban policy from such widespread unrest over today's tax burdens?

First, our reliance on the real property tax as a local revenue source will decline even further. Residential property, especially, will benefit from relatively lower tax exactions. This may mean that states will extend tax abatements less readily in order to preserve the existing tax base which, under tax rate limitations, will generate few dollars for each thousand dollars of fully assessed value. On the other hand, if property tax rates decline, some of the tax deterrents which abatement is meant to overcome will no longer be quite as burdensome. New and renovated urban housing, as well as undeveloped farm land, may be better able to meet the real estate tax burden without the need for an abatement subsidy.

However, if government spending fails to follow property taxes downward to the same degree, alternative taxes, including state and local scales and income taxes, must take up the revenue slack. Thus, insofar as these levies already impact upon land development decisions, or can be manipulated to do so, they will gain the increasing attention of government planners seeking to control urban growth. The next section of this article examines the income tax.

The Income Tax

In discussing the income tax, we will stress federal law although, as we have seen, more than 40 states (and a few cities) also tax income. We do so for several reasons: we know far more about the specifics of the federal tax; in general, state tax measures tend to track the federal law; and in any event, state tax rates still range well below their federal counterpart. To the extent that persons tailor their activities in response to taxability, they are concerned chiefly with the federal statute.[43]

Interest and Tax Deductions: A Stimulus to Homeownership

Federal law allows any taxpayer choosing to itemize his deductions to write off against income his interest expenses[44] and most state and local taxes.[45] The interest deduction, which applies to any business or personal debt, covers the interest payments on a home mortgage, whether the home is the taxpayer's primary residence or a vacation hideaway. The deduction for local taxes applies *inter alia* to all property taxes (other than special assessments)[46] that an owner pays directly. Tenants, by contrast, receive no deduction for that part of their rental payments from which the landlord pays *his* property taxes and mortgage interest.[47] These deductions, taken together, provide an annual tax savings in excess of ten billion dollars, which economists view as an indirect subsidy for home ownership.[48] Although we cannot prove the linkage, these tax benefits may help to explain America's 64 per cent rate of home ownership[49]—the highest in the world. Ironically, except for elderly home owners, most of the "subsidy" beneficiaries have incomes that exceed the national average.

Tax Shelter: A Stimulus to Real Estate Investment

Although we are now seeing a period of change, the federal law has long continued two powerful stimulants to real estate investment: the allowance for depreciation and the favorable treatment of capital gains transactions. Together, they have created what investors call "tax shelter" because of their ability to shield income from the payment of taxes.

The Allowance for Depreciation

The allowance for depreciation is an annual deduction given to the owner of investment or business property.[50] It assumes that when the property reaches the end of its useful life—for example, 40 years for a new apartment house—it will no longer have value; therefore, a tax that fairly measures the taxpayer's income must account for the gradual erosion of his original investment.

Prior to 1954, most owners used a form of write-off which accountants call *straight line* depreciation. This method simply divides the investment by the years of useful life to obtain the annual depreciation. Thus, a one million dollar investment in an asset having a 25-year useful life when purchased would provide an annual deduction of $40,000.

Beginning in 1954, Congress allowed taxpayers to elect alternative modes of depreciation, the so-called accelerated systems of *double-declining balance* and *sum-of-the-years digits*.[51] These methods allowed taxpayers to nearly double their annual depreciation write-offs during the early years of an investment. Often this meant huge paper losses even as the taxpayer was salting away real, tax-free dollars from his property.

Several auxiliary factors magnified the benefits which came from depreciation. First, the depreciation basis—the amount available for annual write-offs—was deemed to include both the taxpayer's equity investment and the original debt against the property.[52] To illustrate: the taxpayer who paid two million dollars for property having a 25-year useful life would receive, via straight line depreciation, an annual $40,000 deduction whether he paid all cash or borrowed the entire purchase price. Second, real estate values tended to rise even as the taxpayer was writing-off his investment. Not uncommonly, the taxpayer could resell at a considerable profit property whose depreciated basis indicated little remaining value. Thus, the annual write-offs did not connote a real value erosion but rather a series of arbitrary deductions which significantly lowered the owner's taxable income. Third, the interplay of depreciation and the favorable rates on capital gains, which we are about to examine, meant that the taxpayer would entirely escape having to repay some of his earlier tax savings.

The Favorable Treatment of Capital Gains

A capital gain results from the profitable sale or exchange of a capital asset which would include any investment property.[53] The gain is measured by the excess of the amount received over depreciated basis.[54] To illustrate: after ten years the taxpayer sells for $1.5 million, property originally costing him $1,000,000. In the years before the sale, the taxpayer had taken $400,000 in depreciation deductions and had adjusted his basis downward to $600,000. The resulting capital gain is $900,000 ($1,500,000—$600,000).

Prior to passage of the Tax Reform Act of 1969, *infra*,[55] the ceiling rate on capital gains was only 25 per cent,[56] whereas the rates on other forms of income ranged upward to 70 per cent.[57] In our example, the taxpayer would pay a maximum tax of $225,000 on his $900,000 capital gain. Note, however, that the capital gain has two components: the appreciated value of asset (*i.e.* $500,000), and the depreciation write-offs prior to sale (*i.e.* $400,000). The "depreciation" component also enjoys the favorable capital gains ceiling rate even though the previous deductions have reduced income which might well have been taxed far more steeply. If our taxpayer's ordinary income placed him in the 50 per cent marginal bracket, depreciation would have saved $200,000 in taxes; yet on the property's resale, he would return only $100,000 (0.25 × $400,000) and would escape entirely any tax on the second $100,000. Moreover, the taxpayer enjoys the interest-free use of the $100,000 which he "repays" in taxes, an advantage that itself can be quite valuable. Finally, by engaging one of the accelerated methods of depreciation which became available in 1954, the taxpayer was able to multiply the benefits described above.[58]

Redesigning the Tax Shelter for Socially Preferred Investment

The decade 1954–1964 offered maximum tax advantages to all forms of real estate activity. This led to the creation of a multi-billion dollar "syndication" industry aimed at wealthy investors who could gain tax shelters through shared ownership of virtually every kind of income-producing structure.[59] Thoroughly alarmed at this hemmorrhage of tax revenue, the Treasury Department campaigned for new restrictions. Congress responded in 1964 by deciding to "recapture" some of the savings the taxpayer enjoyed via *accelerated* depreciation when, and if, he eventually resold the property.[60] Five years later, Congress acted far more ambitiously.

The Tax Reform Act of 1969, more than any earlier legislation, sought to differentiate among various forms of real estate activity, so as to redirect tax shelter incentives into that activity which Congress hoped to promote. In general, the construction of subsidized, lower-income rental housing was intended to become the preferred real estate investment.

To tilt tax incentives away from non-residential investment, the 1969 law provided that:

—Owners of newly built *non-residential* structures could no longer employ the most rapid forms of depreciation write-off.[61]
—Owners of "used" non-residential structures could no longer employ any form of accelerated depreciation.[62]
—The rules for depreciation "recapture" became stiffest for non-residential investment and most lenient for investment in subsidized housing.[63]
—In addition, owners of subsidized housing received an election to defer taxes on resale profit by reinvesting the sales proceeds in another subsidized project.[64]

The post-1969 period saw a renewed flurry of real estate syndication, directed mostly into new residential construction. As Congress had hoped, subsidized housing units were constructed in record-breaking numbers, helped in part by a parallel increase in direct rental subsidies.[65] But at the same time, new apartments for middle- and upper-income families also established construction records.[66]

On balance, the 1969–1976 experience with a redesigned tax shelter was considered a mixed success. One study found that only 11 per cent of the lost revenue resulting from real estate tax shelters led to the construction of subsidized housing. The rest benefited sponsors either of nonsubsidized apartments or non-residential projects. Much of this would have been built anyway and some should not have been built at all. The study concluded that direct subsidies paid to low-income tenants would have met their shelter needs with fewer federal dollars than the present system of offering tax avoidance for well-to-do investors.[67]

In 1976, Congress tried again to direct new construction into subsidized rental housing.[68] The 1976 efforts centered on depreciation recapture and the deductibility of construction period expenses (a complexity we will no discuss). The new recapture rules significantly weaken the incentive to accelerate depreciation for all but subsidized projects.[69] With respect to the construction period changes, Congress made them immediately effective for non-residential ventures, but carefully postponed their start-up until 1978 for unsubsidized apartments and until 1981 for subsidized housing.[70] Experience will show if these changes succeed in rechannelling the flow of real estate investment.

The Renovation of Low Rent Housing

The 1969 Act had one other consequence for urban policy makers: Congress agreed at last that taxes should stimulate the upgrading of the nation's existing dwelling supply. Previously, all tax incentives had greatly favored investment in newly built structures.[71] A new provision, section 167(k), was created to encourage housing renovation for low or moderate income tenants.[72] Section 167(k) offers investors an option, too good to reject, to write off qualifying rehabilitation outlays[73] over a five year period. Absent this rapid write-off, depreciation would normally take 20 to 30 years. For a high-bracketed taxpayer, if the outlays are largely paid for with mortgage financing (the usual case), the tax savings should allow him to recover his equity investment within one or two years. Although it was due to expire in 1977, section 167(k)'s popularity with Congress and the substantial renovation that the five year write-off made economically feasible led to a further extension of the program until 1982.[74]

Historic Preservation

The Tax Reform Act of 1976 made historic preservation a socially preferred activity to be encouraged by tax advantages. Previously, the income
tax system may have worked unwittingly against preservation. After the 1969
reforms, the purchase of an aging structure as a continuing investment offered far less tax shelter possibilities than would tearing the structure down
and replacing it with a new edifice.[75]

The 1976 law sought to redress the tax bias against landmark buildings
and, indeed, to turn it quite heavily in the other direction. The key changes
follow:

—A taxpayer may elect to amortize the cost of "certified rehabilitation" of any
  "certified historic structure" over a five year period.[76] This extends to historic property the rapid write-offs which section 167(k) provides for renovated low-rent housing.[77]
—Alternatively, a taxpayer who "substantially" rehabilitates a "certified historic structure" consistent with its landmark status may depreciate his *entire*
  investment in the property as if he were the *original* owner. This status offers
  the taxpayer the same rate of accelerated depreciation available for new construction.[78]

The choice of write-off method, where the owner qualifies under both alternatives, may depend upon the owner's income from other sources. The first
provision will always provide the faster write-off. On the other hand, if the
owner lacks sufficient other income to absorb fully the heavier depreciation, he may elect the second, more gradual method.

In at least one respect, these provisions may offer less encouragement
towards renovation than at first appears. They do not apply to any part of
the landmark structure which the owner occupies as his personal residence.
Moreover, the quite limited scope of "certified rehabilitation" and,
possibly, the time-consuming certification process may reduce the volume
of potential users.

The 1976 Act also contains two *penalty* features which may discourage an
investor from tearing down or destroying via renovation the character of a
landmark structure. The penalties are as follows:

—In the usual case of a demolition, the owner may write off immediately his
  demolition expense (often sizable) and the residual basis of the demolished
  structure. The 1976 Act would deny this deduction for one who demolishes a
  "certified historic structure" or any other structure in a registered historic
  district (unless the Secretary of the Interior has certified prior to demolition
  that the building has no historic significance). Furthermore, these non-

deductible costs then become part of the basis in the land for which there is no depreciation.[79]
—The investor who replaces a "certified historic structure" or who makes renovations which destroy the building's landmark character may not use any form of accelerated depreciation.[80]

Conservation Easements

The conservation easement is a valuable legal tool for conserving open space and landmark structures. The owner wishing to maintain his parcel's undeveloped or historic character may agree to *donate* a negative easement to the municipality. Having done so, the owner may not make any change that violates the easement. Having obtained the easement, the community may not tax the property at more than its restricted value. Tax abatement is the inevitable *quid* for the easement's *quo*.

In addition to property tax abatement, the owner will also seek an income tax advantage: the right to deduct as a charitable contribution the value of the conservation easement. Section 170 governs the deductibility of charitable contributions.[81] Prior to 1976, the statutory language had cast a shadow on the deductibility of conservation easements, although a series of "clarifying" rulings treated the deduction quite favorably.[82]

Under the 1976 Act, Congress has directly expanded the deductibility privilege. The new law offers a deduction for donations made exclusively for "conservation purposes," which include: the preservation of land areas for public recreation, education, or scenic employment; the preservation of historically important land areas or structures; or the preservation of natural environmental systems. The donated interest may be one of the following: lease, option to purchase, easement of not less than 30 years, or remainder interest in real property. The recipient may be either a governmental entity or any charity organized exclusively for environmental, conservational, or landmark preservation goals.[83]

Conclusion

Tax policy is becoming an active, self-conscious determinant of the nation's urban growth. We can expect this role to gather momentum especially in the efforts to curb unbridled growth, redirect investment into favored activities, and upgrade or preserve our existing real estate plant. Even as we welcome this greater dependence upon tax policy, however, we would also sound a caution. Tax incentives do not always work reliably in achieving their stated goals. Thus, prudence requires that we carefully reevaluate our tax-incentive programs as we gain experience with them.

NOTES

*This article draws extensively from the author's earlier article published *sub nom* Taxation of Immovables as an Aspect of Urban Policy, which appeared at 26 Am. J. Comp. L. 451 (Supp. 1978).

¹A survey completed in 1977 by American pollster Lou Harris confirms a deep skepticism about the nation's capacity for unlimited economic growth and the benefits that growth is supposed to bring. For example, by 63-29 per cent, a majority would prefer to emphasize "learning to appreciate human values more than material values," rather than to "find ways to create more jobs for producing more goods." By 79-17 per cent, the public would place greater emphasis on "teaching people how to live more with basic essentials" than on "teaching higher standards of living". N.Y. Post, May 23, 1977, p. 14, col. 6.

²See, *e.g., Construction Indus. Ass'n. v. City of Petaluma*, 533 F.2d 897 (9th Cir. 1975) (500-unit quota upheld). *Cf. Golden v. Planning Board of Town of Ramapo*, 30 N.Y.2d 359, 285 N.E.2d 291 (1972) (18-year staging of new development upheld).

³See, *e.g., Just v. Marinette Country*, 56 Wis.2d 7, 201 N.W.2d 761 (1972) (bar on landfill operations upheld); *contra, State v. Johnson*, 265 A.2d 711 (Me. 1970).

⁴See, *e.g.,* California's "Coastal Zone Conservation Act of 1972," Cal. Pub. Res. Code §27000 *et seq.* (West Supp. 1976); Fla. Stat. Ann. §§380.012-.11 (Harrison 1975).

⁵42 U.S.C. §§4321-4327 (Supp. 1976).

⁶See, *e.g.,* California's "Environmental Quality Act of 1970," Cal. Pub. Res. Code §§219000-21151 (West Supp. 1976).

⁷Clean Air Amendments Act of 1970, 42 U.S.C.A. §§1857c-4 *et seq.* (Supp. 1976).

⁸See, *e.g.,* New York City Admin. Code ch. 8-A (1971). The United States Supreme Court has recently given landmark protection a firm consititutional footing. *Penn Central Transp. Co. v. City of New York*, 438 U.S. 104, 98 S. Ct. 2646, 57 L. Ed. 2d 631 (1978).

⁹Currier, 51 Ind. L.J. 28 (1975).

¹⁰In many states, school districts are also semi-autonomous units of local government having the power to levy taxes on real property, although not the power to regulate land use.

¹¹Although the property tax generically may include taxes on personal property and intangibles, as well as on real estate, the latter is, by far, the principal source of property tax revenue in most communities.

¹²Bureau of the Census, Summary of Governmental Finances in 1975-76, Table 4. Until the twentieth century, property taxes also provided state governments with much of their revenue. Today, less than 2.5 per cent of state tax revenue is derived from this source, *Id.* The federal government has not levied a property tax since 1862.

¹³1977 Statistical Abstract of the United States 230; Bureau of the Census, Summary of Governmental Finances in 1975-76, Table 4.

The rapid rise in federal social security tax levies, which are generally tied to employment wages, has made the federal income tax somewhat less dominant, but it still produced more than $200 billion in 1978, a three-fold increase since 1960. States, by contrast, turned to the income tax as a significant revenue source only quite recently; within one decade (1965 to 1975) state income taxes climbed from 21.5 to 32.1 per cent of the total revenue, and multiplied more than four times. Local governments, too, have become increasingly income tax reliant; within the same decade, local income tax collections rose seven-fold, *Id.*

¹⁴For discussion of property tax incidence, see Currier, *supra* note 9, at 46-53.

¹⁵Int. Rev. Code of 1954, §§1, 1202. Even at that, these profits enjoy favorable "capital gains" rates where the taxpayer has held the lands for more than one year, and is not in the regular business of subdividing land. See text at pages 18-19 *infra*.

¹⁶Int. Rev. Code of 1954, § 1014. This section provides for a "stepped-up" basis when prop-

erty is received from a decedent. This means that appreciation which the taxpayer does not realize (through a sale or other disposition) during his lifetime forever escapes federal income taxation, although the federal *estate* tax may capture some of that gain.

Congress in 1976 amended the Code so as to reach gains accruing to the decedent's assets after 1976; the beneficiary would no longer enjoy a stepped-up basis to the extent of post-1976 gains. *Id.* §1023. But in 1978 Congress postponed the Amendment's effective date for at least three years. Also, the 1978 Act provides an exclusion from gross income up to $100,000 of realized gain from the sale of a principal residence owned by persons 55 and older.

[17]Since tax "preferences" have an *indirect* cost to the community in the sense that they engender a revenue loss, economists regard these items as equivalent to a subsidy. They are not a direct subsidy like a welfare payment; rather, the tax beneficiary receives an indirect subsidy measured by the reduction in taxes from what he would owe if he had no preference. We sometimes call this loss a "tax expenditure." Some academic critics argue that we should eliminate, not expand, tax expenditures and achieve our social goals by highly visible, measurable direct subsidies. This approach, it is claimed, would expand public discussion on the merits of these "spending" programs. This approach, it is certain, would also eliminate some of the complexities that tax preferences have bred into the system.

[18]Roosevelt, Second Inaugural Address, Jan. 20, 1937.

[19]60 Stat. 888, 42 U.S.C.A. §1401 (1977). For a year or two earlier, the Administration had run a public housing program under the auspices of the Works Progress Administration. A federal court decision halted the program, which relied upon the condemnation of privately held land, as exceeding the federal agency's constitutional powers, *United States v. Certain Lands in City of Louisville*, 78 F.2d 684 (6th Cir. 1935). This case almost certaintly would be decided differently today.

[20]As a rule of thumb, tenants should not spend more than a quarter of their income for shelter. Even this ratio may seem high by contemporary standards abroad.

[21]Tending to keep this ratio relatively high is the American practice of taxing not only the underlying land but also the building improvements. Under Henry Georgian economics, the incidence of any tax on the improvements falls upon the user.

[22]In fact, the tenant paid a small add-on which was returned to the locality "in lieu of taxes." It represented only a minor fraction, however, of the sums that the community would have collected had the unit been fully taxed. This add-on gained the acronym PILOT (payment in lieu of taxes).

[23]1977 Statistical Abstract of the United States 743. This represents fewer than 1.5 per cent of the nation's 77.6 million housing units. *Id* 742.

[24]In 1960, only 2.3 per cent of the units of public housing were occupied by elderly persons. By 1975, the ratio had risen to 24.4 per cent. *Id.*

[25]N.Y. Priv. Hous. Fin. L. §§10–37 (McKinney's 1976).

[26]N.Y. Real Prop. Tax L. §421 (McKinney's Supp. 1976–77).

[27]N.Y. City Admin. Code §J-51 (1975).

[28]Sternlieb, Roistacher, and Hughes, *Tax Subsidies and Housing Investment* (1976) offers a fiscal cost-benefit analysis of New York City's tax abatement programs.

[29]See, *e.g., State v. Johnson*, 265 A.2d 711 (Me. 1970).

[30] U.S. Const. Amend. XIV.

[31]Maryland introduced the "preferential" tax for farmlands about 25 years ago. By the early 1970s, perhaps half the states had followed the Maryland example. One writer describes this practice as "George Henry" taxation, the very antithesis of the single tax philosophy which requires land assessed at its market value to bear the property taxes' entire brunt. Hagman, Urban Planning and Land Development Control Law 349 (1971).

[32]Cal. Gov't. Code §§51200 *et seq.* (West's 1977). 1972 data indicate that 43 of the state's 58

counties have made Williamson Act agreements. However, only six of more than 400 cities have done so. Altogether, 11.43 million acres were receiving preferential assessment, more than one-fifth of the privately owned undeveloped land in California. Landowners not joining the program have, in some instances, faced much higher taxes because of the community's need to offset revenue lost to preferences. (Ironically, this might hasten the decision to sell out to developers—the very evil the Williamson Act sought to avoid.) To meet this problem the state now reimburses local communities for some of their lost revenues. These subventions range from $3.00 per acre for prime farmland within urban areas to $.50 per acre for non-prime land outside urban areas. The 1972 state expenditure came to $3.8 million.

[33]The owner may change his mind, however, and rescind the notice.

[34]The state of Hawaii has gone well beyond California in linking tax and land use policies. For example, tax abatement for acreage placed in Hawaiian "land preserves" requires various findings as to the land's suitability for the intended use and the use's compatibility with the *State's* development plan. Once the landowner gains abatement, he is barred from changing the land use for at least ten years, and faces a stiff gains tax if he then sells the land within five years after its special status ends. Hawaii Rev. Stat. §§205, 246 (Supp. 1978).

[35]See, Beckwith, *Developments in the Law of Historic Preservation and a Reflection on Liberty*, 12 Wake Forest L. Rev. 93, 160–187 (1976), for an exhaustive listing of state preservation laws.

[36]Conn. Gen. Stat. §127a (1977).

[37]N.Y. City Admin. Code §207–8.0 (1976).

[38]N. Mex. Stat. Ann. 1953 §4–27–4–18 (1974).

[39]N.Y. Real Prop. Tax. §§420 et seq. (McKinney's Supp. 1976–77).

[40]Calif. Const. art. XIIIA, 1978 Cal. Legis. Serv. at XXV. When effective, this restriction will lower property tax levies on an average parcel by nearly 60 per cent.

[41]7 Tax Notes 599 (Nov. 20, 1978).

[42]Voters in Alabama, Idaho, Maryland, Missouri, and Nevada approved property tax curbs. The North Dakota electorate voted to cut individual state income taxes. *Id.*

[43]However, one aspect of state and local income tax law may seriously affect a community's development—the disparate rate structure among the various states and, in some instances, the presence or absence of an income tax altogether. For example, New York State and particularly New York City residents and businesses suffer the highest non-federal income tax rates in the country. These stiff rates may have caused many higher-bracket taxpayers and businesses to leave New York for its comparatively tax-free neighbor, Connecticut.

[44]Int. Rev. Code of 1954, § 163. The deduction for home mortgage interest, as well as that for property tax payment, dates from the Civil War income tax laws. Peterson, *Federal Tax Policy and Urban Development*, 8 Tax Notes 3, 5 (Jan. 1, 1979).

[45]Int. Rev. Code of 1954 § 164. Congress in 1978 repealed the deduction for state and local taxes on the sale of gasoline, diesel, and other motor fuels. Rev. Act of 1978, § 111. The repeal covers, however, only personal use of the vehicle.

[46]Int. Rev. Code of 1954, § 164(c).

[47]In what may prove a futile attempt to provide renters with an equivalent tax deduction, the New York legislature has adopted a measure effective in 1979 which would require local assessors to assign an assessed value to each apartment unit, whereupon the tenant becomes "personally liable" for the taxes levied against the unit. The tenant will then pay monthly to the landlord, via separate check, one-twelfth of the unit's yearly tax; the landlord, in turn, must remit the check to the local government. In this fashion, the draftsmen of the measure hope to qualify the tenants' tax payments for the section 164 deduction. N.Y. Sess. Laws 1978, Ch. 471. The federal regulations state that, generally, taxes are deductible only by the person

upon whom they are imposed. Reg. § 1.164–1(a). The Service has yet refused to approve this artifice; until the Service approves, the measure's effective date will be postponed.

⁴⁸Surrey, Warren *et al.*, 1 Federal Income Taxation 126 (Supp. 1977). The estimated tax expenditure for these two items climbed to $11.0 billion in the fiscal year ending Sept. 30, 1979.

⁴⁹As of April 1, 1975, 64.6 per cent of American households owned the units they occupied. 1976 Statistical Abstract of the United States 747.

One attempt to quantify the extent to which tax benefits have contributed to home ownership appears at Peterson, *Federal Tax Policy and Urban Development*, 8 Tax Notes 3, 7 (Jan. 1, 1979). The author estimates that at upper-income levels (household income exceeds $15,000 in 1969 dollars), owner occupancy rates may have increased 16–20 per cent as the result of tax benefits.

⁵⁰Int. Rev. Code of 1954, § 167.

⁵¹Int. Rev. Code of 1954, § 167(b).

⁵²*Crane v. Comm'r.*, 331 U.S. 1 (1947).

⁵³Int. Rev. Code of 1954, § 1221.

⁵⁴Int. Rev. Code of 1954, § 1001.

⁵⁵Pub. L. No. 91–172, 83 Stat. 487, Dec. 30, 1969.

⁵⁶Int. Rev. Code of 1954, § 1201. This was the so-called "alternative" capital gains tax, which prior to 1969 resulted in a 25 per cent ceiling. The stated ceiling rose after 1969 to 35 per cent, but the effective ceiling could approach 50 per cent because of the minimum tax on preferred income and the "poisoning" of earned income. Int. Rev. Code of 1954, §§ 56–58. Congress in 1978 repealed the "alternative" tax on capital gains for individual taxpayers, but as the result of other Code changes, the effective maximum fell to 28 per cent.

⁵⁷Int. Rev. Code of 1954, § 1.

⁵⁸See text at notes 50–51 *supra*.

⁵⁹*See generally* Berger, *Real Estate Syndication: Property, Promotion, and the Need for Protection*, 69 Yale L.J. 725 (1960).

⁶⁰Int. Rev. Code of 1954, § 1250.

⁶¹Int. Rev. Code of 1954, § 167(j)(1).

⁶²Int. Rev. Code of 1954, § 167(j)(4).

⁶³Int. Rev. Code of 1954, § 1250(a).

⁶⁴Int. Rev. Code of 1954, § 1039.

⁶⁵In 1968, Congress introduced the section 236 interest reduction subsidy, a program designed to stimulate housing production for lower income families. Annual program authority soared to $550 million within three years. Housing and Development Act of 1968, § 201(a), Pub. L. No. 90–448, 82 Stat. 476, 498.

⁶⁶Between 1971 and 1973, 2.86 million privately sponsored apartment units underwent construction, the highest three year total on record. *Compare* 1976 Statistical Abstract of the United States 739 *with* U.S. Dep't. of Commerce, Historical Statistics of the United States 639–40 (1957).

⁶⁷4 Housing and Development Rptr. 1162 (1977). The annual revenue loss from real estate tax shelter savings exceeds $1.3 billion.

⁶⁸Tax Reform Act of 1976, § 204(a), adding § 465 to the Int. Rev. Code of 1954.

⁶⁹Int. Rev. Code of 1954, § 1250.

⁷⁰Int. Rev. Code of 1954, § 189.

⁷¹Peterson, *Federal Tax Policy and Urban Development*, 8 Tax Notes 3 (Jan. 1, 1979).

⁷²Int. Rev. Code of 1954, § 167(k). The statute sets income limits for families whose occupancy would qualify the renovation outlays for the five year write-off. In general, these

families are those who would themselves qualify for housing subsidies although the project itself need not be eligible under one of the government housing programs.

[73]Section 167(k) places a floor and upper limits upon qualifying expenses. The investor must spend at least $3,000 per dwelling unit over a two year period. The total expenditure entitled to the rapid write-off cannot exceed $20,000 per dwelling unit (formerly $15,000).

[74]Revenue Act of 1978, § 367.

[75]The 1969 Act had eliminated accelerated depreciation for subsequent owners of non-residential buildings and had greatly restricted rapid write-offs for subsequent owners of residential buildings. The subsequent owner might renovate the structure and obtain accelerated depreciation for his renovation outlays, but this advantage did not require him to preserve the structure's landmark quality.

[76]A "certified historic structure" is defined as a depreciable building or structure which is (1) listed in the National Register, (2) located in a Registered Historic District and certified by the Secretary of the Interior as being of historic significance to the District, or (3) located in an historic district designated as such under a state or local statute, but only if such statute is certified by the Secretary of the Interior as containing criteria which will substantially achieve the purpose of preserving and rehabilitating buildings of historic significance to the district. "Certified rehabilitation" refers to the rehabilitation of a certified historic structure where the Secretary of the Interior has certified that the rehabilitation is consistent with the historic character of such property. Int. Rev. Code of 1954, § 191.

[77]Unlike section 167(k), this provision sets neither a floor nor upper limit on the amount of qualifying expenditure. Int. Rev. Code of 1954, § 191.

[78]Int. Rev. Code of 1954, §§ 167(o), (d). The owner of a new residential structure may use double declining balance or sum-of-the-years digit depreciation. The owner of a new non-residential structure may use 150 per cent declining balance depreciation. The Code defines "substantial rehabilitation" as the greater of $5,000 or the property's adjusted basis.

[79]Int. Rev. Code of 1954, § 280-B. This penalty parallels that imposed upon a taxpayer who acquires property "*with the intention* of demolishing, either immediately or subsequently, the buildings situated thereon." Section 280-B applies, however, not only to an investor who acquires a landmark structure with demolition intent but also to a long-standing owner who decides to tear his structure down.

[80]Int. Rev. Code of 1954, § 167(n).

[81]Int. Rev. Code of 1954, § 170.

[82]Uncertainty centered on statutory language that made nondeductible the donation of "partial interests" in property. However, the Treasury read into other language congressional intent to allow deductions for the donation of a *perpetual* easement. Treas. Reg. § 1.170A-7(b)(1)(ii). *Cf.* Rev. Rul. 75–358, 1975–2 C.B. 76 (restriction on modification of architectural characteristics); Rev. Rul. 75–373, 1975–2 C.B. 66 (restriction on use of beach-front land for public bathing); Rev. Rul. 74–583, 1974–2 C.B. 80 (donation of right-of-way for hiking and skiing).

[83]Int. Rev. Code, §§ 170(f)(3)(B)(iii) and (iv).

IV

Future
Land Use
Considerations

18

New Land Use Economics and Opportunities for the 1980s

Michael C. Halpin

HISTORIC land use patterns and economics are in upheaval. Opportunities are rapidly developing in two divergent directions. On the one hand, urban redevelopment of city core areas is gaining momentum. On the other hand, there is a flight from urban areas to nonmetropolitan areas to escape city costs, environmental pollution, and the frustrations associated with urban living. These two opposing trends are reshaping traditional land use trends and economics.

In the 1960s and 1970s, metropolitan area growth was fueled by both growth in absolute numbers and extension of boundaries. As households migrated further into the suburbs in search of affordable housing and enhanced quality of living, city boundaries expanded outward to incorporate the suburban dwellers. Local governments began to recognize the environmental and economic implications of the infrastructures thus created, and homeowners sought to protect their suburban and country surroundings against the intrusion of further development. No-growth policies and environmental, infrastructural, and economic problems made suburban homesites less available and affordable. As a result, nonmetro areas have become the new frontiers for both employers and households seeking affordable and environmentally attractive working and living conditions.

Impact of Housing–Job Imbalance

Planning agencies are making a concerted effort to mandate that housing, jobs, and retail–service facilities be located in close proximity to one another, as housing affordability and environmental and energy issues

Reprinted with permission from *State Government Journal*, pp. 87–93, Spring 1980. The Council of State Governments, Lexington, Kentucky.

move to the forefront of the decisionmaking process in land use and business location. They are stressing in-filling of land in metropolitan areas where utilities and transportation systems are already in existence. This presents a problem because development costs in established metropolitan areas result in housing too expensive to fill the needs of the preponderance of the jobholders in the market area. In-filling and scattered lot construction are not conducive to the economies that large-volume, single-family tracts or multihousing project construction enjoy. Additionally, low-density infrastructures represent material constraints for subsequent high-density development.

Large employers in metropolitan areas are becoming more aware of the effects of high living costs on their profit margins and competitive position in national and world markets. They are seeking to come up with their own solutions to these problems, having witnessed a lack of effectiveness of planning agencies and developers in coping with the cost-of-living spiral directly attributable to housing and land use planning in metropolitan areas. Areas with high housing costs will experience increasing difficulty in attracting large employers and retaining those already located within their geographic area. The beneficiaries of large employer relocations will be sun belt states, environmentally attractive nonmetro areas, and satellite communities on the border of metropolitan areas. Industry is also gravitating to areas with low-cost electrical power (hydropower), plentiful water, affordable housing, and attractive surroundings, most notably in the northwestern United States. This is a more recent phenomenon and a departure from sun belt migration.

Employers Seek Cost-Effective Locations

Business, to survive, must constantly seek out cost-effective locations for facilities and manufacturing. On a national scale, companies seek out states and counties where costs of manufacturing and sales can be reduced. On a global scale, companies seek out countries where costs can be reduced. To fail in this may mean that a manufacturer cannot compete favorably in his home market with imports from other countries.

One study, *The Nation's Housing: 1975-1985*, recently released by the Joint Center for Urban Studies of MIT and Harvard University, casts light on long-debated social and economic questions and raises new ones. There has been a sharp decline in the number of households living in physically inadequate housing since 1960, but as this number has declined, the number of households paying excessive housing costs has grown by an almost equal amount. One problem has been replaced by another. There is also the problem of neighborhood inadequacy. "Four million households in 1973 were living in adequate housing, not overcrowded, at rents within their means, but found public services or street conditions so objectionable that they wanted to move from the neighborhood." Although housing deprivation has always existed in this country, the recent phenomenon of rapid inflation in housing costs has brought into question the ability of the middle class to obtain affordable housing as well.

At the core of spiraling housing costs is land cost. In a number of major metropolitan markets, lot cost is more than 40 percent the cost of the house, as opposed to 15 to 20 percent in recent years. Lot prices in many markets are rising about three times as fast as new house prices. In many major market areas, lot prices have been increasing 30 percent yearly, with prices escalating by more than 50 percent in some cases. In an attempt to keep land cost, as a percentage of total housing cost, from approaching and exceeding the cost of the structure itself, builders are constructing larger and more expensive structures on high-priced metropolitan land.

Lot costs in metropolitan areas have risen dramatically because of exhaustion of well-located, easy-to-build-on land; antigrowth attitudes which result in numerous direct and indirect obstacles to development; lack of municipal facilities to support new growth and unwillingness to fund expansion of facilities; increased local and state government regulation; federal environmental regulations which add to cost and delays in development; and, in some cases, panic and speculative buying of land or windfall profits. A number of these factors, which add to lot costs, can be mitigated in nonmetro areas.

Phenomenon of Nonmetro Growth

Between 1970 and 1975, there were 131 people who moved into nonmetro areas for every 100 who moved out. In the same period, the south gained 5 million in population and the west 3 million, whereas the northeast gained only 300,000 and the north central states 1 million. The U.S. Bureau of the Census defines nonmetro areas as all counties wherein the largest urban nucleus does not exceed 50,000 population. Those counties where a sizable portion of the population commutes to metropolitan centers for employment are not included.

In 1950, only 10 percent of the nation's rural counties were growing through in-migration; today, almost 70 percent are experiencing this. Between 1970 and 1975, nonmetro population increased by 6.6 percent while metropolitan areas grew 4.1 percent. In every census region except the south, population has grown more rapidly in nonmetro areas. From 1970 to 1975, nonmetro areas claimed 40 percent of the increase in nonfarm employment, expanding the nonmetro share of such jobs to 25 percent. This is the first time such a trend has been observed in modern history. Most large cities—94 out of the 153 that had over 100,000 residents in 1970—are losing population.

The Electronics Revolution

Alvin Toffler, author of *Future Shock* and the just-released *Third Wave*, presents a macro-economic-social transformation taking place within the United States which has profound implications at all levels of the social-economic system. He identifies three waves: the agricultural revolution, the industrial revolution, and the electronics revolution. According to Mr. Toffler, we are beyond the industrial revolution (the second wave) which produced drives to standardize, maximize, and centralize, based on brute force technology linked to fossil fuel energy, with heavy emphasis on maximization of scale and specialization.

The electronics revolution comes at a time when "the biosphere will simply no longer tolerate the industrial assault." The principal direction on the third wave society is toward tremendous diversity no longer requiring masses of blue-collar workers all doing routine, repetitive work. What makes such diversity economically feasible—and even inevitable—is the technological revolution associated with the computer. The convergence of high transportation costs and low communication costs makes it possible to transfer a great deal of work out of centralized factories and offices to decentralized locations or back into the home—the "electronic cottage."

At the forefront of economic and geographic decentralization are high-technology companies serving world markets which have no economic need, or indeed no possibility, of locating within the center of their product's market area. The dispersement of high-technology companies out of California's "silicon valley" to nonmetro locations is a forerunner of more profound decentralization to occur in the 1980s.

As industry decentralizes jobs into economically and environmentally attractive regions (growth pockets), certain regions of the national economy gain in importance while others lose (the economically and socially obsolete regions). Such transitions introduce strains in the national economy to the extent that there is no longer a uniform national economy; further, there are regional economies with sharply different features and in need of quite different economic policies.

Nonmetro Success Stories

Emerson Electric, one of America's premier growth companies, is an example of a large employer which has always believed that small is better. Emerson is not merely following a trend to nonmetro areas, but in a sense has always been there. With 95 domestic plants located mainly in rural areas usually employing fewer than 1,000, Emerson places a strong emphasis on keeping plants small and decentralized.

The preference for smaller plants in smaller towns simply reflects that costs are lower there. Emerson's wage costs are 13 percent below the rest of the industry and a full 16 percent below competitors like General Electric and Westinghouse. This is a major factor in Emerson's ability to be able to compete profitably with far larger competitors and sustain a sales and earnings growth rate appreciably above the growth rate of the markets which they serve. Emerson serves as an example to manufacturers who are experiencing cost pressures in metropolitan areas, showing that there are many benefits to be gained from nonmetro locations. More are getting the message and following the lead.

Volkswagen moved into New Stanton, Pennsylvania (population 3,000 before the move), with a projected $250 million investment and employing 4,000 people in 1978, the start-up year. In 1978, VW was doing business with some 1,800 Pennsylvania firms. Texas Instruments has built massive manufacturing facilities in Texas nonmetro communities in recognition that the cost reductions required to dramatically increase its electronics market share require nonmetro locations. Santa Clara county electronics giants are expanding/relocating into nonmetro areas not only primarily for cost reasons, but also for environmental and sociological reasons.

Effects of Growth on One County

Santa Clara County in California, referred to as "Silicon Gulch" by many because of its concentration of high-technology electronic companies, is a metropolitan county that has reached maturity in terms of economic development and growth. Twenty years ago there were only 489,000 residents in Santa Clara County—fewer people than are now in the city of San Jose alone. The county's population doubled in the next 10 years, and since then has reached 1.2 million. *Fortune Magazine* described the county as having "the deepest concentration of innovative industry anywhere in the world," and it has become known as the venture capital of the world. The median household income for the county is the highest in California and is the sixth highest nationally—$27,000 per year at the end of 1979.

The housing/job imbalance has developed more rapidly in Santa Clara County than it has in other new technology growth centers. Although Santa Clara County's rapid growth period is still relatively new compared to other sun belt metropolitan areas, it is constrained in its land expansion by its location on the San Francisco peninsula—to the east the San Francisco Bay and to the west the Santa Cruz Mountains.

Development north of Santa Clara County is principally limited to in-filling of developed areas. Growth has not been concentric from a central point but channeled along an industrial corridor with employment growing from north to south along the corridor. Palo Alto is located at the northern end of the corridor and San Jose at the southern end.

The capsule view of Santa Clara County presented here is intended to provide a view of how employers are relocating to mitigate environmental and economic problems associated with a maturing metropolitan area. Much of what is happening in Santa Clara County illustrates a phenomenon that is happening or will happen to many metropolitan areas throughout the country.

How the Problem Developed

There has not been a parity between location of jobs and housing in Santa Clara County. Historically, the northern portion of the county (Palo Alto) received the bulk of jobs following the historical development pattern of electronic employers locating as close as possible to Stanford University and gradually moving in a southerly direction as land became unavailable or too expensive. In the earlier stages of this industrial expansion, employees could afford to live in the same geographic area as their employment. As both housing and industrial development intensified, the employee came under pressure to live further from his place of employment.

San Jose, being at the southerly end of the Santa Clara industrial corridor, became the bedroom community, housing those commuting to jobs in the northern portion of the county. San Jose became a leading city of growth within the nation, but experienced more population growth than employment growth.

Housing Cost and Availability

Because the preponderance of households in Santa Clara County prefer single-family housing over multifamily housing, the residential land in Santa Clara County has been developed primarily as single-family dwellings. In 1955, for example, 81 percent of housing was single-family, in 1960 it was 76 percent, and in 1974 it was 78 percent. This form of housing development, providing substantially fewer households per acre than multifamily housing, has brought the inventory of developable residential land in the county to a near saturation point, particularly in the northern portion of the county.

The housing that is located in the northern portion of the county, due to increasing demand and diminishing supply, is experiencing price appreciation that is putting it beyond the means of many who have jobs in the area. In San Jose, where the "affordable" housing is located, the average sale price of a home at the end of 1979 was above $100,000, with housing in the Palo Alto northern county area being much higher.

In every year between 1970 and 1975, more than one half of the houses constructed in the county have been constructed in San Jose. San Jose received 71 percent of the population increase but only 16 percent of the industrial development measured by building permit valuation. Palo Alto, on the other hand, in 1977 had 2.6 jobs for every housing unit.

Attempts to recruit electronics talent to Santa Clara County from other areas of the country often meet with failure. In spite of large pay raises offered, many feel they cannot afford to move becase of housing costs. Substantial housing assistance is necessary to transfer or promote employees from other areas of the country into high-cost housing areas such as Santa Clara County.

Tax Base, Structure

California cities receive one sixth of all state sales tax revenues collected within their boundaries, including the tax on sales of industrial products. San Jose's percentage of the total sales collected in the metropolitan area dropped from 41.2 percent in 1960 to 37.4 percent in 1975, while the city's population increased 161 percent compared with a total county population increase of only about 81 percent. As a result, San Jose is faced with a budget deficit.

San Jose is no longer willing to shoulder the burden of being a bedroom community for industry in other cities and is actively seeking high-technology industrial development with a high ratio of employees per industrial acre. As the Santa Clara County cities compete for the industrial tax dollar, the housing situation deteriorates, resulting in the county becoming less attractive to major industry. As the cities squabble, both major industry and households look elsewhere, thus reinforcing the trend to nonmetro counties.

Transportation

Heavy dependence on the automobile within Santa Clara County results in highway congestion and air pollution. Santa Clara County appears to be the hardest hit of the Bay Area counties by air pollution. As a result, transportation goals are being set by individual cities and planning areas. It appears inevitable that transportation controls will eventually be implemented.

The mounting traffic jam facing most metropolitan areas is pushing more and more commuters into mass transit systems. However, after years of neglect, the nation's bus, rail, and subway fleets are too small and their equipment too old and unreliable to meet the growing demand for service. With money scarce and production backlogs of manufacturers high, there is no hope for a quick expansion of service.

Since transportation systems represent the physical skeletons around which urban centers develop, they have a profound influence on air quality, social segregation in jobs and housing, price of real estate, and fiscal health of governments—influences far beyond transportation. Once a transportation infrastructure is in place in a mature urban area, the infrastructure constrains revisions to the area, particularly revision in density. The problems of implementing high-density planning solutions into low-density infrastructures with low-density transportation systems are immense. This appears to demote urban renewal—the return to downtown—to an incremental defensive strategy and not a wave of the future as a solution to growth.

Reasons for Corporate Relocation

Surveys on moves of corporate headquarters indicate that labor and related costs, such as affordable housing, ranked as a far more significant consideration in relocation than taxes. Face-to-face communication between business suppliers and customers is diminishing in importance in relocation decisions due to rapid advancement in communication technology. Executives are finding that they can locate anywhere along the interstate system which is in proximity to jet airports. With high-technology products and services, plant location is a secondary consideration to state-of-the-art considerations, i.e., high state-of-the-art products and services allow companies providing those services wider geographic options compared to those companies whose primary attractiveness to customers may be convenience of location to the buying public.

For basic industry employers, particularly high-technology employers, the quality of life is a major relocation factor. Considerations such as climate, physical beauty of surroundings, recreational opportunities, and absence of environmental nuisances which plague metro areas are gaining in importance. Employers are learning that, contrary to 10 years ago, quality of life considerations weigh heavily on career decisions of upwardly mobile young executives.

Energy costs are now gaining in importance and rank near labor in determining where a company will locate or expand. Ten years ago, the cost of energy was much further down the scale of priorities. Over the past five years, the price of electricity to business has increased by 100 percent, or 1.5 times the residential rate. There is also a widening gap between the rates charged by different utilities to their industrial and commercial customers. This will accelerate the flight of industry from high utility cost areas to low utility cost areas.

The trend toward greater rate differences among regions will increase over the next 10 years, according to National Utility Service, Inc., the nation's largest utility rate consultant. That is because many utilities currently locked into fossil fuel have few alternatives for switching to other fuels, particularly northeastern utilities. Those utilities, most notably in the northwest, which benefit from hydroelectric power sources and western coal, will experience a lower rate of cost increase.

World vs Regional Markets

In observing industrial employers and how they adjust to social and economic issues, it is helpful to distinguish how locational criteria are quite different for large employers serving world markets and employers serving regional markets.

- Large employers seek locations that allow them to be competitive, price-wise, in national and world markets with proximity to markets being secondary.
- Smaller employers who sell to a regional market seek to be close to their market as a primary concern, with cost in the market a secondary concern.

Large employers who do not necessarily need to be located in close proximity to their market but who must keep their manufacturing costs down can relocate to lower-cost nonmetro locations. This is particularly true for high-technology firms serving world markets. As one executive commented, "It matters little to my worldwide customers if I am located in a metropolitan or nonmetropolitan area. My relationship with customers and suppliers is little affected." In such moves, large employers do not necessarily need an established employee base, but can relocate existing employees and attract others to the new, lower-cost, environmentally attractive areas. Such a relocation creates a real estate boom in the affected area as new employees, suppliers, and service companies follow along. Such relocations can dramatically affect real estate values in the area overnight.

A large industrial company serving national and international markets does not require purchasing power for its products and services in the local market area as do smaller companies supplying regional markets. When the majority of the sales dollars are derived from other than the region in which a production facility is located, the purchasing power within the region diminishes in importance (with costs of operating in the region gaining in importance) as an element of locational analysis. On the other hand, the decision by an international company to locate within a region can add substantial purchasing power to that area to support localized business and economic growth. Companies which funnel new money into a local economy (basic industry employers) create greater economic stimulus to that economy than do companies which compete for a share of the existing locally generated income.

Large employers, aware of their impact on real estate values, are purchas-

ing land far in excess of their own requirements to participate in the real
estate boom they create. In this manner relocation not only reduces
manufacturing costs but creates windfall real estate profits.

In order to maximize the benefits of a relocation, far-sighted companies
are not merely moving further out into the suburbs nearer affordable housing, but leapfrogging urban growth into environmentally attractive nonmetro areas with low land cost and maximum appreciation potential.

To protect real estate investment these companies work with planning officials to shape the master plan and zoning ordinances to facilitate their
developmental goals. The planning area is then transformed in the master
plan to accommodate the type of growth envisioned. The entry of the large
employer provides the immediate demand which fuels the growth envisioned
by the master plan. Enlightened master plans are providing for manufacturing, jobs, housing, and retail/service uses within close proximity to one
another to alleviate the energy and environmental problems affecting the
larger metropolitan areas from which the large employer may be fleeing.

Trade Deficits and Land Economics

The 1940s through the 1960s were the heydays of the emerging U.S.
multinational corporations. The U.S. dollar, "overvalued" in relation to
other currencies, enabled U.S. corporations to purchase companies, land,
plants, and equipment, particularly in countries with "undervalued" currencies, at bargain basement rates. These were also the decades of trade
surplus for the U.S.

During these years, there was also a U.S. payments deficit. This resulted
from U.S. policy to provide aid, loans, and military expenditures outside
the U.S. to cover the European trade deficit with the U.S. and to serve as a
reserve currency to bolster European currencies and economics which were
devastated by World War II. Without such aid, it would not have been
readily possible for these countries to convert each other's currencies and
engage in international trade. During these times, the United States printed
and exported dollar amounts far beyond those needed to balance its trade
surplus with other nations. Long-term aid in loans provided to these countries was funded by short-term U.S. trade surpluses.

A large supply of U.S. dollars had built up around the world. The value
of the dollar during the buildup remained stable due to the dollar's
preeminence as the stabilizing international currency which enabled convert-
ibility of other currencies; that is, there was a greater demand for dollars
than supply, in spite of the fact that the U.S. was printing dollars at a rapid
rate.

However, as an energy-based society, the United States was no longer
self-sufficient in fossil fuels, and oil imports rose more rapidly than the

gross national product. The United States then began running trade deficits. The U.S. dollar was less in demand and in 1978 it was in a state of glut after two years of trade deficits totaling more than $70 billion. At this point, dollar holders everywhere increased their haste in diversifying reserves and bank accounts in currencies other than the dollar. Sellers included American and other multinational corporations seeking to reduce losses from "excessive" dollar holdings. The dollar declined to the point where it is now an "undervalued" currency.

To reduce inflation and bolster the dollar, the government has, among other things, mandated high interest rates with the prime rate at a present 20 percent. High interest rates have increased the desirability of dollar investments to foreign investors. The undervaluation of the dollar has made U.S. plants, equipment, and land attractive to buyers with relatively overvalued currencies, making U.S. assets bargain-basement purchases for investors in other countries.

The combination of high U.S. interest rates and the undervalued dollar has increased the flow of funds into the United States to the point where the U.S. currency has a payment surplus in a reversal of its position in earlier decades. The United States has gone from a trade surplus and payments deficit to a trade deficit and payments surplus. Instead of being suppliers of capital to other countries to balance trade surpluses, the United States now absorbs capital from other countries by liquidating lands, buildings, and companies, keeping interest rates high and collecting returns on previous loans and investments.

With the combination of bargain-basement prices and fear of trade restrictions by the United States because of the trade deficit, foreign multinational corporations and investors find the United States currently very attractive for real estate and plant investment. This outside investment adds to internally generated investment demand for U.S. real estate. Due to the difference in currency valuation and other considerations, foreign investors can generally pay more for U.S. real estate than U.S. investors can. It is apparent, then, that international economic events are directly affecting U.S. land economics on the local and national levels since such foreign investment adds to the demand for real estate.

Major Alternatives for Large Employers

Alternatives for large employers in high-cost geographic areas are:

(1) Manufacture offshore in countries where manufacturing costs can be reduced.

(2) Relocate or expand to new geographic areas within the United States where living and operating costs can be reduced.

(3) Relocate or expand within the existing geographic region to minimize housing and transportation costs and environmental nuisances.

The first alternative is diminishing in attractiveness due to risks inherent in currency fluctuations, new and proposed tax treatment of multinationals, the drop in the dollar relative to other world currencies, and instability of other economies.

The second alternative has in the past resulted in industries fleeing metropolitan areas in the northeast portion of the country for metropolitan areas in the far west and southern portions of the country. However, as these latter metropolitan areas experience more and more of the problems earlier experienced by the northeastern metropolitan areas, industry is compensating by relocating to nonmetro areas.

The third alternative is a compromise of the second alternative whereby industry, not wishing to leave the geographic area, chooses to relocate within the geographic area to mitigate the cost of operating within the area as much as possible. By relocating facilities nearer to affordable housing in the geographic area, a company can reduce housing and transportation costs and hedge against possible gas rationing.

When a large employer moves into a new area, that employer transforms that market in a rather dramatic fashion to create what is termed a "neighborhood in transition." Large employers can transform a market with an immediacy that cannot be matched by either planning changes or speculative development alone. These rapid transitions due to large employer relocations will provide key investment opportunities for both employers and investors/developers who are aware of what is taking place. Indeed, locational decisions of large employers may have more to do with combating housing, energy, and environmental problems than actions of planning agencies and the speculative real estate development community.

Historical development patterns are being disrupted as both government and land users are adopting more innovative solutions to growth problems reflecting today's realities as opposed to historical patterns. There are opposing trends to rebirth of downtown areas and a migration of industry away from metropolitan areas, with profound implications on land values and absorption rates. Understanding these trends requires an analysis of not only local markets but national and international issues which are looming larger in importance.

Where Will Future Growth Pockets Occur?

Pocket growth in nonmetro areas suffers from the chicken-or-egg syndrome. Employers desirous of a nonmetro location may be constrained by a current lack of housing supply and municipal infrastructure in the nonmetro area to accommodate the demand the employer would create. Developers are constrained in developing housing and commercial facilities in the area due to insufficient job growth and household income and lack of supporting infrastructure. Governments and planning agencies in nonmetro areas have constraints to planning for growth and providing an infrastructure due to lack of demand from employers and developers for development sites in their area.

Each party—employer, developer, governmental agency—perceives action on his part to be premature and awaits pressure and opportunity to develop from actions of others. This problem will always exist as long as each party acts independently or, more properly, reacts independently.

The dispersion of employment into nonmetro areas provides opportunities for, and indeed requires, a cooperative effort between employers, developers, and governmental agencies in the establishment of new limited growth communities. The large employer, in providing the demand, is the key factor in establishing feasibility, but not necessarily suited to be the catalyst in creating the opportunity. The developer may be the implementer of the new community, but likewise may not possess the skills and organization to be the catalyst in creating the opportunity. Economic development agencies are not generally best suited to act as a catalyst in creating new opportunities (though they may excel at marketing existing opportunities). What is required is a joint effort between large employers and developers, with governmental agencies as active team members in the establishment of specific nonmetro limited growth communities. A facilitating or catalytic agent is required in the creation of such opportunities to negate the chicken-or-egg syndrome.

Challenges in Planning and Investment

In the 1960s and 1970s, growth patterns were relatively predictable—corridor growth and radial growth from urban centers. Such growth patterns presume a predominant tendency towards centralization, with land values determined by proximity and ease of access to urban centers.

As growth reached further out from urban centers, a pattern of land value was established; that is, land could reasonably be expected to pass through use and value stages—dormant, growth, and maturity—with speculative pressure in user needs fueling the most attractive increases in value during the growth phase.

With the dispersed growth of the 1980s occurring in nonmetro growth pockets, there will be fewer clues as to where these pockets may occur. Many growth pockets of the 1980s would have given no demographic clues in the 1970s to indicate to planners and investors that substantial growth was about to take place. To attempt to speculate where such dispersed growth may take place represents a larger speculative risk than existed in previous decades. This implies a requirement for much greater sophistication on the part of planners and investors.

As relative uncertainty approaches pure uncertainty, analysis diminishes in value in that pure uncertainty is not subject to analysis. A way, but not the only way, to reduce uncertainty to a level which is subject to analysis is to predetermine, with the large employers who create the economic demand, where such growth pockets or skill centers should occur. The commitment of the large employers working in a joint effort with developers and assisted by governmental bodies provides the initial demand and an element of build-to-suit as opposed to total speculation.

Such development need not be overly ambitious and may amount to little more than a mixed-use, planned unit development within the incorporated area of a nonmetro community. High-technology employers, accustomed to and encouraging innovation, are ready candidates for employment dispersal. On the other hand, the more capital-intensive and generally less innovative natural resource companies, with extensive land holdings, have an opportunity to participate in the establishment of growth pockets on their land as land bankers or developers. In such a context, high-technology companies can be perceived as anchor users, much like key retailers are utilized as anchors in regional shopping centers.

On the other hand, some high-technology employers perceive themselves as anchor users, land bankers, and developers of skill centers. This is not a throwback to company towns, which were generally low-technology, single-market enterprises, with a stable and rigid production operation. The new skill centers of the electronic revolution will serve very different needs, though the underlying economic rationale may possess similar characteristics.

As has been pointed out earlier, in-filling of metropolitan areas does not necessarily answer the needs of those businesses and households which are finding the cost and quality of life too expensive in metropolitan areas. Past experience indicates that it is necessary to adjust to free market trends and demands rather than to speculate on how the free market should behave and attempt to manipulate the market.

19

Communications Technology and Land Use

Ithiel de Sola Pool

COMMUNICATIONS technology, for the last 200 years, has been making operation at a distance increasingly easy. Such a steady trend, one might presume, should have engendered as one of its consequences a steady dispersal of population away from crowded city centers. But it is not so! Why did this trend of better long-distance communication, which has indeed promoted exurbia and sprawl recently, appear in an earlier era to have had the reverse effect of encouraging urbanization around superdense downtowns? And why is it different today?

When one finds a cause, at one time having one effect and at another time having another, one suspects that an interaction with a third variable is at work. That is the case. We find intriguing interactions among urban topography and three technologies: production, transportation, and communications. Were we examining an earlier era, we would have to add one more variable, security, as a major factor in human agglomeration, but in the modern world the dominant needs served by common settlements rise from economic pursuits. The rise of the modern city came in part from the assemblage of workers near factories and also from division of labor among producers who lived by exchange in markets.

Contributions of the Telephone and Modern Transportation

In the mid-nineteenth century, if one walked up to one of the big, red brick sheds that housed most American factories along the rivers of the

Reprinted from Ithiel de Sola Pool. "Communications Technology and Land Use." *The Annals of the American Academy of Political and Social Science* 451 (September 1980): 1–12. Copyright © 1980, American Academy of Political and Social Science.

Northeast or to one of the similar sheds in western Europe, one would have found the offices of the company and its president at the front of the same building with the production plant behind. By the 1920s, however, one would have found most corporate headquarters located in Manhattan, or London, or Paris, or sometimes in the downtowns of industrial cities like Pittsburgh, Chicago, Manchester, or Bremen. The factories were not there in the central cities to which the headquarters had moved, but were on the outskirts of the city or in smaller manufacturing towns.[1]

This process of separation of the headquarters office from the plant and the congregation of offices all together is described by Peter Cowen in his book, *The Office*.[2] He notes that in New York "a cluster of central offices . . . began to accumulate in the late 1880s or early 1890s. . . . In London . . . the building of offices got under way during the first part of the century."[3] Cowen attributes the character of office activity to three inventions: the telegraph, the typewriter, and the telephone, especially the last two.[4] The company president located himself at the place where most of his most critical communications took place. Before the telephone, he had to be near the production line to give his instructions about the quantities, pace, and process of production. Once the telephone network existed, however, he could convey those authoritative commands to his employees at the plant and could locate himself at the place where the much more uncertain bargaining with customers, bankers, and suppliers took place.

Before the emergence of telecommunications and power-driven transportation, the limit to the number of people who could assemble in the city was set by the need for people to go on foot to see each other. J. Alan Moyer describes Boston in 1850 as a small city with residences, businesses, and factories intermingled. It was a tightly packed seaport where people normally walked to their jobs, to stores, and to visit friends and relatives. Face-to-face communication was dominant; it was a walking city whose densely settled area was within two miles of city hall.[5]

The combination of the streetcar and the telephone allowed this picture to change, with many more people coming to work in the downtown while living further out. Persons who were engaged in routine production work could be segregated to plants in the remote environs, but everyone who bargained and engaged in decisions found it important to work in the city.

The early telephones and the vehicles of the day were not habile enough devices to substitute for one's being located in person at the center during the day, in easy face-to-face contact with important others. The fidelity of the telephone was poor. It sometimes went out of order. Penetration was low; as a result, one could not count on being able to telephone anyone one wanted to reach. The phone provided a limited link to places where one had arranged for it to be in place; the streetcar served for a daily commute down and up its radial pattern. But for diverse important communications, face-to-face contact had to be available. The limited technologies of the day were neither a substitute for, nor an adequate aid to, personal interaction.

So business first used the new technologies of transportation and communication to assemble in an enlarged commercial center. While quantitatively the separation of corporate offices from manufacturing plants was the most important part of the process of creating a commercial downtown, the same sort of thing was happening in other enterprises besides industry. Before the telephone, doctors, for example, had to live near their offices to be readily available when needed; typically, in fact, the office was in the doctor's home. The telephone, however, allowed many doctors to separate home and office and to put the office where it was convenient for the patients to come.[6]

Before the telephone, businessmen, since they had to be in easy walking distance of their main contacts, located in clusters determined by occupation. The result was a mosaic city. Every city had a furrier's neighborhood, a hatter's neighborhood, a wool neighborhood, a fish market, an egg market, a financial district, a shipper's district, and many others. Businessmen would pay mightily for an office within the few blocks where their trade was centered; their way of doing business was to walk up and down the block and drop in to the places from which one might buy or to whom one might sell. For lunch or coffee, one might drop in to the corner restaurant or tavern where one's colleagues congregated.

Once the telephone was available, business could move to cheaper quarters and still keep in touch. A firm could move outward, as many businesses did, or move up to the tenth or twentieth story of one of the new tall buildings. Instead of an urban pattern of a checkerboard of different specialized neighborhoods, the new urban pattern created a large downtown containing a miscellany of commercial and marketing activities that needed to be accessible to a variety of clients and customers.[7]

The development of skyscrapers permitted more and more people to be packed into that downtown. Recognition of how the telephone contributed to a revolution in modern architecture, namely, by the creation of skyscrapers, appears as early as 1902 in an article in *Telephony*.[8] General Carty, the Chief Engineer at AT&T, used the same arguments in 1908.

It may sound ridiculous to say that Bell and his successors were the fathers of modern commercial architecture—of the skyscraper. But wait a minute. Take the Singer Building, the Flatiron, the Broad Exchange, the Trinity, or any of the giant office buildings. How many messages do you suppose go in and out of those buildings every day. Suppose there was no telephone and every message had to be carried by a personal messenger. How much room do you think the necessary elevators would leave for offices? Such structures would be an economic impossibility.[9]

The prehistory of the skyscraper begins with the elevator in the 1850s; the first Otis elevator was installed in a New York City store in 1857, and with adaption to electric power in the 1880s, the device came into general use.[10] "The need to rebuild Chicago after the 1871 fire, rapid growth, and rising land values encouraged experimentation in construction." In 1884, Jenney erected a ten-story building with a steel skeleton as a frame; the fifty-seven-storied Woolworth Building was opened in 1913. "By 1929 American cities had 377 skyscrapers of more than twenty stories."[11]

There were several ways in which the telephone contributed to that development. We have already noted that human messengers would have required too many elevators at the core of the building to make it economic. Furthermore, telephones were useful in skyscraper construction; the superintendent on the ground had to keep in touch with the workers on the scaffolding, and phones were used for that. So in various ways the telephone made the skyscraper practical and thus allowed a burgeoning of city centers.

Another observation from the early days of suburban commuting was that husbands became more willing to leave their wives miles away in bedroom suburbs for the whole day, and grown children were more willing to leave their parents' neighborhood, once they had telephones and could be in instant touch in emergencies. That, too, facilitated the growth of a commuter-laden downtown.

A Reversal of Trends

Side by side with the process of city growth that has just been described, a second trend was getting under way, first in a small way and then massively. That second trend was dispersion from the city to suburbia and exurbia. That movement had started in the decade before the invention of the telephone and long before the automobile; the streetcar initiated the process. Perceptive observers noted the new trend toward decentralization even in the 1890s. Frederic A. C. Perrine, one of the founders of the profession of electrical engineering in America, noted the beginnings of suburbanization in an article about how electricity would reverse the centralizing effects of the steam engine on society. He stressed the impact of the electric streetcar on the city.[12]

Eight years later, H. G. Wells, in his 1902 *Anticipations* of the twentieth century, forecast centrifugal forces on cities that might lead "to the complete reduction of all our present congestions."[13] A pedestrian city, he said, "is inexorably limited by a radius of about four miles, and a horse-using city may grow out to seven or eight." With street railways the modern city thrust "out arms along every available railway line."

> It follows that the available area of a city which can offer a cheap suburban journey of thirty miles an hour is a circle with a radius of thirty miles. . . . But thirty miles is only a very moderate estimate of speed. . . . I think, that the available area . . . will have a radius of over one hundred miles. . . . Indeed, it is not too much to say . . . that the vast stretch of country from Washington to Albany will be all of it "available" to the active citizen of New York and Philadelphia.

Wells anticipated "that New York, Philadelphia, and Chicago will probably, and Hankow almost certainly, reach forty million." The telephone was one factor Wells listed as fostering this development,[14] for he believed that there was no reason "why a telephone call from any point in such a small country as England to any other should cost more than a postcard."[15] Yet Wells, like Jean Gottmann later, emphasized that urban sprawl did not mean uniformity of density.[16] Shopping and entertainment centers would continue to make for downtowns, even as people in some occupations would prefer to move out to the country or work by telephone from home.[17]

A *Scientific American* article of 1914, "Action at a Distance,"[18] has similar themes, but with special stress on the picturephone as likely to make dispersion possible. "It is evident," it starts out, "that something will soon have to be done to check the congestion" of the city. "The fundamental difficulty . . . seems to be that it is necessary for individuals to come into close proximity to each other if they are to transact business." The article argues that the telephone and picturephone will take care of that.

These anticipations of flight from the city came long before the fact. Even as late as 1940, an evaluation of the telephone's impact on the city stressed its centripetal rather than its centrifugal effect. Roger Burlingame concluded:

> It is evident that the skyscraper and all the vertical congestion of city business centers would have been impossible without the telephone. Whether, in the future, with its new capacities, it will move to destroy the city it helped to build is a question for prophets rather than historians.[19]

He sensed that things were changing. The flight from downtown was perceptible enough for him to note it, but as a qualification to his description of a process of concentration.

Today our attention is focused on the dramatic movement outward and the resulting urban sprawl. We have tended to lose sight of the duality of the movement. The common effect of the telephone, throughout, was to permit a freer choice of residential and work location than in the days of the walking city and the mosaic city. There were two options as neighborhoods broke up, the economics of location changed, and cities grew. One was to move up into the new tall buildings, the other was to move out from the center. Initially, the predominant choice was to take advantage of this new freedom of location to get one's enterprise to the center of the action. Skyscrapers helped make this possible, with millions of daytime workers piled high downtown, but it was only possible thanks to the concurrent availability of mass transport and telecommunications.

Later the pendulum swung, and the predominant direction of movement was outward. Even some headquarters of corporations moved from Manhattan to Westchester or Connecticut. Small enterprises appeared in the fields around Route 128 or Silicon Valley rather than in lofts in an urban ring between the downtown and the slums, as 1930s sociological theory of urban topography would have predicted.

The ring theory of Park's and Burgess's Chicago school of sociologists[20] was essentially American because that model rested on assumptions of a rapidly growing city, with speculative land values graduated downtown from the center, and of heavy taxes proportional to property value. Under those circumstances, one low-rental area in which to put a new and possibly unstable productive plant was in the ring just beyond the downtown, but which was still too far out for high-rise development and in which speculators were holding properties at a loss in the expectation of later appreciation when the downtown spread out. In Europe, with a different fiscal system, a ring of lofts and empty lots at the edge of the downtown was not usual. So, in Europe, earlier than in the United States, manufacturing was extensively located in an outer ring, like Paris's red ring of suburbs, but in Europe the ring hugged tightly the city in which the workers lived. Plant location in scattered green sites well beyond the built-up city was a later and also quite American phenomenon.

The new mid-twentieth century pattern of location was more diverse than that which had preceded it. The typical city that had emerged in the first part of the century had a single hub. A ring theory described it well. What has emerged since the middle of the century is a proliferation of hubs, some of them within the old city but away from the bull's eye, some of them planted beyond the city in green fields, some of them subsidiary downtowns, such as Neuilly or Shinjuku, and some of them specialized single-purpose developments like shoppers' malls or rural industrial parks. The Los Angeles metropolitan area is prototypic of what is likely to develop where there is cheap, good, and universal motor transport and telecommunications. The type of city, as Jean Gottmann emphasizes, is megalopolis and not antipolis.[21] It is not an undifferentiated sprawl of medium-density settlement. It is a highly differentiated, geographically dispersed structure of centers and sub-centers with complex interrelations among them.

Homeseekers and businesses adopted such a megalopolitan and in part even exurban location pattern partly because of improvements in telecommunications, and because they had automobiles. The role of the car in making it possible to both live and produce in very scattered locations is obvious. The millions of persons who live in suburbs well beyond the reach of public transport and without walkable neighborhood shopping streets, who carpool or bus their children to school, go to movies at a drive-in, and drive for shopping to a shopping mall could not exist without cars. And there are also many scattered plants where these people work and to which virtually everyone arrives by car. In the instance of Route 128, the very name of the development is the road which it straddles.

However, good and fast as it might be, transportation by car, with cheap gasoline, would not by itself have permitted such a topography of settlement to emerge. If every message, question, order, instruction, or change of instruction from and to such dispersed homes and plants required that someone jump into a car and drive for 20 to 45 minutes in order to communicate, no such dispersal of settlement would have taken place. The ability to pick up a telephone and get a message through without moving was just as essential as the car.

The improvements in telecommunications technology between about 1910, when the telephone was mainly found useful in pushing activities into the downtown, and about 1960, when it was more important in allowing activities to migrate out, were not very dramatic, but they were significant.

In the first place, in the United States telephones had become universal over that half century, and with that their use changed. It was all very well in 1910 for the remote office or plant to have a telephone, but its effective use depended on others whom one wanted to reach also having one. To avoid running an errand, to cancel an appointment, or to find out if something or someone was ready to be picked up required a telephone at both ends. One could not assume that a sick worker would telephone in or that a substitute could be telephoned in order to tell him to drive right out. One could not track down a deliveryman easily or always expect to be able to reach a customer with a question or with information. The universality of telephones made them more valuable to each subscriber.

In the second place, in the early years the quality of telephone service depended heavily on one's location. The gradually growing investment in telecommunications plants was concentrated where users in large numbers could share the cost. Rural subscribers had to be content with party lines and sometimes had to pay for running a line out to their location. Even when a business user was willing to pay for stringing lines to his premises, his rural exchange might not have capacity for added lines. In a rural area, with less redundancy of equipment to fall back on, when a line went out the outage was apt to be more protracted. Also the degradation of the signal with distance was a major problem in the early days and was more severe for scattered customers. That problem was only gradually fully overcome; only young people today fail to react with surprise when a caller from thousands of miles away sounds as though he were calling from next door. Automatic switching was introduced to urban exchanges first, and as direct distance dialing came in, that, too, was in the major commercial exchanges first. So in the early years, one reason for preferring a central location was its superior telecommunications facilities.

Third, the telephone facilities a business subscriber can have on his own premises have improved. Now he is likely to have a fully automatic PABX allowing calls to be made without waiting for a switchboard operator, and incoming calls may go directly to his Centrex line, also without operator intervention. Long-distance calls may be made over private lines or WATS lines at a marginal cost that the employee does not have to think about. For an employee who spends much of his day on the telephone, these are important efficiencies.

Fourth and finally, data communication in forms much faster and cheaper than telex has become available. For the past decade, in most large companies, employees from many locations have had access to the company's computers either in time-sharing or remote job entry mode. Orders and inventory information can pass to and from terminals.

Everything so far described is now history. We are describing changes in communications technology that were already pervasive enough in the 1960s and 1970s to help explain the numerous decisions made both by business firms and individuals to locate in noncentral and even remote and isolated places. These telecommunications developments were prerequisite to the viability of such new centers as Rosslyn, Bethesda, and McLean near Washington; or Shinjuku, Saitama, and Skuba around Tokyo; as well as to the much more modest sub-subcenters, such as a shopping plaza cut out of green fields or a housing development folded into woodlands.

Now, however, let us consider more advanced telecommunications developments that may become common over the next decades and which may serve to make remote locations even more attractive.

A Look to the Future

One particular development clouds our crystal ball. For the first time in the last two centuries, the trends in transportation do not parallel those in communications. In the late nineteenth century, both the streetcar and the telephone provided improved intercourse between selected pairs of points. The convenience this achieved, though considerable, was modest by modern standards, and the topography of both services was rigid. However, as we have already noted, by the mid-twentieth century, universalization of availability of cheap motor transport and of telecommunications was achieved, as was greater flexibility in the topography of both systems and in their uses. All these developments were common to both communications and transportation.

Now for the first time, the prospect in transportation is of rising prices and consequent restriction of liberal use, while the prospect in communications is of falling prices and abundance. How the balance between concentration and dispersion will work out in this new situation, time alone can tell. Without predicting the net balance, we can, nonetheless, analyze fairly well the direction that will come from communications technology. It is toward more diffusion.

Communications facilities in the past have tended to be organized in a hierarchical geographical structure. At the lowest level were local nodes, perhaps united under regional structures and united under a national one. There can be two, three, or more levels. The American press consists of a simple two-level system in which city newspapers are fed by national networks. The most complex of the networks is the telephone system, sometimes described as the largest machine ever built. Subscriber premises are linked to local exchanges by wire pairs called "the local loop." The local exchanges are connected, ordinarily, by coaxial cable to nearby local exchanges and to a toll exchange on the long-distance network. That toll exchange is connected by microwave, or satellite, or cable to other toll exchanges and then on down in symmetrical fashion to the subscriber at the other end. Before satellites, the network structure reflected rather closely the volume of traffic, with much bandwidth installed, for example, between New York and Washington, but with little capacity installed on low-traffic routes.

The network of the year 2000 is likely to be quite different. The two technical developments underlying that difference are the coming availability of abundant, low-cost bandwidth from end to end and the low cost of digital switching.

Optical fibers are likely to carry great bandwidth capacity all the way to the customer's home or office allowing him to connect computers, videophones, or almost any communications device directly to the network. Wherever the optical fibers reach—and eventually that may be everywhere —the customer can have top-grade communications services. Also, insofar as the long-distance links are by satellite, the structure of a network with some heavy traffic routes and some thin routes gives way to random access. Every point at which an earth station is placed (within the satellite's beam) is reachable in the same way as every other. There is no difference in cost regardless of the distance traversed, and there is the same quality of service to every point. So the future broadband transmission system will equalize the service to all locations.

Low-cost switching has important effects, too. It is simply one aspect of the revolution in microelectronics. A digital switch is a digital computer that is being used for routing control. With the progress in microelectronics, such computing capability can be embodied on tiny chips all through the network. "Distributed intelligence," as it is called, means that there can be a computer operating as a switch—and also for other purposes—in the customer's telephone itself, elsewhere on his premises, on telephone poles outside his building, at any concentrator along the line, in telephone company exchanges, and elsewhere. One configuration which gets entirely away from having exchanges is a packet network. For that kind of service, each terminal has a line to the network to which it is connected by a small interface switch which reads the address on the packet and forwards it, switch to switch, to the interface at the destination that is recorded on the header. There need be no hierarchy at all among the interface switches.

Another configuration which gets away from the historical hierarchy of exchanges is that of a switched satellite system. In such a system, the customer's telephone has a line to a concentrator and then on to the earth station. From there the signal, along with an address, is transmitted up to the satellite, and there, 22,300 miles above the equator, it is switched to a beam that will reach the particular earth station to which the receiver is connected.

Even a circuit-switched terrestrial system on a future all-digital network —what is called an "integrated services digital network" (ISDN)—may not have a geographic hierarchy of exchanges. On an ISDN, different functions, like billing, storing of messages when no one is home, and testing the availability of lines, may all be performed by specialized equipment at different places on the network. The distinction between local and long-distance calls may disappear. Some very local calls may never even enter an exchange, being switched at the local concentrator on a pole. Other local calls may be processed for some functions by special equipment hundreds of miles away.

The implication of all these technical facts is that the future telecommunications system is likely to eliminate the disparities in the quality of communications service now found in different locations. Until the energy crisis of 1973, it was a common fantasy in popular literature that advances in communications would engender reruralization. Exhibits at the world's fairs and articles in popular magazines depicted the home/office of the twenty-first century, set in an idyllic countryside with its resident enclosed in a cocoon of a room, sitting at a console with a video screen, carrying on his business with anyone, to the ends of the earth, by telecommunications. That fantasy in its fullness was always silly, but it captured a small element of reality, namely, that whatever expanded communications facilities the market will offer to customers two or three decades hence can be expected to be available just as well in a rural as in an urban environment. In all locations, be they metropolitan centers or remote hinterlands, the most sophisticated kinds of communications service should be available.

At a price, the customer of such a future communications system can be serviced with pictures of any fidelity he needs, with electronic mail, with word processing, and with voice processing, too. The barrier of price is an important one, but it is a very different kind of barrier from that of technical impossibility. In the past there were a limited number of things one could do with a telecommunications line. In the early days, one could use it for poor-quality, high-value voice conversations or for telegrams to limited destinations. Later, one could use it to almost anywhere, but still only for relatively standard voice output. For the future, a fairly accurate statement is that one will be able to have at any given terminal whatever quality of video, audio, or text representation one is willing to pay for and will be able to have these at any location without penalty for distance.

Given the rising cost of transportation, it will pay in many situations to substitute investment in sophisticated communications for the expense of travel. How far the energy crunch will lead to geographic reconcentration of activities in urban centers will depend on the cost of communications services good enough to be a satisfactory substitute.[22]

Much of the literature on the tradeoff between telecommunications and travel makes the naive assumption that if people have the means to communicate to a long distance, they will travel less. That is quite untrue. In the first place, traveling and communicating reinforce each other; people travel to see people with whom they have established a communicative relationship, and people communicate with people to whom or from whom they travel.[23] There is a significant positive correlation between long-distance telephone traffic and travel.

These comments, however, do not contradict what has just been said. We did not ask previously whether the improvement of communications facilities would in and of itself stop people from traveling. We asked what people would do in a situation in which an exogenous third variable, energy prices, forced them to curtail their travel. Under those circumstances, the geographically dispersed availability of very flexible communications devices could curb what otherwise might be a strong shift back into concentrated urban centers.

A Closing Observation

The process described can be generalized in a closing observation about technological determinism. Usually the physical nature of a technology in its early and primitive form is fairly determinative of its use. At that primitive stage there is little understanding either of the underlying laws that are embodied in the device or of the technical alternatives. If the technology is to be used at all, it must be used with the existing hardware. Technological determinism is, therefore, a powerful force at the early stage.

Later, intellectual understanding of the technology advances, and as technicians learn how to make the device do what they want it to do, the degree of technological determinism declines. Social values, goals, and policies take over, and the technology is shaped to serve them.

In its early days, telecommunications technology had a significant effect on the character of the modern city, mainly leading to urban concentration. Later, a more flexible telecommunications technology allowed people increasingly to escape urban concentration.

In prospect now is a still more flexible and malleable communications technology that will give people still more choices about how they will use it. One choice that seems very likely to be frequently made in the near future is to use telecommunications as a way to resist the renewed force toward urban concentration that stems from the rising cost of energy.

NOTES

[1] Cf. Jean Gottmann, Ronald Abler, and J. Alan Moyer in *The Social Impact of the Telephone*, ed. I. Pool (Cambridge, MA: MIT Press), 1976.

[2] New York: American Elsevier, 1969.

[3] Ibid., p. 29.

[4] Ibid., p. 30.

[5] Pool, *Social Impact*, p. 344.

[6] "Telephone and the Doctor," *Literary Digest* 44:1037 (May 18, 1912).

[7] Cf. Pool, *Social Impact*.

[8] "Application of the Modern Telephone," 4:(2):94–5.

[9] John Kimberly Mumford, "This Land of Opportunity, The Nerve Center of Business," *Harper's Weekly* 52:23 (August 1, 1908). This point was first made in the trade journal *Telephony* 4:(2) (1902).

[10] Charles N. Glaab and A. Theodore Brown, *A History of Urban America* (New York: Macmillian, 1967), pp. 144–5.

[11] Ibid., p. 280.

[12] *Electrical Engineering* 3:(2):39 (1894).

[13] H. G. Wells, *Anticipations* (New York: Harper Bros., 1902), pp. 51 ff.

[14]Ibid., p. 65.

[15]Ibid., p. 58.

[16]*Megalopolis* (Cambridge, MA: MIT Press, 1961).

[17]Wells, *Anticipations*, p. 66.

[18]Suppl. no. 1985 77:39 (Jan. 17, 1914).

[19]Roger Burlingame, *Engines of Democracy* (New York: Charles Scribner's Sons, 1940), p. 96; cf. also Arthur Page, "Social Aspects of Communication Development," *Modern Communication*, ed. Page (Boston: Houghton Mifflin, 1932). He notes the relation of the phone to both the skyscraper and suburb, and says it "allows us to congregate where we wish to." p. 20.

[20]Cf. Ernest W. Burgess, "The Growth of the City," in *The City*, eds. Robert E. Park, Ernest W. Burgess, and Roderick D. McKenzie (Chicago: Univ. of Chicago Press, 1967), first published in 1925.

[21]*See* his chapter in Pool, *Social Impact*.

[22]On the possibilities of telecommunications substituting for travel, *see* John Short, Ederyn Williams, and Bruce Christie, *The Social Psychology of Telecommunications* (London: John Wiley & Sons, 1976); Alex Reid, "Comparing Telephone With Face-to-Face Contact," in Pool, *Social Impact*; and Starr Hiltz and Murray R. Turoff, *Network Nation* (Reading, MA: Addison-Wesley, 1978).

[23]Ithiel de Sola Pool, "The Communications/Transportation Tradeoff," in *Current Issues in Transportation Policy*, ed. Alan Altshuler (Lexington, MA: D.C. Health, 1979).

Bibliography

100. Factors Affecting Land Use Demand

101. Benson, Jim. "Getting on the Right Path: Constituency Building Through Energy Planning." *Alternative Sources of Energy*, No. 49, May –June 1981, pp. 20-24.
102. Blair, William G. E. "Visual Resource Management." *Environmental Comment*, June 1980, pp. 6-15.
103. Brueckner, Jan K. and Burkhard von Rabenan. "Dynamics of Land-Use for a Closed City." *Regional Science and Urban Economics*, February 1981, pp. 1-17.
104. Buck, Peter L. *Modern Control of Land Development*. New York: Practicing Law Institute, 1980.
105. Byrne, Robert M. "Industries, Cities and Air." *Environmental Comment*, April 1980, pp. 4-7.
106. California Office of Planning and Research. *Filling in the Blanks: Using Unused Urban Land*. Sacramento, CA: n.p., 1981.
107. Cason, Forrest M. "Land Use Concomitants of the Urban Fiscal Squeeze." *Urban Affairs Quarterly*, Vol. 16, No. 3, March 1981, pp. 337-355.
108. Cigler, Beverly A. "Local Growth Management: Changing Assumptions About Land?" *Current Municipal Problems*, Spring 1980, pp. 443-454.
109. CONEG Policy Research Center, Inc. *Energy Costs and Housing: A Background Paper*, Washington, D.C.: The Center, 1980.
110. Conway, H. McKinley. *Disaster Survival: How to Choose Secure Sites and Make Practical Escape Plans*, Atlanta, GA: Conway Publications, 1981.
111. Cooper, Norman L. "Land Use and Land Use Planning." *Right of Way*, Vol. 27, No. 5, October 1980, pp. 18-23.
112. Diamond, Douglas B., Jr. "The Relationship Between Amenities and Urban Land Prices." *Land Economics*, February 1980, p. 21-32.
113. Dowall, David E. "U.S. Land Use and Energy Policy—Assessing

Potential Conflicts." *Energy Policy* (U.K.), Vol. 8, No. 1, March 1980, pp. 50–60.

114. Erley, Duncan and David Mosena. "Energy-Conserving Development Regulations: Current Practice." *Planning Advisory Service Report*, No. 352, 1980, entire issue.

115. Erley, Duncan and William T. Kookelman. "Reducing Landslide Hazards: A Guide for Planners." *Planning Advisory Service Report*, No. 359, March 1981, entire issue.

116. Feaver, Douglas B. "Does Mass Transit Save Energy?" *ITE Journal*, Vol. 50, No. 5, May 1980, pp. 29–31.

117. Foster, Harold D. *Disaster Planning: The Preservation of Life and Property*. New York: Springer-Verlag, 1980.

118. Frieden, Bernard J. "Allocating the Public Service Costs of New Housing." *Urban Land*, Vol. 39, No. 1, January 1980, pp. 12–16.

119. Gates, W. E. and Associates, Inc. *Technology Assessment for Water Resource Management in Urbanizing Areas*. Springfield, VA: NTIS, 1980.

120. Goodisman, L. D. and F. Caslich. "A Model for Land Use and Water Quality." *Water Supply and Management*. Vol. 4, No. 5–6, 1980, pp. 371–377.

121. Grethner, David. "The Effects of Nonresidential Land Uses on the Prices of Adjacent Housing: Some Estimates of Proximity Effects." *Journal of Urban Economics*, Vol. 8, No. 1, 1980, pp. 1–15.

122. Guarino, Michael A. "Disaster Preparedness and the Building Official." *APWA Reporter*, Vol. 48, No. 4, April 1981, pp. 14–15.

123. Guterbock, Thomas M. "Sociology and the Land-Use Problem." *Urban Affairs Quarterly*, Vol. 15, No. 3, March 1980, pp. 243–267.

124. Halpin, Michael C. "New Land Use Economics and Opportunities for the 1980s." *State Government*, Spring 1980, pp. 87–93.

125. Harrison, David, Jr. *Income and Urban Development*, Cambridge, MA: Harvard University, Department of City and Regional Planning, 1979.

126. Hartgen, David T. "Transportation Energy Assessment for Local Governments." *ITE Journal*, Vol. 51, No. 7, July 1981, pp. 20–25.

127. Harrison, David, Jr. and Michael H. Shapiro. *The Local Government Role in Energy Policy*. Cambridge, MA: Harvard University, Department of City and Regional Planning, 1979.

128. Hassell, John S. "How Effective has Urban Transportation Planning Been?" *Traffic Quarterly*, Vol. 34, No. 1, January 1980, pp. 5–20.

129. Hauschen, Larry D. "Increasing Water Scarcity: Some Problems and Solutions." *VOICE*, December 1979, pp. 2–12.

130. Hildebrand, Michael S. *Disaster Planning Guidelines for Fire Chiefs:*

Final Report. Washington, D.C.: International Association of Fire Chiefs, 1980.

131. Houstoun, Lawrence O., Jr. "Market Trends Reveal Housing Choices for the 1980s." *Journal of Housing*, Vol. 38, No. 2, February 1981, pp. 73-79.

132. Houstoun, Lawrence O., Jr. "The New Non-Metropolitan Growth: Where do Blue Collar Residents Fit In?" *Small Town*, Vol. 11, No. 5, March-April 1981, pp. 8-24.

133. Hudson, Steve. "Managing the Impact of the Energy Crisis: The Role of Local Government." *Management Information Service Report*, Vol. 12, No. 2, February 1980, entire issue.

134. Huffmire, N. M. and F. C. Reitman. *Regulation of Land Use Practices for Areas Surrounding Acquifers—Economic and Legal Implications.* Springfield, VA: NTIS, 1979.

135. Jackson, Richard H. *Land Use in America.* New York: John Wiley and Sons, 1980.

136. Johnson, Donald L. and Gary Schanbacher. "Using Residential Space Wisely." *Urban Land*, Vol. 40, No. 10, November 1981, pp. 16-20.

137. Kain, John F. *The Future of Urban Transportation: An Economist's Perspective.* Cambridge, MA: Harvard University, Department of City and Regional Planning, 1979.

138. Kuss, Fred R. and John M. Morgan III. "Estimating the Physical Carrying Capacity of Recreation Areas: A Rationale for Application of the Universal Soil Loss Equation." *Journal of Soil and Water Conservation*, Vol. 35, No. 2, March-April 1980, pp. 87-89.

139. Lefcoe, George. "The Market's Place in Land Policy." *Urban Law and Policy*, Vol. 3, No. 3, 1980, pp. 205-216.

140. Lord, William B. "Water Resources Planning: Conflict Management." *Water Spectrum*, Summer, 1980, pp. 1-11.

141. Major, D.C. "Planning Theory: Multi-Objectives." In *Applied Water Resource Systems Planning.* Englewood Cliffs, NJ: Prentice-Hall, 1979, pp. 29-36.

142. "Managing the Impact of the Energy Crisis: The Role of the Local Government." *Management Information Service Report*, Vol. 12, No. 2, February 1980, entire issue.

143. Mather, J.R. *The Influence of Land-Use Change on Water Resources.* Springfield, VA: NTIS, 1979.

144. Meehan, Patrick J. "Guidelines for Climatic Residential Planning." *Urban Land*, Vol. 40, No. 5, May 1981, pp. 6-21.

145. Miller, Jay. "Assessing Residential Land Price Inflation." *Urban Land*, Vol. 40, No. 3, March 1981, pp. 16-20.

146. Moriarty, Barry M. and David J. Cowen. *Industrial Location and*

Community Development. Chapel Hill, NC: University of North Carolina Press, 1980.

147. Mosher, Lawrence. "If There's a National Water Crisis, You Can't Tell it to Washington: Outside the Capital, Reports of Drought, Pollution and Waste Are Abundant; but Federal Policy Makers are Engaged in a Debate that Critics Insist Misses the Point." *National Journal,* Vol. 13, July 25, 1980, pp. 1332–1335.

148. Niethammer, William. "Underwater Land and Value." *Real Estate Report,* Vol. 9, 1st Quarter, 1980, pp. 5–7.

149. Northeastern Illinois Planning Commission. *Guidelines for Energy-Efficient Community Development: Site Planning and Subdivision Design.* Chicago, IL: n.p., 1981.

150. O'Banion, Kerry. "Modeling Land Use Conflicts and Constraints for Energy Development." *Environmental Science and Technology,* Vol. 14, No. 12, December 1980, pp. 1438–1444.

151. Ordway, Nicholas and Jack Harris. "The Dynamic Nature of Highest and Best Use (Urban Land Use and Value)." *Appraisal Journal,* 49: 325–34, July, 1981.

152. Osteen, Craig et al. "Managing Land to Meet Water Quality Goals." *Journal of Soil and Water Conservation.* Vol. 36, No. 3, May–June 1981, pp. 138–141.

153. Pechman, Joseph A., ed. *Setting National Priorities: Agenda for the 1980s.* Washington, D.C.: Brookings Institute, 1980.

154. Pederson, E.O. *Transportation in Cities.* Elmsford, NY: Pergamon, 1980.

155. Peltier, L.C. "Land Use as an Environmental Science." *Journal of Environmental Science,* Vol. 24, July–August 1981, pp. 11–14.

156. Perloff, Harvey S. *Planning the Post-Industrial City.* Chicago, IL: American Planning Association, 1980.

157. Perry, Ronald W. *Evacuation Decisionmaking and Emergency Planning.* Seattle, WA: Battele Human Affairs Research Center, 1980.

158. Popper, Frank. *The Politics of Land-Use Reform.* Madison, WI: University of Wisconsin Press, 1981.

159. "Public Transit and Downtown Development: Mobility and Growth Must Go Together." *Metro,* May–June, 1980, pp. 48–54.

160. Rabin, Yale. "Federal Urban Transportation Policy and the Highway Planning Process in Metropolitan Areas." *Annals of the American Academy of Political and Social Science,* Vol. 451, September 1980, pp. 21–35.

161. Real Estate Research Corporation. *Local Government Approaches to Energy Conservation.* Washington, D.C.: U.S. Government Printing Office, 1979.

162. Real Estate Research Corporation. *Urban Infill: The Literature*, Washington, D.C.: U.S. Government Printing Office, 1980.

163. Regional Northeast Energy Conference. *Community Energy Planning —A Local Solution: Proceedings*. Ithaca, NY: Cornell University, Northeast Regional Center for Rural Development, 1981.

164. Ridgeway, James. *Energy-Efficient Community Planning: A Guide to Saving Energy and Producing Power at the Local Level*. Emmaus, PA: JG Press, 1979.

165. Rogers, Elizabeth C. and Stan R. Nikkel. "The Housing Satisfaction of Large Urban Families." *Housing and Society*, Vol. 6, No. 2, 1979, pp. 73–87.

166. Romanos, M.C. et al. "Transportation Energy Conservation and Urban Growth." *Transportation Research*, Vol. 15A, May 1980, pp. 215–222.

167. Rosenberg, Robert C. "Future of Residential Housing: A Decent Home—The American Dream." *Vital Speeches*, June 15, 1981, pp. 523–525.

168. Siebert, Horst, Ingo Walter and Klaus Zimmermann, eds. *Regional Environmental Policy: The Economic Issues*. New York: New York University Press, 1979.

169. Siegel, Richard A. and Thomas V. Martin. "The Why and How of Locating in the City." *Industrial Development*, November–December 1980, pp. 8–11.

170. Simpson, Robert H. and Herbert Riehl. *The Hurricane and Its Impact*. Baton Rouge, LA: Louisiana State University Press, 1981.

171. Smit, Barry. "Prime Land, Land Evaluation and Land Use Policy." *Journal of Soil and Water Conservation*, Vol. 36, No. 1, July–August 1981, pp. 209–212.

172. Starr, Richard E. "Infill Development—Opportunity or Mirage." *Urban Land*, March 1980.

173. Stellar, Joseph D. "Residential Development in the '80s: A Preview of Practices, Products, Practicalities." *Urban Land*, Vol. 40, No. 8, September 1981, pp. 18–21.

174. Tamakloe, E.K.A. "Spatial Equity in Regional Transportation Investment Policies." *Traffic Quarterly*, Vol. 34, No. 10, October 1980, pp. 605–626.

175. Treadway, Peter. *The Economic Environment for Housing: 1980 and Beyond*. Federal National Mortgage Association, Washington, 1980.

176. U.S. Comptroller General. *Water Supply for Urban Areas: Problems in Meeting Future Demand*. Washington, D.C.: U.S. General Accounting Office, 1979.

177. U.S. Congress. House Committee on Banking, Finance and Urban Affairs. Subcommittee on the City. *New Urban Rail Transit: How Can Its Development and Growth-Shaping Potential be Realized?* Washington, D.C.: U.S. Government Printing Office, 1980.

178. U.S. Congress. House Committee on Banking, Finance and Urban Affairs. *Compact Cities: Energy-Saving Strategies for the Eighties.* Washington, D.C.: U.S. Government Printing Office, 1980.

179. U.S. Department of Agriculture. *National Agricultural Lands Study.* Final Report. Washington, D.C.: U.S. Government Printing Office, 1981.

180. U.S. Federal Highway Administration. *The Land Use and Urban Development Impacts of Beltways: Summary.* Washington, D.C.: U.S. Government Printing Office, 1980.

181. U.S. General Accounting Office. *Domestic Housing and Community Development, Issues for Planning: Study.* Washington, D.C.: U.S. General Accounting Office, 1980.

182. U.S. General Accounting Office. *Land Use Issues: Study.* Washington, D.C.: U.S. General Accounting Office, 1980.

183. U.S. General Accounting Office. *Greater Energy Efficiency Can Be Achieved Through Land-Use Management.* Washington, D.C.: U.S. General Accounting Office, 1980.

184. U.S. General Accounting Office. *Transportation Issues in the 1980s.* Gaithersburg, MD: U.S. General Accounting Office, 1980.

185. U.S. Library of Congress. Congressional Research Service. *State and National Water Use Trends to the Year 2000: A Report.* Washington, D.C.: U.S. Government Printing Office, 1980.

186. Viesman, Warren, Jr. *Assessing the Nation's Water Resource: Issues and Options.* Washington, D.C.: U.S. Government Printing Office, 1980.

187. Werth, Joel T., ed. "Energy in the Cities Symposium." *Planning Advisory Services Report*, No. 349, 1980.

188. Wheaton, William C. *Interregional Movements and Regional Growth.* Washington: The Urban Institute, 1979.

189. Worth, Joel T. "Energy in the Cities Symposium." *Planning Advisory Service Report*, No. 349, April 1980, entire issue.

190. Wrenn, Douglas. "Computer-Assisted Land Development." *Environmental Comment*, Oct. 1981, entire issue.

191. Zech, Charles E. "Fiscal Effects of Urban Zoning." *Urban Affairs Quarterly*, Vol. 16, No. 1, September 1980, pp. 49–58.

200. Institutional Controls on the Supply of Land

201. Andrus, Cecil D. "Have Now, Pay Later: Buying a Farm Land Crisis on the Installment Plan." *AMICUS Journal*, Vol. 2, No. 4, Spring 1981, pp. 22–25.
202. Barror, Richard F. "Effective Wastewater Management Planning for Small Communities—Part 1." *Public Works*, August, 1980, pp. 76–80.
203. Baumann, Duane D. and John J. Boland. "Urban Water Supply Planning." *Water Spectrum*, Fall 1980, pp. 33–41.
204. Bills, Nelson L. and Kenneth Gardener. *Perinton, New York: A Case Study in Farmland–Open Space Preservation*. Ithaca, N.Y.: Cornell University, Northeast Regional Center for Rural Development, 1980.
205. Bjork, Gordon C. *Life, Liberty, and Property: The Economics and Politics of Land-Use Planning and Environmental Controls*. Lexington, MA: Lexington Books, 1980.
206. Brown, H. James et al. "Land Markets at the Urban Fringe: New Insights for Policy Makers." *American Planning Association Journal*, April 1981, pp. 131–144.
207. Briggs, Darwyn and E. Yurman. "Disappearing Farmland: Conservation." *Soil Conservation*, Vol. 45, No. 6, January 1980, pp. 4–7.
208. Burby, Raymond J., Stephen P. French and Edward J. Kaiser. *Managing Flood Hazard Areas: A Conceputal Framework for Evaluating Program Effectiveness*. Chapel Hill, NC: University of North Carolina, Center for Urban and Regional Studies, April 1980.
209. Burchell, Robert W. and David Listokin. *Energy and Land Use*. New Brunswick, N.J.: Rutgers University, The Center for Urban Policy Research, 1982.
210. Bryant, C.R. and L.H. Russwurm. "The Impact of Non-Farm Development on Agriculture." *Plan Canada*, June, 1979, pp. 122–139.
211. Butline, J.A., ed. *Economics of Environmental and Natural Resources Policy*. Boulder, CO.: Westview Press, 1981.
212. Callies, David L. "The Quiet Revolution Revisited." *American Planning Association Journal*, April 1980, pp. 135–144.
213. Chan, Arthur H. "The Structure of Federal Resources Policymaking." *Journal of Economics and Sociology*, Vol. 40, April 1980, pp. 115–127.
214. Chasis, Sarah. "The Coastal Zone Management Act." *American Planning Association Journal*, April 1980, pp. 135–144.
215. Conservation Foundation. *Coastal Environmental Management: Guidelines for Conservation of Resources and Protection Against Storm Hazards*. Washington, D.C.: The Foundation, 1980.
216. Coplan, Norman. "Zoning Regulations Limiting Family Units." *Progressive Architecture*, Vol. 61, No. 2, February 1980.

217. Coughlin, Robert E. "Farming on the Urban Fringe: Where Are the Farmlands Going?" *Environment*, Vol. 22, No. 3, April 1980, pp. 33–39.
218. Cook, Earleen H. *Taxation, Urbanization, Zoning, and the Vanishing Farm*. Monticello, IL.: Vance Bibliographies, 1979. (Vance Bibliographies P-257).
219. Coughlin, Robert E. and John C. Keene. "Commentary—The Protection of Farmland: An Analysis of Various State and Local Approaches." *Land Use Law and Zoning Digest*, Vol. 33, No. 6, June 1981, pp. 5–11.
220. Daugherty, Arthur B. "Preserving Farmland Through Federal Income Tax Incentives." *National Tax Journal*, Vol. 33, No. 1, March 1980, pp. 111–115.
221. Davis, Gordon E. "Special Area Management-Resolving Conflicts in the Coastal Zone." *Environmental Comment*. October 1980, pp. 4–7.
222. Dzwik, Andrew A. "Floodplain Management Trends." *Water Spectrum*, Summer 1980, pp. 35–42.
223. Fischel, William A. "Zoning and the Exercise of Monopoly Power: A Reevaluation (Whether Zoning Restrictions Are Used to Restrict the Supply of New Housing, Which in Turn Raises the Value of Existing Homes and Raises the Money Wages in Metropolitan Areas)." *Urban Economist*, 283–293, November 1980.
224. Fischel, William A. *Zoning and Suburban Housing Costs: The Effects of Legal Rights and Government Structure*. Springfield, VA: NTIS, 1981.
225. Folkman, P.J. *Some Implications of Water Law and Rights toward Land Use Planning*. Springfield, VA: NTIS, 1980.
226. French, Steven P. and Raymond J. Burby. *Managing Flood Hazard Areas: The State of Practice*. Chapel Hill, NC: University of North Carolina, Center for Urban and Regional Studies, January 1980.
227. Geier, Karl E. "Agricultural Districts and Zoning: A State-Local Approach to a National Problem." *Ecology Law Quarterly*, Vol. 8, No. 4, 1980, pp. 655–696.
228. Graf, William L. "Riparian Management: A Flood Control Perspective." *Journal of Soil and Water Conservation*, Vol. 35, No. 4, July–August 1980, pp. 158–161.
229. Grieson, Ronald E. "The Effects of Zoning on Structure and Land Markets." *Journal of Urban Economics*, November 1981, pp. 271–285.
230. Griffith, David. "Coastal Hazard Management: A Challenge for Florida." *Florida Environmental and Urban Issues*, Vol. 7, No. 2, January 1980, pp. 6–8f.
231. Gustafson, Greg C. "Farmland Protection Policy: The Critical Area Approach." *Journal of Soil and Water Conservation*, Vol. 36, No. 1, July–August 1981, pp. 194–198.

232. Hagman, Varir S. "Temporary or Interim Damages Award in Land Use Control Cases." *Zoning and Planning Law Report*, Vol. 4, No. 6, June 1981.

233. Huddleston, Jack R. and Thomas M. Kruskopf. "Further Evidence Concerning Local Control of Land Use." *Land Economics*, November 1980, pp. 471–476.

234. Jain, R.K. et al. *Environmental Impact Analysis: A New Dimension in Decision Making*. Ann Arbor, MI: Ann Arbor Science, 1979.

235. Jamczyk, Joseph T. and William C. Constance. "Impacts of Building Moratoria on Housing Markets within a Region." *Growth and Change*, Vol. 11, No. 1. January 1980, pp. 11–19.

236. Jensen, David R. *Zero Lot Line Housing*. Washington, D.C.: Urban Land Institute, 1981.

237. Jud, G. Donald. "The Effects of Zoning on Single-Family Residential Property Values: Charlotte, NC." *Land Economics*, Vol. 56, No. 2, May 1980, pp. 142–154.

238. Kahn, Sanders A. "Zoning and Transfer of Development Rights." *Appraisal Journal*, October 1981, pp. 556–562.

239. Kendig, Lane, Susan Connor, Cranston Byrd and Judy Heyman. *Performance Zoning*. Washington, D.C.: Planners Press, American Planning Association, 1980.

240. Kusler, Jon A. *Regulating Sensitive Lands*. Cambridge, MA: Ballinger Publishing Co., 1980.

241. Lieberman, Nancy H. "Contract and Conditional Zoning: A Judicial and Legislature Review." *Urban Land*, Vol. 40, No. 10, November 1981, pp. 10–12.

242. Liroff, Richard A. "NEPA—Where Have We Been and Where Are We Going?" *American Planning Association Journal*, Vol. 46, No. 2, April 1980, pp. 154–161.

243. Little, Charles E. "On Saving Farmland." *American Land Forum Magazine*, Vol. 2, No. 1, Winter 1981, p. 8f.

244. Little, Charles E. "Too Much Development and too Little Farmland." *Business and Society Review*, No. 36, Winter 1980–81, pp. 4–8.

245. Lowry, G. Ken, Jr. "Policy-Relevant Assessment of Coastal Zone Management Programs." *Coastal Zone Management Journal*. Vol. 8, No. 3, 1980, pp. 227–255.

246. "Managing Coastal Development." *Environmental Comment*, October 1980, entire issue.

247. McAllister, Donald M. *Evaluation in Environmental Planning: Assessing Environmental, Social, Economic and Political Tradeoffs*. Cambridge, MA: MIT Press, 1980.

248. McEachern, William A. *Large-Lot Zoning in Connecticut: Incentives*

and Effects. Storrs, CT: University of Connecticut, Center for Real Estate and Urban Economic Studies, School of Business Administration, 1979.

249. Neiman, Max. "Zoning Policy, Income Clustering and Suburban Change." *Social Science Quarterly,* December 1980, pp. 666–675.

250. Netter, Edith. *Linking Plans and Regulations: Local Responses to Consistency Laws in California and Florida.* Chicago, IL: American Planning Association, 1981.

251. Nordstrom, Karl F. and Norbert P. Psuty. "Dune District Management: A Framework for Shorefront Protection and Land Use Control." *Coastal Zone Management Journal.* Vol. 7, No. 1, 1980, pp. 1–23.

252. Ognibene, Peter J. "Vanishing Farmlands Selling Out the Soil." *Saturday Review,* May 1980, pp. 29–32.

253. Pearce, B. "Property Rights vs. Development Control: A Preliminary Evaluation of Alternative Planning Policy Instruments." *Town Planning Review,* Vol. 52, pp. 47–60, January 1981.

254. Peirce, Neal R. and George M. Hatch. "Can the Nation Preserve Its Farmland?" *National Journal,* August 16, 1980, pp. 1357–1361.

255. Peirce, Neal. "Preservation Is to Seek Government Help as Farmland Gives Way to Developers: A Federal Agricultural Land Study and a Wave of State and Local Tax Laws and Land Use Plans Seek to Guide Developers away from the Nation's Farmland." *National Journal,* Vol. 12, No. 33, August 16, 1980, pp. 1357–1361.

256. Public Technology, Inc. *Community and Environmental Impact Assessment: A Management Report for State and Local Governments.* Washington, D.C.: U.S. Department of Housing and Urban Development, Office of Policy Development and Research, 1980.

257. Richman, Roger. *Federal Transportation Policy and the Coastal Zone Management Program.* Washington, D.C.: U.S. Department of Transportation, Office of University Research, April, 1980.

258. Rosener, Judy B. "Intergovernmental Tension in Coastal Zone Management: Some Observations." *Coastal Zone Management Journal,* Vol. 7, No. 1, 1980, pp. 95–109.

259. Scott, Stanley. *Coastal Conservation: Essays on Experiments in Governance.* Berkeley, CA: University of California, Institute of Governmental Studies, 1981.

260. Scott, Stanley. *Policies for Seismic Safety: Elements of a State Governmental Program.* Berkeley, CA: University of California, Institute of Governmental Studies, 1979.

261. Semmes, Martha Mason. "The Potential Role of Land Use Planning in Air-Quality Control. *Environmental Comment,* May 1981, pp. 7–9.

262. Steiner, Frederick. *Ecological Planning for Farmlands Preservation: A*

Sourcebook for Educators and Planners. Pullman, WA: Washington State University Cooperative Extension, 1980.

263. Stevenson, Lisa and Marie Hayman. *Local Government Disaster Protection: Final Technical Report.* Washington, D.C.: International City Management Association, 1981.

264. Stohes, Samuel N. "Rural Conservation," *Environmental Comment.* May 1980, pp. 10–15.

265. Swartz, S.I. et al. *Controlling Land Use for Water Management and Urban Growth Management: A Policy Analysis.* Springfield, VA: NTIS, 1979.

266. Travis, Edna Hubbard. "Assault on the Beaches: 'Taking' Public Recreational Rights to Private Property." *Boston University Law Review,* November 1980, pp. 933–949.

267. U.S. Advisory Commission on Intergovernmental Relations. *The Federal Role in the Federal System: The Dynamics of Growth; Protecting the Environment: Politics, Pollution, and Federal Policy.* Washington, D.C.: n.p., 1981.

268. U.S. Congress. Senate Committee on Agriculture, Nutrition, and Forestry. *Agricultural Land Availability: Papers on the Supply and Demand for Agricultural Lands in the United States.* Washington, D.C.: U.S. Government Printing Office, 1981.

269. U.S. General Accounting Office. *Problems Continue in the Federal Management of the Coastal Zone Management Program: Report to the Secretary of Commerce.* Washington, D.C.: U.S. General Accounting Office, 1980.

270. U.S. National Agricultural Lands Study. *Where Have the Farmlands Gone?* Washington, D.C.: n.p., January 1981.

271. U.S. National Oceanic and Atmospheric Administration. *The Federal Coastal Programs Review: A Report to the President.* Washington, D.C.: The Administration, 1981.

272. Wilson, David Eugene. *The National Planning Idea in U.S. Public Policy: Five Alternative Approaches.* Boulder, CO: Westview Press, 1980.

273. Taylor, Barbara. "Inclusionary Zoning: A Workable Option for Affordable Housing?" *Urban Land,* Vol. 40, No. 3, March 1981, pp. 6–12.

274. White, Dennis A. *Farmland Preservation Program Options*: Howard County, Ellicott City, MD: n.p., 1980.

275. Whiteman, Michael K. "Planning for Disaster: The Preparedness Dimension in Emergency Assistance." *Development Digest,* Vol. 19, No. 2, April 1981, pp. 93–97.

276. "Wetlands: The Destruction Continues, but Protection is Growing." *Great Lakes Communicator,* Vol. 11, No. 9, June 1981, entire issue.

300. Modifying Land Use Regulation

301. Berger, Curtis J. "Controlling Urban Growth Via Tax Policy." *Urban Law and Policy*, Vol. 2, No. 4, December 1979, pp. 295–314.

302. Block, Walter. "Is Zoning Obsolete? Free Urban Land Markets." *Vital Speeches*, August 15, 1980, pp. 659–662.

303. Brace, Paul. "Urban Aesthetics and the Courts." *Environmental Comment*, June 1980, pp. 16–19.

304. Bundy, Lydia S. "Lenders Discover Advantages and New Market with Community Reinvestment Act." *Journal of Housing*, March 1980, pp. 136–138.

305. Douglas, Richard W., Jr. "Site Value Taxation and the Timing of Land Development." *American Journal of Economics and Sociology*, July 1980, pp. 289–294.

306. Dowall, David E. "Reducing the Cost Effects of Local Land Use Controls." *American Planning Association Journal*, Vol. 47, No. 2, April 1981, pp. 145–153.

307. Eagleton, Annette Kolis. "Recent Trends in Conditional Rezoning Validation." *Urban Land*, Vol. 40, No. 10, November 1981, pp. 21–23.

308. Farr, Cheryl. "Modifying Land Use Regulations for Economic Development." *Management Information Service Report*, December 1980, entire issue.

309. French, Steven P. et al. *Managing Flood Hazard Areas: A Field Evaluation of Local Experience*. Chapel Hill, NC: University of North Carolina, Center for Urban and Regional Studies, February 1980.

310. Frieden, Bernard J. "Housing Development Is Stifled by Environmental Growth Control Regulation." *Journal of Housing*, Vol. 38, No. 1, January 1981, pp. 25–29, 32.

311. Goetz, Michael L. and Larry E. Wofford. "The Motivation for Zoning: Efficiency or Wealth Redistribution?" *Land Economics*, Vol. 55, No. 4, November 1979, pp. 472–485.

312. Heffley, Dennis R. *Transferable Development Rights: A Spatial Equilibrium Analysis*. Storrs, CT: University of Connecticut, Center for Real Estate and Urban Economic Studies, School of Business Administration, 1979.

313. Jones, Roscoe H. "Houston: City Planning without Zoning." In *Zoning: Its Costs and Relevance for the 1980s*. Walter Black, ed. Vancouver, Canada: Fraser Institute, 1980.

314. Jorgansen, Paul V. "Tearing Down the Walls: The Federal Challenge to Exclusionary Land Use Laws." *Urban Lawyer*, Spring 1981, pp. 201–220.

315. King, Sally. *Assuring Sunshine to Your Solar Heating System through Solar Easements*. Seattle, WA: n.p., 1980.

316. Kmiec, Douglas W. "The Role of the Planner in a Deregulated World." *Land Use Law & Zoning Digest*, June 1982.

317. Knight, Robert L. "The Impact of Rail Transit on Land Use: Evidence and a Change of Perspective." *Transportation*, March 1980, pp. 3–16.

318. Kolis, Annette. "Curbing Uncertainties in the Development Approval Process." *Urban Land*, Vol. 38, No. 11, December 1979, pp. 23–25.

319. Kozlow, David. "Should Industrial Land Be Preserved?" *Urban Land*, Vol. 40, No. 3, March 1981, pp. 13–15.

320. Kron, N.F., Jr. *Development Regulation Changes Local Elected Leaders Can Make to Promote Energy Conservation*. Springfield, VA: NTIS, 1980.

321. Leffler, Mary L. "Municipal Perspectives: Local Decision-Makers Need to See Potential for Waste Emergencies." *Solid Wastes Management–RRJ*, Vol. 24, No. 7, 1981, pp. 80f.

322. Marcus, Norman. "A Comparative Look at TDR, Subdivision Exactions and Zoning as Environmental Protection: The Search for Dr. Jekyll Without Mr. Hyde." *Urban Law Annual*, Vol. 20, 1980, pp. 3–73.

323. McClendon, Bruce W. "Reforming Zoning Regulations to Encourage Economic Development: Beaumont, Texas." *Urban Land*, April 1981, pp. 3–7.

324. Minnesota Metropolitan Council of the Twin Cities Area. *Streamlining the Housing Development Approval Process: A Joint Report of the . . . and the Association of Metropolitan Municipalities*. St. Paul, MN: Metropolitan Council, 1979.

325. National League of Cities. *Parallel Goals—Clean Air and Economic Development: Exploring New Strategies for Urban Areas*. Washington, D.C.: U.S. Environmental Protection Agency, 1980.

326. Rice Center. "The Potential Impacts of Air Pollution Controls in Two Metropolitan Areas." *Environmental Comment*, April 1980, pp. 8–16.

327. Rhodes, John J. "Developing a National Water Policy: Problems and Perspectives on Reform." *Journal of Legislation*, Vol. 8: Winter 1980, pp. 1–15.

328. Rider, Robert. "Decentralizing Land Use Decisions." *Public Administration Review*. Vol. 40, No. 6, November–December, 1980, pp. 594–602.

329. Schnidman, Frank. "Selling Air Rights Over Public Property." *Urban Land*, Vol. 40, No. 10, November 1981, pp. 3–9.

330. Stemmler, Hal. "Industrial Zoning: New Wave or Washout?" *Western City*, Vol. 56, No. 8, August 1980, pp. 13–15f.

331. Strong, Ann Louise. *Land Banking: European Reality, American Prospect*. Baltimore: Johns Hopkins University Press, 1979.

332. Toner, William. *Zoning to Protect Farming: A Citizen's Guidebook.* Washington, D.C.: National Agricultural Lands Study, 1981.
333. Vranicar, John, Welford Sanders and David Mosena. *Streamlining Land Use Regulation: A Guidebook for Local Governments.* Chicago, IL: American Planning Association, 1980.
334. Washburne, Randel F. "Carrying Capacity Assessment and Recreational Use in the National Wilderness Preservation System." *Journal of Soil and Water Conservation,* Vol. 36, No. 3, May–June 1981, pp. 162–166.
335. Weaver, Clifford L. and Richard T. Babcock. "The Age of Experiment: Academic and Otherwise." In *City Zoning: The Once and Future Frontier.* Chicago, IL: Planners Press, American Planning Association, 1980.

400. Future Land Use Considerations

401. Bradshaw, Bob. *Protecting Solar Access Through Land Use Planning.* Harrisburg: Pennsylvania Department of Community Affairs, 1981.
402. Conway, H. McKinley. *The Airport City: Development Concepts for the 21st Century.* Atlanta, GA: Conway Publications, 1980.
403. de Sola Pool, Ithiel. "Communications Technology and Land Use." *Annals of the American Academy of Political and Social Science,* Vol. 451, September 1980, pp. 1–12.
404. Hoose, Phillip M. *Building an Ark: Tools for the Preservation of Natural Diversity through Land Protection.* Covelo, CA: Island Press, 1981.
405. Hopcraft, David. "Nature's Technology: The Natural Land-Use System of Wildlife Ranching." *Vital Speeches,* May 15, 1980, pp. 465–469.
406. Jaffe, Martin and Duncan Erley. *Residential Solar Design Review: A Manual on Community Architectural Controls and Solar Energy Use.* Washington, D.C.: U.S. Dept. of Housing and Urban Development, 1980.
407. Levinson, Herbert S. "The 21st Century Metropolis: A Land-Use and Transportation Perspective." *ITE Journal,* Vol. 51, No. 7, July 1981, pp. 54–58.
408. Papaioannon, John G. "The City of the Future Project (COF)." *Ekistics,* May–June, 1980, pp. 175–228.
409. "Report on Ecumenopolis, City of Tomorrow (Part One)." *Ekistics,* Vol. 47, No. 282, May–June 1980, entire issue.

410. Rutter, Lawrence. "Strategies for the Essential Community: Local Government in the Year 2000." *Futurist*, June 1981, pp. 19–28.

411. Van Till, Jon. "A New Type of City for an Energy-Short World." *Futurist*, Vol. 14, No. 3, June 1980, pp. 64–70.

412. Vidich, Charles. *Overcoming Land Use Barriers to Solar Access: Solar Planning Recommendations for Local Communities*. Waterbury, CT: Central Naugatuck Valley Regional Planning Agency, 1980.

Index